# ARGUING TO LEARN

# COMPUTER-SUPPORTED COLLABORATIVE LEARNING

## VOLUME 1

The *Computer-Supported Collaborative Learning Book Series* is for people working in the CSCL field. The scope of the series extends to 'collaborative learning' in its broadest sense; the term is used for situations ranging from two individuals performing a task together, during a short period of time, to groups of 200 students following the same course and interacting via electronic mail. This variety also concerns the computational tools used in learning: elaborated graphical whiteboards support peer interaction, while more rudimentary text-based discussion forums are used for large group interaction. The series will integrate issues related to CSCL such as collaborative problem solving, collaborative learning without computers, negotiation patterns outside collaborative tasks, and many other relevant topics. It will also cover computational issues such as models, algorithms or architectures which support innovative functions relevant to CSCL systems.

The edited volumes and monographs to be published in this series offer authors who have carried out interesting research work the opportunity to integrate various pieces of their recent work into a larger framework.

# Arguing to Learn

## Confronting Cognitions in Computer-Supported Collaborative Learning Environments

Edited by

**Jerry Andriessen**

*Department of Educational Sciences,*
*Utrecht, The Netherlands*

**Michael Baker**

*GRIC Laboratory, C.N.R.S. & University Lyon 2, France*

and

**Dan Suthers**

*Department of ICS,*
*University of Hawai'i at Manoa, Honolulu*

KLUWER ACADEMIC PUBLISHERS

DORDRECHT / BOSTON / LONDON

A C.I.P. Catalogue record for this book is available from the Library of Congress.

ISBN 1-4020-1382-5

Published by Kluwer Academic Publishers,
P.O. Box 17, 3300 AA Dordrecht, The Netherlands.

Sold and distributed in North, Central and South America
by Kluwer Academic Publishers,
101 Philip Drive, Norwell, MA 02061, U.S.A.

In all other countries, sold and distributed
by Kluwer Academic Publishers,
P.O. Box 322, 3300 AH Dordrecht, The Netherlands.

*Printed on acid-free paper*

Printed in the Netherlands.

# TABLE OF CONTENS

# LIST OF CONTRIBUTORS

JERRY ANDRIESSEN is an Associate Professor at the Faculty of Educational Sciences at Utrecht University. His main research area is argumentative discourse production, especially within computer-supported collaborative learning, in various contexts of practice.

MICHAEL BAKER is a permanent Senior Research Scientist of the Centre National de la Recherche Scientifique, working in the Groupe de Recherches sur les Interactions Communicatives at University Lyon 2 (France). His main research areas are dialogue analysis, argumentation and computer-supported collaborative learning.

PIERRE COIRIER is a permanent Senior Research Scientist of the Centre National de la Recherche Scientifique, working in the Laboratory for Language and Cognition at the University of Poitiers (France). His main research is written text production, especially argumentative writing by young learners.

PIERRE DILLENBOURG is Professor of Pedagogy and Training Technologies at the Swiss federal Institute of Technology in Lausanne. His main research area is computer-supported collaborative learning.

GIJSBERT ERKENS is an Associate Professor at the Faculty of Educational Sciences at Utrecht University. His main research areas are dialogue analysis, argumentative text production and computer-supported collaborative learning.

PATRICK JERMANN is a Senior Scientist at the Swiss Federal Institute of Technology Lausanne (EPFL), working in the Center for Research and Support of Training and its Technologies (CRAFT). His main research area is interaction regulation and computer-supported collaborative learning.

PAUL A. KIRSCHNER is Professor of Educational Technology at the Educational Technology Expertise Center of the Open University of the Netherlands. His main research areas are affordances (technological, social, and educational) for collaborative learning, collaborative learning in (a)synchronous distributed groups, and the acquisition of complex skills and competencies.

TIMOTHY KOSCHMANN is an Associate Professor in the Department of Medical Education at Southern Illinois University. His research focuses on the ubiquitous and typically taken-for-granted practices by which participants in joint activity, routinely and accountably provide instruction to each other. He examines these practices through microanalytic studies of interaction in concrete, practical settings (e.g., small-group learning meetings in medical education, the operating room of a teaching hospital).

NANNO PETERS is working as an instruction designer of e-learning applications at Bright Alley. His main interests are collaborative learning processes and case based learning supported with new media.

RACHEL PILKINGTON is Senior Lecturer in Information and Communication Technology at the University of Birmingham, England. Her main research areas are dialogue for educational interaction with through and around computers, collaborative learning and Virtual Learning Environments.

BARUCH SCHWARZ is Professor of Education at the Hebrew University, Jerusalem, Israel. His main research areas are cognition and instruction, cognitive development and social interactions, and mathematics education.

DAN SUTHERS is an associate professor of Information and Computer Sciences at the University of Hawai`i. His research areas include representational support for collaborative learning and other aspects of the design of technology for online learning and collaboration.

JAN VAN BRUGGEN is an Educational Technologist at the Educational Expertise Center of the Open University of the Netherlands. His main research interest is in the area of graphical representation of argumentation.

CATHY VAN DE LAAK is presently researcher for the TNO Human Factors Research Institute, Department of Training and Instruction. In her work at TNO she focuses on e-learning and the application of agent technology and user profiles to improve adaptivity.

ARJA VEERMAN is working as a senior educational researcher at TNO Human Factors, the Netherlands. Her interests are distance education and training, collaborative learning with ICT and representational support of argumentation.

AISHA WALKER is based at the University of Leeds, UK. Her research interests include computer-mediated communication, argument, writing and academic discourse.

PIERRE DILLENBOURG

# PREFACE

For many years, individualizing was the motto of learning technologies. However, since we had more students than computers, it appeared that pairs of students often perform better than individuals. At the same period, late eighties and early nineties, learning theories paid an increasing attention to the impact of social interactions. Moreover, connecting computers to the network progressively became an obvious necessity, and the Web appeared. All the conditions -theoretical, technical and empirical- were met for the emergence of new ways to use computers for education/training. The computer was not anymore perceived as a fake teacher but as an environment where groups solve problems, construct objects, conduct inquiries or projects.

Ten years later, CSCL became the dominant use of technology in education. The community grew from a few pioneers to thousands of researchers. This book series aims to foster quality research in CSCL. No futuristic predictions, no overstatement over the impact of technology. This is not a 'guru' series. Instead, the editorial board aims to encourage serious empirical studies, solid computational models, innovative pedagogical scenarios and robust conceptual frameworks. The best CSCL researchers should find here the space they need to report their findings with the level of details required to convince the reader.

I am very proud to present the very first book of the CSCL series. Several other books will be published in the near future, ranging from basic research to practical guidelines. I am convinced that our efforts will contribute to grasp the educational value of networked technologies and, thereby, to improve the quality of our educational system, for our kids and for us.

JERRY ANDRIESSEN, MICHAEL BAKER AND DAN SUTHERS

# ARGUMENTATION, COMPUTER SUPPORT, AND THE EDUCATIONAL CONTEXT OF CONFRONTING COGNITIONS

## THE KNOWLEDGE AGE

The current period in the history of mankind has been coined as the knowledge age (Brown & Duguid, 2000; Bereiter, 2002). This term serves to distinguish this period from its predecessor, the information age. In contrast to information, knowledge entails a knower, is hard to detach from its owner, and seems to be something that we digest rather than hold. Knowledge lies less in databases than in people, and has to be disclosed by some form of collective activity, and people have to learn how be engaged in collaborative activities that produce new knowledge. In professional contexts at least, the people who construct knowledge are called 'knowledge workers', a term that can be associated with slavery, under those who coordinate them, and who need knowledge for economic reasons. Because knowledge does not really have ownership, it can be turned into economic value by anyone who knows how to do it. Whatever the undertone, currently there is a more than humanitarian interest in collaborative learning, especially in forms of collaboration that allow people to display and develop their knowledge.

The information age was a label indicating a period characterised by rapid developments in information technology, initially inspired by a naive belief that computers, as storage and retrieval devices, could meet all demands for relevant information, and thereby solve most of our learning problems. Now we know better, but what we still do not fully understand is how to construct *knowledge* technology (Roschelle & Pea, 2002). On the one hand, we suppose that knowledge is highly situational rather than general, and activity-bound rather than a product that can be held. This calls for specific solutions in the form of tools that support situational activities. On the other hand, collaboration is still taken as a general skill, so people can do it, or they cannot. This calls for the opposite type of solution: general, and content free tools, that can be implemented in many collaborative situations. For researchers, the concept of knowledge worker is interesting, because it requires us to think about how to integrate conceptions about knowledge with those of collaborative work, especially in the context of new technologies, without detaching the activities from the individuals and their situation.

The chapters in this book all focus on collaborative learning from the perspective of the learners and their situations. The situations that we examine in our research

1

*J. Andriessen, M. Baker, and D. Suthers (eds.), Arguing to Learn: Confronting Cognitions in Computer-Supported Collaborative Learning environments (1-25).*
© *2003 Kluwer Academic Publishers. Printed in the Netherlands*

are learning situations, which are traditionally designed for the acquisition of knowledge. In parallel with new views on knowledge, but lagging behind to different degrees, education is working on the implementation of collaborative learning, with or without support from new technologies. Information technologies, supporting learning and instruction, as in Intelligent Tutoring Systems, computer simulations, hypertext information systems, focused on content; and the student's main task was to understand this content. New technologies — or instructional artefacts as they are currently termed (e.g. Sutter, 2002) — will support collaborative learning, by supporting the practice of *meaning making* in the context of joint activity (Stahl, 2002; Koschmann, 2002). Schools are to become communities engaged in knowledge creation by processes of inquiry and discovery, not unlike the case of scientific research (Bereiter, 2002). This implies a change of focus for studying learning, from primarily content-based, to being activity- or process-based, and from the individual to the group learning process. The chapters in this book can be characterised as studies of learners being in the uncertain process of transition from one perspective to the other.

The transition in uncertain, as there is no clear existing notion of support for schools or students for achieving these ambitious goals. Even worse, there is no clear picture about how to understand and implement the necessary educational change. There is a need for carefully and sincerely documented practice, showing how changes can be achieved, what problems emerge during such a process, and what improvements that could lead to. As researchers within the CSCL (Computer-Supported Collaborative Learning) community, we study collaborative learning with technology in various learning contexts. The extent to which such contexts display awareness about particular views on learning has a relationship with the nature of the research questions that can be asked. In the section about pedagogical scenarios of this introductory chapter, we try to elaborate a framework to describe the contributions to this volume in this respect.

We claim that the field of CSCL research is now sufficiently mature for it to be worthwhile to focus on learning from one particular type of collaborative activity: argumentation. In this book we understand the term argumentation in a very open way, as any form of collaborative activity that involves *confronting cognitions and their foundations*. For example, a CSCL environment designed to foster learning from argumentation, in this wide sense, could be based on requiring students to confront their individual reasoning in the form of a diagram, it could be based on stimulating and supporting a constructive debate on a particular topic, or it could involve collaborative writing of an argumentative text (with or without argumentative interaction).

The general issue addressed in this volume, and that provides coherence to it, concerns *the roles of argumentation with technologies supporting meaning-making activities in various educational practices*. The present chapter serves as an introduction to the book, and as an attempt to combine issues from different research communities, with respect to learning from argumentation with technology in educational situations: argumentation, argumentation and learning, electronic tools, and the pedagogical context. Rather than summarising each chapter in detail, we provide a set of more general intellectual tools for the reader, in the form of an analysis of activities, tools and situations associated with argumentative practices in education. Whilst this book presents something of a state of the art on these complex issues, it is not yet possible to present a complete integration, to answer such detailed questions as "what types of argumentation should be fostered, and in what way, within a community of secondary school learners being engaged in an assignment where they collaboratively are to discuss two controversial essays about using new media for learning, to what types of knowledge and learning would that give rise, and how should their practice be changed in order to improve the depth of their argumentation?".

Instead, the chapters in this book address various perspectives on the main questions stated above, that is, how to design computer-supported collaborative learning environments that favour: (1) collaborative learning interactions with representational support (chapters 2 and 7), (2) argumentative interactions with respect to scientific notions (chapters 3 and 9), (3) argumentative interactions during collaborative writing about societal issues (chapter 4), (4) argumentative activities during electronic discussions in academic practice (chapters 5 and 8), and (5) development of argumentation skills in a community (chapter 6).

One dimension on which the contributions can be aligned may be distinguished here. The perspective on educational practice can be from top-down or bottom up viewpoints. From the top down, there are ideas about how learning to argue should be organised, how participants can be subjected to a task design and task sequence, which provides ideas about how such settings lead to specific changes in argumentative activities. This may be accompanied by a relatively great involvement of teachers and researchers in actually getting the students to be engaged in the desired types of activities. From the bottom up, the idea is that practice is characterised in a specific manner, and the goal of the researcher is to find out how to characterise argumentative activities within that practice, supported by an electronic tool. This may involve greater responsibility for learners for engaging in learning activities. This combination of approaches across the chapters should allow readers to take on a dynamic perspective, so that bottom-up and top-down positions can be integrated.

In the next sections, we first discuss our general notion about confronting cognitions and the role of argumentation in learning, giving pointers towards how certain chapters approach this notion. We then present a general discussion about electronic support for argumentation, in relation to each chapter.. Finally, we present three general pedagogical approaches with respect to collaborative learning and try to situate contributions to this volume within these approaches. By moving from the general to the specific, we feel that perspectives from a CSCL-sub domain can provide inspiration to the CSCL field in general.

## CONFRONTING COGNITIONS

This book is about learning from confronting cognitions in argumentative interactions, in situations where students use Computer-Supported Collaborative Learning (CSCL) environments. These are computer-based learning environments that are designed to be used across networks for the type of group work that is potentially favourable to collaborative learning. The book focuses on the processes and medium of collaborative learning from argumentation, in relation to its products.

Although typewritten and graphical computer-mediated communication can be viewed as an obstacle to free expression and smooth cooperation in groups (cf. Clark & Brennan, 1991), it is now becoming increasingly recognised that CSCL environments can provide new and rich opportunities for complex collaborative learning. This is because learners can access multiple distributed learning resources provided by the Web and specialised multimedia interfaces, within environments whose overall characteristics — including especially the form of interactions — can be shaped towards pedagogical ends. Thus, rather than viewing CSCL environments as group learning situations without co-presence, it is more fruitful to see them as groups of new integrated resources that can favour collaborative learning, using varied learning resources, structured interaction histories, interaction management tools and multiple representations of both problem-solving domain and interaction tasks. The advent of CSCL environments can therefore be seen as an opportunity for revitalising work in collaborative learning research on understanding the relations between types of interactions and types of learning.

For most researchers working on collaborative learning, the notion of 'confronting cognitions' is no doubt reminiscent of research carried out in the socio-cognitive conflict paradigm (Doise & Mugny, 1981), together with some negative results that have recently been reported with respect to it (e.g. Blaye, 1990). With a number of other researchers, we claim that insufficient attention has been given to the *processes* by which conflicts or confrontations are addressed, in complex learning situations. In other words, the roots of collaborative learning are most likely to be found in the cooperative attempt to resolve different views by argumentation, rather than in the mere incidence of conflicts (Mavarech & Light, 1992).

The aim of the book is therefore to bring together state of the art work on learning from argumentation (in our sense of the term) in CSCL environments, in order to synthesise the contribution of work in this field to research on collaborative learning with distributed technologies. Each chapter takes a firm stance on the questions of what it means to confront cognitions, or to engage in argumentation, how CSCL environments can be used to support such processes in a constructive way, and on what types of learning occur as a result. Several chapters present comparable studies of different tasks being performed with the same CSCL environments.

Before moving on to say more about argumentative activities, , we need to say a little more about the attractive yet enigmatic term "confronting cognitions".

If cognitions are viewed as representations in the mind, or as structures in the brain, then of course they cannot be "confronted" in any direct sense of the word. What can be confronted are expressed statements, claims, points of view and … arguments. Although it might be tempting, therefore, to see argumentation as essentially a language-based activity, we take a wider view, which is that it is both *semiotic* and *epistemic*. It is a semiotic activity to the extent that views and arguments can be expressed in a variety of sign-systems, such as formal languages and diagrams (see e.g. Suthers, *this volume*); it is an epistemic activity since it involves expressing knowledge (at least from the point of view of the people involved), and more specifically, relations between 'pieces' of knowledge. In fact, 'knowledge' in this sense corresponds to the original meaning of the term 'cognition' (the faculty or object of knowing — latin *cognitio*). Finally, by 'confronting' we simply mean mutually apprehending or considering.

In sum, therefore, when we say that students confront their cognitions, we just mean that they produce and mutually apprehend a variety of semiotic representations in a relation to a specific knowledge domain. As we discuss below, confronting does not only mean that cognitions are viewed as opposed, but also that students deliberate as to which is most acceptable, by examining arguments for and against each. The process of confronting cognitions will be viewed as leading to learning in the case where the semiotic representations the students produce are improved (according to some norm) across new situations, in a relatively stable form.

## THE VARIETY OF UNDERSTANDINGS OF ARGUMENT(ATION)

As is well-known, researchers working on 'argument' and 'argumentation' over around the last three thousand years have given quite different meanings to these terms (see e.g. van Eemeren, Grootendorst & Snoeck-Henkemans, 1996). Without claiming to review the whole field, nor attempting to propose a single unified approach, it is worth saying something here about the variety of approaches as a basis for understanding how argumentation relates to learning.

If asked what argument or argumentation is, most researchers would probably give one or both of the three following replies: "it's about giving reasons" (justification), "it's about trying to persuade or convince" (rhetoric, dialectic) and "it's about demonstrating a point of view" (logic). Whilst these replies are adequate as far as they go, for our purposes here — understanding argumentation and collaborative learning with technical artefacts — they are each too restrictive. Firstly, 'having an argument' is not just about giving reasons, since people also often examine coherence between them (for example "if you already claim x then you can't also claim y, you're contradicting yourself"). Secondly, people also sometimes argue when they have no genuine hope of persuading or convincing their audience: they simply want to show that their point of view is at least defendable or worthy of consideration. Finally, the idea of argumentation as demonstration restricts the type of reasoning involved to the mathematico-logical kind, associated with proof and validity: not all ('valid') reason and argument is of this kind.

Before sketching a wider view of argument(ation), let us briefly deal with the two terms "argument" and "argumentation" (as well as, in passing, the term "reasoning"). In the English language, the terms "argument" and "argumentation" can both be used interchangeably to describe a more or less heated discussion or debate involving several parties. But more restricted meanings of each restrict the term "argument" to a "reason advanced" and the term "argumentation" to a "methodological (line of) reasoning". Clearly, it is not reasonable to make prescriptions in these matters; but we think it is useful here to use these more restricted meanings. Thus "an argument" (singular) is a meaningful expression (e.g. an utterance), that is meant to *support* another (and the converse with a "counter-argument"). What "support" means depends on the situation in which the expression is produced — it could mean "prove to be true", or "defend from attack", or "render more acceptable, believable, plausible", and so on. An "argumentation" then, is simply a series, set or chain of arguments, linked by theme or reasoning, materialised, for example, in the form of a text or a dialogue. "Reasoning" is the process by which arguments are generated (as opposed to retrieved from memory). These proposed definitions, whilst requiring further fleshing out, are not so anodyne as they may seem: they have analytical consequences. For example, an interaction in which doubt is expressed, and a single argument is produced, would not be termed an argumentation, since no further inter-linked arguments have been produced. In general, argumentation situations require some kind of *diversity* — of claims and/or of arguments for and against them —, as well as some kind of situational *constraint* that pushes participants to deliberate or choose with respect to them (otherwise, they could simply let the matter drop).

Let us now return to our general characterisation of argumentation situations. We propose that types of argument and argumentation can be characterised in terms of five main factors: *object, reasoning, medium, activity* and *goal*.

The *object* of argumentation is what it is about, what it bears upon. For example, one argumentation could be about the acceptability of authorising experiments on genetically modified organisms in nature, another could be about the possible causes of dinosaurs becoming extinct, and yet another about the validity of a mathematical proof. Although such objects can be conceived in disciplinary terms — e.g. argumentation in mathematics, science, religious studies, history, and so on — it is likely that different types of argumentation, in this sense, can occur within each discipline, from a more abstract or trans-disciplinary point of view. For example, argumentation about factual statements, that could be (in)validated by recourse to experience, can be distinguished from axiological (concerning judgements), doxastic (concerning commonly held beliefs) and deontic (concerning rights and obligations) argumentation. The object of argumentation can make a great deal of difference with respect to how the latter does and can take place, since statements are, by their nature, more or less *debatable* (c.f. Golder, 1996). For example, a factual claim such as "metals are colder than wood" could be invalidated by the appeal to common experience "but you don't want to sit on the corrugated bike-shed roof when it's been in the sun in August, it's much hotter than the wooden fence!". However, an argumentation concerning the ethics of capital punishment, whilst perhaps making appeal to factual arguments, could also reach a stalemate when participants' define implications of the facts in different ways.The *reasoning* involved in argumentation should naturally be appropriate to its object. As discussed above, given objects will nevertheless often involve different types of reasoning. For example, in defending a particular mathematical proof, it would be possible to use *analogical* reasoning with respect to a similar problem, *plausible* reasoning by stating that the result is approximately of the right order of magnitude, or that it is an even number (which is surely what the teacher would have intended) and of course, mathematical (deductive, inductive, etc.) reasoning for checking stages of the proof. Traditional categories of types of arguments are commonly based on types of reasoning (e.g. by analogy, by cause), as are types of fallacies.

Argumentation can take place in different *media*, by which term we here combine both physical means of expression (speech, writing, television, Internet, telephone) and types of semiotic representations (linguistic, symbolic, diagrammatic, pictural, etc.). Clearly, such factors can greatly influence the degree of determinateness and 'sharpness' of a cognitive confrontation — for example, an argumentation based on diagrams or logical formulæ could be quite different from one expressed in relatively vague and evanescent spoken language. Isolating this feature of argumentation, in learning situations, reveals an interesting connection to be explored, with research on the cognitive properties of multiple external representations (Van Someren, Reimann, Boshuizen, & de Jong, 1998).

By the *activity* associated with argumentation, we mean quite simply the overall social situation in which it is produced, including the person or persons involved, the extent to which they can or can not interact in co-presence, and the problem-solving task (if any) in which they are engaged. Clearly, an argumentation produced in a school problem-solving setting is likely to be different in important ways from one where an important decision needs to be made, with much at stake, or from one in everyday conversation where the interpersonal relation is likely to be primary. Written argumentation, or spoken monologue with little feedback from the audience, is likely to be more orderly than argumentation produced in a largely unpredictable interaction, in which speakers have to both present their own points of view and criticise their partners'. The activity is relatively independent of the medium since, for example, a given problem could be solved interactively either by face-to-face speech or across another medium such as Internet.

Finally, the *goal* of argumentation is usually closely related to the activity within which it is produced, and yet can be distinct from it. Thus, the goal of the argumentation can be quite simply to contribute to solving a common problem — for example, cooperatively searching for the most adequate solution. But on an *intersubjective* level, goals can include *convincing* one's partner that one's own position is to be accepted, *refuting* one's partner's position, demonstrating the *defensibility* of one's position, and so on. On an *interpersonal* level, goals can relate to facework, and include demonstrating personal superiority in different respects. Walton (1989) has produced a useful classification of types of (argumentation) dialogue in terms of their situations (c.f. "activity", above), methods (c.f. "reasoning" above) and goals, that is useful in characterising the research described in this book (reproduced below in Table 1).

*Table 1. Types of argumentation dialogue (Walton, 1989, p. 10).*

| Dialogue | Initial Situation | Method | Goal |
|---|---|---|---|
| Quarrel | Emotional disquiet | Personal attack | "Hit" out at other |
| Debate | Forensic contest | Verbal victory | Impress audience |
| Persuasion (critical discussion) | Difference of opinion | Internal and external proof | Persuade other |
| Inquiry | Lack of proof | Knowledge-based argumentation | Establish proof |
| Negotiation | Difference of interests | Bargaining | Personal gain |
| Information-seeking | Lacking information | Questioning | Find information |
| Action-seeking | Need for action | Issue imperatives | Produce action |
| Educational | Ignorance | Teaching | Imparting knowledge |

We think it likely that the situations described in this book will contain all of these types of dialogue to a greater or lesser extent, despite the fact that the objective is usually to emphasise knowledge-based argumentation, debate, critical inquiry and even (peer) teaching.

In summary, argumentation involves producing and comparing arguments using a variety of types of reasoning. The nature of what is being argued about, the media of expression, the wider situation and activity, as well as local goals of argumentation, all have determining influences on the overall form it takes. Such a general analysis provides a means by which readers can situate the different contributions in this book.

The objects of argumentation dealt with here are quite varied, not least in the way in which they are defined by authors and the importance attributed to choice of the topic. Thus, chapters by Baker, by Schwarz and Glassner and by Suthers focus on argumentation about scientific problems or scientific controversies (the nuance is important), chapters by Jermann and Dillenbourg, and by Veerman study argumentation about the relations between educational theories and technologies at university level, and chapters by Andriessen, Erkens, van de Laak, Peters and Coirier, and by Pilkington and Walker address societal questions that are or should be motivating to students (labour policy, existence of aliens, roles of men and women in the family, etc.). Van Bruggen and Kirschner discuss argumentation about a general class of so-called "wicked" problems, such as design of cars. The media of argumentation considered are quite varied, including CHAT or classroom discussion, individual or collective text writing, and individual or collective drawing of argumentative graphs. Whilst some authors deal with a single medium such as CHAT, structured or otherwise, others focus precisely on argumentation as a multisemiotic or multirepresentational activity, where, for example, argument graphs are considered as both a means of expressing arguments and as a focus for argumentative discussion. It is perhaps instructive to compare the variety of ways in which the authors of each chapter in this volume theorise the general process or activity of argumentation, in relation to the type of reasoning involved and its goals:

- argumentation as a form of negotiation about content of a common argumentative text (Andriessen, Erkens, van de Laak, Peters and Coirier);

- argumentation as interlocutionary problem-solving (Baker);

- argumentation as justification or explanation for individuals' answers to a question, and as argumentative discussion of arguments (Jermann and Dillenbourg);

- argumentation as a chain of varied individual and cooperative dialectical activities (Schwarz and Glassner);

- argumentation as a set of speech acts that aim to convince (Pilkington and Walker);

- argumentation as expressing and discussing evidential relations between data and hypotheses (Suthers);

- argumentation as a multi-representational activity oriented towards solving open-ended problems (Van Bruggen and Kirschner);

- argumentation as a type of constructive and multi-representational exchange (Veerman).

It appears that argumentative activities and situations can thus be surprisingly varied. A final question that is worth meditating here concerns the specificity of argumentative activities: are they restricted human activities, or is argumentation much more ubiquitous? Does all thinking involve argumentation or not? From Billig's (1987) point of view, for example, argumentation is a general model of human thinking and action, to be compared with 'theatrical' (role-playing) and 'game' (rule-following) models. For linguists such as Ducrot (1980), *all* language is argumentative in the sense that it is oriented towards certain conclusions rather than others. Thus the scope of argumentation is an important question here, in determining the applicability and generalisability of results and tools.

## ARGUMENTATION AND LEARNING

As we have discussed, argumentation is a complex and varied activity. Before discussing how learning might take place as a result of it, we briefly discuss *what* can be learned, focussing on the case of *debate* (interactive argumentation produced in a normatively constrained and structured situation). Similar reflexions apply to other forms of argumentation.

We term the first type of learning **learning *from* the debate**. By this we mean deepening understanding about the topic debated, and concepts associated with it. For example, in debating the desirability of cloning human beings, debaters could gain deeper understanding of the concept of a "person", and perhaps better understanding of cellular biology.

The second type of learning is **learning *about* the debate**, which basically means becoming better acquainted with the full diversity of points of view and common types of arguments with respect to a topic. For example, suppose a student is firmly against allowing cars in city centres on grounds relating to public health. As a result of debating the topic, the student might become better acquainted with an economic point of view on the question, with its associated arguments.

Finally, although children already possess argumentation skills from a quite early age (around three years — Stein & Bernas, 1999), many situations also provide opportunities for **learning *to* debate**, with respect to specific topics. As with any type of learning, learning to argue is closely associated with learning a technical vocabulary or language (symbolic or graphical). Whilst learning a language of argumentation (e.g. of connectors in texts, of types of arguments, claims and so on; see Suthers, *this volume*) can be seen as an impediment to learning from argumentation over a relatively short period of time, in the long term, such an acquisition can be seen as essential to learning to argue.

The chapters in this book consider a variety of pedagogical goals associated with argumentation, including understanding scientific concepts (Baker; Schwarz and Glassner; Suthers), learning general literacy skills (Pilkington and Walker; Schwarz and Glassner; Suthers), learning to reason in science (Schwarz and Glassner; Suthers) and in education (Jermann & Dillenbourg; Veerman), learning to solve open-ended problems in general (Van Bruggen and Kirschner) and learning domain concepts in general (Andriessen, Erkens, van de Laak, Peters and Coirier).

But *how* might students learn in argumentation situations, thus broadly defined? The first possible mechanism relates to the *production of (counter-)arguments* in an interactive context. In a manner analogous to the mechanisms underlying the "self-explanation effect" (Chi et al., 1989), the expression of arguments could itself lead to reflexion and knowledge restructuring. More generally, the expression of views under criticism could lead the speaker to elaborate a more coherent discourse on the topic being discussed (c.f. Crook, 1994). However, evidence from analyses of argumentative interactions now suggests that students do not always express the knowledge that genuinely underlies their views, but rather reconstruct appropriate arguments in a way that is situated within their argumentative goals (Baker, 1996, 1999). Learning from expression of arguments can take place in both spoken and written dialogues via computer-mediated communication. In the latter case, synchronous CHAT argumentative interactions could inherit learning mechanisms from both dialogue and writing (c.f. Alamargot & Andriessen, 2002).

Secondly, within a rhetorical point of view on argumentation, arguments are generally produced with a view to modifying underlying attitudes, such as beliefs, comittments, and so on. Thus the acquisition or dropping of beliefs as a result of argumentation could correspond to a type of learning. Whilst the most obvious case would be dropping an erroneous belief in a thesis that is refuted, more subtle changes can occur, such as adopting less rigid or certain attitudes with respect to a question, as a result of discussing it (c.f. Nonnon, 1996). It has been found that in general, students' beliefs are weakened as a result of argumentation, which functions as a means of eliminating 'flawed' claims, rather than as a way of convincing partners to accept views (Baker, 1999).

Thirdly, new knowledge and understanding can be co-constructed in argumentation, especially as a means of achieving a compromise between divergent views. In addition, the interpersonal 'pressure' imposed by disagreement (especially in face-to-face situations) can lead students to refine meanings of key concepts that are being discussed. Similarly, argumentation can lead to dissociating concepts from one-another (c.f. Perelman & Olbrechts-Tyteca, 1958/1988). Most chapters in this book emphasise all three of these learning mechanisms in collaborative argumentative interactions.

Fourthly, learning can occur as a result of expression of argumentation using different types of (graphical, textual) representations, and in making transitions between them (see notably chapters by Suthers and by Van Bruggen and Kirschner, *this volume*).

Finally, given that these learning mechanisms have been described primarily for face-to-face interactions, the question arises as to how the kinds of argumentation that take place in CSCL environments will lead to different kinds of learning mechanisms. For example, whilst working at a distance over the network should lead students to be less inhibited in expressing disagreement, this lowered social-interactional pressure might also mean that they will expend less effort in resolving the disagreement. Similarly, whilst a slowed-down typewritten interaction allows more time for reflexion and argument generation, the higher cognitive-motor costs of utterance production would make co-constructing meanings and knowledge more difficult. These examples illustrate gross differences between face-to-face versus computer mediated modes of interaction. Yet tremendous variation is possible in the design of CSCL environments. We turn now to consideration of how design choices *within* the computer medium might influence learning.

## TOOLS FOR SUPPORTING ARGUMENTATION IN RELATION TO LEARNING

How might CSCL technologies be designed to most optimally support "arguing to learn"? This question can be approached by considering the ways in which technology can potentially influence learning processes and outcomes. It is natural to first consider the properties of technologies as communication channels, for without communication no argumentation would be possible. Yet, computational media are not limited to being means of communication. They also present opportunities to aid and guide argumentation and learning through their dynamic and representational properties. We will therefore also consider the more general question of how CSCL tools can help facilitate argumentative communication.

*Computer Mediated Communication*

We first consider computational media as communication channels. The study of computer-mediated communication (CMC) has demonstrated, among other things, that problems arise from the limitations placed on communication in the computer medium (Clark & Brennan, 1993; Olson & Olson, 1997). The loss of nonverbal cues (such as intonation, facial expressions and gesture) and the increased cost of utterance production (such as when using a keyboard) can make any discourse, including argumentation, more difficult. However, other advantages may be realized in comparison to face-to-face discourse. For example, persons who are inhibited from participating in face-to-face discussion have greater opportunities online. As another example, it is possible to review the written record of discourse in CMC, which is not possible without recording face-to-face conversations. Learners can use this record as a learning resource.

CMC is generally used when face-to-face communication is not possible due to spatial or temporal separation of the interlocutors. *Synchronous* CMC tools address spatial separation, and *asynchronous* tools address temporal (and possibly spatial) separation. Synchronous interaction such as "chat" tends to be fast paced with short utterances, like a verbal conversation. The immediacy of synchronous interaction has social advantages: participants may be more motivated to engage, and interpersonal negotiations are easier to carry out in synchronous media. With appropriate scaffolding, chat can support productive argumentation (Pilkington & Walker, this volume). Yet the fast pace of chat is also a disadvantage. Asynchronous communication encourages more reflective dialogue, as there is time to think through and compose a considered response, unlike in either face-to-face communication or synchronous CMC.

Face-to-face discourse – whether argumentation or not – often involves reference to and manipulation of artifacts such as pictures, figures, diagrams, and textual documents under discussion. Many CMC tools provide poor or no support for discourse about artifacts other than the text of the messages themselves. Documents attached to email or other messages exist only with in the context of the message. In many applications, this dependency should be reversed: artifacts should exist independently as part of the context of the ongoing discussion, with messages attached to the appropriate artifacts. Solutions to this problem include document annotation systems in which messages and threads are associated with documents or parts of documents (e.g., Buckingham-Shum & Sumner, 2001).

*Structuring Interactions*

If messages (synchronous or asynchronous) are simply listed in the order they are contributed, it may be difficult to keep track of the different threads of conversation that emerge as multiple participants reply to each others' messages. Two contiguous messages may not have any thing to do with each other, violating a basic assumption behind the coherence of spoken dialogue (Herring, 1999). This problem is typically addressed by enabling contributors to indicate the message to which they are responding, and displaying the messages according to the resulting reply structure.

Yet, such "threaded" discussions present other problems. They are notorious for their lack of convergence, a situation that has been blamed on the fact that the reply relations build an inherently divergent representation: a tree (Hewitt, 1997). Furthermore, the representation reflects the historical development of the discussion rather than its conceptual content (Turoff et al., 1999) making it difficult to quickly grasp and assess the status of the discourse and hence to make contributions that move it forward. Argumentation tools may require representations that capture the conceptual structure of argumentation, a topic to which we return shortly.

Some tool designers address problems of coherence and convergence by tracking and constraining the learners' interactions. A common approach is to provide and require the use of a usually fixed set of classifications for messages, whether synchronous or asynchronous. In synchronous environments, these classifications often take the form of communicative acts (Baker, this volume) or of sentence openers (McManus & Aiken, 1995). In asynchronous environments, messages may be classified as posing a question, providing information, offering a theory, etc. Proponents claim that utterance classifiers and sentence openers (1) increase the efficiency of online communications by reducing cost of message production (saving typing); (2) guide interlocutors into argumentation by prompting them with an appropriate set of argument moves; (3) increase refection on the part of interlocutors by requiring that they identify the intent of their communications; and thereby (4) increase the success of online communications by making intentions more explicit. Results of studies are mixed. If not sufficiently trained and motivated, users of such systems may form the habit of using the most convenient (e.g., first item in the menu) or most generic ("I think ...") markers (Robertson et al, 1998). On the other hand, some work has shown that structured interfaces can lead to a greater percentage of task-oriented (if not argumentative) communications (Baker, this volume). Other benefits may accrue from automated guidance enabled by tracking the dialogue. Yet, given that the choice of communicative acts imposes an additional cognitive burden on the users, designers might ask whether their users perceive direct benefits for making these choices.

*Argument Representations*

We have just discussed ways to structure the argumentation *process*. Another approach is to structure argument *products*, including intermediate forms. Software is provided that enables interlocutors to construct a map of one or more beliefs and the argumentation about these beliefs in some usually pre-determined notation. Externalization of beliefs and arguments in visual knowledge representations has several potential advantages.

Every notation has its representational biases, which may be exploited to guide the direction of argumentation. Chapters by Suthers and van Bruggen & Kirschner discuss possible mechanisms by which representational tools can influence the content of learners' argumentation, and chapters by Suthers, Jermann & Dillenbourg, and Veerman summarize empirical studies of the influence of tool on argumentation. This influence begins before learners construct a representation: the notation's ontology influences learners' conceptualization of the problem. A partially constructed representation may prompt for particular constructive activities, such as linking new claims to an existing argument graph or filling in cells of a table. Once beliefs and the argumentation underlying those beliefs are externalized in a visual representation, it becomes easier for interlocutors to share and compare their conceptualizations, and thereby to recognize potential points of conflict for further discussion. The ease with which this comparison can be done depends on the properties of the representational notation used.

The concepts of epistemological and heuristic adequacy, which we borrow from the artificial intelligence literature, can clarify the importance of well-considered representation design in CSCL tools. A representation is epistemologically adequate if it captures the distinctions (e.g., between types of entities and relationships between them) needed to expose differences to be worked out via argumentation. A representation is heuristically adequate if the important differences are immediately salient to the interlocutors (rather than requiring some effort to recover from the notation). For example, natural language text has high epistemological adequacy (it can express virtually any concept) but low heuristic adequacy (we cannot tell at a glance, or sometimes even after a quick read, the argumentative structure of a text or the points of conflict between two texts). As an example of the other extreme, evidence mapping notations such as used in Belvedere (Suthers, this volume) have low epistemological adequacy (they do not capture many of the nuances of argumentation we might need) but high heuristic adequacy *within the scope of their epistemological adequacy* (it is easy to assess and compare the content of evidence maps). These examples suggest the possibility of a fundamental tradeoff in the design of representational tools, termed the "techno-cognitive paradox" by Baker (this volume): epistemological adequacy seems to come at the cost of heuristic adequacy, and vice-versa. If we want our guidance we apparently must pay for it with our freedom of expression.

Representational tools play other roles in addition to prompting users for certain ideas and enabling assessment and comparison of expressions of those ideas. The very act of constructing a representation together changes the interaction. Interlocutors acting on a shared representation may feel some level of obligation to obtain agreement or permission from one's group members, leading to explication and negotiation of representational acts in advance of their commission. Thus, the creative acts afforded by a given representational notation may affect which negotiations of meaning and belief take place. The components of a collaboratively constructed representation, having arisen from these negotiations, evoke in the minds of the participants rich meanings, and therefore can serve as an easy way to refer to ideas previously developed through deixis rather than complex verbal descriptions (Clark & Brennan, 1993). In this manner, collaboratively constructed external representations facilitate subsequent negotiations; increasing the conceptual complexity that can be handled in group interactions and facilitating elaboration on previously represented information. The shared representation also serves as a group memory, reminding the participants of previous ideas (encouraging elaboration on them) and possibly serving as an agenda for further work. Representational guidance pervades these roles: the utility of a representation with respect to constructing and comparing arguments depends on its biases.

*Active Guidance of Argumentation*

To this point, we have discussed only passive forms of support for argumentation as a learning process. Drawing upon the field of intelligent tutoring systems (or, more generally, artificial intelligence in education), tool designers may elect to build in active guidance of the argumentation process. Although there has been much work on coaching individual problem solving, coaching of collaboration is more rare. Approaches can be classified according to whether they are based on dialogue models or actions in the workspace (Muehlenbrock, 2000). An example of a dialogue-based approach is the Group Leader Tutor (McManus & Aiken, 1995). Students' use of sentence openers is tracked and compared to an ideal model of interaction to generate a tutoring plan, applied when students ask for suggestions or when they do not use the sentence openers properly. An example of a workspace-based approach is COLER (Constantino-Gonzales, 2000). After constructing individual solutions to a database-modelling problem, students construct a group solution. COLER compares each individual's workspace to the group workspace and encourages students to address differences they may have with the group solution.

COLER was designed with a particular activity sequence in mind: differences between individual problem solutions provide the basis for argumentation in the group phase. This dependency of tool on activity illustrates an important point: one cannot expect too much of the tool alone. Several chapters of this volume attest to the importance of designing appropriate activities and indeed environments for argumentation (see for example the chapters by Andriessen et al.; Baker; and Schwartz & Glassner), a topic to which we now turn.

## PEDAGOGICAL SCENARII

From a pedagogical perspective, collaborative tasks may serve different roles in educational practice. It seems reasonable to suppose that in this practice, the stakeholders' assumptions about learning and knowledge will reciprocally interact with the design of learning environments and how one participates in those environments (Barab & Duffy, 2000). What people think knowing something entails affects the likelihood of accepting new knowledge, belief revision or conceptual change (Kuhn, 2001). The discussion of confronting cognitions and instructional technologies cannot be detached from discussing classroom or work practices of which they are a part. Because of the wide range of options available to participants in a collaborative learning task, a range that is necessary for personal beliefs and knowledge to be at stake, in order for learning by argumentation to take place, it is crucial to consider the role of the educational context. This is the purpose of this section.

The educational contexts under which specific learning goals are to be realized can be captured in the form of pedagogical scenarios. Scenarios stand for educational arrangements, that is a designed combination of tasks or task sequences, instructions, and tools that enable learner activities, serving the attainment of specific learning goals. Andriessen & Sandberg (1999) proposed three prototypical scenarios, covering most educational practices, that can be distinguished on the basis of underlying assumptions about learning, goals typically associated with learning assignments, types of learning activities involved and the associated roles of the participants in the learning situation. While most learning situations involve a blend of scenario ingredients, a more abstract approach to characterise these practices helps clarifying the relationships between argumentation and its educational context, specifically with respect to epistemology and pedagogy.

*Transmission scenarios*

The first prototypical pedagogical scenario was called *transmission*. In transmission, knowledge is supposed to be an object to be imparted into the minds of learners. The goal of education is the transmission of domain knowledge from the expert to the learner. Learners have to understand what experts mean, and their lack of personal understanding is treated as misconceptions that have to be repaired. Transmission based teaching, which characterizes most formal education, centres on the acquisition of declarative or statable knowledge and a limited number of critical skills, by a system of lectures, textbooks, and testing. Transmission scenarios favour closed assignments with criteria determined by the instructor. Learning by being taught, by examples and demonstrations, by drill and practice, or by discovery all should lead to the attainment of fixed learning goals. The ideal transmission-based learning environment is one with an inspiring tutor teaching with clear demonstrations, expositions, narratives, arguments and examples. In transmission, collaboration may support participants in trying to understand ideas, by explanation and comprehension processes. The success of the collaboration in transmission depends on the (effective and efficient) attainment of domain-specific knowledge.

In transmission, argumentation is mainly considered as a reasoning process, in which learners try to articulate strong and relevant arguments to arrive at an approved conclusion. The situational constraint that drives the argumentation in the first place is the teacher (who has the roles of domain expert, discussion moderator and evaluator at the same time), not the interests or personal goals of the participants themselves. Hence, what is being confronted during argumentation between two students concerns not only their personal representations, but also those of experts, represented in the teacher's words or the textbook contents. In other words, for the participants the issue at stake during argumentation in knowledge transmission is: is this information *correct*? Ideally, this would require on-line expert feedback and prompting, originally one of the main goals of Intelligent Tutoring Systems (Andriessen & Sandberg, 1999).

If correctness of knowledge is the principal issue, participants in a discussion will be constrained to the extent of their lack of confidence in the strength and relevance of their personal knowledge. The paradox of transmission with respect to the role of argumentation as a learning tool is that the less knowledge you have, and so the more you can benefit from argumentative discussion, the less inclined you may be to deeply engage in such a discussion. As a consequence, participants do not tend to bring in more than facts and opinions they feel relatively certain about, resulting in less understanding (especially less refinement of goals and concepts) than would have been possible. In other words, in transmission, the learners' argumentative *goals* do not match those required for constructive debate, from a learning perspective.

Another characteristic of transmission scenarios is their focus on *individual learning* or *personal understanding*. Individual conflict is a driving force of knowledge transmission, not interpersonal disagreement. Obviously, handling interpersonal conflict during confrontation of cognitions involves a social component as well, which is tightly interwoven with the cognitive aspects of the collaborative situation. However, learners' social skills for handling conflicts are not linked to school tasks, but to their personal interactions outside the context of school assignments. When students collaborate they are used to distributing tasks, as in writing a paper where each writer produces a section of the text, after which all sections are assembled. The social skills of students necessary to handle socio-cognitive conflicts in constructive epistemic discussions are not developed in this way. This relates to a paradox referred to by Baker (*this volume*): if the dialogue is to have any point, then students must, to some extent, address cognitive conflicts as they arise; but the more they go deeper into cognitive disagreement, the greater the threat to their interpersonal relationship.

Furthermore, due to the focus on individual knowledge in transmission, students involved in a collaborative discussion do not have great interest in sharing ideas. It is more likely an act of benevolence when a student with more understanding of some aspect of the domain explains this understanding to another student. The receiver of this information would better not try to challenge this gift too much. As a consequence, conflicts may not be sought as often as they potentially could be, from a learning perspective.

A number of findings reported by authors in this book (e.g. Baker, Veerman, Andriessen et al.) may be (at least partly) explained by the role of user expectations in a transmission scenario. Some of the common findings addressed in these chapters are that (1) students tend to focus on solutions, rather than processes, even if the problems to be solved are open and complex, (2) students tend to divide subtasks between them, rather than working together, (3) students feel stuck by constraints, rather than trying to overcome them, (4) students use provided information and task structure as given, not as negotiable or discussible, and (5) because of their inflexibility, users are extremely sensitive to specific design features of the computer environment. In addition, concerning argumentation, (6) students depend on explanations to guide their knowing rather than on evidence (Baker, 2002; Kuhn, 2001).

It would be easy to raise more issues concerning problems with most current educational contexts, which have been described as 19th century Tayloristic, based on the wrong ideas about what knowledge is, and lacking in authenticity with respect to real life tasks (e.g. Resnick, 1987; Harasim, 1997; Petraglia, 1998; Bereiter, 2002). As a consequence, the effectiveness of argumentation as an educational activity in such contexts is limited to the extent that the participants in this activity are truly committed to knowledge improvement. This is not very likely to happen in transmission scenarios, and only with enigmatic teachers and socially highly skilled and motivated students.

*Studio scenarios*

The second educational scenario distinguished by Andriessen and Sandberg (1999) was called studio. Instead of focusing on personal understanding of normative information as in transmission, the studio scenario concerns the acquisition of metacognitive skills and learning to learn. The learning environment is explicitly considered, as it is seen as a collection of tools and tasks to be used by learners to adapt their learning to their needs and goals. Collaborative learning is one of the skills that learners are supposed to master. Instead of collaboration being acquired as a by-product of knowledge acquisition, now it is addressed in a number of different tasks in which different functions of collaboration and roles of participants are the focus of attention. While studio scenarios presuppose that learners have the ability to understand given information, the new focus is now on their individual roles as learners and collaborators that have to apply and extend their understanding to different tasks. Typically, the tasks are open, with no fixed solutions or solution paths, and allow adaptation to specific individual knowledge and skills. In studio, learners are learning to arrive at shared understanding, by dialogue and communication of information and knowledge through the use of various tools available in the environment. This involves, among other things, discussing different viewpoints, and integrating personal beliefs, other peoples' ideas and information from different sources in a process of argumentative learning (Stahl, 2000).

The general reason why argumentation is supposed to involve more committed users in studio than in transmission is that in studio collaboration is an integral part of the curriculum and a skill explicitly to be acquired during the learning process. In studio, context is ripe for the development and use of CSCL environments that (1) adequately *support* (as opposed to enable) collaborative (and argumentative) learning, (2) allow using *generic tools* that are not task- and domain-specific as in transmission, and (3) do not treat collaboration as a single type of activity, but instead allow attention for *development* of users, differentiation of user *roles* and distinction of different *phases* in task-based discussions.

Although an implementation of a studio scenario according to the criteria we described here is not known to us, there are many attempts to create studio-type CSCL environments. In this book, the chapter by van Bruggen & Kirschner addresses issues for the development of tools that support several types of argumentation in the context of complex open problems, such as design and investigation. Their chapter offers interesting and important suggestions for a framework for designing external representations for studio-type CSCL environments, and more specifically for representation and support for argumentation in such environments. One of their main points is that the richer the ontology the representational system offers to the users, the harder it would be to use the representation, at least for beginners.

This assumption is also derived from results reported in the chapter by Suthers (*this volume*) in which it was found that in the case of constructing graphical representations to map scientific debate, the labels of categories on the buttons led students to trying to classify their contributions in terms of these labels, rather than developing their own thinking and reasoning. Similarly, Veerman (*this volume*) found that the limitations of the linear interface that supported electronic communication during open problem solving were a greater obstacle for students that focused on concepts and their meaning than for students that had a more product oriented goal. In terms of the pedagogic scenarios one would be tempted to examine such results in terms of differences in flexibility of learners in different scenarios.

The contribution by Jermann & Dillenbourg (*this volume*) also addresses the interface issue. They report a study situated in actual teaching practice that explicitly attempts to foster active interaction between students in an electronic environment, called the TECFA virtual campus. The scenario, serving to promote the acquisition of declarative knowledge about design principles for computer support in education, includes making students' ideas available for discussion by graphically representing them as a collective output. What the authors try to show is that when the computer tool (by its design) orients the students towards expressing differences in opinion, students abandon their usual 'standing pat' attitude (Baker, 1994), an attitude that was discussed above as a characteristic of behaviour in a transmission scenario. Certain tool features served to perceive the task in a different way, which worked out in the context of the studio-type scenario designed by Jermann & Dillenbourg.

The chapter by Schwarz & Glassner (*this volume*) discusses the Kishurim project, an impressive and well-founded attempt to integrate argumentation-based activity in classroom practice. Although it is not explicitly described as such, the project can be taken (among other things) as an attempt to establish the transition from transmission to studio, and beyond, in educational practice. By discussing the role of argumentation in education the authors note the lack of adequate learning environments for students, leading them not to engage in argumentation. This is because (1) the students do not know how to link many natural arguments to personal knowledge and beliefs, and (2) the students tend to take scientific arguments as true rather than challenging them, in other words, they are blind (1) and paralytic (2) with respect to argumentative activities. Schwarz & Glassner go on to discuss several principles, at the level of educational design, with and without technology, to develop a goal-directed program in which students learn and experience argumentation in several forms, and during which students can have different roles.

The role of argumentation is taken much more seriously in studio than in knowledge transmission. Although the focus is still on individual learning, the need for a collaborative context for a learner to be engaged in several forms of meaningful learning is acknowledged. Three chapters in this book explicitly address important issues related to the studio scenario, at the level of design of representations in the CSCL environment (van Bruggen & Kirschner), at the level of task design (Jermann & Dillenbourg), and at the level of educational design (Schwarz & Glassner). Although there is not much evidence to support this, it is expected that argumentation may help to realize more and more versatile learning goals in studio than in transmission. However, in order for such learning to be realized in a collaborative task, a relatively high degree of mutual understanding (grounding) between collaborators has to be established, at the pragmatic level (learning to collaborate, play roles, in different tasks) to arrive at meaning making at the semantic level (Baker, Hansen, Joiner & Traum, 1999). Hence, the focus in studio is on the *pragmatics* of collaborative argumentation (when, why, and how to argue, and for what purpose?) with the aim of (1) reducing the space of misunderstanding during collaborative learning (Dillenbourg, 1999), (2) increasing metacognitive awareness of learning, collaboration and the role of argumentation (e.g. Kuhn, Shaw & Felton, 1997), and (3) preparing learners for the practice of group work and knowledge building discourse (e.g. Bereiter, 2002).

*Negotiation scenarios*

The third (and final) prototypical scenario distinguished by Andriessen & Sandberg (1999) is called the *negotiation* scenario. Negotiating implies individuals communicating and debating points of view in order to reach agreement or understanding. The goal of education in this scenario is to establish learning groups (within and between schools) engaged in knowledge building: creating new knowledge by sharing and negotiating content. All professional practices have found their current shape by long-term interaction and negotiation processes (Saljo, 1996). Participating in professional groups implies the ability to understand the important debates and problems and to use the right language to examine and influence ongoing discussion. Learning in the negotiation scenario is to a large extent learning to produce and comprehend the discourse of the community (Lemke, 1987; Pea, 1993). The idea that learning may be negotiated is not, of course, new. It closely relates to what Bennett (1976) termed the "progressive approach" to teaching, which Bruner (1986) described a decade later as follows:

> "... induction into the culture through education, if it is to prepare the young for life as lived, should also partake of the spirit of a forum, of negotiation, of the recreating of meaning. But this conclusion runs counter to traditions of pedagogy that derive from another time, another interpretation of culture, another conception of authority - one that looked at the process of education as a transmission of knowledge and values." (Bruner 1986, p. 123)

While in studio, learners' activities focus on arriving at shared understanding through multiple forms of collaboration, in the negotiation scenario, learners focus on the process of creating new knowledge on the basis of what is shared (which does not necessarily imply *agreed*). This scenario is about arriving at and building on meaning making practices, making ideas the focus of inquiry and the product an achievement that represents the best of a collaborative effort (c.f. Scardamalia, 1997).

The chapter by Andriessen et al. (*this volume*) discusses the process of *knowledge negotiation* in collaborative writing, which they describe as discussion for agreement about the meaning of concepts and their interpretations in the context of a learning task. Negotiation may be about problem solutions, meanings of concepts, and other things. Argumentation is one of the forms that dialogues in negotiation may take (Baker, 1994; Dillenbourg and Baker, 1996). The extent to which negotiation fosters individual learning depends on specific meaningful exchanges between individual participants. The chapter by Andriessen et al. shows that university students that collaboratively produce an argumentative text through electronic communication do not tend to negotiate each item of content extensively. When they do, as in elaborate argumentation, this immediately increases the variety of arguments in the discussion, in terms of their orientation, pro- and counter the main position of the text. In addition, much of this information discussed as elaborate argumentation is immediately entered into the text under construction. However, in most of the discussion, participants are all too eager to accept ideas put forward by the other. It seems straightforward to attribute this behaviour to the context of transmission-based university education.

The negotiation *scenario*, however, is not merely about individual learning, it is about getting the best out of groups. Knowledge is seen as a (by-) product of group activities, displayed by their discursive practice (Gergen, 1995). In order to construct negotiation scenarios, educational designers must be able to understand concepts such as collective thinking (Allwood, 1997), collaborative knowledge building (Brown & Campione, 1991; Stahl, 2000; Bereiter, 2002), communities of practice (Wenger, 1998), and knowledge management (Brown & Duguid, 2001). Research in this area is in its exploratory phases, and frequently involves case-studies in business contexts, which are beyond the scope of this chapter. The chapter by Pilkington & Walker (*this volume*), however, can be taken as an attempt to study the role of electronic communication in the development of a learning community which can be linked with characteristics of a negotiation scenario.

Pilkington & Walker reason that in order for young students to develop argumentation skills it is first necessary to develop a culture of interaction in which constructive debate is possible. They study this development in a setting outside the school context, a community centre that provides an environment for disadvantaged children (10-15 years old) that need extra support to develop their literacy skills (among other things). The medium is synchronous text-based chat, which was supposed to facilitate communication by reducing writing apprehension and inequality. One of their research questions was whether it is possible to learn children to engage in debate-style 'substantive conflict' (explicit disagreement, considering alternatives) through the use of this medium, to engage in better argumentation, and to produce better individually written compositions. Characteristic for their approach is the study of developments over a long period, using different media, tasks and specific task goals, implementing different teacher roles and a variation of individual and collaborative phases. Note that the study by Schwarz & Glassner (*this volume*) explicitly states a similar approach in these respects. Both studies involve the goal of 'learning to argue', which is not taken as the mastery of argumentative schemas, but as a form of practice in a social and educational context, to be exercised in open and complex domains such as scientific reasoning or written text production.

The differences between the two studies relate to the context of the research (community centre and classroom) and the balance between top-down (teacher or researcher-designed) and bottom-up (student choices and responsibility) goals set during the experiments. Hence, argumentation in the Schwarz & Glassner study concerned bridging the gap between scientific reasoning and the students' personal reasoning. This requires for their students quite precise reflections on the content and formulation of arguments. In contrast, in the Pilkington & Walker study, the development of argumentation skills served to improve literacy in different contexts. This is studied in a context in which interpersonal communication is at least as important as the content of the arguments put forward during this communication.

*Confronting cognitions in different scenarii*

Arguing to learn serves different goals in the different pedagogic scenarios. Different goals affect the argumentative activities users are engaged in, which is directly related to the learning outcomes of these activities. Scenarios focusing on meaning making practice rather than on the product, and on collaboration and group processes rather than individual knowledge were considered as better test-beds for the study of learning from argumentation. All chapters in this book address issues that are relevant to these distinctions. However, educational practice seems to be lagging behind in may respects. A fundamental problem is thus to understand how to help teachers to provide help to learners to better exploit the co-constructive potential of their argumentative interactions.

## CONCLUDING REMARKS

In this introductory chapter, rather than summarising the book, we have tried to map out a space of argumentative activities and pedagogical situations in relation to CSCL tools that can support them, whilst giving pointers to different chapters. We hope that these reflexions will stimulate readers to actively work on the chapters.

By way of conclusion, we restrict ourselves to two brief remarks that may be worth reflecting upon when reading this book.

Firstly, for a book on the apparently restrictive topic of confronting cognitions in argumentation-based CSCL environments, the chapters describe a surprisingly varied ensemble of situations and complex sequences of pedagogical tasks, activities, and scenarii, with their associated sets of tools. But this is perhaps not so surprising if one accepts that knowledge-based argumentation is one of the most complex cognitive, linguistic and communicative tasks required of human beings, who not only have to generate cognitions, but also refine them by examination of their foundations, in confrontation with others people's cognitions. Pedagogical activities for argumentation-based learning will thus have to be correspondingly knowledge-rich and complex.

Secondly, although this book concentrates on argumentation, in a very wide sense of the term, we do not wish to suggest that everything could or should be learned in this way. There are surely limits to learning from confronting cognitions in CSCL environments, however well situations are designed in terms of collaborating partners, communication tools, associated information and pedagogical scenarii. What are those limits? We can only hope that this book contributes not to answering that question, but rather to laying foundations for ... a constructive debate.

## REFERENCES

Alamargot, D. & Andriessen, J. (2002). The "power" of text production activity in collaborative modeling: Nine recommendations to make a Computer Supported situation work. In P. Brna, M. Baker, K. Stenning & A. Tiberghien (Eds.), *The Role of Communication in Learning to Model* (pp. 275-302). Mahwah, New Jersey: Lawrence Erlbaum Associates.

Alwood, J. (1997). Dialog as collective thinking. In Pylkkänen, P., Pylkkö, P. & Hautamäki, A. (Eds.). *Brain, Mind and Physics (pp. 205-210)*. Amsterdam, IOS Press.

Andriessen, J. E. B. & Sandberg, J. A. C. (1999). Where is Education heading and how about AI? International Journal of Artificial Intelligence in Education *10*, 2, 130-150.

Baker, M. J. (1994). A Model for Negotiation in Teaching-Learning Dialogues. *Journal of Artificial Intelligence in Education*, 5(2), 199-254.

Baker, M. J. (1996). Argumentation et co-construction des connaissances. *Interaction et Cognitions* 2 (3), 157-191.

Baker, M. J. (1999). Argumentation and Constructive Interaction. In G. Rijlaarsdam & E. Espéret (Series Eds.) & J. Andriessen and P. Coirier (Vol. Eds.) Studies in Writing: Vol. 5. *Foundations of Argumentative Text Processing*, (pp. 179 – 202). Amsterdam: University of Amsterdam Press.

Baker, M. J. (2002). Argumentative interactions, discursive operations and learning to model in science. In P. Brna, M. Baker, K. Stenning & A. Tiberghien (Eds.), *The Role of Communication in Learning to Model* (pp. 303-324). Mahwah N.J.: Lawrence Erlbaum Associates.

Baker, M., Hansen, T., Joiner, R. & Traum, D. (1999). The role of grounding in collaborative learning tasks. In P. Dillenbourg (Ed.), *Collaborative Learning: cognitive and computational approaches* (pp. 31-63). Oxford: Pergamon.

Barab, S. A. & Duffy, T. M. (2000). From practice fields to communities of practice. In: D. Jonassen & S. M. Land (Eds.), *Theoretical foundations of learning environments*, (pp. 25-56). Mahwah, New Jersey: Lawrence Erlbaum Associates.

Bennett, N. (1976). *Teaching Styles and Pupil Progress*. London: Open Books.

Bereiter, C. (2002). *Education and mind in the Knowledge age*. Mahwah, New Jersey: Lawrence Erlbaum Associates.

Billig, M. (1987). *Arguing and thinking: A rhetorical approach to social psychology*. Cambridge: Cambridge University Press / Paris: Éditions de la Maison des Sciences de l'Homme.

Blaye, A. (1990). Peer Interaction in Solving a Binary Matrix Problem: Possible Mechanisms Causing Individual Progress. In H. Mandl, E. De Corte, N.Bennett & H.F. Friedrich (Eds.) *Learning and Instruction* Vol 2,1. London: Pergamon Press.

Brown, A. L. & Campione, J. C., (1981). Inducing flexible thinking: A problem of access. In M. Friedman, J.P. Das & N. O'Connor (Eds.), *Intelligence and learning* (pp. 515-529). New York: Plenum.

Brown, J. S. & Duguid, P. (1991). Organizational learning and communities of practice: Toward a unified view of working, learning, and innovation. *Organization Science 2* (1), pp. 40-57.

Bruner, J.S. (1986). *Actual Minds, Possible Worlds*. London: Harvard University Press.

Buckingham Shum, S. & Sumner, T. (2001). JIME: An Interactive Journal for Interactive Media. *First Monday*, 6, (2), Feb. 2001. [http://firstmonday.org/issues/issue6_2/buckingham_shum/]. To be reprinted in Learned Publishing, 2001. PrePrint (with high resolution screens images) available as a PDF: Technical Report KMI-TR-99, Knowledge Media Institute, Open University, UK (2001) [http://kmi.open.ac.uk/tr/abstracts/kmi-tr-99.html].

Chi, M. T. H., Bassok, M., Lewis, M. W., Reimann, P. & Glaser, R. (1989). Self-Explanations: How Students Study and Use Examples in Learning to Solve Problems. *Cognitive Science* , 13 (2), 145-182.

Clark, H. H & Brennan, S. (1991). Grounding in communication. In L.B. Resnick, J.M. Levine & S.D. Teasley (Eds.) *Perspectives on Socially Shared Cognition*, pp. 127-149. Washington DC: American Psychological Association.

Clark, H. H. & Brennan, S. E. (1993). Grounding in Communication. In R. M. Baecker (Ed.), Readings in Groupware and Computer-Supported Cooperative Work (pp. . San Mateo, CA: Morgan Kaufmann Publishers.

Constantino-González, M. A. (2000). *A Computer Coach to Support Collaboration in a Web-based Synchronous Collaborative Learning Environment*. Unpublished dissertation, ITESM (Instituto Tecnológico y de Estudios Superiores de Monterrey), México.

Crook, C. (1994). *Computers and the Collaborative Experience of Learning*. London: Routledge.

Dillenbourg, P. & Baker, M. J. (1996). Negotiation Spaces in Human-Computer Collaboration. In Actes du colloque *COOP'96, Second International Conference on Design of Cooperative Systems*, pp. 187-206, INRIA, Juan-les-Pins, juin 1996.

Dillenbourg, P. (1999) Introduction: What do you mean by 'collaborative learning'? In P.Dillenbourg (ed.) *Collaborative learning, cognitive and computational approaches,* (pp. 1-19). Oxford: Pergamon.

Doise, W. & Mugny, G. (1981). *Le développement social de l'intelligence* [The social development of intelligence]. Paris : InterÉditions.

Ducrot, O. (1980). Les Échelles Argumentatives [Argumentative Scales]. Paris: Les Éditions de Minuit.

Gergen, K. (1995). The social constructionist movement in modern psychology. *American Psychologist,* 40(3), 266-275.

Golder, C. (1996). *Le developpement des discours argumentatifs* [The development of argumentative discourses]. Lausanne: Delachaux & Niestle.

Harasim, L. (1997, march). Network learning: what have we learned and what does it mean? Presented at the AERA annual meeting, Chicago, Il.

Herring, S. C. (1999, January). Interactive coherence in CMC. In *Proceedings of the 32$^{nd}$ Hawai`i International Conference on the System Sciences (HICSS 32).* (CD-ROM). Maui, Hawai`i: Institute of Electrical and Electronics Engineers, Inc. (IEEE).

Hewitt, J. (1997). Beyond threaded discourse. Paper presented at WebNet'97. Available: http://csile.oise.utoronto.ca/abstracts/ThreadedDiscourse.html

Koschmann, T. (2002). Dewey's contribution to the foundations of CSCL Research. In G. Stahl (ed.), *Computer Support for Collaborative Learning*. Proceedings of CSCL 2002, (pp. 17-22). Boulder, Colorado.

Kuhn, D. (2001). How do people know? *Psychological Science, 12 (1),* 1-8.

Kuhn, D., Shaw, V. & Felton, M. (1997). Effects of dyadic interaction on argumentative reasoning. *Cognition and Instruction, 15(3),* 287-315.

Lemke, J. L. (1989). *Using language in the classroom.* Oxford: Oxford University Press.

Mevarech, Z. R. & Light, P. H. (1992). Peer-based interaction at the computer : looking backward, looking forward. *Learning and Instruction* , 2, 275-280.

McManus, M. M. and Aiken, R. M. (1995). Monitoring Computer Based Collaborative Problem Solving. *Journal of Artificial Intelligence in Education* , 6(4) , 308-336.

Muehlenbrock, M. (2000). Action-based collaboration analysis for group learning. Ph.D. thesis, Department of Mathematics/Computer Science, University of Duisburg.

Nonnon, E. (1996). Activités argumentatives et élaboration de connaissances nouvelles: le dialogue comme espace d'exploration. *Langue Française, 112,* 67-87.

Olson, G. M. & Olson, J. S. (1997). Research on computer-supported cooperative work. In M. Helander, T. K. Landauer, & P. Prabhu (Eds), Handbook of Human-Computer Interaction (2nd Edition), Amsterdam: Elsevier.

Pea, R. D. (1993). Learning scientific concepts through material and social activities: Conversational analysis meets conceptual change. *Educational Psychologist, 28* (3), 265-277.

Perelman, C. & Olbrechts-Tyteca, L. (1958/1988). *Traité de l'argumentation. La nouvelle rhétorique* [Treatise on argumentation. The new rhetoric]. Bruxelles: Editions de l'Université de Bruxelles.

Petraglia, J. (1998). *Reality by Design: The rhetoric and technology of authenticity in education.* Mahwah, New Jersey: Lawrence Erlbaum Associates.

Resnick, L. B. (1987). Constructing knowledge in school. In L. S. Liben (ed.), *Development and learning: Conflict or congruence?* (pp. 19-50). Hillsdale, New Jersey: Lawrence Erlbaum Associates.

Robertson, J., Good, J., & Pain, H. (1998). BetterBlether: The design and evaluation of discussion tool for education. *International Journal of Artificial Intelligence in Education*, 9, 219-236.

Roschelle, J. & Pea, R. (2002, January). A Walk on the WILD side: How wireless Handhelds may change CSCL. In G. Stahl (ed.), *Computer Support for Collaborative Learning.* Proceedings of CSCL 2002, (pp. 51-60). Boulder, Colorado.

Scardamalia, M. (1997, march). *Networked Communities Focused on Knowledge Advancement.* Presented at the AERA annual meeting, Chicago, Il.

Stahl, G. (2000). A model of collaborative knowledge-building, In: *Proceedings of the Fourth International Conference of the Learning Sciences* (ICLS 2000), (pp. 70-77). Ann Arbor, MI.

Stahl, G. (2002, january). Introduction, Foundations for a CSCL community. In G. Stahl (ed.), *Computer Support for Collaborative Learning.* Proceedings of CSCL 2002, (pp. 1-2). Boulder, Colorado.

Stein, N. L. & Bernas, R. (1999). The Early Emergence of Argumentative Knowledge and Skill. In G. Rijlaarsdam and E. Espéret (Series Eds.) & J. Andriessen and P. Coirier (Vol. Eds.) Studies in Writing: Vol. 5. *Foundations of Argumentative Text Processing*, (pp. 97–116). Amsterdam: University of Amsterdam Press.

Sutter, B. (2002, January). Instructional Artifacts. In G. Stahl (ed.), *Computer Support for Collaborative Learning.* Proceedings of CSCL 2002, (pp. 33-42). Boulder, Colorado.

Turoff, M., Hiltz, S. R., Bieber, M., Fjermestad, J., & Rana, A. (1999). Collaborative discourse structures in computer mediated group communications. *Journal of Computer Mediated Communication, 4*(4). Online: http://jcmc.huji.ac.il/

van Eemeren, F. H., Grootendorst, R. & Snoeck Henkemans, F. (1996). *Fundamentals of Argumentation Theory: A Handbook of Historical Backgrounds and Contemporary Developments.* Mahwah, New Jersey: Lawrence Erlbaum Associates.

Van Someren, M. W., Reimann, P., Boshuizen, H. P. A., & de Jong, T. (1998). Learning with Multiple Representations. Amsterdam: Elsevier Science, Ltd.

Walton, D. N. (1989). *Informal Logic: a handbook for critical argumentation.* Cambridge: Cambridge University Press.

Wenger, E. (1998). *Communities of practice: Learning, Meaning, and Identity.* Cambridge: Cambridge University Press.

DANIEL D. SUTHERS

# REPRESENTATIONAL GUIDANCE FOR COLLABORATIVE INQUIRY

## INTRODUCTION

For a number of years, my colleagues and I (see acknowledgments) have been building, testing, and refining a diagrammatic environment ("Belvedere") intended to support secondary school children's learning of critical inquiry skills in the context of science (Suthers, Connelly, Lesgold, Paolucci, Toth, Toth, & Weiner, 2001; Toth, Suthers, & Lesgold, 2002). The diagrams were first designed to engage students in complex scientific argumentation with the help of an intelligent tutoring system. (For the purposes of this chapter, scientific argumentation is a dialectic in which participants mutually evaluate alternative hypotheses according to their consistency with empirical evidence and related criteria such as plausibility of the proposed causal explanations and reliability of the evidence. Participants may but need not necessarily take conflicting positions.) The diagrams were later simplified to focus on evidential relations between data and hypotheses. This change was driven in part by a refocus on collaborative learning (Koschmann, 1994; Slavin, 1980; Webb & Palincsar, 1996), which led to a major change in how we viewed the role of the interface representations. Rather than being a medium of communication or a formal record of the argumentation process, we came to view the representations as resources (stimuli and guides) for conversation and reasoning (Collins & Ferguson, 1993; Roschelle, 1994). Laboratory and field trials with Belvedere provided many examples of situations in which Belvedere's diagrammatic representations appeared to be influencing learner's argumentation. Meanwhile, various other projects with similar goals (i.e., critical inquiry in a collaborative learning context) were using substantially different representational systems (to be reviewed in this chapter). Finding that the literature lacked systematic research on this variable, I undertook a program of exploring the hypothesis that the expressive constraints imposed by a representation and the information (or lack of information) that it makes salient may have facilitative effects on students' argumentation during collaborative learning.

This chapter provides a summary of the thinking behind this work and the empirical studies that my colleagues and I undertook. The chapter begins with an overview of the core claims of a theory of representational guidance and discussion of these claims from cognitive and social standpoints. I then exemplify applications

27

*J. Andriessen, M. Baker, and D. Suthers (eds.), Arguing to Learn: Confronting Cognitions in Computer-Supported Collaborative Learning environments (27-46).*

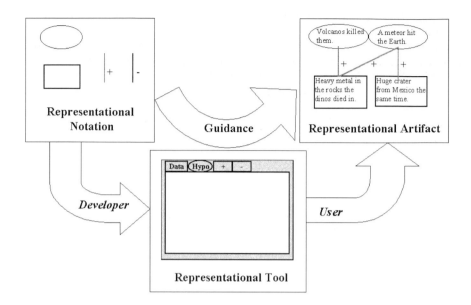

*Figure 1. Flow of Representational Guidance across Notations, Tools and Artifacts*

of the theory by making predictions about the effects of various representational systems found in the literature on software for inquiry learning. The third major section of the chapter summarizes research undertaken to test these predictions, including laboratory research that focused on process measures, and classroom research that focused on students' work products. Results in both cases indicated that predicted representational effects are present, although there are interactions with other variables indicating that further study will be productive.

## THEORY

In this section I outline my initial theory of how variation in features of representational tools used by learners working in small groups can influence learners' knowledge-building argumentation and learning outcomes. In later sections I will summarize predictions I made concerning the effects of selected features of representational tools, and tests of these predictions. The discussion begins with some definitions.

### Representational Guidance

Representational tools are software interfaces in which users construct, examine, and manipulate external representations of their knowledge. My work is concerned with symbolic as opposed to analogical representations. A notation/artifact distinction (Stenning & Yule, 1997), depicted in Figure 1, is critical to the theory. A *representational tool* is a software implementation of a *representational notation* that provides a set of primitive elements out of which *representational artifacts* can be constructed. For example, in Figure 1, the representational notation (following Belvedere) is the collection of primitives for making hypothesis and data statements and "+" and "-" links, along with rules for their use. The software developer chooses the representational notation and instantiates it as a representational tool, while the user of the tool constructs particular representational artifacts in the tool. For example, in Figure 1 the representational artifact is the particular diagram of evidence for competing explanations of mass extinctions.

Each given representational notation manifests a particular representational guidance, expressing certain aspects of one's knowledge better than others. The concept of representational guidance has its origins in artificial intelligence, where it is called "representational bias" (Utgoff, 1986). I use the phrase *guidance* to avoid the negative connotation of bias. My formulation was influenced by writings on "epistemic forms and epistemic games" (Collins & Ferguson, 1993) and the role of simulations in "mediating collaborative inquiry" (Roschelle, 1994). The concept of *affordances* was also influential. Indeed, it was tempting to use the phrase "representational affordances," but see Norman (1999) for a discussion of the misuse of "affordances." Representational guidance is closer to Norman's "perceived affordances" than it is to Gibson's original concept of affordances, although conventional uses of symbol systems (i.e., "epistemic games") are also a factor.

The phrase *knowledge unit* will be used to refer generically to components of knowledge one might wish to represent, such as hypotheses, statements of fact, concepts, relationships, rules, etc. The use of this phrase does not signify a commitment to the view that knowledge intrinsically consists of "units," but rather that users of a representational system may choose to denote some aspect of their thinking with a representational proxy.

Representational guidance manifests in two major ways:

*Constraints*: limits on expressiveness, and on the sequence in which knowledge units can be expressed (Stenning & Oberlander, 1995).

*Salience*: how the representation facilitates processing of certain knowledge units, possibly at the expense of others (Larkin & Simon, 1987).

As depicted in Figure 1, representational guidance originates in the notation and is further specified by the design of the tool. It affects the user through both the tool and artifacts constructed in the tool.

*Central Claims*

The central claims of the theory may now be stated as follows: Representational tools mediate collaborative learning interactions by providing learners with the means to represent emerging knowledge in a persistent medium, inspectable by all participants, where the knowledge then becomes part of the shared context. The representational notation in use constrains what knowledge can be expressed in the shared context, and makes some of that knowledge more salient and hence a likely topic of argumentation. Salience of missing information and ways in which the representation can be extended also influence students' subsequent information seeking activities. These direct effects on argumentation and information seeking may in turn influence learning outcomes. See Baker (2003, this volume) for a discussion of the influences of argumentation on learning.

The following sections clarify this thesis from cognitive and social standpoints, detailing several ways in which constraints and salience are claimed to influence argumentation processes.

## The Origins of Constraints and Salience

Zhang (Zhang, 1997) distinguishes cognitive and perceptual operators used in reasoning with representations. Cognitive operations operate on internal representations; while perceptual operations operate on external representations. Expressed in terms of Zhang's framework, the present analysis is concerned primarily with perceptual operations on external representations rather than cognitive operations on internal representations. This is because my work is concerned with how representations that reside in learners' perceptually shared context mediate collaborative learning interactions. While cognitive operations on internal representations do influence interactions in the social realm, software designers do not design internal representations—they design tools for constructing external representations. These external representations are accessed by perceptual operations, so the perceptual features of a representational notation are of interest for designers of collaborative learning systems.

Stenning and Oberlander (Stenning & Oberlander, 1995) distinguish constraints inherent in the logical properties of a representational notation from constraints arising from the architecture of the agent using the representational notation. This corresponds roughly to my distinction between constraints and salience. Constraints are logical and semantic features of the representational notation. Salience depends on the perceptual architecture of the agent. Differences in degrees of salience can be understood in terms of Zhang's definition of the "directness" of perception as the extent to which information is recoverable from a representation by automatic perceptual processing rather than through a controlled sequence of perceptual (and in our case, cognitive) operators.

It should be understood from Figure 1 and the foregoing discussion that the present work focuses on properties of representational systems with which learners construct representations, not on the properties of pre-constructed representations. Therefore, I consider the cognitive and social (argumentative) activities that are prompted by a representational system and by partially constructed representations, not just the ease of interpretation of a completed representation that is shown to its users. In this respect, as well as the fact that I am concerned with representations of arguments rather than quantitative information, this work is distinct from the voluminous research on the visual display of information (see Lohse, 1997 for a review).

*Representational Guidance and Distributed Cognitions*

External representations have long been a subject of study in the context of learning and problem solving by individuals, with research showing that choice of representation can affect learners' conceptions of a problem and hence impact significantly on problem solving success. See for example Kotovsky & Simon (1990), Novick & Hmelo (1994), and Zhang (1997). One might ask whether it is sufficient to extrapolate from this work, predicting representational effects on groups by aggregating effects on individuals. While much can be gained from such reasoning, I believe that the shared use of representations by distributed cognitions (Salomon, 1993) involves additional emergent phenomena. The interactions of the cognitive processes of several agents differ from the reasoning of a single agent (Okada & Simon, 1997), and therefore may be affected by external representations in different ways. Specifically, external representations play at least three roles that are unique to situations in which a group is constructing and manipulating shared representations as part of a constructive activity:

1. initiating negotiations of meaning,

2. serving as a representational proxy for purposes of gestural deixis, and

3. providing a foundation for implicitly shared awareness.

These roles are discussed below.

1. *Initiating negotiations of meaning.* An individual who wishes to add to or modify a shared representation may feel some obligation to obtain agreement from one's group members, leading to negotiations about and justifications of representational acts. This discourse will include negotiations of meaning and shared belief that would not be necessary in the individual case, where one can simply change the representation as one wishes. The creative acts afforded by a given representational notation may therefore affect which negotiations of meaning and belief take place.

2. *Serving as a representational proxy for purposes of gestural deixis.* The components of a collaboratively constructed representation, having arisen from negotiations of the type just discussed, evoke in the minds of the participants rich meanings beyond that which external observers might be able to discern by inspection of the representations alone. These components can serve as an easy way to refer to ideas previously developed, this reference being accomplished by gestural deixis (reference to an entity relative to the context of discourse by pointing) rather than verbal descriptions (Clark & Brennan, 1991). In this manner, collaboratively constructed external representations facilitate subsequent negotiation, increasing the conceptual complexity that can be handled in group reasoning and facilitating elaboration on previously represented information.

3. *Providing a foundation for implicitly shared awareness.* The shared representation also serves as a group memory, reminding the participants of previous ideas (encouraging elaboration on them) and possibly serving as an agenda for further work. Individual work also benefits from an external memory, but in the group case there is an additional awareness that one's interlocutors may be reminded

by the representation of prior ideas, prompting oneself to consider potential commentary that others will have on one's proposals. That is, it becomes harder to ignore implications of prior ideas if one is implicitly aware that one's interlocutors may also be reminded of them by the representations (Michelene Chi, personal communication, February 1998).

In summary, there is good reason to believe that representational effects will extend to collaborative argumentation in ways worthy of study in their own right. In the following sections, I apply this theory by predicting several ways in which the constraints and saliences of representations commonly used in CSCL will influence collaborative learning. For further discussion of ways in which external representations can aid or hinder collaborative problem solving, see Van Bruggen and Kirschner (this volume).

## REPRESENTATIONS USED IN CSCL SYSTEMS

The research described in this chapter began with a review and analysis of representational notations used in Computer Supported Collaborative Learning (CSCL) systems for "critical inquiry" and "scientific argumentation" as of about 1997. A brief revisitation of this review will provide a collection of representations that I will draw upon as examples when I present three hypotheses concerning representational guidance of argumentation. The purpose of this discussion is to characterize major representational approaches in CSCL systems rather than to provide a review of the systems themselves.

Hypertext/hypermedia systems include CLARE (Wan & Johnson, 1994), the Collaboratory Notebook (O'Neill & Gomez, 1994), CSILE (Scardamalia & Bereiter, 1991; Scardamalia, Bereiter, Brett, Burtis, Calhoun & Smith, 1992), and Web-Camile and Web-SMILE (Guzdial, Hmelo, Hubscher, Nagel, Newstetter, Puntambekar, Shabo, Turns & Kolodner 1997). Seminal systems include gIBIS (Conklin & Begeman, 1987) and NoteCards (Harp & Neches, 1988), which were not developed for educational applications. These systems all have in common a hyperlinking of different comments relevant to an issue, usually with categorization of the hyperlinks or their targets with labels such as "answer," "argument," "problem," "solution," "comment," etc. The representations used vary widely: some take the form of a threaded discussion or other tree structure that may be viewed in summary form, while others support construction of graphs of "nodes" or "cards" through which one navigates, viewing one card at a time.

Argument mapping environments, a variation on concept mapping (Novak, 1990), include Belvedere (Suthers & Weiner, 1995; Suthers, Toth & Weiner 1997; Suthers, et al. 2001), ConvinceMe (Ranney, Schank & Diehl, 1995), and Euclid (Smolensky, Fox, King & Lewis, 1987). All of these tools utilize node-link graphs representing rhetorical, logical, or evidential relationships between assertions (usually categorized as "hypothesis" versus "data" or "evidence"). The entire graph is viewed and manipulated at once, distinguishing these systems from hypermedia environments in which one normally views and manipulates one node of the graph or tree at a time.

SenseMaker (Bell, 1997) exemplifies an intermediate approach. Statements are organized in a 2-dimensional space and viewed all at once, as in argument graphs. However, SenseMaker uses containment rather than links to represent the relationship of evidential support: an empirical statement is placed inside the box of the theory it supports. This notation does not enable one to discriminate between negative evidence and lack of relevance.

Finally, another representation is an evidence or criteria matrix. Such matrices organize hypotheses (or solutions) along one axis, and empirical evidence (or criteria) along another, with matches between the two being expressed symbolically in the cells of the matrix. Puntambekar, Nagel, Hübscher, Guzdial & Kolodner (1997) experimented with such representations in a paper-based collaboration tool. Belvedere 3 and 4 provide matrix views on evidential models (in addition to graphs).

When I undertook this survey in 1997, there appeared to be no systematic studies comparing the effects of external representations on argumentation, although a number of valuable studies had been conducted on software utilizing single representational notations. An informal survey of colleagues revealed that, like me, several designers of systems exemplified above had chosen designs based on informed intuition. Given that these representations define the fundamental character of software intended to guide collaborative learning, I concluded that a systematic comparison was overdue, and initiated the work described in this chapter.

## THREE HYPOTHESES CONCERNING REPRESENTATIONAL GUIDANCE

In this section, I summarize three specific hypotheses concerning effects of constraints and salience that guided my early work, and illustrate these hypotheses with predictions about the affordances of the types of representations outlined above. (The discussion is not intended to pick a "winner" from among the systems reviewed above. Rather, it seeks to identify the kinds of interactions, and therefore learning, that each representational notation encourages. It may well be the case that all of the above representations are useful, albeit for different learning and problem solving phases or task domains.) After these illustrations, we will be fully prepared to review the studies undertaken with Belvedere.

### Hypothesis 1: Representational Notations Influence Learners' Ontologies

The first hypothesis claims that important guidance for learning interactions comes from ways in which a representational notation limits what can be represented (Reader, unpublished; Stenning & Oberlander, 1995). A representational notation provides a set of primitive elements out of which representational artifacts are constructed. These primitive elements constitute an ontology of categories and structures for organizing the task domain. Learners will see their task in part as one of making acceptable representational artifacts out of these primitives. Thus, they will search for possible new instances of the primitive elements, and hence (according to this hypothesis) will be guided to think about the task domain in terms of the underlying ontology.

For example, Belvedere's node-link notation requires users to categorize their statements as *data*, *hypothesis*, or *unspecified,* and to relate statements with consistency and inconsistency relations. Earlier versions of Belvedere presented users with a much richer ontology, but we simplified the ontology to the two most essential distinctions – empirical versus theoretical and consistency versus inconsistency – because the plethora of choices confused students. In fact, this experience motivated Hypothesis 1. As an example, this hypothesis predicts that learners using Belvedere will make use of concepts such as data and hypothesis more often than users of a text editor, which allows use of any concepts but does not prompt for any particular one. This claim would not be of interest if learners merely talked about features of the software tool being used. Rather, the claim is that the representations underlying the software tools will influence learners' use of epistemological concepts.

### Hypothesis 2: Salient Knowledge Units Receive More Elaboration

This hypothesis states that learners will be more likely to attend to, and hence elaborate on, the knowledge units that are perceptually salient in their shared representational workspace than those that are either not salient or for which a representational proxy has not been created. This is for two reasons:

*Reminding:* the visual presence of the knowledge unit in the shared representational context serves as a reminder of its existence and any work that may need to be done with it.

*Ease of Reference:* it is easier to refer to a knowledge unit that has a visual manifestation, so learners will find it easier to express their subsequent thoughts about this unit than about those that require complex verbal descriptions (Clark & Brennan, 1991).

These claims apply to any visually shared representations. However, to the extent that two representational notations differ in kinds of knowledge units they make salient, these functions of reminding and ease of reference will encourage elaboration on different kinds of knowledge units. The ability to manipulate learners' elaborations is important because substantial psychological research shows that elaboration leads to positive learning outcomes, including memory for the knowledge unit and understanding of its significance (Chi, Bassok, Lewis, Reimann, & Glaser 1989; Craik & Lockhart, 1972; Stein & Bransford, 1979).

For example, consider the three representations of a relationship between two hypotheses and two empirically-based statements shown in Figure 2. The topmost notation (threaded discussion) implicitly represents a relevance relationship between statements, but does not capture the reason for this relevance. (Some variations address this problem by allowing one to tag contributions.) The other two notations represent a relationship of evidential support. The middle notation (exemplified by SenseMaker) uses containment to represent evidential support, while the bottom-most notation (exemplified by Belvedere) uses a link. The notations differ in the degree to which the statements and relations are represented with perceptually

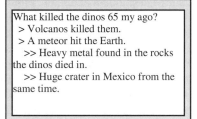

*(a)*   *Threaded   Discussion:*   limited *representation of relation.*

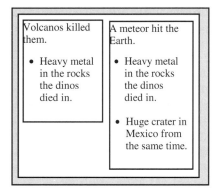

*(b)*        *Containment:*        Implicit *representation of relations.*

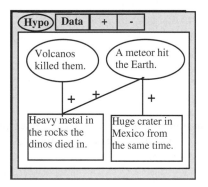

*(c)* *Graph:* Relationship as object of *perception.*

*Figure 2. Example of Elaboration Hypothesis*

distinct visual objects. Data and hypotheses are represented with increasingly distinct objects as one moves down the figure. Hence, Hypothesis 2 predicts that these statements will receive more elaboration in the bottommost representational notation. Similarly, it becomes easier to perceive and refer to the relationship as an object in its own right as one moves from the top to the bottom of the figure. Hence Hypothesis 2 claims that relationships will receive more elaboration in the bottommost representational notation.

A viable argument exists for the opposite prediction. Learners may see their task as one of putting knowledge units "in their place" in the representational environment. I call this the *Pigeonhole hypothesis*. For example (according to this hypothesis), once a datum is placed in the appropriate context (Figure 2b) or connected to a hypothesis (Figure 2c), learners may feel it can be safely ignored as they move on to other units not yet placed or connected. Hence they will not elaborate on represented units. This possibility suggests the importance of making missing relationships salient.

*Hypothesis 3: Salience of Missing Knowledge Units Guides Information Search*

Some representational notations provide structures for organizing knowledge units, in addition to primitives for construction of individual knowledge units. Unfilled fields in these organizing structures, if perceptually salient, can make missing knowledge units as salient as those that are present. If the representational notation provides structures with predetermined fields that need to be filled with knowledge units, the present hypothesis predicts that learners will try to fill these fields. For example, a two dimensional matrix has cells that are intrinsic to the structure of the matrix: they are there whether or not they are filled with content. Learners using a matrix will look for knowledge units to fill the cells.

Figure 3 shows artifacts from three representational notations that differ in salience of missing evidential relationships. In the textual representation, no particular relationships are salient as missing: no particular prediction about search for new knowledge units can be made. In the graph representation, the lack of connectivity of the volcanic hypothesis to the rest of the graph is salient. However, once some connection is made to one data item, the hypothesis will appear connected, so one might predict (by the Pigeonhole hypothesis) that only one relationship involving each object will be sought. In the matrix representation, all undetermined relationships are salient as empty cells. The present hypothesis predicts that learners will be more likely to discuss all possible relationships between objects when using matrices.

I conclude this section by applying the foregoing hypotheses to the specific representational paradigms identified in the review of CSCL systems.

Maybe volcanos killed them. Or a
meteor hit the Earth. Some scientists
found heavy metal in the rocks the
dinos died in. Others found a big
crater in Mexico from the same time.

*(a)* ***Text:*** *No relation is saliently*
*missing.*

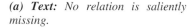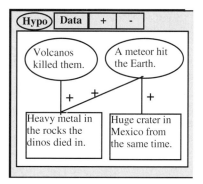

*(b)* ***Graph:*** *Partial salience of*
*missing relations.*

| + | - | | |
|---|---|---|---|
| *Data \ Hypo* | Volcanic | Meteor | |
| Heavy metal in the rocks. | | + | |
| Huge crater in Mexico. | | + | |

*(c)* ***Matrix:*** *Salience of all missing*
*relations.*

*Figure 3. Example of Salient Absence Hypothesis*

*Operational Hypotheses: A Comparison of Selected Notations*

Based on the discussion of this section, the following predictions are made. The symbol ">" indicates that the discourse phenomenon at the beginning of the list (*concept use*, *elaboration*, or *search*) will occur at a significantly greater rate in the treatment condition(s) on the left of the symbol than in those on the right

*Concept Use:* Graph > Matrix > Container > {Text, Threaded Discussion}. The Graph and Matrix representations require that one categorize statements and relations, and Container requires that one categorize statements. Prompting is most explicit in Graph, which provides a palette of shapes for each concept, and strong in Matrix, which labels the axes, while Container, provides only implicit categorization of statements. Categorization of relations is explicit in Graph and Matrix and implicit or absent in the others.

*Elaboration on Relations:* Graph > Matrix > Container > {Text, Threaded Discussion}. Graphs and Matrices make relations explicit as objects that can be pointed to and perceived, while this is not the case in the other two representations. More tenuously, the ability to link relations to other relations in Graphs may increase elaboration on relations relative to Matrices, if this facility is used. The appearance of one statement inside another's container constitutes a more specific assertion of evidence than the reply relation of Threaded Discussion or contiguity of statements in plain Text. Hence, participants are more likely to talk about whether a statement has been placed correctly in the Container representation than in the textual representations.

*Search for Missing Relations:* Matrix > Graph > Container > {Text, Threaded Discussion}. The matrix representation provides an empty field for every undetermined relationship, prompting participants to consider all of them. The Graph and Container representations make unrelated statements salient, but this salience disappears as soon as a link is drawn to the statement in question or another is placed in its container, respectively. Hence, these representations do not prompt for exhaustive consideration of relations. Graph is given precedence over Container for procedural reasons: one must make a copy of a datum in order to involve it in multiple relations in Container, while multiple links are easy to add in Graph. Threaded Discussion and Text do not make missing relationships salient in any perceptual manner.

## STUDIES WITH BELVEDERE

A series of studies undertaken with Belvedere tested these hypotheses on selected representations and illuminated other aspects of the nature of representational guidance for collaborative inquiry. These studies include informal observations of collaborative use of Belvedere undertaken during our formative evaluations, a formal classroom study, and formal laboratory studies. Having already alluded to our informal observations in the foregoing discussion, I will summarize our formal studies in this section, with references to publications where details may be found. The classroom study provided evidence that representational guidance influences students' work in "natural" settings. For logistical reasons we were only able to observe students' work products in the classroom study. The laboratory studies fill in the picture with a closer look at the effects of representational guidance on learning *processes* under controlled conditions.

*Guidance for Inquiry in a Classroom Setting*

Eva Toth, Arlene Weiner and I developed a comprehensive method for implementing Belvedere-supported collaborative inquiry in the classroom. The method includes student activity plans worked out in collaboration with teachers. Students work in teams to investigate real world "science challenge problems," designed with attention to National Science Education Standards to match and enrich the curriculum. A science challenge problem presents a phenomenon to be explained, along with indices to relevant resources. The teams plan their investigation, perform hands-on experiments, analyze their results, and report their conclusions to others. Investigator roles are rotated between hands-on experiments, tabletop data analysis, computer-based literature review, and use of computer simulations and analytic tools as well as Belvedere. Assessment rubrics are given to the students at the beginning of their project as criteria to guide their activities. The rubrics guide peer review, and help the teacher assess non-traditional learning objectives. See Suthers et al. (1997) or Toth et al. (2002) for further information on this integrated approach to classroom implementation.

As part of this work, we conducted a classroom study comparing two forms of guidance for inquiry with respect to quality of inquiry process and conclusions (Toth et al., 2002). The forms of guidance included Belvedere's graphical representations of evidential relations, and assessment rubrics. Version 2.1 of Belvedere was used. The assessment rubrics were paper-based charts that included detailed criteria, in Likert-scale format, for progress in each of four components of scientific inquiry: data collection, evaluation of information collected, quality of reports, and quality of peer presentations. The rubrics were provided to students at the outset of the study with explicit instructions concerning their use during the activity to guide inquiry. A 2x2 design crossed Graph (Belvedere) versus Text (Microsoft Word) conditions with Rubric versus No-rubric conditions across four 9th grade science classes. Students spent about 2 weeks on each of three science challenge problems, including problem introduction, investigation, preparation of reports, and presentations to peers.

The data analysis was based primarily on artifacts produced by groups of students, namely their Belvedere graphs or Word documents, and their final report essays. The amount of information recorded did not differ significantly between groups. Significant results were obtained on the categorization of information and the number of evidential relationships recorded. Specifically, a factorial ANOVA indicated that the Graph groups recorded significantly more inferences than the Text

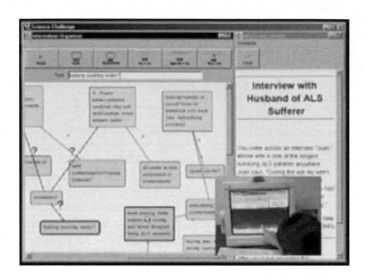

*Figure 4. Experimental Setup, Graph Version, Belvedere 3.0*

groups, and the Rubrics users recorded significantly more inferences than those groups who did not use the rubrics for explicit reflection. An interaction between the type of representational tool and the use of rubrics prompted a closer look at differences in mean scores. A post-hoc paired comparison of the four treatment groups' performance using Tukey's HSD indicated that the combination of graphing and rubrics resulted in a larger number of inferences formulated and recorded compared to all other conditions; while the use of either graphing or rubrics alone did not result in a significantly higher performance compared to either of text groups. Further analysis showed that this interaction was primarily due to the Graph/Rubrics students having recorded significantly more inconsistency relations. Thus, there appears to be a synergistic effect between effective representations and guidelines for their use, particularly with respect to attending to discrepant evidence. Best results were obtained with the combination of rubrics encouraging students to look for and record disconfirming as well as confirming information and explicit representational devices for recording such inferences.

*Comparing Three Representations in a Laboratory Setting*

Subsequent laboratory studies were undertaken to observe representational guidance of argumentation processes that were not accessible to us in the trans-Atlantic classroom study. With the capable assistance of Christopher Hundhausen and Laura Girardeau, I conducted a study comparing three alternative notations for recording evidential relationships between data and hypotheses (free text, graphs, and matrices) with respect to participants' amount of talk about evidential relations

(Suthers & Hundhausen, 2003). We employed a single-factor, between-subjects design with three participant groups defined by the software they used. Dependent measures included: (a) the percentage of utterances and participant actions in the software focused on evidential relations; (b) ability to recall the data, hypotheses, and evidential relations explored in a multiple-choice test; and (c) ability to list, in a written essay, the data, hypotheses, and evidential relations that a scientist familiar with the problem would deem important.

Sixty students were recruited out of introductory science courses in self-selected, same gender pairs, Participant pairs were randomly assigned to the three treatment groups such that there were no significant differences between the groups' mean Grade Point Average (a measure of academic performance). Participant pairs worked with software with two main windows, one containing a workspace for creating either text, graph, or matrix representations, and the other presenting a science problem (what causes a mysterious neurological disease in Guam?) as a fixed sequence of 15 information pages. Participants were instructed to visit each page in the sequence, and to record data, hypotheses, and evidential relations. Once finished, they were individually given a post-test, and then asked to work together on an essay summarizing their findings. This work was undertaken with a research version of Belvedere 3.0. A sample interface using the graph representation is shown in Figure 4.

All 30 sessions were videotaped and transcribed, including both verbal utterances and actions performed with the software. Transcript segments were coded on several dimensions, including content categories of special interest such as whether participants were discussing issues of evidence or using empirical or theoretical concepts. Essays were scored according to the strength and inferential difficulty of the evidential relations they cited, as determined by a systematic analysis.

Using a non-parametric Kruskall-Wallis test, we found significant differences with respect to overall percentages of evidential relations segments, and with respect to the percentages of verbal evidential relations segments. A post-hoc Fischer PLSD test determined that, in both cases, the significant differences were between Matrix and Graph and between Matrix and Text. These results confirm our prediction that notation significantly impacts learners' discussion of evidential relations. The data on ontological bias was inconclusive. In order to provide equivalent instructions to all groups, the instructions provided to Text users modelled labelling of sentences with "Data" and "Hypothesis." Apparently participants faithfully complied with these instructions, leading to just as much use of these concepts in Text as in the other groups.

Further analyses of the same data focused on the contents of participants' representations and their elaborations on (revisitations and reuse of) information and beliefs once they are represented. The results of these analyses indicate that visually structured and constrained representations can provide guidance that is not afforded by plain text. Users of Matrix and Graph revisited previously discussed ideas more often than users of Text, as was predicted from the greater salience of ideas and prompting for missing relations in the more structured representations. However, analyses of the contents of representational artifacts, of how participants revisited prior content, and of essay content suggest that not all guidance is equal, and more is not necessarily better. Comparison of participants' represented content to our own analysis of the problem domain indicates that Text and Matrix users represent more hypotheses than an expert might derive from the problem materials, and Matrix users represent far more evidential relations than can be considered relevant by our analysis. Matrix users revisit prior data and hypotheses mainly to fill in the matrix cells that relate them. They revisit relations far more often than Text or Graph users, but often appear to be doing this because they are attempting to make relationships between weakly or equivocally related items due to the exhaustive prompting of the matrix. Whether the increased talk about evidence prompted by Matrix is valuable is a pedagogical decision that must be made in light of the possibility that many of the evidential relationships considered may be irrelevant. A representation such as Graph may guide students to consider evidence without making them unfocused.

With respect to learning outcomes, analyses of variance found no significant differences between the groups' post-test scores and essay scores, although all trends were in the predicted direction. These results were disappointing, but not surprising. Participants spent less than an hour on task, and this may not have been enough time for learning outcomes to develop fully.

### *The Roles of Representations in Face-to-Face and Online Collaboration*

All of the foregoing studies were undertaken with face-to-face collaboration of participants, yet online learning is becoming increasingly important, especially in higher education. We conducted a follow-up study designed to explore how the roles of representations in online learning might shift, with possible implications for the relevance of representational guidance (Suthers, Hundhausen & Girardeau, submitted). This study was undertaken with a version of the Belvedere 3.0 research software that supported synchronous computer-mediated communication (CMC) with a textual "chat" provided in addition to the graph representation and information pages. Our focus was on understanding how the particular results reported above might change in an online paradigm. There are of course many variables of interest in CMC and a large literature; see Veerman (this volume) for a brief review and a comparison of the effects of three CMC systems (including Belvedere 2.0) on the types of contributions in argumentation.

We conducted sessions with 10 pairs of students using the CMC version of Belvedere 3.0, and compared these sessions to the face-to-face graph sessions from the previous study in order to identify how the roles of representations in supporting collaboration might change. Two hypotheses were considered without prejudice:

(H1)	Visual knowledge representations will play less of a role in guiding discourse online because without co-presence the representations do not as easily function to convey "taken as shared" information or support deixis.

(H2) Visual knowledge representations will play a greater role in supporting discourse online because participants will make use of them to make up for the reduced bandwidth of the verbal modes of interaction.

Our quantitative results provided adequate evidence for the second hypothesis. In the online condition, there was a clear shift to a greater number of communicative acts being undertaken in the graphical knowledge representation as opposed to spoken or chat communications. We found an increased focus on categories supported by the the software (i.e., evidential relations and epistemic classifications). We also observed a shift in the role of the graph representation from object of discourse in the FTF condition to medium of discourse in the CMC condition. Online participants introduce new ideas directly in the graph medium (rather than in the chat) far more often than than face-to-face participants, who always introduced and discussed new ideas verbally before modifying the graph representation.

However, there was also qualitative evidence for the first hypothesis. Our informal review of the transcripts shows many examples of poorly coordinated activity in the online groups, such as disconnects between the activity in the workspace and the verbal activity in the chat. The two hypotheses are not in direct conflict, and may be synthesized as follows: Lack of mutual awareness of orientation towards shared representations may result in poorer coordination of immediate activity and the thinking behind it (H1). At the same time, greater reliance may be placed on those very representations as the medium *through* which activity takes place, biasing activity towards actions best supported by the representations (H2). Online discourse will not be confined to the medium provided for natural language interaction: it will be distributed across all mutable representations and influenced by the properties of those representations. Therefore, close attention must be paid to the design of affordances for argumentation in *all* representations provided to online collaborators.

## CONCLUSIONS

In this chapter, I explored the hypothesis that the expressive constraints imposed by a representation and the information (or lack of information) that it makes salient may have important effects on students' argumentation during collaborative learning. This hypothesis was examined from both theoretical and empirical standpoints. I sketched a theoretical analysis of the role of constraints and salience in representational guidance, and applied this analysis to the representations used by Belvedere and related CSCL systems. Results of two studies were reported showing that appropriate representational guidance can result in increased consideration of evidential relations during an investigation and in the products of the investigation, especially when coupled with additional guidance in the form of rubrics, and that representations can differ in the extent to which represented information is revisited within the representation and used in subsequent work undertaken without the representation present. A third study showed that knowledge representations take on more of the communicative burden online, and therefore representational properties may have a greater opportunity to influence these communications. Two of these three studies also showed representational guidance of the use of epistemological concepts. Further work is needed to address influences on learning outcomes (see for example Schwarz & Glassner, this volume).

My research strategy of comparing representations does not constitute a commitment to mutual exclusivity of the representations. Each representation has its own strengths and weaknesses, and each may be the best choice for different cognitive tasks, learning objectives, and populations. In fact, recent versions of Belvedere integrate three representational "views" (Graph, Matrix, and a Hierarchy representation not discussed here) of evidence models in one tool, providing an interesting platform for future studies. I speculate that Graph will be most useful for gathering and relating information by the relationships that motivated its inclusion; Matrix for subsequently checking that no important relationships have been missed and for scanning for patterns of evidence; and Hierarchy for performing selective queries on a complex evidential model. This line of work promises to inform the design of future software learning environments and to provide a better theoretical understanding of the role of representations in guiding learning through argumentation.

## ACKNOWLEDGMENTS

I am grateful to Alan Lesgold, who initiated the Belvedere project, for his mentorship; Violetta Cavalli-Sforza for work on Belvedere 1.0's argumentation language; Eva Toth and Arlene Weiner for substantial contributions to Belvedere's curriculum and classroom implementation; Dan Jones for work on the client-server architecture and collaborative database; Kim Harrigal for work on the client; Massimo Paolucci, Joe Toth, John Connelly and Sandy Katz for related work on Belvedere not reported here; Laura Girardeau, Cynthia Liefeld, Chris Hundhausen, and David Pautler for assistance with recent and ongoing studies; and Micki Chi, Martha Crosby, and John Levine for discussions concerning the role of representations in learning, visual search, and social aspects of learning, respectively. Work on Belvedere, development of these ideas, and the experimental sessions were funded by DARPA's Computer Aided Education and Training Initiative and DoDEA's Presidential Technology Initiative while I was affiliated with the University of Pittsburgh, and by NSF Learning and Intelligent Systems grant #9873516 under my present affiliation at the University of Hawai`i at Manoa.

## AFFILIATION

*Daniel D. Suthers, Laboratory for Interactive Learning Technologies, Department of Information and Computer Sciences, University of Hawai'i at Manoa, 1680 East West Road, POST 309, Honolulu, HI 96822, USA. Email: suthers@hawaii.edu WWW: http://lilt.ics.hawaii.edu/*

# REFERENCES

Baker, M. (2003). Computer-mediated argumentative interactions for the co-elaboration of scientific notations. To appear in J. Andriessen, M. Baker, & D. Suthers (Eds.) *Arguing to Learn: Confronting Cognitions in Computer-Supported Collaborative Learning Environments*. Kluwer, 2003 (this volume).

Bell, P. (1997, December). Using argument representations to make thinking visible for individuals and groups. In *Proceedings of the Computer Supported Collaborative Learning Conference '97*, 10-19. University of Toronto.

Chi, M.T.H., Bassok, M., Lewis, M., Reimann, P., & Glaser, R. (1989). Self-explanations: How students study and use examples in learning to solve problems. *Cognitive Science*, 13,145-182, 1989.

Clark, H.H. & Brennan, S.E. (1991). Grounding in communication. In L.B. Resnick, J.M. Levine and S.D. Teasley (Eds.), *Perspectives on Socially Shared Cognition* (pp. 127-149). (need city): American Psychological Association.

Collins, A. & Ferguson, W. (1993). Epistemic forms and epistemic games: Structures and strategies to guide inquiry. *Educational Psychologist*, 28(1), 25-42.

Conklin, J. & Begeman, M.L. (1987). gIBIS: A hypertext tool for team design deliberation. In *Hypertext'87 Proceedings* (247-252). New York: ACM.

Craik, F. I. M., & Lockhart, R. S. (1972). Levels of processing: A framework for memory research. *Journal of Verbal Learning and Verbal Behavior*.11, 671-684.

Guzdial, M., Hmelo, C., Hubscher, R., Nagel, K., Newstetter, W., Puntambekar, S., Shabo, A., Turns, J., & Kolodner, J. L. (1997, December). Integrating and guiding collaboration: Lessons learned in computer-supported collaborative learning research at Georgia Tech. In *Proceedings of the 2nd International Conference on Computer Supported Collaborative Learning* (CSCL'97) (pp. 91-100). Toronto: University of Toronto.

Harp, B. & Neches, R. (1988, March). Notecards: An everyday tool for aiding in complex tasks. In *Proceedings of the Architectures for Intelligent Interfaces Workshop* (pp. 287-304). Monterey, CA: ACM/SIGCHI.

Koschmann, T. D. (1994). Toward a theory of computer support for collaborative learning. *The Journal of the Learning Sciences*, 3 (3), 219-225.

Kotovsky, K. and H. A. Simon (1990). What makes some problems really hard: Explorations in the problem space of difficulty. *Cognitive Psychology* 22, 143-183.

Larkin, J. H. & Simon, H. A. (1987). Why a diagram is (sometimes) worth ten thousand words. *Cognitive Science* 11(1), 65-99. 1987.

Lohse, G. L. (1997). Models of graphical perception. In M. Helander, T. K. Landauer, & P. Prabhu (Eds.), *Handbook of Human-Computer Interaction* (pp. 107-135). Amsterdam: Elsevier Science B.V.

Norman, D. N. (1999). Affordance, conventions, and design. ACM *interactions* 6(3), 38-43

Novak, J. (1990). Concept mapping: A useful tool for science education. *Journal of Research in Science Teaching* 27(10), 937-49.

Novick, L.R. & Hmelo, C.E. (1994). Transferring symbolic representations across nonisomorphic problems. *Journal of Experimental Psychology: Learning, Memory, and Cognition* 20(6), 1296-1321.

Okada, T. & Simon, H. A. (1997). Collaborative discovery in a scientific domain. *Cognitive Science* 21(2): 109-146.

O'Neill, D. K., & Gomez, L. M. (1994). The collaboratory notebook: A distributed knowledge-building environment for project-enhanced learning. In *Proceedings of Ed-Media '94*, Charlottesville, VA: Association for the Advancement of Computing in Education.

Puntambekar, S., Nagel, K., Hübscher, R., Guzdial, M., & Kolodner, J. (1997, December). Intra-group and intergroup: An exploration of learning with complementary collaboration tools. In *Proceedings of the Computer Supported Collaborative Learning Conference '97* (207-214). Toronto: University of Toronto.

Ranney, M., Schank, P., & Diehl, C. (1995). Competence versus performance in critical reasoning: Reducing the gap by using Convince Me. *Psychology Teaching Review* 4(2).

Reader, W. (1997). Structuring Argument: The Role of Constraint in the Explication of Scientific Argument. Unpublished manuscript.

Roschelle, J. (1994, May). Designing for cognitive communication: Epistemic fidelity or mediating collaborative inquiry? *The Arachnet Electronic Journal of Virtual Culture*, 2(2).

Salomon, G. (Ed.) (1993). *Distributed cognitions: psychological and educational considerations.* Cambridge, England; New York, NY: Cambridge University Press.

Scardamalia, M., & Bereiter, C. (1991). Higher levels of agency for children in knowledge building: A challenge for the design of new knowledge media. *The Journal of the Learning Sciences* 1(1),37-68.

Scardamalia, M., Bereiter, C., Brett, C., Burtis, P.J., Calhoun, C., & Smith Lea, N. (1992). Educational applications of a networked communal database. *Interactive Learning Environments*, 2(1), 45-71.

Schwarz, B. B. & Glassner, A. (2003). The blind and the paralytic: Supporting argumentation in everyday and scientific issues. To appear in J. Andriessen, M. Baker, & D. Suthers (Eds.) *Arguing to Learn: Confronting Cognitions in Computer-Supported Collaborative Learning Environments.* Kluwer, 2003 (this volume).

Slavin, R. E. (1990). *Cooperative learning: Theory, research, and practice.* Englewood Cliffs, NJ: Prentice-Hall.

Smolensky, P., Fox, B., King, R., & Lewis, C. (1987). Computer-aided reasoned discourse, or, how to argue with a computer. In R. Guindon (Ed.), Co*gnitive Science and Its Applications for Human-Computer Interaction* (pp. 109-162). Hillsdale, NJ: Erlbaum.

Stein, B. S., & Bransford, J. D. (1979). Constraints on effective elaboration: Effects of precision and subject generation. *Journal of Verbal Learning and Verbal Behavior* 18,769-777.

Stenning, K. & Oberlander, J. (1995). A cognitive theory of graphical and linguistic reasoning: Logic and implementation. *Cognitive Science* 19(1), 97-140. 1995.

Stenning, K. & Yule, P. (1997). Image and language in human reasoning: A syllogistic illustration. *Cognitive Psychology* 34, 109-159.

Suthers, D., Connelly, J., Lesgold, A., Paolucci, M., Toth, E., Toth, J., and Weiner, A. (2001). Representational and Advisory Guidance for Students Learning Scientific Inquiry. In Forbus, K. D., and Feltovich, P. J. (2001). *Smart machines in education*: The coming revolution in educational technology. Menlo Park, CA: AAAI/Mit Press, pp. 7-35.

Suthers, D. & Hundhausen, C. (2003). An Empirical Study of the Effects of Representational Guidance on Collaborative Learning. Accepted to the *Journal of the Learning Sciences* for publication in 2003.

Suthers, D., Hundhausen, C. & Girardeaue, L. (submitted). Comparing the roles of reprsentations in face-to-face and online computer supported collaborative learning. Submitted August 2003 to *Computers in Education.*

Suthers, D., Toth, E., and Weiner, A. (1997, December). An integrated approach to implementing collaborative inquiry in the classroom. In *Proceedings of the 2nd International Conference on Computer Supported Collaborative Learning* (CSCL'97) (272-279). Toronto: University of Toronto.

Suthers, D. and Weiner, A. (1995, October). Groupware for developing critical discussion skills. CSCL '95, *Computer Supported Cooperative Learning*, Bloomington, Indiana.

Toth, E., Suthers, D., & Lesgold, A. (in press). Mapping to know: The effects of evidence maps and reflective assessment on scientific inquiry skills. To appear in *Science Education.*

Utgoff, P. (1986). Shift of bias for inductive concept learning. In R. Michalski, J. Carbonell, T. Mitchell (Eds.) *Machine Learning: An Artitificial Intelligence Approach, Volume II* (pp. 107-148). Los Altos: Morgan Kaufmann.

Van Bruggen, J. M. & Kirschner, P. A. (2003). Designing external representations to support solving wicked problems. To appear in J. Andriessen, M. Baker, & D. Suthers (Eds.) *Arguing to Learn: Confronting Cognitions in Computer-Supported Collaborative Learning Environments.* Kluwer, 2003 (this volume).

Veerman, A. (2003). Constructive discussions through electronic dialogue. To appear in J. Andriessen, M. Baker, & D. Suthers (Eds.) *Arguing to Learn: Confronting Cognitions in Computer-Supported Collaborative Learning Environments.* Kluwer, 2003 (this volume).

Wan, D., & Johnson, P. M. (1994, October). Experiences with CLARE: a Computer-supported collaborative learning environment. *International Journal of Human-Computer Studies* 41, 851-879.

Webb, N. & Palincsar, A. (1996). Group processes in the classroom. In D. Berlmer & R. Calfee, (Eds.), *Handbook of Educational Psychology.* New York: Simon & Schuster Macmillian.

Zhang, J. (1997). The nature of external representations in problem solving. *Cognitive Science*, 21(2), 179-217.

MICHAEL BAKER


# COMPUTER-MEDIATED ARGUMENTATIVE INTERACTIONS FOR THE CO-ELABORATION OF SCIENTIFIC NOTIONS


## INTRODUCTION

It is now well recognised that argumentative interactions can be vehicles of collaborative learning, especially on a conceptual plane (see e.g. Andriessen & Coirier, 1999). Information and communication technologies such as Computer-Supported Collaborative Learning ("CSCL") environments can play an important role in such learning to the extent that they enable task sequences and interpersonal communication media to be structured in ways that favour the co-elaboration[1] of knowledge (e.g. Baker, 1996, 1999; Baker, de Vries, Lund & Quignard, 2001).

This chapter adopts a general perspective in educational psychology and technology according to which understanding the cognitive, linguistic and interpersonal *processes* of interactive learning is a primary basis for design of learning situations, together with the tasks and tools that comprise them. Such an emphasis on the study of interactive learning processes now crosscuts theoretical perspectives and currents as diverse as situated learning, social psychology, as well as Vygotskian and post-Piagetian psychologies of learning (e.g. Resnick, Levine & Teasley, 1991; Pontecorvo, 1993; Gilly, Roux & Trognon, 1999), in the general attempt to understand how understanding emerges from interaction (e.g. Roschelle, 1992). If we could gain better understanding of the processes by which different types of knowledge are elaborated in argumentative interactions, this could enable us to better design CSCL environments that exploit this learning potential.

Within this perspective, we present a case study analysis of a corpus of interactions that was collected in a situation where students used the "CONNECT" CSCL environment (Baker, de Vries & Lund, 1999; De Vries, Lund & Baker, 2002) to collaboratively solve a problem of interpreting a sound phenomenon in physics. CONNECT enables dyads of students to critically reflect upon and to collaboratively write texts across the Internet. As background for the analyses, we first sketch a theoretical approach to understanding the relations between argumentation, interaction and collaborative problem solving, out of which emerge a number of reasons why learning might occur as a result of engaging in an

47

*J. Andriessen, M. Baker, and D. Suthers (eds.), Arguing to Learn: Confronting Cognitions in Computer-Supported Collaborative Learning environments (47-78).*
© *2003 Kluwer Academic Publishers. Printed in the Netherlands*

argumentative interaction. We then briefly describe the CONNECT study and present illustrative analyses of the corpus that was collected during it. Our analyses emphasise the way in which the dialectical game of argumentation relates to expressed changes of attitudes towards solutions, and how the playing out of this game goes hand in hand with renegotiation of the conceptual background within which it is situated. In conclusion, we discuss potentials and limits of CSCL environments in relation to productive argumentative interactions.

## ARGUMENTATIVE INTERACTION, COLLABORATIVE PROBLEM-SOLVING AND COLLABORATIVE LEARNING

### Argumentative interaction and collaborative problem-solving

Understanding how argumentative interaction can lead to collaborative learning requires setting it in the context of collaborative problem-solving activity. Within such a research goal, we see argumentative interaction fundamentally as a type of *dialogical or dialectical game* that is played upon and arises from the 'terrain' of *collaborative problem solving*, and that is associated with *collaborative meaning-making*. Although negotiation of meaning is of course an integral part of any communicative interaction, our conjecture is that the interpersonal and interactive pressures imposed by the necessity to deal with conflicting points of view are particularly conducive to collaborative sense-making.

Although argumentation can occur with respect to any aspect of a problem space, as classically defined by Newell and Simon (1972), it will be convenient here to restrict our discussion to possible *solutions* to (sub-)problems in the task domain, that may be proposed by collaborating problem solvers. Let us term the task domain problem "$P$", and name different possible solutions that are proposed for it $s1$, $s2$, etc. Suppose that a single solution is proposed and is mutually accepted; in that case, problem solving presumably proceeds without notable interruption. Argumentation can get off the ground in the case where either more than one solution is proposed, or else where a single proposed solution is not mutually accepted. We term the extent to which an interlocutor is willing to accept (believe, endorse, commit to, etc.) a solution its *epistemic status*, "$e$", from the point of view of that interlocutor. The starting point for argumentation in collaborative problem-solving situations thus requires a certain degree of *diversity* — either in terms of solutions that are proposed for the task domain problem, and/or else in terms of the epistemic statuses of one or more solutions. The existence of such diversity creates a second level interlocutory problem, "$I$" (c.f. Quignard, 2000)[2]: which of the $s$ for $P$, with their associated $e$, should be chosen? We assume that it is inherent in the problem-solving situation that either a single $s$ must be chosen, or possibly that $s$'s should be ranked in order of their epistemic statuses[3].

Thus far, an interlocutory problem $I$ (i.e. one that rises in exchange between interlocutors) has arisen from a task domain problem, $P$. But how can $I$ be solved? On the first level, the answer is clearly: by *transforming epistemic statuses of solutions*, so that one appears more acceptable, believable, etc., than others. This intuition is in fact one of the bases of the classical *rhetorical* approach to argumentation (see van Eemeren, Grootendorst & Henkemans, 1996, for a modern account), according to which argumentation fundamentally aims at persuasion, or changing an auditory's point of view. But clearly, not all argumentative interactions are of this type; speakers' goals could be simply to decide which solution is to be preferred, without necessarily trying to impose their own views (Walton, 1989). Similarly, argumentation can take place in interaction with respect to several solutions proposed by a single speaker, whose interlocutor cooperates in helping to make a choice. To that extent, argumentation in collaborative problem-solving situations can often be seen more as a cooperative exploration of a dialogical space (Nonnon, 1996) than as an adversarial confrontation of well-elaborated and entrenched points of view.

But how can epistemic statuses of solutions be transformed, so as to decide which solution to prefer? We propose that there are two main and complementary ways: firstly, by *argumentation*, and secondly, by *negotiation of meaning*.

As a *discursive* activity, argumentation involves establishing specific types of (inferential or other) relations between the solutions being discussed, *s*, and other sources of knowledge, *k*, the establishment of which potentially influences the epistemic statuses of the solutions. An "argument" strengthens the epistemic status of a solution, and a "counter-argument" weakens it, from interlocutors' points of view. The sources of knowledge, *k*, must be different from the views to which they relate; they must *not* be understandable as developments, paraphrases, redefinitions, etc., of views (otherwise, the interaction becomes negotiation of meaning, or else explanation, in certain cases). A typology of (counter-)argumentation can be defined in terms of the nature of the inferential links, whether they are intended to strengthen or weaken epistemic statuses, and the nature of knowledge sources, *k*, drawn upon.

As a *dialogical* activity, argumentation involves somewhat more than linking in new knowledge sources to the ongoing discussion. Along its dialogical, or dialectical dimension, it is useful in the present context to theorise argumentation using certain elements of formal dialectics (Barth & Krabbe, 1982) and pragma-dialectics (van Eemeren & Grootendorst, 1984). Firstly, interlocutors' views with respect to epistemic statuses can become somewhat stabilised into *stances*, or *dialectical roles* — opponent and proponent — and the solutions under discussion then take on the form of *theses*. Although in formal dialectical models such roles must be stable (e.g. an opponent must be systematically *contra* all of the proponent's statements), in real students' interactions, positions can naturally shift in a more flexible way. Secondly, interlocutors must play the game of producing (counter-)arguments according to certain (usually implicit) *ground rules*. These ground rules are partly logical — e.g. logical contradiction will usually be pointed out, as will inconsistent expression of dialectical roles, such as being both *pro* and *contra* a given statement — and partly pragmatic or cooperative (in a Gricean sense). Pragmatic/cooperative rules fulfil the function of enabling the discussion to move forward to a determinate outcome: given the arguments that have been expressed as dialectical moves (attacks, defenses, retractions, etc.), which thesis has 'won out'? For example, arguing round in repetitive circles may be legitimately sanctioned, and the outcome of the discussion must be expressed explicitly. As a result of such dialogical games, however flexible the roles may be, the interlocutors may be in a position to decide which of the solutions-theses should be retained, as a function of dialectical roles to be adopted towards them, which in turn encapsulate epistemic statuses with respect to domain problem solutions. Of course, participants may have their own private or unexpressed opinions; but dialectical models maintain that argumentation functions fundamentally in terms of what has been publicly expressed and recognised.

As stated above, the second way of resolving an interlocutionary problem is by negotiation of meaning. By this we mean any interactive and communicative means by which interlocutors transform, redefine or reformulate linguistic expressions relating to the domain of discourse. Clearly, such negotiation of meaning goes hand in hand with argumentation in interaction, since in any exchange, interlocutors express the way in which they have interpreted the preceding dialogue (c.f. Clark & Shaefer, 1989). A number of argumentation theorists have already described ways in which debate is associated with negotiation of meaning. Thus Walton (1992) has described how topics of debate often shift gradually towards more fundamental issues (he gives the example of a conversation about the institution of tipping in the USA that is transformed into a debate about the role of the state in regulating commercial practices). Naess (1966) has proposed that the process of making theses more precise is intrinsic to argumentation itself: a debate about the legitimacy of taking a human life is more likely to result in a refined understanding of the concept of human life than in a determinate dialectical outcome. There are two further ways in which negotiation of meaning can occur in argumentative interaction. The first is by dissociating concepts from each other (Perelman & Olbrechts-Tyteca, 1958/1988), thus redefining their meanings, and the second is by so-called compromise outcomes, in which new solutions are created by complex combinations and elaborations of existing ones. In all of these cases, it is clear that once meanings of statements or utterances shift, then so do their epistemic statuses. Whether you accept a statement or not obviously depends on what is meant by it. It is perhaps more precise to say that the epistemic statuses of the original solutions do not change, but rather than new solutions or even domain task problems are defined in a way that 'dis-solves' rather than 're-solves' the original problem (Baker, 1999).

This general theoretical perspective on argumentation and collaborative problem solving, that forms the basis for analysis techniques to be described in a subsequent section, is summarised in Figure 1.

The diagram represents the point of view of a single speaker; clearly, different people can have different understandings of all elements of the diagram, especially the nature of the problem, $P$. In the problem space, two solutions are shown (there could be others), with their epistemic statuses. In the dialectical space, the problem is to choose between the solutions for $P$, each of which become theses ($T$) with associated dialectical roles. New knowledge sources ($k$) are linked to the theses as (counter-)arguments. This process leads to clarification of dialectical roles with respect to the theses, that 'feed back' into choice of solution for $P$. In their interactions,

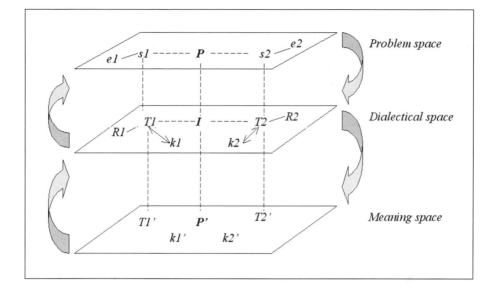

*Figure 1. Basic approach to analysing argumentative interactions in cooperative problem-solving situations.*

students usually glide seamlessly between these two types of problems, the interlocutionary problem arising from the task-level one, and task-level problem solving being resumed when students stop attempting to solve the interlocutionary problem (because they believe it to be solved, because they redefine it, because they 'let it drop', and so on). Concomitantly, the meaning of theses, arguments, and even the original problem $P$, can be negotiated. Thus, the semi-circular arrows in the diagram (Figure 1) represent possible transitions between the spaces: dialectics arises out of diversity and necessity for choice in the problem space, then in turn feeds back into it; dialectics involves and requires negotiation of meaning, that in turn influences the course of the argumentative interaction. Although this is not represented in the diagram, negotiation of meaning can of course occur in problem-solving outside dialectical contexts (i.e. a direct arrow between problem and meaning spaces).

*Argumentative interaction and collaborative learning*

Given the above characterisation of argumentative interactions in collaborative problem-solving situations, it is now easier to understand how these complex collective activities could lead to elaboration of new knowledge and understanding.

The first process by which this can occur relates to the discursive dimension of argumentation, by which new knowledge sources, $k$, are linked to theses in an attempt to solve an interlocutionary problem, $P$, i.e. production of arguments or counter-arguments. One possibility would be to see argument generation as a process of rendering explicit explanations for solutions that could lead to knowledge restructuring in a manner analogous to the "self-explanation effect" (Chi et al., 1989). More generally, verbalisation of problem-solving processes in the context of a communicative interaction can enable interlocutors to elaborate more coherent points of view (Crook, 1994) or, at the very least, to become acquainted with the diversity of points of view.

The second potentially productive process relates to the dialectical dimension of argumentation that is orientated towards clarifying dialectical roles and ultimately the epistemic statuses that are ascribed to problem solutions: what are the problem solutions that students are led to (publicly) accept or reject? The most straightforward cases would be dropping or acquiring beliefs in solutions (c.f. Harman, 1986) as a result of successful dialectical refutations or defenses, respectively. Clearly, students' dialogical activity, even assuming it is completely frank and sincere, is not a simple determinant of more stable changes in their knowledge. But the acceptance of a proposal, in the sense of agreeing to use it as a basis for continuing joint reasoning (Cohen, 1992), may lead to its being appropriated in a deeper sense. In addition, changes in perceived epistemic status are of course not necessarily all or nothing; in fact more subtle and potentially beneficial changes may correspond to the simple realisation that a proposal is not as sure as was originally thought, and thus merits further inquiry. In all of these cases, when students argue without a teacher's supervision, and they can find no conclusive (counter-)arguments in the problem-solving situation, there is of course no guarantee that normatively preferred proposals will not be commonly rejected.

Finally, it is clear that the processes of negotiation of meaning, conceptual dissociation and knowledge elaboration, referred to above as integral parts of the argumentative process, are potentially the primary means by which collaborative learning can occur, especially on a conceptual level.

Our aim in the rest of this chapter will be to analyse and examine these processes at work in a specific corpus of computer-mediated interactions, collected with the CONNECT CSCL environment.

## THE CONNECT ENVIRONMENT AND EMPIRICAL STUDY

### *CSCL interface design*

CONNECT[4] (Baker, de Vries & Lund, 1999; de Vries, Lund & Baker, 2002) is a CSCL environment for collaborative critical comparison and writing of texts, via Internet. It was developed as part of a long-term research programme (see Baker, de Vries, Lund & Quignard, 2001, for a short synthesis), involving several CSCL interfaces, the main aim of which was to understand what aspects of the overall learning environment were most conducive to enabling students to engage in "epistemic interactions" bearing on scientific notions. In analogy with Ohlsson's (1996) notion of epistemic discourse, by an epistemic interaction we mean an interaction in which goes beyond stating problem solutions and methods, to discussion of conceptual foundations of problem solving. Our hypothesis is that such interactions will be predominantly argumentative and explicative.

In previous work on the C-CHENE CSCL environment (Baker & Lund, 1997), we had remarked that collaborating students rarely argued or explained their solutions during problem-solving itself, when starting together 'from scratch', and that when we presented them with alternative solutions, their choice between them was usually based on very superficial analysis. In CONNECT we tried to remedy this by a combination of means. Firstly, students produce individual problem-solutions before coming together to collaborate, which enables them to elaborate initial knowledge to be discussed, and enables the researcher to create working groups on the basis of maximising conceptual distances between individual solutions[5]. Secondly, a phase devoted to reflexion upon and comparison of solutions/texts was separated from the main problem-solving phase, so as to leave room for epistemic interaction. This phase is carried out using the interface shown in Figure 2.

The screen is divided into main upper and lower parts. The upper part is for typewritten synchronous communication across the network, with full screen sharing. Students (or the teacher) can take the floor by clicking on the speech balloons, and can also use some structured communication buttons. The lower part of the screen is for critical comparison of texts. On the right hand side, two students' texts have been segmented into statements; on the left hand side, students use check boxes to express their opinions — restricted to "YES, "NO" and "?" — with respect to every text segment, including segments of their own texts. The idea of asking students to do this was to find a means of requiring them to read actively their texts. As a function of pairs of attitudes for each text segment (e.g. "YES"/"NO", "?"/"YES", etc.), CONNECT generates some advice (a short statement) on how the students could go about discussing that segment. In this way, we hoped to help students to focus on key points, differences and similarities in or between their texts, which could be profitably discussed and explained. The text advice relating to attitude pairs is shown in Table 1.

From a methodological point of view, asking students to express their attitudes its interesting, since it enables us to study the precise relations between types of dialogue and types of changes in attitudes (see analyses below).

Once they have finished discussing individual texts, the students move onto the next phase of the activity, during which they are given an interface (the precise details of which are not our principal concern here) for collaboratively writing a new text on the basis of their individual texts. At the end of the task sequence, the students' interaction log-files are passed to teachers for analysis, as a basis for subsequently going on-line to help the students improve their solutions and understandings (c.f. Lund & Baker, 1999). The overall task sequence lasts around three hours.

ConNeCT

| Student 1 | Teacher | Student 2 |
|---|---|---|

| | Yes | No |
|---|---|---|
| | Ok? | I don't agree |
| | I'll do it | You do it |
| | Hello? | Are we done? |

| | Yes | No |
|---|---|---|
| | Ok? | I don't agree |
| | I'll do it | You do it |
| | Hello? | Are we done? |

| | Yes | No |
|---|---|---|
| | Ok? | I don't agree |
| | I'll do it | You do it |
| | Hello? | Are we done? |

Tambourines : Phase 1

Phase 1 ▼

Show Situation

Student 2 : Should we read the thing first?
Student 1 : Yes, but what thing? The document?
Student 2 : I'll do it
Student 1 : You do it

| Student1 | Student2 | ToDo | | Text of Student1 |
|---|---|---|---|---|
| Yes ▼ | Yes ▼ | verify | 1 | The molecules in the middle of the propagation, between the two tambourines, run into each other. |
| Yes ▼ | Yes ▼ | verify | 2 | There is a propagation from tambourine 1 to tambourine 2. The propagation hits tambourine 2. |
| Yes ▼ | Yes ▼ | verify | 3 | The tambourine 2's skin vibrates. The ball jumps because it's in contact with the skin of tambourine 2. |
| Yes ▼ | Yes ▼ | verify | 4 | The A molecules are pushed towards the B molecules. |
| Yes ▼ | Yes ▼ | verify | 5 | In their turn, the B molecules push the C molecules which hit tambourine 2. |
| Yes ▼ | Yes ▼ | verify | 6 | If we hit more strongly, the little ball jumps farther out. |
| Yes ▼ | ? ▼ | explain | 7 | The skin vibrates a lot less because the waves emitted by T1 are longer and the skin isn't as tight. |

| Student1 | Student2 | ToDo | | Text of Student2 |
|---|---|---|---|---|
| Yes ▼ | Yes ▼ | verify | 1 | When the sound is emitted from T1, it moves and emits a vibration. This is a displacement of air molecules. |
| Yes ▼ | Yes ▼ | verify | 2 | When the vibration gets to T2, the air molecules hit T2. It moves and makes the ball move. |
| Yes ▼ | Yes ▼ | verify | 3 | The A molecules go to the right, push those in B, which push those in C. |
| ? ▼ | No ▼ | explain | 4 | When these molecules have hit T2, they go to the right and push the B ones, which push those in A. |
| ? ▼ | Yes ▼ | explain | 5 | But during every A-C path, the molecules go less quickly and push less strongly. |
| Yes ▼ | Yes ▼ | verify | 6 | The molecules move more quickly and hit more quickly than the others. The ball will "jump" higher. |
| No ▼ | ? ▼ | explain | 7 | The skin isn't as tight so it streches more and maybe emits a sound. |

*Figure 2. First interface of CONNECT (comparing texts and expressing attitudes)*

*Table 1: Attitude pairs and discussion instructions in CONNECT*

| Attitude combinations | Discussion type | Instructions |
|---|---|---|
| YES-YES, NO-NO | verify | verify both of you that you understand the same thing by the sentence |
| YES - NO | discuss | discuss in order to reach agreement, each one defending their points of view |
| YES - ?, NO - ? | explain | explain what you meant to say to your partner who put the "? " |
| ? - ? | to be seen … | both of you verify that it's really what you meant to put |

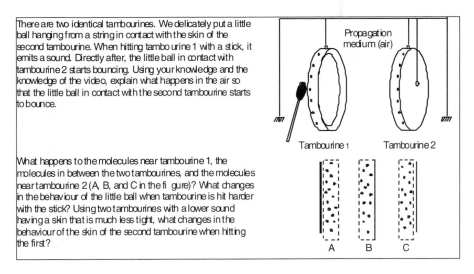

There are two identical tambourines. We delicately put a little ball hanging from a string in contact with the skin of the second tambourine. When hitting tambourine 1 with a stick, it emits a sound. Directly after, the little ball in contact with tambourine 2 starts bouncing. Using your knowledge and the knowledge of the video, explain what happens in the air so that the little ball in contact with the second tambourine starts to bounce.

What happens to the molecules near tambourine 1, the molecules in between the two tambourines, and the molecules near tambourine 2 (A, B, and C in the figure)? What changes in the behaviour of the little ball when tambourine is hit harder with the stick? Using two tambourines with a lower sound having a skin that is much less tight, what changes in the behaviour of the skin of the second tambourine when hitting the first?

*Figure 3. The sound task carried out with CONNECT*

## An empirical study with CONNECT

An empirical study was carried out using CONNECT, in the domain of interpreting sound phenomena in physics. The students' task was to interpret a simple situation in terms of a molecular model of air: two tambourines are suspended from a support, a short distance apart, with a small ball being suspended so that it touches the outer skin of the second tambourine; when the first tambourine is struck, the ball against the second moves in a certain way (see Figure 3 below).

We chose to study this task since it is known that students typically have a variety of different mental models of sound (Maurines, 1998; Linder & Erickson, 1989), the confrontation of which in interaction was, we hypothesised, likely to lead to productive epistemic interactions. For example, according to a microscopic perspective, students may conceive of sound as being 'carried' by individual molecules, or as being transferred from one another. From a macroscopic perspective, sound can be conceived as a travelling 'substance' or else as a travelling pattern. The task shown in Figure 3 is partly designed so as to enable us to identify these different ways of conceiving of sound. For example, indicators of students' different understandings are likely to turn around the question as to whether the "A" molecules will be in contact or not with the "C" molecules: if they are, this could be an indicator of a 'travelling impetus' perspective, otherwise, together with other indicators, perhaps of a 'travelling pattern' perspective. Considerations of this kind were used to pair students together on the basis of the different perspectives on sound underlying their texts.

In reality, what is at stake for the teacher is that the students should come to understand that sound is a type of *displacement* of *vibrations* of air molecules — in a sense, a movement of a vibration. Since vibration is also a certain type of movement, the conceptual difficulty is to grasp the notion of sound as a "movement of a movement".

We worked with a class of secondary school students (aged 16-17 years) and their teacher, from whose individual texts we were able to create and study seven dyads, within each of which the students had different mental models of sound. Due to technological constraints, the working session was carried out in computer rooms in our laboratory.

At the end of the session (lasting a little over 3 hours), we collected the automatically recorded log files (time-stamped typewritten interventions, interwoven with actions on the task interfaces, including all modifications of the texts).

## CORPUS ANALYSES

A first qualitative-quantitative analysis of the CONNECT corpus was carried out, with a view to identifying the extent to which the students engaged in epistemic interaction. Results were globally encouraging (see de Vries, Lund & Baker, 2002, for details) in that during the text comparison/discussion phase, 23% of the interaction was argumentative and 33% was explanatory.

We now present and discuss results of further qualitative analyses of the argumentation sequences that were analysed according to the theoretical perspective described earlier in this chapter. In the discussion phase, 7 argumentation sequences[6] occurred in all, across the complete corpus collected for the 7 dyads. All of the sequences apart from one were "simple conflicts" (Barth & Krabbe, 1982), to the extent that a single segment of one student's text was discussed. However, in some cases, changes in attitudes with respect to one text segment logically triggered changes elsewhere, as the following student utterance illustrates: "since you put "no" for the 3 [3rd text segment] you should also put "no" there [for the 4th segment]".

Our analyses focus on attempting to explain different types of expressed attitude changes, as a function of characteristics of the argumentative interaction. We shall introduce the necessary analytical machinery as required.

*Changes in epistemic status*

As mentioned above, during the discussion phase of the CONNECT task sequence, students were first asked to express their attitudes — "YES", "NO" or "?" — with respect to each text segment. At the end of each argumentation sequence (as well as in other sequences), the students updated their attitudes on the interface as they felt appropriate. Such explicit changes therefore provide us with a set of phenomena to be explained: why, as a function of their interaction, did the students change their attitudes in the way that they did? For example, when one student initially expresses the attitude "YES" towards her own statement "Since the groups of A and B mol arrive towards the C mol, they make an impact with the tam", then, following a short discussion with her partner, changes this attitude to "NO", why, in this concrete case, did she do that? To what extent can an explanation be found in interactive processes?

As a preliminary, it is necessary to point out that from our theoretical point of view, the fact that there may be a difference between what the students "really think" and the attitudes they express is besides the point for the analysis of argumentative interaction. Argumentative interaction is concerned with "dialogical attitudes", such as commitments (c.f. Winograd & Flores, 1986) and acceptances (Cohen, 1992), and as such bears an indirect relation to more deep-seated beliefs. It is clear that argumentative concession does not necessarily imply a deep change of belief or opinion (c.f. Dennett, 1981); but what is important is that a student *did* in fact (publicly) concede, and can thus be held responsible for his or her public dialogical acts. What is said is said and cannot be unsaid. We will never know what people 'really think' (admitting that that expression is in fact meaningful) 'behind' their dialogue (Edwards, 1993); we can only interpret their discourse, in a wide sense of the term. Dialogue is not a "window on the mind", it a manifestation of minds in operation.

We analyse the ways in which students' attitudes could change into the following three categories[7]:

1. no expressed change (e.g. "YES" ➔ "YES"),
2. strengthening in epistemic value ("NO" ➔ "?" ➔ "YES "), or
3. weakening in epistemic value ("YES" ➔ "?" ➔ "NO").

Table 2 below summarises the seven argumentation sequences in the CONNECT corpus, in terms of epistemic statuses accorded to text segments by two speakers, A and B, before and after discussion, using the three values "YES", "NO" and "?", expressed by the students on the interface (e.g. "A: NO" means that speaker "A" expressed the attitude "NO" with respect to a given text segment currently under discussion). In the second column, the attitude that has changed is marked in bold. In fact, there are eight types of attitude change in all, since in one sequence, two attitude changes occurred with respect to two different text segments. In an argumentative interaction, the "?" symbol is interpreted (by students and by the researcher) as expressing doubts, or as requesting a defense of a view. In an explanatory interaction it would be interpreted as expression of lack of understanding.

*Table 2: Changes in expressed attitudes as a result of discussion in the CONNECT corpus*

| Attitudes before discussion | Attitudes after discussion | Type of attitude change | N |
|---|---|---|---|
| *Dialectical opposition:* | A: **NO** I B: NO | Weakening | 2 |
| A: YES I B: NO | A: YES I B: **YES** | Strengthening | 1 |
| | A: **?** I B: **?** | Weakening | 1 |
| *Interrogative* | A: YES I B: ? | No change | 2 |
| *opposition:* | A: **?** I B: ? | Weakening | 1 |
| A: YES I B: ? | A: **NO** I B: **NO** | Weakening | 1 |

From Table 2 it can be seen that argumentation more often leads to weakening of attitudes (5 changes out of 8) than to no change (2 out of 8) and strengthening (1 out of 8). In two cases, each of which involve weakening of attitudes, both students' attitudes change, whereas in the other six cases, only one student's attitude changes.

We now examine examples of argumentation sequences associated with each of these types of attitude change (weakening, strengthening and no change). Fundamentally, our analyses and explanations of results depend on three main factors (see Baker, 1999):

the dialectical interplay of argumentative attacks and defenses;

the types of knowledge and understandings that are appealed to; and

the way in which meanings are transformed or negotiated.

The dialectical interplay should, as we previously mentioned, function in a way that relates to externalised argumentation outcomes, with their associated attitude changes. Understanding the types of knowledge and understandings[8] expressed in debates is also important with respect to overall outcomes, given that certain types of arguments 'weigh' more than others. In the present case, types of understandings correspond principally to the students' models[9] of the sound phenomena, as described above.

*Strengthening of attitudes*

The single case of strengthening of attitudes in the corpus, where Andrew's "NO" is changed to a "YES", is shown in Table 3. As with similar tables reproduced below, the text typed by the students is translated from the original French, whilst attempting to transliterate spelling and typing errors. Students' names are changed whilst preserving their gender. The first column shows the time (in minutes and seconds) elapsed since the beginning of the session, and the second column consists of a simple numbering of interventions. An intervention corresponds to the text typed by a single student, that is then sent to the interaction history (see upper middle of interface shown in Figure 2) by pressing the return key.

In this sequence the problem, $P$ is the second question shown in Figure 3: "What happens to the molecules near tambourine 1, the molecules in between the two tambourines, and the molecules near tambourine 2, and the molecules near tambourine 2 … ?". The first solution, $s1$, proposed by John, corresponds to the second part of statement 1 of his text: "*…They move away from each other*". S1 becomes a dialectical thesis, T1, once Andrew has criticised it (line 32) and John has defended his thesis from this criticism (line 40). It has become a thesis since, by their dialogical actions, the students have adopted the dialectical roles of proponent and opponent.

*Table 3: Example of a sequence leading to attitude strengthening (CONNECT corpus)*

| T(m:s) | L | Andrew | John |
|--------|-----|--------|------|
| | | | Statement 1: "It perturbs the air molecules contained between t1 and t2. They move away from each other" |
| | | Attitudes before:<br>**NO** | **YES** |
| 8:19 | 32 | They don't move away from each other, they all go towards t2 | |
| (…) | (…) | <Section omitted: Andrew completes his expression of opinions towards John's other statements, using the check boxes> | |
| 14:08 | 40 | | my 1: in the film we saw that the air molecules that were positioned in a certain way stretched out towards the front, here T2, thus creating a greater space between the molecules than before OK?YES OR NO |
| 14:13 | 41 | Yes | |
| (…) | (…) | <Section omitted: different argumentation sequence with respect to John's statement 7> | |
| 4:12 | 60 | | To my sentence that you can see, you replied YES: why haven't you written it in the opinions table. Perhaps you weren't completely in agreement. |
| 5:53 | 61 | You mean why I haven't written in the text? | |
| 6:27 | 62 | | look at what I'm going to show you <designates the opinions check boxes on the screen with the mouse pointer> |
| 7:16 | 63 | Q | |
| 7:27 | 64 | | ritt yo read |
| 9:01 | 65 | Stop writing at the same time as me. | |
| 10:07 | 66 | | there it wasnnxt me let's begin |
| 10:09 | 67 | No | |
| 13:04 | 68 | I haven't replied to your question. When I wrote that I didn't remember the film.<br>O | |
| 14:12 | 69 | SSTO P !!!!!! We can begin. | |
| 14:17 | 70 | | Yes |
| | | Attitudes after:<br>**YES** | **YES** |

*Basic principles of dialectical analysis*

In order to present the dialectical analysis of this sequence, we shall introduce a little notation, to be used below (see Baker, 1996, 1999, for further details).

Each dialectical move is analysed into three aspects, namely a *type of content*, a *speech act category* and a *pragmatic function*, as follows:

*Contents* of moves can be propositions in the domain of discourse, notated "A, B, C, etc", predications of dialectical roles (*pro* or *contra*, or sometimes *no-commitment*) with respect to such propositions, or else references to ground rules of the debate, notated "GR-1, GR-2, GR-3, etc." (see below). A special marker "(?)P" is used for hypothetical statements, glossed as "I am willing to defend P in this debate", or "might not P be the case?". Where moves involve complex propositions (see subsequent analyses), the reasoning involved will be reconstructed. To that extent, reasoning is clearly distinguished from argumentation, in a dialectical sense of the term.

*Speech act categories* apply to propositions, and are given force indicators: "?" for interrogatives (questions, requests), absence of an indicator for assertives, and "!" for exclamatives. The "!" indicator will most often be used with respect to special propositions, that represent the ground rules of debate. For example, Barth and Krabbe (1982) define a special move called "*Ipse dixisti!*", or "You already said it yourself!", which signals that the interlocutor has just attacked a statement that (s)he previously defended. In a less restricted dialectical system, such as a "forensic debate" in the sense of Walton (1989), involving a cooperative search for the truth of the matter, *Ipse dixisti* would not necessarily be viewed as a foul move, but rather as part of the game. Our aim here is clearly not to impose a normative system, but rather to describe the ground rules with which the students appear to be operating, and to which they explicitly refer.

The *pragmatic character* of a dialectical move refers to its function with respect to the debate. The principal functions are "attacks" on statements (theses) and defenses of statements/theses, which can be either direct supports of a thesis, or counteractive defenses (attacks on attacks). Pragmatic character is distinct from the speech act used in a move since, for example, an attack can be made by raising a question or else by making a new assertion, whose content would show the attacked statement to be unacceptable in some way.

It is important to emphasise that such dialectical analyses are deliberately reductionist: they only represent purely argumentative dimensions of interaction, to the exclusion of all others, such as negotiation of meaning, the type of knowledge involved, and social dimensions of interaction. Our proposal is that by separating out dimensions in this way, we can better see their interrelations.

*Dialectical analysis of the example*

A dialectical analysis of the interaction sequence reproduced in Table 3 is shown in Table 4 below.

*Table 4: Dialectical analysis of attitude strengthening sequence*[*]

| L | Andrew | John | Pragmatic character of dialectical move |
|---|--------|------|------------------------------------------|
| — | | A, B | John's first statement in his text, the second part of which (B) retroactively becomes a thesis to be defended. |
| | contra(A,B) | pro(A,B) | Andrew's and John's expression contra and pro roles on interface check-boxes |
| 32a | ¬ B | | *Contra* B, by expression of negation of |
| 32b | C | B. | |
| | | | Attack on B. |
| 40a | | D | Direct defense of thesis, B. |
| 40b | | [pro(D) ∨ contra(D)]? | Request for clarification of dialectical role |
| 41 | pro(D) | | Concession of D |
| 60a | | pro(A,B)? | Request for clarification of dialectical outcome |
| 60b | | GR-1! | "Infraction against GR-1!" |
| | pro(A,B) | | Concession of John's thesis A,B, explicitation of dialectical outcome |

[*] *Key:*

A: It [t1] perturbs the air molecules contained between t1 and t2
B: They[the air molecules contained between t1 and t2] move away from each other
C: They [the air molecules contained between t1 and t2] all go towards t2
D: in the film we saw that the air molecules that were positioned in a certain way stretched out towards the front, here T2, thus creating a greater space between the molecules than before
GR-1: The outcome of the debate must be externalised.

In purely dialectical terms, what is interesting about this sequence is that John, from line 60 onwards, has to insist so that Andrew makes the outcome of the sequence explicit, i.e. John has successfully defended his thesis, B. John points out, in line 60, that since Andrew conceded D, which defends B, then he should also make clear, on the opinions interface, that he concedes B (or rather the statement A;B) as well. But in fact, Andrew moves on to considering other statements in the interval between lines 41 and 60. One possible interpretation of John's request that Andrew make the outcome explicit is to see this as an implicit reference to what Barth and Krabbe (1982) term an "externalisation" rule of formal dialectics. The provision of check boxes for expression of attitudes can in fact be seen as encouraging this. But why did Andrew not openly admit defeat? One possible reason lies in his expression of annoyance at his partner typing at the same time: is this only frustration with the interface, or does it also reveal the fundamentally social character of argumentation (Muntig & Turnbull, 1998), i.e. losing an argument means losing 'face'?

To complete our brief analysis of this short, yet interesting, sequence, let us finally make some remarks about the types of knowledge expressed and about negotiation of meaning.

The two students' utterances can here be easily interpreted as expressions of different 'models', or understandings, of the way in which sound works on a molecular level. For Andrew, sound is a sort of wind, or displacement of substance, whereby all molecules are pushed along from left to right. John's understanding is closer to a vibration model of sound, in that he speaks of molecules moving away from each other to leave a space. It turns out that John's understanding is closer to objectives of physics teaching; but was this why he managed to make Andrew concede? Perhaps. But another possibility could lie in the fact that he makes explicit reference to an introductory film that both students saw ("in the film we saw that …"): seeing — or rather having seen — is believing. This interpretation would be coherent with our previous results (Baker, 1999), where it was shown, for a different physics problem-solving task, that students' debates were almost always resolved by making appeal to perceptual (and thus 'undeniable') facts, either within the experimental situation, or else derived from everyday experience.

With respect to negotiation of meaning, this short sequence can also be seen as a process of explaining, elaborating, or making more precise the students' (opposed) views. At the beginning of the sequence, Andrew states that it is the second part of John's statement (B) with which he does not agree. Andrew's defense, using D, can be seen as an explanation of the expression "move away from each other", i.e. the molecules are "stretched out", leaving a "greater space". To that extent, in this case argumentation does seem to have an "other-explanation" function, since students are led to make their underlying understandings explicit, under the interactional pressure of their interlocutionary problem, and to further develop them in interaction.

In conclusion to the analysis to this sequence, why, therefore, did a student who was against a statement about a sound phenomenon then say that he was in favour of it? The answer cannot of course be simple. It appears that the student could find no reason to deny something that he himself had seen; but his partner had to work hard to make him admit openly that this showed his thesis to be successfully defended. An interesting conjecture would be that this latter fact underlines the importance of social dimensions of interaction, as influenced by the CSCL communication situation.

*Weakening of attitudes*

We now turn to summarised analyses of two examples of weakening of attitudes. In the first example (see Table 5 below), one girl changed her "YES" to a "NO. The second example (see Table 7 below) is complex, in that two statements are discussed together, and all four attitudes weaken towards uncertainty ("?").

*Table 5: First example of attitude weakening ("YES" to "NO")*

| T(m:s) | L | Linda | Elaine |
|---|---|---|---|
| | | | Statement 3: "Since the groups of A and B mol arrive towards the C mol, they make an impact with the tam" |
| | | *Attitudes before:* | |
| | | NO | YES |
| 9:36 | 36 | it was nice of you to have put yes to everything for me, but for the 3, I think that the "a" mol aren't in contact with the "c" mol | |
| 14:40 | 37 | | of course they are, because if you have a wave all the molecules, like billiard balls, will be displaced because the hit on the tambourine it's as if we'd pushed them all the mols will mix up and hit on the tam no, |
| 17:39 | 38 | ah! after all perhaps you're right, but I ask myself whether they'll mix together as much as all that, don't you think that the "b" will create a barrier between the "a" and the "c" | |
| 20:36 | 39 | | i don't know maybe i'm wrong so i'm going to chang[e] and after we change question to go onto the 6 |
| | | *Attitudes after* | |
| | | NO | NO |

In the sequence reproduced in Table 5, the same problem, *P*, is discussed as with the sequence shown in Table 3 — what happens to the A, B and C molecules between the two tambourines?

The dialectical analysis of this sequence is shown in Table 6.

The sequence appears to be a straightforward refutation, since Elaine was forced to concede Linda's attack on her idea of the molecules mixing up together, according to which the B molecules would create a barrier between the A and C molecules. However, something significant is not sufficiently highlighted in this analysis, which is that the students use many modal expressions, such as "perhaps you're right", "I think that", "I ask myself", "I don't know, maybe i'm wrong". These expressions indicate the students' general lack of certainty with respect to their proposals, and probably the social dimension of politeness in interaction. It is worth noting that although Elaine has several reasons in favour of her proposal, it is refutation that determines the outcome of this dialectical game. As with the previous sequence analysed above (Tables 3 and 4), the pressure of argumentation forces the students to negotiate the meaning of certain expressions (e.g. "arrive towards" is more precisely defined as a wave, and in terms of "mixing up"), and to express their

*Table 6: Dialectical analysis of first attitude weakening sequence*[*]

| L | Linda | Elaine | Pragmatic character of dialectical move |
|---|---|---|---|
| | | A | Statement 3 of Elaine's text |
| | *contra*(A) | *pro*(A) | Expression of attitudes on check-boxes |
| 36 | B | | Attack on A |
| 37a | | ¬ B | Counter-active defense of A: attack on B (that attacks A) |
| 37b | | C | Defenses of ¬ B |
| 37c | | D | |
| 38a | D? | | Calling D into question; request for justification of D. |
| 38b | E | | Attack on D |
| 39 | | (?)*pro*(E) | Concession of E (attack on D, that defended thesis A), in an hypothetical form "perhaps". |
| | | *contra*(A) | Concession of refutation of A, expressed on interface check-box |

[*] *Key:*
A: Since the groups of A and B mol arrive towards the C mol, they make an impact with the tam.
B: the "a" mol aren't in contact with the "c" mol
C: if you have a wave all the molecules, like billiard balls, will be displaced because the hit on the tambourine it's as if we'd pushed them
D: all the mols will mix up and hit on the tam
E: the "b" will create a barrier between the "a" and the "c"

different understandings. Perhaps surprisingly, it is again the less elaborate understanding of sound — a wave or wind of molecules that are all displaced — that is eliminated from consideration.

Our second example of weakening of attitudes is shown in Table 7, between the same two students as above. In fact, there is a complex set of related changes of attitudes: Elaine's two "YES"s weaken to "?", and Linda's "?" remains unchanged, whilst her "NO" slightly strengthens to a "?".

For considerations of space, we shall not present a detailed dialectical analysis of this sequence, but shall rather restrict ourselves to discussion of a new aspect that is important for understanding why the students' change their expressed attitudes. This key aspect is revealed by Elaine's statement that "[since] we are not sure ... we shouldn't take a firm view". It is as if the students function according to a principle of consensus in uncertainty. In other words, since a view has been called into question, all that can be said is that "*we* are not sure".

*Table 7: Second example of weakening of attitudes (all to "?")*

| T(m:s) | L | Linda | Elaine |
|--------|---|-------|--------|
| | | | Statement 4: The mol which will be in C will leave again with the mol in A and in B towards the left<br>Statement 6: The little ball will jump faster with a greater frequency |
| | | *Attitudes before:*<br>**Statement 4: ?**<br>Statement 6: NO | **Statement 4: YES**<br>Statement 6: YES |
| 23:24 | 43 | there's **[Elaine's statement 6]** a thorny issue ! since it jumps higher it takes more time to come down again therefore the frequency is perhaps not more rapid | |
| 28:27 | 44 | | i'm not sure so we'll take away "with a greater frequency". for the 4 i'll explain it to you: since I thought they would mix up together and that they would strike each other, I thought they would come back together no? |
| 30:05 | 45 | yes, that's logical but since you put "no" for the 3 you should put "no" also | |
| 30:25 | 46 | | <Expresses "NO" for Elaine's Statement 4> |
| 30:28 | 47 | | <Expresses "?" for Elaine's Statement 4> |
| 30:38 | 48 | | <Expresses "?" for Elaine's Statement 6> |
| 30:41 | 49 | Expresses "?" for Elaine's Statement 6 | |
| 33:02 | 50 | | that we are not sure so we shouldn't take a firm view in the text and we'll start it now since everything's sorted out |
| | | *Attitudes after:*<br>**Statement 4:?**<br>Statement 6: ? | **Statement 4: ?**<br>Statement 6: ? |

This general point is in accordance with results of argumentation analysis for another physics problem-solving task (drawing energy chains), with respect to which it was found that argumentation functioned as a mechanism for "weeding out flawed proposals", rather than as a means for imposing them (Baker, 1996, 1999). In Miller's (1986) terms, a view that is contested cannot become part of the "collectively valid".

*No change in attitude*

Finally, we analyse a complex sequence that resulted in no explicit change of attitude. The sequence is interesting given the complexity of the reasoning involved, as well as the range of types of knowledge appealed to, and processes of negotiation of meaning by conceptual dissociation. The example sequence is reproduced in Table 8 below.

*Table 8. Example of no explicit change in attitudes.*

| T(m:s) | L | Alan | John |
|--------|---|------|------|
|  |  |  | Statement 7: "With the less tight skin, it is easier for the molecules to make it shift but the ball shifts less." |
|  |  | *Attitudes before:* ? | **YES** |
| 16:19 | 43 | If the skin shifts more why does the ball shift less? | |
| 19:15 | 44 | | the skin shifts more because it is less tight but the pressure that the air exerts is the same. This skin "marries" [wraps around] thus the form of the ball. |
| 21:24 | 45 | Not agreed. In my opinion the skin of T2 shifts less (see my 7). <Statement 7 of Alan, to which both marked "YES", is: "The less tight skin of tambourine 2 absorbs vibrations more, and thus vibrates less itself"> | |
| 27:20 | 46 | | difficult to know when one looks at the skin, one sees it shift more that has the tighter skin when you hit on something hard, that is stable in space, it won't shift whereas a rag that is not stretched tight, for example, yes [it will] |
| 33:14 | 47 | Another explanation: take a string that is not tight. If you touch [strike] it it will shift a lot but it will vibrate little. By contrast, a tight string, like a guitar one, it will shift little but vibrate a lot. | |
| 36:37 | 48 | | i agree with your 7 but at one point I thought you didn't agree with mine. For me, the two sentences are right, they simply don't explain the same thing(vibrations and movements) |

*Table 8 (continued). Example of no explicit change in attitudes.*

| T(m:s) | L | Alan | John |
|--------|---|------|------|
| 39:23 | 49 | NO. If a less tight skin vibrates less it shifts more, therefore the ball must shift more as well. | |
| 40:34 | 50 | pardon, have you understood? | |
| 43:29 | 51 | | Hypothesis: with the same force of the air exerted on T2: a tight skin will vibrate more than a less tight skin but will shift less than it |
| 43:37 | 52 | <changes "NO" to "YES" for opinion with respect to John's statement 1: "It perturbs the air molecules contained between t1 and t2. The molecules go away from each other."> | |
| 43:44 | 53 | Yes | |
| 43:47 | 54 | Yes | |
| 47:55 | 55 | | for the ball, I think it will shift less with the not-tight skin because it will vibrate less thus it will "transmit" many less vibrations |
| 48:27 | 56 | | Agreed? |
| 49:09 | 57 | Perhaps | |
| | | *Attitudes after:* | |
| | | **? (no change marked)** | **YES (no change marked)** |

Given the complexity of the students' reasoning, drawing on "more" or "higher" and "less" or "lower" values for factors such as force, pressure and tension, in some cases we shall represent this in the dialectical analysis using the following predicates: "x shifts" = "$S(x)$"; "x moves" = "$M(x)$"; "the tension of x" = "$T(x)$"; "x vibrates" = "$V(x)$"; "pressure of x" = "$P(x)$"; "$W(x,y)$" = "x wraps around y"; "x absorbs y" = "$A(x,y)$"; "x transmits to y" = "transmits(x,y); "x increases, is higher, etc." = $\uparrow(x)$"; "x is lower, decreases, etc." = "$\downarrow(x)$"; "x remains the same, is constant, etc." = "$\leftrightarrow(x)$"; "x" can refer to objects such as skin, strings, a ball, etc.

The students' reasoning is expressed in many linguistic forms, such as: "x since y", "x because y", "x thus y", "x causes or leads to y", and so on. For simplification of the analysis, we shall (brutally) reduce all such expressions to an IF/THEN form, "$x \rightarrow y$".

In order to highlight operations on meaning, we shall represent a reformulated version of a proposition X, or a version that makes its meaning explicit ("in other words ..."), as X'. The predicate "$n\text{-}c()$" represents a non-committed dialectical role. To avoid repeating whole complex propositions, they will sometimes be referred to by their line numbers (e.g. "45c").

We use the verb "to shift", rather than "to move", in this case for an important reason, which is that in the original French, two distinct words are used to refer to movement in general: "*bouger*", which is an everyday familiar word, that we have translated by "to shift", and "*mouvement*", that can be a more scientific term, that we have translated by "movement". For learning viewed as appropriation of language (e.g. Wertsch, 1991), the interplay of everyday and scientific discourse is important here. As will be seen, the students' discussion in everyday language ("bouger", to shift) culminates in a (proposed but not accepted) distinction between movement and vibration.

The dialectical analysis of the sequence reproduced in Table 8 is shown in Table 9.

*Table 9. Dialectical analysis of sequence with no explicit attitude change.*

| L | Alan | John | Pragmatic character of dialectical move |
|---|------|------|------------------------------------------|
| | | $\downarrow$T(skin) $\wedge$ $\uparrow$S(skin) $\wedge$ $\downarrow$S(ball) | John's statement 7. Thesis T1 |
| | *n-c*(T1) | *pro*(T1) | Dialectical roles expressed on interface |
| 43 | ( $\uparrow$S(skin) $\wedge$ $\downarrow$S(ball) )? | | Attack on part of T1: how do you defend that? |
| 44a | | $\downarrow$T(skin) $\wedge$ $\leftrightarrow$P(air) $\rightarrow$ $\uparrow$S(skin) $\rightarrow$ | Defense of why skin shifts more |
| 44b | | W(skin, ball) $\rightarrow$ $\downarrow$S(ball) | Defense of why ball shifts less |
| 45a | *contra*($\uparrow$S(skin)) | | Attack on proposition that skin shifts more. |
| 45b | $\downarrow$S(skin) | | |
| 45c | $\downarrow$T(skin) $\rightarrow$ $\uparrow$A(skin,V(x)) $\rightarrow$ $\downarrow$V(skin) | | Defense of skin shifting less, using a statement that John has already conceded (Alan's statement 7). |
| 46a | | *n-c*($\downarrow$V(skin)) | Partial concession. |
| 46b | | (?)$\uparrow$T(skin) $\rightarrow$$\uparrow$S(skin) | Intended defense of first part of T1 |
| 46c | | $\uparrow$T(x) $\rightarrow$$\downarrow$S(x) | Attack on 45c, that states that low tension leads to low vibration (a type of "shifting") |
| 46d | | $\downarrow$T(x) $\rightarrow$$\uparrow$S(x) | |
| 47a | $\downarrow$T(string) $\rightarrow$$\uparrow$S(string) $\wedge$ | | Defense of own statement 45c *and* of John's 46c: attempt to resolve by dissociating "shifting" from "vibration". |
| 47b | $\downarrow$V(string) $\uparrow$T(guitar-string) $\rightarrow$$\downarrow$S(string) $\wedge$ $\uparrow$V(string) | | |

*Table 9 (continued). Dialectical analysis of sequence with no explicit attitude change.*

| L | Alan | John | Pragmatic character of dialectical move |
|---|---|---|---|
| 48a | | *pro*(45c) | Concedes Alan's defense using his statement 7. |
| 48b | | *pro*(T1)? | |
| 48c | | *pro*(45c ∧ T1) | Request for clarification of dialectical role with respect to own thesis T1. |
| 48d | | M(x) ≠ V(x) | Attempted resolution of conflict: both are correct, but not equivalent. |
| 49a | *contra*(45c ∧ T1) | | Attempted resolution not accepted! |
| 49b | ↓T(skin) → ↓V(string) → ↑S(skin) → ↑S(ball) | | Attack on second part of T1 (the ball must shift *more*), using own statement 47a, which was not denied by John. |
| 50 | *pro*(49b)? | | Request for expression of dialectical role |
| 51 | | ↑T(skin) → ↑V(skin) ∧ ↓S(skin) | Concession of 47b |
| 53-4 | *pro*(51) | | Ratifies concession |
| 55 | | ↓T(skin) → ↓V(skin) → ↓transmits(skin, V(skin)) → ↓S(ball) | Attack on 49b: with a slacker skin, ball moves less not more! |
| 56 | | *pro*(55)? | |
| 57 | *n-c*(55) | | |

When looked at under the microscope of analysis, the above sequence is highly complex. We shall restrict ourselves to a few main points relating to co-elaboration of understanding in a dialectical framework, without commenting every detail of the analysis.

In contrast to the previous examples, the task problem, *P*, that the students address here is as follows: "Using two tambourines with a lower sound, having a skin that is much less tight, what changes in the behaviour of the skin of the second tambourine when hitting the first?". John's proposed solution, *s1*, is firstly, that when the skin is less tight, it can be *moved (shifted) more easily*, and secondly, that in this case, however, *the ball moves less*. From a dialectical point of view, the sequence proceeds by focussing on the second statement, then the first, then returning to the second. To Alan's attack, "If the skin shifts more, why does the ball shift less?", John replies with an imaginative image — "the slack skin wraps around the ball" — to which he returns at the end of the sequence, stating that a slack skin will not transmit much vibration.

In order to strengthen his attack, Alan refers to his own statement (7), in which he states that a slack skin absorbs vibration and so vibrates less." From then on, the whole sequence can be seen as an attempt to make more precise what *shifting*, *movement* and *vibration* mean, and how they are to be dissociated from each other. At certain points, it seems that by "shifting" of the skin, John means something like its *amplitude*, the extent of movement, and at others, the 'amount' of movement, or its *frequency*. To that extent, the students touch upon the key concepts at stake here — sound as a *displacement of a vibration*, or, in a sense, a 'movement of a movement'. However, although John and Alan recognise that movement and vibration need to be dissociated (they have opposed "more" and "less" values: higher vibration means lower movement and lower vibration means more movement), this does not really help them to gain a clearer understanding of each notion. The fact that each student is, in a sense, talking about something different, helps to explain why the debate, despite numerous attacks, defenses and concessions, can not come to a conclusive outcome, producing explicit attitude changes concerning what is explicitly debated.

However, it appears that the necessity to express his view about John's statement 7, leads Alan to change his mind (line 52) with respect to another of John's statements (number 1): since John speaks of molecules moving away from each other, this is closer to Alan's insistence on the notion of vibration, so he changes his NO to a YES. This is perhaps an example of argumentative interaction leading to a more coherent discourse (see reference to Crook, 1995, above).

Finally, in order to try to resolve their interlocutionary problem, the students draw extensively on their everyday life experience, of rags and guitar strings. This does not, however, help them to dispel confusion, since the notions of movement they are working with are not sufficiently defined.

*Synthesis of analysis results*

In conclusion to this section, we summarise the main results of our analyses, to be discussed in the final section of the chapter.

The corpus analysed here was collected in a situation where pairs of students used a specific interface of the CONNECT CSCL environment to solve a problem of understanding sound, in physics, using a molecular model. That interface invites students to express their attitudes — "YES", "NO" or "?" — towards each segment of each of their texts, as a means of focussing critical analysis, reflexion and discussion. As a result of discussion, students can, and often did, change the attitudes they expressed. The CONNECT corpus thus lends itself to attempting to understand the interactive processes that potentially relate to those attitude changes.

After having identified the seven argumentative interaction sequences in the corpus, we categorised them into types of attitude changes, as follows: strengthening of attitudes (e.g. "NO" → "YES"), weakening of attitudes (e.g. "YES" → "?"), and no explicit change in attitudes (e.g. "NO" → "NO"). Our analyses were presented as a function of these three types of changes.

Only one example of *attitude strengthening* occurred, in which a student changed his attitude from a "NO" to a "YES", with respect to one of his partner's statements. In this case, the 'winning' student had to work hard to oblige his partner to explicitly represent this attitude change on the CONNECT interface. We analysed this as an implicit reference to a ground rule of dialectics that requires externalisation of outcomes of the debate, and speculated that failure to immediately comply with this rule illustrated the social dimension of facework (face-loss, in this case) of argumentative interaction. In this example, a more elaborated understanding of sound was successfully defended. The students' interaction was also analysed as a process of making explicit and more precise the meaning of an aspect of the more elaborated sound model, involving the notion of molecules moving away from each other.

*Attitude weakening* was the case with 5 out of 8 argumentative sequences. We analysed two examples, involving dialectical refutation[10] ("YES" → "NO") and a common movement towards being unsure ("?" for each student). Weakening is associated with expressions of uncertainty ("I don't know", "I ask myself"), and modal expressions ("perhaps", "could") that were analysed as 'softeners' of loss of face, on the level of social interaction. In one case, given that doubts had been raised, students agreed on a type of consensus in uncertainty. Attitudes were weakened with respect to less elaborated models of sound.

When there was *no manifest change in attitudes*, this was associated with, and explained by, the fact that the students' understandings of important domain notions had been renegotiated. We analysed a complex case in which the students attempted to dissociate everyday and possibly scientific notions of movement and vibration, the latter being a specific case of the former.

Our principal results, with respect to the CONNECT corpus, can thus be summarised as the following five points. These results apply also to the sequences (3 out of 7) whose analyses have not been presented here.

*Attitudes weaken rather than strengthen.* Attitude strengthening is rare; attitude weakening and absence of change in attitudes, in that order, are more frequent.

*Students' argumentative interactions display dialogical rationality.* Attitude changes, when they occur, can be analysed as adhering to a certain dialogical rationality; they can be explained as a function of dialectical moves (e.g. failure to defend against an attack means losing the game) and in terms of adherence to certain ground rules, such as a requirement for clarification of the outcome.

*Understandings are co-elaborated.* In argumentative interaction, students are led to render explicit, to co-elaborate and to make more precise their discourses on their understandings of the task domain. Argumentative interaction goes hand in hand with negotiation of the meaning of the notions at stake.

*Less adequate understandings are eliminated.* When more and less adequate models of sound are confronted, and associated with an attitude change, in these cases, the less adequate understanding is eliminated from consideration, or the more adequate understanding wins out.

*Argumentative interaction is social interaction.* The playing out of the dialectical game, often involving winners and losers, is intimately associated with attempts to manage and maintain a viable social interaction, involving expression of emotional disquiet and minimisation of loss of face.

## DISCUSSION

We interpret these results in terms of the interrelations between three main dimensions of the CSCL collaborative problem-solving situation: *epistemological-cognitive*, *socio-interactional* and *technological*. The first concerns the nature of the problem-solving domain, the students' understanding of it, and the sequence of tasks. The second concerns the nature of the students' interpersonal relationship, as it evolves in the interaction, along factors such as face threatening/preserving, friendliness/hostility, positive/negative emotions, within a socio-institutional situation that defines them as equals in the hierarchy (both are "students" of the same class). The technological aspect concerns specific characteristics of the interface tools, such as the fact that no visual contact is provided, each can overtype at the same time, etc. These are analytical, not empirical dimensions: it could be maintained that in practice, the three are inseparable, or should not be dissociated. In particular, the interface can only be meaningfully analysed with respect to the task for which it is intended.

Why does there seem to be a general tendency for attitudes to weaken, with respect to problem solutions? One possible reason lies in the epistemological-cognitive dimension in the collaborative learning situation. As discussed previously, the problem to be solved is potentially suitable for argumentative discussions, given the range of alternative understandings that students can have with respect to it. In addition, we created dyads precisely to maximise these differences between students, and created a phase for solving the interlocutory problem (see above) that was separated from problem solving in the task domain. However, as Nonnon (1996) has pointed out, there is a paradox with respect to argumentative discussions in learning situations: in learning situations, new knowledge is supposed to be co-constructed; so it is unlikely that students will be in a position to adopt firm attitudes with respect to such knowledge. Rather, students' positions will most probably be quite volatile, shifting for and against, as they explore around the problem, dialectical and meaning spaces. What is remarkable in this corpus is that collaboration between students with different interpretations of sound leads to less elaborate or adequate solutions being eliminated. Why should this be the case, when students usually are able to defend solutions irrespective of their quality? Is there something about a better solution that is 'just obvious'?

A second possible line of explanation for attitude weakening lies in the nature of the students' interpersonal relations. In several cases, the students' attitudes seem to weaken because it would be only 'fair' to their partners to weaken their attitudes a little, given that doubts have been raised with respect to a statement. In one case, this requirement for fairness went so far as a consensus in uncertainty. The fact that the students' are communicating at a distance, with no face-to-face contact, does not appear to prevent the students from using linguistic resources to 'soften' the possible loss of face associated with criticism and refutation.

Our proposal that students' argumentative interactions could be analysed in terms of ground rules for "rational discussions", derived from formal dialectical models (Barth & Krabbe, *op. cit.*), may appear contentious. In particular, we propose that students' adherence to the two following rules is a plausible analysis of their interaction: "argumentative outcomes must be made explicit", "an attack must be followed by a defense, otherwise you lose the game". To these we can add "attacks and defenses must not be repeated", given that the students always redefined and re-elaborated their defenses and attacks, along the dimension of negotiation of meaning. Our claim may appear less contentious given the following two points. The first point is that dialogical rationality is not the same as individual rationality. In cognitive science the latter has often been conceived as a matter of acting in a way that one believes will maximise achievement of one's goals. But dialogical rationality is about how one acts in communication and cooperation with others. It is thus plausible that groups will impose stronger constraints on rationality than individuals will upon themselves. The second point relates to the nature of dialectical rules in accordance with dialogical rationality. Such rules should not be seen as restricted to a specific and idealised form of interaction. In fact, they are expressions of more general principles of cooperation and communication (c.f. Allwood, 1976). It is thus not surprising that students' communicative inter-actions can be interpreted in terms of these rules and principles.

Finally, interpreting the extent to which students explain their understandings and negotiate the meaning of notions in the task domain requires, in addition to the above points, an examination of the characteristics of the CSCL interface tools. Constraints associated with synchronous typewritten communication across the network (e.g. Clark & Brennan, 1991) are now well known. For example, one could predict that typewritten communication inhibits free expression of elaborate ideas in complex types of interaction, and that absence of non-verbal clues at a distance would lead to problems in establishing intercomprehension. What is it, then, about the CONNECT CSCL situation — by "situation" we mean the tools-task-situation-social actors — that favours or allows expression and elaboration of understandings in the task domain? One possibility is that the careful choice of the task and of participants in dyads was able to outweigh interface constraints. Another is that the provision of check boxes for expressing attitudes for each segments of texts enabled the students to *focus* on the important points to be discussed, or, as we defined them above, the interlocutionary problems. Finally, it is not certain that some form of constraint on expression of ideas in typewritten CMC is necessarily negative from the point of view of problem solving. For example, Tiberghien and de Vries (1997) have shown that in CMC interactions, students restrict themselves to expressing the most complex operations of modelling in physics. Perhaps CMC helps to cut out verbiage, whilst not obviating the necessity to maintain an adequate interpersonal relation?

## CONCLUSION

In this chapter, we have presented a theoretical approach to understanding how students engaged in collaborative problem solving can co-elaborate new understandings in and by argumentative interactions. The approach depends on describing interrelations between three "spaces": the problem space, the dialectical space and the meaning space. This approach was applied in the analysis of a corpus of interactions that was collected when dyads of students used the CONNECT CSCL environment to solve a problem of interpreting a sound phenomenon in physics.

In conclusion, we discuss the generalisability of our results, and provide some indications on further work.

Generalisation of our results beyond the CONNECT corpus requires a painstaking inductive approach (accumulation of supplementary evidence), involving similarly detailed analyses to the ones presented above. The analyses would need to cover a wide range of variations in tasks, groups and interfaces. Such an enterprise represents a major and daunting challenge for the cognitive science of collaborative learning. We make the conjecture that the most effective way of achieving this goal is to develop strong theories and models, and to apply them to the deep analysis of specific cases.

It turns out that our results are largely concordant with those obtained from the analysis of a corpus of spoken interactions, collected with respect to an analogous problem involving modelling energy in physics (Baker, 1996, 1999). For example, in that research it was found that students' argumentative interactions mostly functioned as means of eliminating proposals that were seen to be 'flawed' in some way, rather than as a means of defending and commonly adopting proposals (see result 1 above). An alternative to the inductive approach would be to see our results as existential statements that falsify universal ones (the existence of a black swan falsifies the statement that all swans are white, i.e. not black). For example, our results would contradict the belief (assuming that it was widespread) that typewritten CMC communication necessarily prevents production of potentially constructive epistemic interactions.

We have shown that students can interact with and via the CONNECT CSCL environment students in order to choose better problem solutions and to co-elaborate deeper understandings in and as a result of engaging in argumentative interactions. But there are clearly limits to what students can achieve in their argumentative interactions, without outside help. Clearly, students need a teacher's help in order to resolve certain questions, and to integrate what they believe to have learned into their existing knowledge, within constraints inherent in the educational system. One line of research that we are currently exploring aims to define the teacher's role in CSCL environments based on the pedagogical power of argumentative interactions.

## AUTHOR'S CONTACT ADDRESS

*Dr. Michael Baker, Chargé de Recherche au CNRS*
*UMR 5612 GRIC — Groupe de Recherches sur les Interactions Communicatives*
*Interaction & Cognition Research Team, C.N.R.S. & Université Lumière Lyon 2*
*5, avenue Pierre Mendès-France, 69676 BRON Cedex, France*
*Telephone: (+33) (0)4 78 77 31 17; Fax: (+33) (0)4 78 77 40 19*
*Email: Michael.Baker@univ-lyon2.fr ; Web: http://gric.univ-lyon2.frgric5/*

## ACKNOWLEDGEMENTS

The CONNECT interface, together with its related empirical study, was designed, implemented and carried out in collaboration with Erica de Vries and Kristine Lund, during Erica de Vries' postdoctoral work in the GRIC laboratory. I would also like to thank teachers and pupils who participated in the studies, as well as members of the COAST research team. Over a period of at least five years, this research has received financial support from the Centre National de la Recherche Scientifique, the French Education Ministry and the Rhône-Alpes Region.

## REFERENCES

Allwood, J. (1976). *Linguistic Communication in Action and Co-operation: A Study in Pragmatics.* Gothenburg Monographs in Linguistics 2. University of Gothenburg, Department of Linguistics, Sweden.

Andriessen, J. & Coirier, P. (Eds.) (1999). *Foundations of Argumentative Text Processing.* Studies in Writing, (Series Eds.) G. Rijlaarsdam & E. Espéret. Amsterdam: Amsterdam University Press.

Baker, M.J. & Lund, K. (1997). Promoting reflective interactions in a computer-supported collaborative learning environment. *Journal of Computer Assisted Learning.* 13, 175-193.

Baker, M.J. (1994). A Model for Negotiation in Teaching-Learning Dialogues. *Journal of Artificial Intelligence in Education,* 5(2), 199-254.

Baker, M.J. (1995). Negotiation in Collaborative Problem-Solving Dialogues. In *Dialogue and Instruction: Modeling Interaction in Intelligent Tutoring Systems,* (eds.) Beun, R.J., Baker, M.J. & Reiner, M., pp. 39-55. Berlin: Springer-Verlag.

Baker, M.J. (1996). Argumentation et co-construction des connaissances [Argumentation and co-construction of knowledge]. *Interaction et Cognitions* 2 (3), 157-191.

Baker, M.J. (1999). Argumentation and Constructive Interaction. In G. Rijlaarsdam & E. Espéret (Series Eds.) & Pierre Coirier and Jerry Andriessen (Vol. Eds.) Studies in Writing: Vol. 5. *Foundations of Argumentative Text Processing,* 179 – 202. Amsterdam: University of Amsterdam Press.

Baker, M.J. (2000). Explication, Argumentation et Négociation : analyse d'un corpus de dialogues en langue naturelle écrite dans le domaine de la médecine [Explanation, Argumentation and Negotiation: analysis of a corpus of typewritten natural language dialogues in the domain of medicine]. *Psychologie de l'Interaction,* N° 9-10, 179-210.

Baker, M.J., de Vries, E. & Lund, K. (1999). Designing computer-mediated epistemic interactions. *Proceedings of the International Conference on Artificial Intelligence and Education,* Le Mans, July 1999. S.P. Lajoie & M. Vivet (Eds.) *Artificial Intelligence in Education* (pp. 139-146). Amsterdam: IOS Press.

Baker, M.J., de Vries, E., Lund, K. & Quignard, M. (2001). Computer-mediated epistemic interactions for co-constructing scientific notions: Lessons learned from a five-year research programme. In P. Dillenbourg, A. Eurelings & K. Hakkarainen (Eds.) *Proceedings of EuroCSCL 2001: European Perspectives on Computer-Supported Collaborative Learning,* Maastricht McLuhan Institute (ISBN 90-5681-097-9), pp. 89-96. Maastricht, March 22-24, 2001.

Barth, E.M. & Krabbe, E.C.W. (1982). *From Axiom to Dialogue: A philosophical study of logics and argumentation.* Berlin: Walter de Gruyter.

Chi, M.T.H., Bassok, M., Lewis, M.W., Reimann, P. & Glaser, R. (1989). Self-Explanations: How Students Study and Use Examples in Learning to Solve Problems. *Cognitive Science*, 13 (2), 145-182.

Clark, H.H. & Schaefer, E.F. (1989). Contributing to Discourse. *Cognitive Science*, 13, 259-294.

Clark, H.H., & Brennan, S.E. (1991). Grounding in communication. In L.B. Resnick, J.M. Levine, & S.D. Teasley (Eds.), *Perspectives on socially shared cognition* (pp. 127-149). Washington DC: American Psychological Association.

Cohen, L.J. (1992). *An Essay on Belief and Acceptance.* Oxford: Clarendon Press.

Crook, C. (1994). *Computers and the Collaborative Experience of Learning.* London: Routledge.

De Vries, E., Lund, K. & Baker, M.J. (2002). Computer-mediated epistemic dialogue: Explanation and argumentation as vehicles for understanding scientific notions. *The Journal of the Learning Sciences*, 11(1), 63—103.

Dennett, D.C. (1981). How to Change your Mind. In *Brainstorms: Philosophical Essays on Mind and Psychology*, pp. 300-309. Brighton (UK): Harvester Press.

Edwards, D. (1993). But What Do Children Really Think ?: Discourse Analysis and Conceptual Content in Children's Talk. *Cognition and Instruction* 11 (3 & 4), 207-225.

Gilly, M., Roux, J.-P. & Trognon, A. (Eds.). *Apprendre dans l'Interaction [Learning in Interaction].* Nancy: Presses Universitaires de Nancy / Publications de l'Université de Provence.

Harman, G. (1986). *Change in View: Principles of Reasoning.* Cambridge Mass.: MIT Press.

Johnson-Laird, P.N. (1983). *Mental Models.* Cambridge: Cambridge University Press.

Linder, C. J. & Erickson, G. L. (1989). A study of tertiary physics students' conceptualizations of sound. *International Journal of Science Education*, 11, 491-501.

Lund, K. & Baker, M.J. (1999). Teachers' collaborative interpretations of students' computer-mediated collaborative problem-solving interactions. *In Proceedings of the International Conference on Artificial Intelligence and Education*, Le Mans, July 1999. S.P. Lajoie & M. Vivet (Eds.) Artificial Intelligence in Education (pp. 147-154). Amsterdam: IOS Press.

Maurines, L. (1998, January). Les élèves et la propagation des signaux sonores [Students and the propagation of sound signals]. *Bulletin de l'Union des Physiciens*, 92, 1-22.

Meyer, M. (1986). *De la problématologie. Philosophie, science et langage* [On problematology. Philosophy, science and language]. Brussels: Pierre Mardaga.

Miller, M. (1986). Argumentation and cognition. In M. Hickmann (Ed.) *Social and functional approaches to language and thought* (pp. 225-249). New York: Academic Press.

Muntig, P. & Turnbull, W. (1998). Conversational structure and facework in arguing. *Journal of Pragmatics*, 29, 225-256.

Naess, A. (1966). *Communication and argument. Elements of applied semantics.* London: Allen and Unwin.

Newell, A. & Simon, H. A. (1972). *Human problem solving.* Englewood Cliffs, NJ: Prentice-Hall.

Nonnon, E. (1996). Activités argumentatives et élaboration de connaissances nouvelles: le dialogue comme espace d'exploration [Argumentative activities and elaboration of new knowledge: dialogue as a space for exploration]. *Langue Française, 112* (décembre 1996), 67-87.

Ohlsson, S. (1996). Learning to do and learning to understand: A lesson and a challenge for cognitive modeling. In P. Reimann & H. Spada (Eds.), *Learning in humans and machines* (pp. 37-62). Oxford: Elsevier.

Perelman, C. & Olbrechts-Tyteca, L. (1958/1988). *Traité de l'argumentation. La nouvelle rhétorique [Treatise on argumentation. The new rhetoric].* Bruxelles: Editions de l'Université de Bruxelles.

Pontecorvo, C. (Ed.) (1993). Discourse and Shared Reasoning [Journal Special Issue]. *Cognition and Instruction*, 11 (3 & 4).

Quignard, M. (2000). *Modélisation cognitive de l'argumentation dans le dialogue: étude de dialogues d'élèves en résolution de problème de sciences physiques.* [Cognitive modelling of argumentation in dialogue: a study of students' problem-solving dialogues in physics] Thèse de doctorat de sciences cognitives [PhD thesis in Cognitive Science], Grenoble, Université Joseph Fourier.

Resnick, L.B., Levine, J.M. & Teasley, S.D. (eds.) (1991). *Perspectives on Socially Shared Cognition.* Washington D.C.: American Psychological Association.

Roschelle, J. (1992). Learning by collaborating: Convergent conceptual change. *Journal of the Learning Sciences*, 2, 235-276.

Tiberghien, A., & De Vries, E. (1997). Relating characteristics of learning situations to learner activities. *Journal of Computer Assisted Learning*, 13, 163-174.

van Eemeren, F. and Grootendorst, R. (1984). *Speech Acts in Argumentative Discussions*. Dordrecht: Foris.

van Eemeren, F.H., Grootendorst, R. & Henkemans, F.S. (1996). *Fundamentals of Argumentation Theory: A Handbook of Historical Backgrounds and Contemporary Developments*. Mahwah New Jersey: Lawrence Erlbaum Associates.

Walton, D.N. (1989). *Informal Logic: a handbook for critical argumentation*. Cambridge: Cambridge University Press.

Walton, D.N. (1992). *Plausible Argument in Everyday Conversation*. State University of New York Press: Albany, N.Y.

Wertsch, J. V. (1991): *Voices of the Mind. A Sociocultural Approach to Mediated Action*. USA: Harvester Wheatsheaf.

Winograd, T. & Flores, F. (1986). *Understanding Computers and Cognition*. Reading, Mass.: Addison-Wesley.

# NOTES

[1] Throughout this chapter we shall use the terms "co-elaborate" and "co-elaboration", rather than the more common "co-construct" and "co-construction", for a specific reason. We view the term "co-construction" as an architectural metaphor, that could lead to the view that collaboration involves each partner adding a new separable element to the solution, in the way that builders might add bricks to a building. In fact, from our previous research (Baker, 1994, 1995), we propose that collaboration proceeds by each participant ("co-") *transforming*, or elaborating, previous contributions. A better metaphor would therefore be that of a group of people each moulding a common piece of clay until the result satisfies them.

[2] The theoretical perspective according to which argumentation can be seen as the attempt to solve these two types of problems is a basis of M. Quignard's PhD thesis in Cognitive Science (Quignard, 2000), research for which was carried out in the GRIC Laboratory, Lyon, under the supervision of M. Baker and J. Caelen. Echos of this approach are also to be found in the "problematology" of Meyer (1986).

[3] See, for example, Baker (2000), for an analysis of argumentative interactions in which experienced and less experienced doctors discussed alternative medical diagnoses in order to rank them in order of plausibility.

[4] "CONNECT" means "CONfrontation, NEgotiation and Construction of Text".

[5] For precise details on the procedure for pairing students, together with other experimental details, readers are referred to de Vries, Lund & Baker (2002).

[6] Strictly speaking, we should rather say "sequences in which argumentation is the predominant discursive process", rather than "argumentation sequences", since argumentation almost never occurs as a 'pure' genre, usually being combined with explanation, negotiation of meaning and different types of interaction management.

[7] Clearly, even more fine-grained categories could be used, that exploit individuals' attitude changes in the group. For example, there are many ways in which attitudes could be weakened: from YES/YES to YES/?, YES/NO, ?/?, NO/?, NO/NO, and so on. Examples of only some of these possibilities are presented here, for reasons of brevity.

[8] By the terms "knowledge" and "understanding" in this context, we do not mean to say that what the students think is true. Rather, we mean an understanding of a problem solving situation, in a sense closer to the French term *connaissance* rather than to *savoir*.

[9] Elsewhere in this chapter we shall use the less theoretically-charged terms "understandings" and "points of view", instead of (mental) models (Johnson-Laird, 1983). Given our preoccupation with discourse in interaction, we do not necessarily mean to imply that the students possess fully elaborated and coherent mental representations, whether they correspond to scientific models or not.

---

[10] Dialectical refutation of a thesis means that its proponent lost the dialectical game, i.e. was unable to provide a defense against an attack. This is not the same as 'genuine refutation', in some normative sense of the term.

JERRY ANDRIESSEN, GIJSBERT ERKENS, CATHY VAN DE
LAAK, NANNO PETERS & PIERRE COIRIER

# ARGUMENTATION AS NEGOTIATION IN ELECTRONIC COLLABORATIVE WRITING

## INTRODUCTION

The goal of our research is to analyse the relationship between communication and task execution in computer supported collaborative learning. The current paper is about a collaborative writing situation in which pairs of students have to produce an argumentative text, while collaborating via an electronic network. In our perspective, this is a task from which students are supposed to learn about the concepts that are discussed and written about. Learning happens because in this situation participants negotiate about text content. We will specifically address the issue of how argumentation contributes to the knowledge negotiation process in collaborative electronic writing: to what extent is text content negotiated? What forms of negotiation can be observed? Are there relationships between the types of negotiation and the content that is discussed?

It is generally acknowledged that writing can be very useful in the process of knowledge transformation. Several studies have, on the other hand, found clear evidence that writers do not engage in knowledge transformation in all cases (Bereiter & Scardamalia, 1985). Similar conclusions have been put forward concerning argumentation and collaboration (Baker, 1998; Veerman, 2000). In our research, we look for specific information about argumentative exchanges during collaborative tasks in networked environments. That is, we consider both the content and the form of communicative exchanges, and try to relate these exchanges to specific processes in the collaborative task. For this purpose, the task execution process is divided into three phases, which are compared for types of exchanges. This division allows differentiating conclusions concerning specific processes implied in each of the distinguished phases.

*J. Andriessen, M. Baker, and D. Suthers (eds.), Arguing to Learn: Confronting Cognitions in Computer-Supported Collaborative Learning environments (79-115).*
© *2003 Kluwer Academic Publishers. Printed in the Netherlands*

## COORDINATION OF INTERACTION AND PERFORMANCE IN COLLABORATIVE LEARNING

Cooperation or collaboration[1] on a cooperative task concerns a complex interaction between task strategies and communication processes. Cooperation requires that the collaborating subjects acquire a common frame of reference to negotiate and communicate about their individual viewpoints and inferences. Obtaining a *common ground* is crucial in every communicative situation (Clark and Brennan, 1991). One problem with collaboration is that the processes of representation formation and communication often take place implicitly. Natural language communication is implicit by nature, that is, viewpoints are not always advanced, task strategies are not always open to discussion, and so forth. Although implicitness may be ineffective because it masks differences in knowledge, viewpoints, and attitudes, it also results in efficient and non-redundant transfer of information.

In normal educational settings, we can define a *co-operative learning situation* as one in which two or more students work together to fulfil an assigned task within a particular domain of learning to achieve a joint product. In ideal co-operation, the collaborating partners must have a common interest in solving the problem at hand. Furthermore, they should be mutually dependent on the information and co-operation of the other to reach their (shared) goals. Only when the participants have abilities or information that are complementary, co-operation can be fruitful and will be looked for. For this reason, in our experiments, we often distribute information between participants.

The learning situations we are examining serve to foster *knowledge negotiation*, that is, discussion for agreement about the meaning of concepts and their interpretations in the context of a learning task (Baker, 1994; Dillenbourg and Baker, 1996). Negotiation may be about problem solutions, meanings of concepts, and other things. Students tend to differ in their tendency to focus on problem solutions or on concept meanings (Veerman, Andriessen and Kanselaar, 2000). In educational tasks, participants differ (by default) in their knowledge and experience, and their knowledge is supposed to be incomplete, and consequently, negotiation is not always a balanced process. This may be a reason why some students are not very fond of such learning tasks. The learning goal of collaborative tasks in education is not only to learn to produce optimal solutions (such as an argumentative text), but, more importantly, concerns the active exploration and elaboration of the space of debate during negotiation itself. The long-term question underlying our research is: what is the relationship between knowledge negotiation and learning in collaborative writing?

To answer the question how interaction and task performance during collaboration are related, a detailed, process oriented analysis of collaborative dialogues is required. Task-content goals, the current dialogue context, conversational conventions, the current topic, expectations about the partner, and individual knowledge or processing of information all have an effect on the interpretation or the generation of utterances in dialogues (Erkens, 1997).

Technically speaking, these factors constrain the type and the propositional content of utterances at a certain moment. The degree to which an utterance satisfies the numerous constraints, relates to the coordination between information exchange and interactive knowledge construction, and between external and internal control in the dialogue. It is for this reason that we think that a pragmatic analysis of collaborative dialogues without reference to content matters (task goal, problem solving strategies and aspects of knowledge construction) is not sufficient to give an answer to the question of how interaction and performance are related. Therefore, we propose an analysis of the concepts involved during task execution.

## ARGUMENTATIVE WRITING

Three major processes are usually distinguished in individual writing: planning, translating and revising. Process analysis of individual writing has shown a number of activities with different activation over time during these three processes (Flower & Hayes, 1980; van den Bergh & Rijlaarsdam, 1996, 1999; Alamargot & Chanquoy, 2001).

According to Bakhtine (1981), argumentation may be considered as "un discours à plusieurs voix" (a discourse with multiple voices), requiring the integration of a dialogue into the form of a monologue. This requires careful use of specific linguistic means (conceptual, rhetoric, linguistic) to articulate this goal (Coirier, Andriessen & Chanquoy, 1999). The ultimate criterion for the success of an argumentative text is the acceptance by the addressee of the main position. Hence, one important difference of argumentative text production in comparison with the production of other types of texts (narratives, expositions, etc.) is that a writer more explicitly has to deal with the addressee. Because of the important role of the addressee in argumentation, even the situation of individual text production can be seen as virtual negotiation (Coirier & Andriessen, 2000).

As an example, one of the most interesting discourse actions requiring such cooperativity is counter argumentation, that is the attempt to refute evidence put forward in defence of the adversary's point of view. From a developmental perspective, counterarguments appear relatively late in children's writing, that is around 13-14 years of age (Espéret, Coirier, Coquin-Viennot, & Passerault, 1987). One explanation could be that the knowledge relevant for the adversary's point of view is less developed than the knowledge pertaining to one's own point of view (Stein & Miller, 1993). This is one of the reasons why collaboratively constructing argumentative texts could be a potential learning experience: one may acquire more information about the other standpoint. Counter argumentation can be observed in a text as concessions, restrictions, and modulations of arguments, each of which is linked to specific use of linguistic operations, which are only rarely found before the age of 16-17 in written text production (De Bernardi & Antolini, 1996; Coirier & Golder, 1993; Golder, 1992; Marchand, 1993).

Argumentative text production presents many specific problems to writers, and accordingly offers many opportunities for learning (Coirier, Andriessen & Chanquoy, 1999; Alamargot & Andriessen, 2002). This contribution focuses on the dialogue between two participants collaboratively constructing an argumentative text, a situation in which both partners may each serve as the other's audience. Of this dialogue, we analysed meaning negotiation, that is, those utterances that explicitly addressed content, as opposed to procedures or social talk.

We view collaborative writing as a negotiation task because participants have to discuss the production of a single text. The negotiation that we specifically address concerns the content of the argumentative text. Many aspects of this content could be addressed, such as the strength and relevance of individual arguments, their persuasiveness with respect to a target audience, the completeness of reasoning, issues of text coherence, etc. Our main question concerns the characteristics of the negotiation about content and the role of argumentation in this process.

## NEGOTIATION AND LEARNING BY ARGUMENTATION

### Argumentation and negotiation

Collaboration is analysed in this chapter with respect to the conceptual and interactive dimensions (Baker, 1999). We suppose that during this process, participants confront concepts by proposing, explaining, arguing and evaluating with respect to the goal of the task, which is to produce a text that defends a specific point of view. These actions are part of the process of *knowledge negotiation*, which serves to reach agreement, in our case about the concepts (reasons, arguments) to use in the text.

Baker (1994) explored the role of knowledge negotiation in several teacher-student and student-student dialogues and described three different negotiation strategies, each associated with specific communicative acts: refining knowledge, argumentation and standing pat. In refining knowledge, participants modify and build on each other's knowledge by proposing and accepting information. This can be done symmetrically (both participants propose and accept information), or asymmetrically (one participant stands pat; the other one elaborates). In argumentation, participants do not accept a particular piece of information and try to convince each other of their own viewpoints.

Argumentation (as a dialogue action) is taken as a subclass of knowledge negotiation. Argumentation can be seen as a more or less explicit attempt at confrontation. This conception of argumentation is pragmatic, as opposed to formal, and we distinguish three types of requirements for classifying part of a dialogue as argumentative, based on Coirier, Andriessen & Chanquoy (1999) and Baker (1999):
1.  Argumentation minimally involves a participant stating a position, and another participant questioning it.
2.  In elaborate argumentation, we observe defence and attack moves, at least one for each participant. This may imply counter argumentation.
3.  In a dialogue, the argumentation can be resolved by an (explicit or implicit) acceptance of the defended position, or the alternative position.

Argumentation may lead to one or more of three conceptual goals, each of which we tend to call a learning result: (1) sharing knowledge: argumentation leads to both participants better understanding each other; (2) knowledge constitution: argumentation leads to deeper understanding of a concept; (3) knowledge transformation: argumentation leads to a different belief and/or idea.

Baker (1996) studied argumentation strategies in greater depth, in relation to students' conceptual change in collaborative problem-solving dialogues. He found that in all cases where arguments had a dialectical outcome (a 'winner' and 'loser'), arguments were refuted rather than defended. However, no clear relationships were found between argumentation, conceptual change and the quality of the problem solution produced. In another study (Baker, De Vries & Lund, 1999), aimed at promoting epistemic interactions in a CSCL environment, the authors concluded that conceptual change could be achieved by dissolving conceptual differences as well as by resolving conflicts in a dialectical sense. Hence, realising what was not understood could be as much a start for learning as encountering conflict and disagreement.

The relationship between argumentation and learning by collaboration is not direct. It seems that, among other things, specific task characteristics are important here. One of the possible distinctions at this level is between problem solving and conceptual reasoning, already introduced in section 2. Veerman (2000; this volume) showed that if students interpret the assignment as problem solving, they tend to negotiate problem *solutions*, at the cost of discussing the meaning of relevant concepts.

*Representing meaning negotiation in writing*

The comparison between the concepts that are negotiated during collaboration and the concepts that are entered in the text actually produced during collaborative writing may allow specifying to what extent negotiation actually contributes to the content of text production. In a previous study (Erkens, Andriessen & Peters, in press), we characterised this process as meaning co-construction, represented as a landscape of peaks and valleys of concepts across discussion cycles (see Figure 1). The landscape model (van den Broek, Risden, Fletcher & Thurlow, 1996) is based on the activation of concepts during the reading process, leading to the formation of a content representation. We proposed to discuss the collaborative writing process as one of collective knowledge co-construction, in which individual dispositions combine to a (virtual) landscape of concepts that are activated at a specific moment by making them explicit. Under ideal circumstances, cycles of individual knowledge construction may be confronted in a collective landscape of concepts that are activated and discussed. This process is visualized in figure 1. We use the landscape metaphor to represent (collective) knowledge building rather than individual learning or mental representation. Our landscape is located *outside* the individuals participating in the dialogue but it is supposed to represent the concepts that individuals are conscious about to differing degrees. One of the roles of negotiation could be the (re-) activation of concepts, that is, raising their activation level in the landscape. Argumentation could represent a more brutal and global form of activation, for example as avalanches or earthquakes. Grounding could be represented as the extent to which individual participants share a common view of the landscape. Knowledge constitution and transformation is extending the range and the form of the landscape.

It is beyond the scope of the current text to explore these ideas much further. However, the notion of a collective landscape is somewhat similar to that of the conversational record as proposed by Thomason (1990) and earlier by Stalnaker (1978). One difference with these ideas is that the landscape characterizes the temporary activation of concepts, allowing a more dynamic model.

Taken as a meaning negotiation task, collaborative writing involves activation, generation, negotiation and revision of conceptual information during or as a result of formulation of content. The collective landscape represents the fluctuation in activation of concepts expressed by participants in various dialogue patterns.

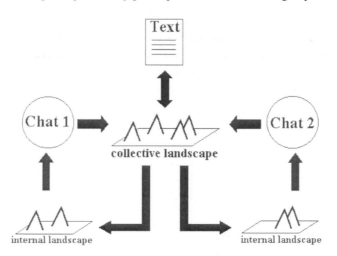

*Figure 1: Topography of a collaborative writing task*

## The collaborative writing environment

At our laboratory in Utrecht, we study electronic collaborative text production with respect to the relationship between characteristics of interaction on the one hand and learning and problem solving on the other. A network-based (Collaborative Text Production: CTP) tool has been developed which combines a shared word-processor, chat-boxes and private information sources to foster the collaborative distance writing of texts. Collaboration and the sharing of windows are restricted to dyads of students.

The working screen of the program displays several private and shared windows (see Figure 2):

- TASK (upper-left): contains the task assignment
- ARGUMENTS (upper-right): displays additional information: texts or pictures
- CHAT (lower left): The lower chat box is for the student's current contribution, the other for the incoming messages of his partner. Every typed letter is immediately conveyed to the partner via the network, so that both boxes are WYSIWIS: What You See Is What I See. The scrollable window holds the chat history.
- SHARED TEXT (lower right): A word processor (also WYSIWIS) in which the shared text can be composed while taking turns, and a turn-taking device.

The tool allows logging of all keystrokes during task execution. The CTP-tool is currently replaced by a new tool, which is described in Erkens, (Tabachneck)-Schijf, Jaspers & van Berlo (2000). The data we report here are from an earlier study (Andriessen, Erkens, Overeem & Jaspers, 1996), the analysis is new.

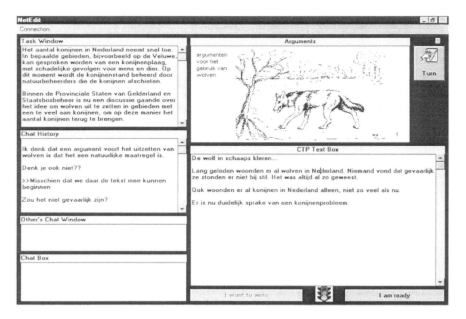

*Figure 2: The CTP-tool interface*

In what follows, when we mention discussion or communication, we are referring to what happens in the Chat Box. When we mention the text, we are referring to the content of the shared Text Box. This distinction supposes that participants discuss in the chat-interface, while they are producing text in the other window. From a negotiation perspective, this distinction is not entirely correct. We return to this issue in the discussion section.

*Electronic communication*

The slow pace and physical constraints of keyboard communication may put off a knowledge negotiation process. In one study (Veerman, Andriessen & Kanselaar, 2000) we found that a linear chat interface was ill suited for conversation about complex information (that is: multiple themes), especially with more than two people involved. Confusion about what theme a reaction referred to, and the problem of reacting to multiple issues probably gives rise to many missed opportunities for learning. This happens in oral conversation, but maybe to an even greater extent when communicating with typical linear chat interfaces. In general, the electronic environment may severely constrain the negotiation mode (shifting between task, content or interaction) and the negotiated content, as well as the complexity (supported dialogue moves), the flexibility (the liberty to realise dialogue moves), the systematicity (consistent realisation of attitudes), and degree of directness (the possibility of expressing illocutionary force) of the communication (Dillenbourg & Baker, 1996). What could be a reason for still using such an environment, apart from our interest in electronic learning? In our view, the benefits can still be found in the possibility of explicitly facilitating communication, argumentation and/or problem solving. We are currently involved in a number of studies that investigate some of these possibilities (e.g. Erkens et al, in press; van der Puil & Andriessen, 2002; Munneke & Andriessen, 2000). In principle, in a constructive electronic environment, relatively slow-moving synchronous electronic communication might tolerate more reflection, when compared to speaking, while still keeping some of the advantages of deliberate written communication. Our current hypothesis is that the results of such educational arrangements are about problems with communication and collaboration, rather than with argumentation and writing. In the mean time, we should be aware of the problem that we lack knowledge about necessary features of chat interfaces, and that required chat interface characteristics may be different for different tasks or between different phases of a complex task (Alamargot & Andriessen, 2002).

In the next sections we describe the result of an experiment in electronic collaborative writing. First, we describe the method used. Then, we summarize the results of an analysis of focusing, which is reported elsewhere in more detail. Then, the most important part of this paper involves the analysis of meaning negotiation and argumentation.

## DESCRIPTION OF THE TASK

Collaborative writing is an extremely complex task that can have many arrangements and goals (e.g. Posner & Baecker, 1992; Neuwirth, Kaufer, Chandhok & Morris, 1994). In our case, the joint writing situation we examine involves two equal participants (university students), collaborating synchronously over a network, exchanging chunks of information containing one or a small number of sentences, in order to produce an argumentative text with a length between one and two pages.

In the experiment 74 university students participated. There were students of various departments, such as educational sciences, psychology, geography and philosophy, all of the University of Utrecht. The mean age of the students was 22,9 years, 61 % female and 39 % male. The participants received financial compensation for their efforts. The students were randomly assigned to dyads.

The task concerns writing two argumentative texts defending assigned positions (a or b) on two topics. Each pair of subjects had to produce two texts on one topic each. The two topics and their positions were:

1. Nature preservation (the overpopulation of rabbits): (a) Wolves: reintroduction of wolves to regulate overpopulation (b) Professional hunters: assign hunters to regulate overpopulation
2. Labour policy (employment principles): (a) Flexible jobs: flexible employment, no steady contracts; (b) Steady jobs: long term contracts.

The goal of the experiment was to examine content elaboration. Three reasons were provided to each participant in favour of one of the alternative viewpoints. These reasons were the reasons in favour or against the positions stated above that were most frequently mentioned in a survey by students of the same group. Participants were free to use these as reasons in their texts. Reasons were presented either in pictorial or textual format. In the picture condition, we tried to represent the propositions represented in the textual format as closely as possible. In this contribution we will discuss results of students who received reasons in the textual format and about the labour policy topic.

To determine the opinion of the subjects on the four different viewpoints, an opinion-test was administered. In order to minimise its effect on the writing-tasks, the relevant questions were mixed with questions about opinions on other matters. Two pre-tests were developed to measure knowledge and interest in the topics at hand. Each test contained 10 multiple-choice items on general information in these domains. After taking the pre-tests and opinion-test the students received a short instruction describing the task and the interface of the program. The students were allowed to collaborate for 75 minutes to produce one text, and after a 15-minute break, the second text was written. A maximum of 8 students (4 dyads) were writing at the same time in the same room in the experiment. By means of screens the dyads were prevented to have visual eye contact with their partner. After the two tasks were completed, the students answered an evaluation questionnaire and were allowed to talk to each other. The questionnaire revealed very positive attitudes towards an experience that was new to most of them.

The task instruction is included in the Appendix.

## ANALYSIS 1: CO-CONSTRUCTION

The results described in this section are reported more extensively in Erkens et al. (in press) and Peters (1999). The goal of this analysis was to compare the concepts put forward in the dialogue and those written in the text. Two questions were addressed: (1) what is the relationship between the concepts produced in the chat and those in the resulting texts, measured during three phases of collaborative interaction, and (2) is this relationship affected by the content of the position to be defended, that is, is it affected by the nature of individual dispositions? To that end, the task execution protocols were split (post-hoc) into three phases, each phase starting with a chat, and ending with a text. The first period ended when the participants had written a first part of text, the third period ended with the final text and the second period is determined by the middle text between the first and final drafts.

We analysed the phases by comparing the concepts the dyads used in their chat discussions and during their writing. To answer the research questions, we particularly focused on corresponding concepts, that is, the concepts that appear in the chat as well as in the text. Figure 3 serves to display this idea. The figure shows the intersections of ideas in the chat and in the text in the three phases. Some ideas will be mentioned in the chat as well as in the text, some only in the chat, while others appear in the text only. The size of the different diagrams illustrates that we expect the number of ideas in the three drafts to grow, but those in the chat to decrease between phases.

We mentioned before that we exclusively analysed utterances that focused on meaning of concepts. To give an idea about the role of such utterances in the writing task, table 1 displays the percentages of utterances focusing on meaning and on task strategy (e.g. "Let's start with the arguments", or "I think it is best to write down the arguments first and then to make a nice text at the end") in each of the three phases (Ingenluyff, 1999).

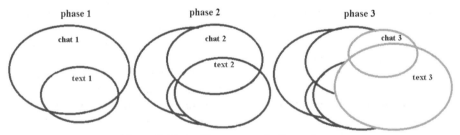

Figure 3. The writing process in three phases

Table 1. Percentages of utterances in the dialogue focusing on content or on task strategy in each of the three phases.

| Phase | Content | Strategy |
|---|---|---|
| 1 | 45.1 | 45.2 |
| 2 | 24.8 | 53.0 |
| 3 | 20.9 | 57.5 |
| Overall | 39.9 | 47.2 |

Table 1 shows that content focused discussion diminishes between the three phases, while strategy oriented discussion seems to become more important. As we did not analyse the strategy-oriented discussion, we cannot interpret this difference. In addition to content or strategy, utterances could focus on social aspects and on technical issues, dealing with the software.

The analysis of utterances focusing on content involved only the protocols on the employment issue written as a first text (N=14). All data were analysed on a propositional level. A *proposition* is defined here as a sentence or part of a sentence, which contains one concept, or the description of the concept. A *concept* is a unit of content linked to the topic of discussion by a predicate relationship. In total we distinguished 96 concepts, dyads use on the average 33.4 concepts. We define *topic* as the concept towards which the argumentative position is oriented. The dyads selected for this analysis were assigned one of two possible topics: flexible work and steady work. The topic doesn't have to be mentioned explicitly in a proposition. To illustrate these variables we give an example in Table 2.

We obtained interrater agreement percentages of 92% for topic and 65% for the concepts (Cohen's kappa's: 0.77 & 0.63). Taking into account the complexity of interpreting semantic categories we consider these percentages and kappas acceptable.

*Table 2. Example of a protocol fragment: concepts, topics and propositions*

| Actor | Concept | Topic | proposition |
|---|---|---|---|
| 1 | specialisation | steady work | What do you think about the argument: with steady work people are becoming professionals in their work |
| 2 | specialisation | steady work | yes, but it is restricted to the company where he is working; he will get a limited idea about his working area |
| 2 | commitment | steady work | I think that he or she is more committed to the company or institute |
| 2 | loyal employee | steady work | and that is more important than with a flexible worker |
| 1 | commitment | steady work | Commitment because of steady work, I think |
| 2 | contacts | flexible work | eeeeh.... I think that is an argument supporting flexible work because you will have more contacts |
| 1 | contacts | flexible work | so supporting flexible work -> many contacts |
| 2 | exchange | flexible work | supporting flexible work ->easy exchange |

*Table 3. Results of the analysis of corresponding concepts.*
*Two types of questions can be answered by inspecting this table:*
*(1) In bold face: what is the average amount of concepts in each phase for chat and text (in*
*absolute number and as a percentage of the total number of concepts in all phases)? For*
*example: chat2 contained 9.2 concepts, or 29% of all concepts mentioned.*
*(2) The average amount of concepts in common between chat and text in the three phases.*
*For example: 2.4 concepts mentioned in chat3 were also mentioned in chat1.*

|  | chat 1 | | chat 2 | | chat 3 | | text 1 | | text 2 | | text 3 | |
|---|---|---|---|---|---|---|---|---|---|---|---|---|
|  | n | % | n | % | n | % | n | % | n | % | n | % |
| chat1 | **16.4** | **48.9** | | | | | | | | | | |
| chat2 | 3.0 | *9.0* | **9.2** | **29.3** | | | | | | | | |
| chat3 | 2.4 | *7.1* | 1.5 | *4.6* | **6.6** | **19.6** | | | | | | |
| text1 | 3.2 | *9.6* | 0.9 | *2.7* | 0.8 | *2.4* | **5.3** | **15.8** | | | | |
| text2 | 5.5 | *16.6* | 4.9 | *14.7* | 1.3 | *3.9* | 4.6 | *13.8* | **15.7** | **46.9** | | |
| text3 | 8.5 | *25.4* | 6.4 | *19.0* | 4.7 | *14.1* | 5.2 | *15.6* | 14.3 | *42.8* | **22.6** | **67.5** |

Table 3 displays the main results of the analysis. We interpreted these complicated results as corresponding to a linear model of text production. Phase1 can be characterised as a phase of **concept generation**, as many concepts are generated in the chat (a mean of 16.4 concepts, which equals 48.9% of the total), but only a few of these (19.4%, not shown in the table) are written down into text1, of which nearly 45% of the concepts (5.3 − 3.2) is not discussed in chat1. This was interpreted as indicating high disagreement, a strict selection criterion, inefficient co-construction, and/or a low amount of decision making during that phase.

In contrast, during chat2 fewer concepts (n = 9.2, or 29.3%) are discussed than in chat1, of which nearly one third (n = 3.0) is taken over from chat1. So, there is substantially less mention of new concepts in chat2. Conversely, more than half of the information discussed in this phase is transferred to text2 (4.9/9.2), indicating stronger agreement, a lower selection threshold, more efficient co-construction and/or more effective decision-making. It seems that compared to the previous phase, the subjects are more involved in writing the text. This is the most important phase of **text production** and maybe negotiation with regard to the actual writing of the text. This conclusion is corroborated by the fact that during this phase, compared to phase1, we find a high proportion of strategic discussion (see table 1), and also a significant correlation (.61, p < .001) between the frequency of strategic utterances in that phase and the quality of the resulting text. No other correlations between the focus of utterances and text quality in either phase were significant (Ingenluyff, 1999).

In chat3 even less concepts are being discussed (6.6 or 19.6%), and most of these concepts (2.4 + 1.5) are taken over from chats1 and 2. Most concepts discussed in chat3 end up in the text (4.7/6.6 = 71%). Text3 is for one third based on text2, but still contains 6.9 more concepts. It seems that during this phase we find much agreement, a less strict selection criterion, good co-construction and efficient decision-making. These seem to be characteristics of an efficient **completion** process.

With respect to the second research question, whether the correspondence between the concepts in the chats and texts relate to the content of the position to be taken, different results were obtained for each of the two positions. In the chats and texts of dyads supporting *flexible work* the concepts that are mentioned relate in majority to the flexibility topic. In the texts written during the three phases almost all concepts are bound to this topic. In the chats 85% of the concepts are about flexible work, whereas only 15% are related to steady work. It seems safe to conclude that in texts defending the flexible position (recall this position is *assigned*), chats and texts merely focus on one side of the position. However, the students defending the alternative position (*steady work*) refer to both topics in a more balanced way. In these chats about half of the concepts focused on steady work. However, while discussing how to defend steady work participants frequently mention concepts related to flexible work. In the texts a similar distribution occurs, and in text1 the alternative position is emphasized even more (68%). It is clear that differences in knowledge and/or attitude with respect to the different positions affect both the discussion and the selection of information. This leads to more elaborated, but one-sided, discussion for the 'flexible' position, but to more balanced texts, which have higher ratings, in the case of 'steady work' (Overeem, 2000).

## ANALYSIS 2: NEGOTIATION DURING DIALOGUE

The results of the previous analysis reveal differences between phases as well as between argumentative positions. It is obvious that task strategy as well as knowledge factors affect the content of discussion and text. In this section, we study the dialogue in more detail. We examine the meaning negotiation process: what types of negotiation about content can be distinguished and what is its role for content selection? To what extent is meaning negotiation argumentative and what is the specific role of argumentation in negotiating content for collaborative writing?

*Method of analysis*

The content analysis discussed in the previous section was the basis for a new analysis directed at the dialogues and the roles of negotiation and argumentation in collaborative writing (van de Laak, 2000). The idea was to examine differences in the dialogues between the three phases, specifically with respect to the characteristics of content negotiation. The following analyses were undertaken:

- The propositions distinguished in the content analysis were first classified according to the *dialogue action* as shown in table 4. Again, only dialogue actions referring to content were classified.

*Table 4: Dialogue actions*

| Communicative function | Dialogue action on concept | Proposition examples |
|---|---|---|
| Information | DSC (describe illustration) STM (Statement) | My next picture shows two companies and two persons (DSC) The contacts with colleagues (STM) |
| Argumentation | EXP (explain, give example, background info) | Maybe it is simply much easier (STM), you don't have to enlist all the time, change insurances, etc. etc. (EXP). |
| | THN (Consequence) | So, more possibilities for the future (THN) |
| | RST (restrict your own reason) | .., but if you don't have a steady job, this is quite possible (RST) |
| | CNT (counter: indicates disagreement) | Yes, but …. (CNT) |
| Elicitation | CHK (check) | But does flexible work also include people working in a factory? (CHK) |
| | CHL (challenge) | Why do you say that? But what if…? (CHL) |
| Evaluation | EVL (positive evaluation) | I prefer the second reason (EVL) |
| | NOT (negative evaluation) | Let's skip this one (NOT) |

- To be able to distinguish reasons in favour or against the main point of view expressed in the text we coded *the argumentative orientation* of dialogue actions as being in favour (Z+) or against (Z-) the main viewpoint, or in favour (A+) or against (A-) the alternative viewpoint, indicated by the sentence topic. In addition, we included in this code the source of the information (given or new), as each participant received three reasons by the experimenter free to use or not to use.

- On the basis of focus shifts (Grosz, 1978), 11 *dialogue patterns* were distinguished. The criteria were: either (1) Explicit proposition of a new or different reason (STM); or (2) Explicit elicitation (CHK, CHL), argumentation (EXP, CNT) or evaluation (EVL) concerning a new or different reason; or (3) An explicit closing comment; or (4) Explicit use of a clue expression (OK) to close an argument. The dialogue patterns are displayed in table 5.

- We distinguished *informative* and *argumentative* negotiation. Argumentative negotiation required elicitation, a counter and at least two arguments. The 'function' column in table 5 shows the dialogue patterns that meet this requirement.

- We selected concepts that elicited most elaborate negotiation or most minimal negotiation. For these concepts, we carried out a number of detailed analyses, with respect to topic, argumentative orientation, whether they appeared in the text or not, and in which phase.

Several protocols were analysed by two coders. After several improvements in formulation of the criteria, dialogue acts could be scored with Cohen's Kappa of .81, which we consider quite acceptable. Function could be scored reliably (Kappa = .902) because concepts had already been assigned in a previous analysis.

## Results

### Dialogue patterns

The fifth column of table 5 shows the frequencies of each of the dialogue patterns, column 6 displays their average length. It can be observed that most instances of dialogue patterns can hardly be called a pattern, as they most of the time involve a single statement only (numbers below refer to the same numbers in table 5):

1. *Proposal*, almost always a statement (STM) that is not discussed, nor explicitly acknowledged. After the proposal, focus shifts to a next concept.

2. *Elicitation*, 90%[2] of the time a CHK, which is not reacted to (or at least not immediately).

3. *Evaluation*, 96% positive (EVL), and 4% negative (NOT), without acknowledgement or discussion.

4. *Information*, a somewhat longer dialogue pattern, consisting of explanation (EXP: 42%) and/or a reason (STM: 26%), without counter information or argumentation. Sometimes there is a question (CHK), evaluation (EVL) or even an argumentative action (CNT, RST, THN), but these are rare and not reacted to.

We propose to refer to the above 4 dialogue patterns as indicative of *minimal negotiation*. This term refers to the task situation supposed to being one of negotiation, but in these cases, the dialogue does not explicitly reflect this supposition. Minimal negotiation comprises 71% of the dialogue patterns.

The next four patterns display moderate negotiation, that is, there is acknowledgement and some lines of dialogue:

5. *Evaluated Proposal*: a proposal that is explicitly accepted or rejected.

6. *Elicited Information*: a question (CHK: 35% or CHL: 13%) answered by explanation (EXP: 16%) or a reason (STM: 19%)

7. *Evaluated Information*: Reasons (STM: 18%) or explanations (EXP: 26%) that are positively evaluated (EVL: 28%).

8. *Argumentation*: a counter (CNT: 33%), which is acknowledged, by a positive evaluation (EVL: 33%), or by explanation (EXP: 13%).

*Table 5. Dialogue patterns in 14 protocols (see above for explanation)*

| Dialogue pattern | Agreement | Counter | Function | Frequency (n=344) | Avg. length |
|---|---|---|---|---|---|
| 1. PRP (Proposal) | Implicit | - | Inf | 158 | 1.1 |
| 2. ELI (Elicit) | - | - | Inf | 9 | 1.2 |
| 3. EVL (Evaluate) | Explicit or Implicit | - | Inf | 22 | 1.1 |
| 4. INF (Inform) | Explicit or Implicit | - | Inf | 56 | 4 |
| 5. PRP-EVL (Proposal-Evaluate) | Explicit | √ | Inf | 15 | 3.5 |
| 6. INF-ELI (Inform-Elicit) | Implicit | √ | Inf | 12 | 3.5 |
| 7. INF-EVL (Inform-Evaluate) | Explicit | √ | Inf | 28 | 3.8 |
| 8. ARG (Argumentation) | Implicit | √ | Arg | 2 | 7.5 |
| 9. ela INF-EVL (elaborate Inform-Evaluate) | Explicit | √ | Inf | 9 | 6.3 |
| 10. ela ARG (elaborate Argumentation) | Implicit | √ | Arg | 25 | 8.6 |
| 11. ela ARG-EVL (elaborate Argumentation-Evaluation) | Explicit | √ | Arg | 8 | 9.1 |

Moderate negotiation comprises 57 dialogue patterns, or nearly 17% of all patterns. It is negotiation, as content proposed or focused on is acknowledged by the two participants in the dialogue, which either seems to lead to explicit acceptance or rejection, or to explanation and possibly grounding (that is, better mutual understanding and agreement) of the information. The remaining 12% of the dialogue patterns have been classified as *elaborate negotiation*, but this term should be taken as relative to the current task:

9. *Elaborate inform/evaluate* patterns involve an elicitation (ELI: 10.5%), then explanations (EXP: 38.6%) and then (positive) evaluation (EVL: 25%).

10. *Elaborate argumentation* involves the same dialogue actions, but we find more of the argumentative categories, more questions, and less evaluation.

11. *Elaborate argue/evaluate* is our 'highest' category, which is similar to the previous one, except that there always is a (positive) evaluation of the outcome of the discussion.

Concepts, put forward in whatever pattern, were almost always positively evaluated or not explicitly evaluated at all. Elaborate negotiation involved many kinds of dialogue actions, but included only 12% of the distinguished dialogue patterns. Note, that moderate and elaborate negotiation patterns could involve multiple concepts. Most instances of negotiation in this task appeared to be implicit and minimal (71%). Only three of the pattern types were classified as argumentative, comprising 10.2% of all patterns. We classified 43% of the dyads as mainly minimal negotiators, while the remaining 57% at least showed some moderate and elaborate negotiation. To more closely examine the *functions* of dialogue patterns, in the next sections we discuss the effects of the argumentative orientation of the patterns, and the differences between the three phases.

*Effect of topic*

The content analysis showed that 'flexible jobs' raised more concepts than the 'steady jobs' topic. The dialogue analysis confirms that most dialogue patterns (63.7%) are about flexibility, and this applies to all patterns, except to the patterns 1 (PRP) and 3 (EVL).

*Argumentative orientation*

Tables 6a and 6b show the proportional relations between each of the three types of negotiation and each type of argumentative orientation. Several results are important to note:

- Given reasons (Z+given and A+given), that is, the reasons that were provided to each of the participants, either in textual or in pictorial format, lead to minimal negotiation. It seems they are taken for granted by the participants, and merely proposed.

- In contrast, we find between 37% and 52% elaborate argumentation involving *new* reasons, also about those against the main point of view.

- About 50% of the dialogue patterns are about Z+, that is, most negotiation involves reasons in favour of the goal of the text.

If we do not include the given reasons, the proportion of elaborate negotiation in the dialogue is raised substantially. From a learning and negotiation perspective, it seems that participants do not tend to discuss information provided by the experimenter. Furthermore, participants negotiate most about the reasons in favour of the goal position, which is a common result in argumentation research (e.g. Coirier et al., 1999). With respect to the degree of negotiation for each type of argumentative orientation (table 6b), it is striking that, while most negotiation of any type involves Z+ arguments, there seems no strong relation between argumentative orientation and type of negotiation.

*Table 6a: Argumentative orientation [Z: goal to defend; A: alternative goal; +: in favour; -:
against] and type of negotiation (minimal, moderate, and elaborate); columns add up to
100%*

|  | Z+ given | A+ given | Z+ new | A+ new | Z- new | A- new |
|---|---|---|---|---|---|---|
| MIN | 72 | 68 | 35 | 37 | 23 | 37 |
| MOD | 12 | 15 | 20 | 20 | 25 | 26 |
| ELA | 16 | 17 | 45 | 43 | 52 | 37 |

*Table 6b: Negotiation and argumentative orientation; rows add up to 100%*

|  | Z+ given | A+ given | Z+ new | A+ new | Z- new | A- new | Rest[3] |
|---|---|---|---|---|---|---|---|
| MIN | 16 | 7 | 39 | 7 | 6 | 17 | 7 |
| MOD | 6 | 3 | 43 | 8 | 12 | 25 | 4 |
| ELA | 3 | 2 | 49 | 8 | 12 | 17 | 8 |

*Table 7. The dialogue patterns in the three phases (%)*

| Pattern | phase 1 | phase 2 | phase 3 | Total |
|---|---|---|---|---|
| 1. PRP | 43.2 | 40.4 | 60.0 | 45.9 |
| 2. ELI | 3.6 | - | 1.5 | 2.6 |
| 3. EVL | 8.1 | 5.3 | 1.5 | 6.4 |
| 4. INF | 15.3 | 19.3 | 16.9 | 16.3 |
| 5. PRP-EVL | 5.0 | 3.5 | 3.1 | 4.4 |
| 6. INF-ELI | 4.1 | 5.3 | - | 3.5 |
| 7. INF-EVL | 7.2 | 12.3 | 7.7 | 8.1 |
| 8. ARG | .5 | 1.8 | - | .6 |
| 9. ela INF-EVL | 2.7 | 3.5 | 1.5 | 2.6 |
| 10. ela ARG | 8.6 | 7.0 | 3.1 | 7.3 |
| 11. ela ARG-EVL | 1.8 | 1.8 | 4.6 | 2.3 |
| Total | 100 | 100 | 100 | 100 |
|  |  |  |  |  |
| **Negotiation** |  |  |  |  |
| Minimal | 63.7 | 15.1 | 21.2 | 100.0 |
| Moderate | 65.5 | 22.4 | 12.1 | 100.0 |
| Elaborate | 68.3 | 17.1 | 14.6 | 100.0 |
| Total | 64.5 | 16.6 | 18.9 | 100.0 |

*Differences between the three phases*

The content analysis gave rise to the idea that the three phases could be characterised differently, with respect to task strategy. The first phase was to be about content generation, the second about formulation and negotiation, and the third phase as task completion, with quick and efficient decision-making. Table 7 presents the frequencies of dialogue patterns in the three phases. The following conclusions are drawn from the analysis:

- Phase1: Most negotiation is found in the first phase, without many differences between types, in the sense that about two third of negotiation of each type can be found during this phase. The most frequent types are PRP (propose), and then INF (inform) and, maybe surprisingly, elaborated ARG (argumentation).

- Phase2: In this phase we find relatively more moderate negotiation, especially INF-EVL (information-evaluation). There seems to be a tendency towards more explanatory discussion during this phase (INF, INF-EVL and elaborate INF-EVL).

- Phase3: Relatively speaking, there is much implicit negotiation in the third phase, as we can see that 60% of the concepts are simply proposed, without explicit acceptance or rejection (PRP). In addition, there is a rise in elaborate ARG-EVL, but a drop in elaborate ARG, without evaluation.

From a negotiation and learning perspective, the first phase of the collaborative writing task is most interesting, as we find more elaborated negotiation in that phase. Recall this phase as being characterised as concept generation. It is the phase during which the landscape is formed. From a writing and problem solving perspective, it may be that the second phase is more interesting, but this needs to be supported by analysing the strategy oriented communication. Content negotiation in the second phase may be characterised as moderate. This process seems to rely in part on reinstatement of concepts from earlier discussion, because much information in the text is based on earlier chat (Erkens et al, in press).

*Negotiation about specific concepts*

In this section we try to analyse the way specific concepts are negotiated in the collaborative writing task. For each concept distinguished in the content analysis, we determined the dialogue pattern(s) by which the concept was discussed. Table 8 presents the results for concepts found more than 10 times in all protocols together.

Table 8 displays numerous differences between concepts. First, the most frequent concepts are discussed more often in minimal and in elaborate negotiation than in moderate negotiation. Because in elaborate negotiation patterns involve more concepts than the other two types of negotiation, these data are different from those presented above. As already may have been expected, 4 of the 5 concepts that appear most frequently in minimal negotiation, are given concepts. The analyses that follow below concern the five concepts most often discussed as minimal (allocation44, diversity, expertise, income and loyal employees), and those 5 most often discussed as elaborate *(employment agency, age, project work, expenditure,*

*Table 8: Most frequent concepts (N=number of fragments these concepts appeared in) and type of negotiation (%=relative proportion of type of negotiation), underlined concepts were provided by instruction, percentages in* **bold** *indicate concepts selected for further analysis*

| Negotiation Concept | Minimal N | Minimal % | Moderate N | Moderate % | Elaborate N | Elaborate % | Total N | Total % |
|---|---|---|---|---|---|---|---|---|
| allocation | **13** | **76.5** | 3 | 17.6 | 1 | 5.9 | 17 | 100 |
| diversity | **17** | **65.4** | 5 | 19.2 | 4 | 15.4 | 26 | 100 |
| employment agency | 1 | 9.1 | 0 | 0.0 | **10** | **90.9** | 11 | 100 |
| spending | 9 | 42.9 | 4 | 19.0 | 8 | 38.1 | 21 | 100 |
| bonus | 6 | 27.3 | 4 | 18.2 | 12 | 54.5 | 22 | 100 |
| contacts | 13 | 31.0 | 8 | 19.0 | 21 | 50.0 | 42 | 100 |
| continuity | 15 | 50.0 | 6 | 20.0 | 9 | 30.0 | 30 | 100 |
| economic aspects | 0 | 0.0 | 5 | 41.7 | 7 | 58.3 | 12 | 100 |
| experience | 11 | 40.7 | 11 | 40.7 | 5 | 18.6 | 27 | 100 |
| expertise | **14** | **70.0** | 1 | 5.0 | 5 | 25.0 | 20 | 100 |
| flexible | 1 | 10.0 | 3 | 30.0 | 6 | 60.0 | 10 | 100 |
| function | 3 | 15.8 | 3 | 15.8 | 13 | 68.4 | 19 | 100 |
| family | 6 | 40.0 | 9 | 60.0 | 0 | 0.0 | 15 | 100 |
| income | **35** | **83.3** | 1 | 2.4 | 6 | 14.3 | 42 | 100 |
| scaffolding | 8 | 61.5 | 0 | 0.0 | 5 | 38.5 | 13 | 100 |
| jubilee | 5 | 31.3 | 1 | 6.3 | 10 | 62.5 | 16 | 100 |
| age | 0 | 0.0 | 1 | 6.3 | **15** | **93.8** | 16 | 100 |
| loyal employees | **17** | **73.7** | 5 | 26.3 | 0 | 0.0 | 22 | 100 |
| society | 6 | 35.3 | 4 | 23.5 | 7 | 41.2 | 17 | 100 |
| market oriented | 6 | 46.2 | 0 | 0.0 | 7 | 53.9 | 13 | 100 |
| disadvantage | 7 | 63.6 | 0 | 0.0 | 4 | 36.4 | 11 | 100 |
| dismiss | 6 | 26.1 | 4 | 17.4 | 13 | 56.5 | 23 | 100 |
| project work | 3 | 16.7 | 2 | 11.1 | **13** | **72.2** | 18 | 100 |
| travelling | 15 | 42.9 | 10 | 28.6 | 10 | 28.6 | 35 | 100 |
| social aspects | 2 | 13.3 | 12 | 80.0 | 1 | 6.7 | 15 | 100 |
| stress | 3 | 25.0 | 4 | 33.3 | 5 | 41.7 | 12 | 100 |
| expenditure | 2 | 14.3 | 1 | 7.1 | **11** | **78.6** | 14 | 100 |
| exchange | 3 | 30.0 | 0 | 0.0 | 7 | 70.0 | 10 | 100 |
| bonding | 10 | 41.7 | 5 | 20.8 | 9 | 37.5 | 24 | 100 |
| advantages | 8 | 53.3 | 4 | 26.7 | 3 | 20.0 | 15 | 100 |
| freedom | 3 | 18.8 | 7 | 43.8 | 6 | 37.5 | 16 | 100 |
| employer | 8 | 50.0 | 2 | 12.5 | 6 | 37.5 | 16 | 100 |
| unemployment | 3 | 27.3 | 0 | 0.0 | **8** | **72.7** | 11 | 100 |
| working hours | 13 | 28.3 | 6 | 13.0 | 27 | 58.7 | 46 | 100 |
| security | 16 | 35.6 | 13 | 28.9 | 16 | 35.6 | 45 | 100 |
| Total | 285 | 39.6 | 144 | 20.0 | 290 | 40.3 | 719 | 100 |

and *unemployment)*. All conclusions below pertain to these concepts only (called 'frequent concepts'), unless stated otherwise.

## Effect of topic

Frequent concepts that are discussed during elaborate negotiation are linked to the flexibility topic in 92.7% of the cases. In contrast, minimally negotiated frequent concepts are equally often linked to the 'flexible' as to the 'steady' topic.

*Table 9. Degree of elaboration and argumentative orientation for frequent concepts (row adds up to 100%)*

| Concept | Z+given | A+given | Z+ | A+ | A- | Z- |
|---------|---------|---------|------|------|-----|------|
| Minimal | 40.2 | 18.5 | 29.3 | 2.2 | 9.8 | - |
| Elaborate | - | - | 58.8 | 11.8 | 7.8 | 21.6 |

*Argumentative orientation*

For the set of frequent concepts we compared the argumentative orientations for which they were used. Table 9 shows the results. Both minimal and elaborate negotiation is most frequent for the point of view to be defended. Minimally negotiated concepts are most often given concepts. In contrast, all elaborate negotiation involved new concepts.

*Phase in the writing process*

Concepts that are minimally negotiated are most often proposed during the *first* phase (see Table 10). In addition, such concepts are relatively rare during the second phase. With respect to the elaborately negotiated concepts, we find relatively higher instantiation during the first and third phases. There are differences between concepts, however. The concepts 'unemployment', 'age' and 'employment agency' are mainly discussed during the first phase. In contrast, 'project work' is found in both first and third phases, while 'expenditure' is more frequently discussed during the third phase. The lack of elaborate negotiation for these concepts in the second phase does not match the general tendency for all concepts.

*Table 10: Phase in the writing process and type of negotiation for frequent concepts*

| | phase 1 | phase 2 | phase 3 | Total |
|---|---------|---------|---------|-------|
| Allocation | 76.9 | 15.4 | 7.7 | 100.0 |
| Diversity | 76.5 | 11.8 | 17.6 | 100.0 |
| Expertise | 78.6 | 7.1 | 14.3 | 100.0 |
| Income | 58.8 | 14.7 | 26.5 | 100.0 |
| Loyal Employee | 85.7 | 14.3 | - | 100.0 |
| **Minimal negotiation** | 73.1 | 12.0 | 17.4 | 100.0 |
| | | | | |
| Employment Agency | 90.0 | - | 10.0 | 100.0 |
| Age | 76.9 | - | 23.1 | 100.0 |
| Project work | 50.0 | - | 50.0 | 100.0 |
| Expenditure | 18.2 | 18.2 | 63.6 | 100.0 |
| Unemployment | 100.0 | - | - | 100.0 |
| **Elaborate negotiation** | 64.7 | 3.9 | 31.4 | 100.0 |
| | | | | |
| **All concepts** | 64.5 | 16.6 | 18.9 | 100.0 |

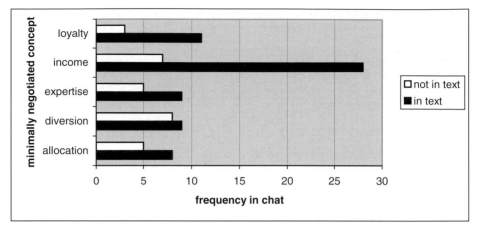

*Figure 4a. Frequency in chat (number of dialogue fragments) of minimally negotiated frequent concepts appearing or not appearing in the text.*

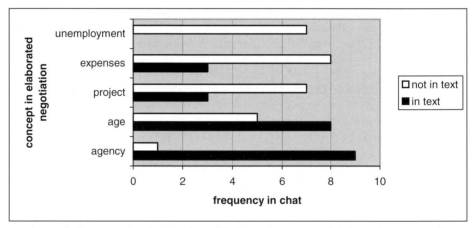

*Figure 4b Frequency in chat (number of dialogue fragments) of elaborately negotiated frequent concepts appearing or not appearing in the text.*

*Negotiated concepts and text produced*

First, we examined for each selected concept wether or not it would appear in the text to be written. Figures 4a and 4b show the results for each concept. For the concepts that have been minimally negotiated, chances are greater that they will appear in the text than that they will be rejected. In contrast, for concepts that experience elaborate negotiation, rejection chances seem slightly greater than those for acceptance. The most striking example is the concept 'unemployment', which is much used in elaborate negotiations, but which never appears in the text. Apparently, it has been used to support other concepts and arguments. On the other hand, the chances that a concept will appear in the text seem to depend more on the nature of the concept itself than on the degree to which it is negotiated, as we also find two concepts that are negotiated in an elaborate way for which the chances they appear in the text are quite positive. The concepts 'age' and 'agency' seem to be discussible and relevant for these subjects in this assignment.

Next, we analysed for each of the selected concepts in which phase they appeared in the text. Figures 5a and 5b display the results for minimal negotiation and for elaborate negotiation, respectively.

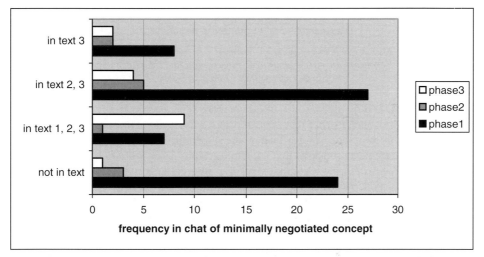

*Figure 5a. Frequent concepts in minimal negotiation and the phase in the writing task during which they appear in the text*

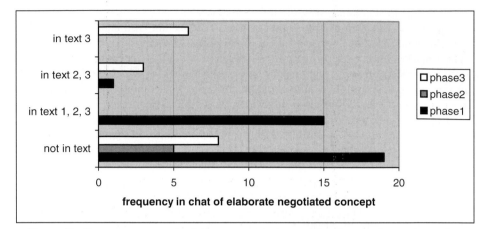

*Figure 5b: Frequent concepts in elaborate negotiation and the phase in the writing task during which they appear in the text*

Figures 5a and 5b show some unexpected results. Firstly, it appears that 44.6% of the frequent concepts that had appeared in minimal negotiation in the first phase only appear in the text during a later phase. Secondly, compared to the two other phases, more frequent concepts that appeared in minimal negotiation during the first phase do not appear in the text at all. Thirdly, minimal negotiation in the third phase also involves concepts that had been proposed in the first phase, so these are repeated in the last phase. Most concepts that are in minimal negotiation in the last phase appear in the text.

With respect to elaborate negotiation, the picture is different. Although also the majority of concepts discussed in the first phase do not appear in the text at all, 41.2% of the concepts discussed in this phase do appear in text 1. Concepts appearing in elaborate negotiation during the second phase do not appear in the text. Finally, a relatively large amount of concepts appearing in elaborate negotiation during the third phase do not appear in the text, but again, the chances that a concept appears in the text when in elaborate negotiation in the third phase still is 37.5%.

*Relationship between negotiation and text*

In this section, we return to all dialogue actions and concepts discussed. We look at the efficiency of negotiation, that is, the chances that a specific dialogue pattern leads to concepts being selected in the text. Table 11 presents these results, in combination with a summary of other relevant data, some of which were discussed earlier in this chapter. In terms of efficiency, elaborate argumentation is most efficient, and the third phase displays more efficient negotiation than the other two phases. Minimal negotiation is very efficient in the third phase, but not in the first phase, and it seems this type of negotiation has a different function in the two phases.

*Table 11. Summary table*

|  | Phase 1 | Phase 2 | Phase 3 | Total |
|---|---|---|---|---|
| Mean nr. of concepts in chat | 16.4 | 9.2 | 6.6 | 24.4 |
| Mean nr. of concepts in text | 5.3 | 15.7 | 22.6 | 23.1 |
| % overlap chat>text | 19% | 53% | 90% | - |
| Total nr. of dialogue patterns | 222 | 57 | 65 | 344 |
| % minimal negotiation | 70.3% | 64.9% | 80.0% | 71.2% |
| % moderate negotiation | 17.1% | 22.8% | 10.8% | 16.9% |
| % elaborate negotiation | 12.6% | 12.3% | 9.2% | 11.9% |
| % in text with minimal negotiation | 12.8% | 48.6% | 88.5% | 71.0% |
| % in text with moderate negotiation | 18.9% | 66.7% | 57.1% | 69.6% |
| % in text with elaborate negotiation | 58.6% | 62.5% | 83.3% | 83.7% |
| % implicit agreement | 76.2% | 75.4% | 82.8% | 77.3% |
| % explicit agreement | 23.8% | 24.6% | 17.2% | 22.7% |

## SUMMARY OF RESULTS

As the result of a collaborative electronic writing task, 14 discussion protocols and texts were examined with respect to concepts discussed and dialogue actions involved. We assumed that this task is an assignment during which participants negotiate the concepts to include in the text. We conceptualised negotiation as the type of dialogue pattern by which the participants discussed conceptual information. The task was divided (post-hoc) into three phases, characterised as concept generation, text production and task completion, respectively. Negotiations were distinguished by their function (informative or argumentative) and their elaboration (minimal, moderate and elaborate).

The majority of negotiation (71%) was of the minimal type. Most negotiation (77.3%) did not involve explicit agreement. Concepts that were provided in the instruction were almost always only proposed, even though each participant received different (defending the other viewpoint) concepts. Most negotiation of any type involved defending the assigned position; however, opposed arguments (Z- and A+) were more frequently discussed as elaborate negotiation, that is, they showed argumentation. Argumentative negotiation involved only 10.2% of the dialogue patterns, but when the provided reasons are not included in the count, we found proportions of elaborated negotiation between 37% and 52%, depending on the argumentative orientation of the dialogue pattern.

It seems safe to conclude that in this task,

- subjects are not inclined to discuss provided information, and
- mainly argue in favour of the preferred point of view. On the other hand,
- participants are quite more willing to negotiate new information, whatever its argumentative orientation with respect to the main position to defend.

In terms of efficiency, that is the chance that a concept discussed in the chat will appear in the text, elaborate argumentation is most efficient, and the third phase displays more efficient negotiation than the other two phases. Minimal negotiation is very efficient in the third phase, but not in the first phase, and it seems this type of negotiation has a different function in the two phases.

An analysis of the relationship between types of negotiation in the three phases for 10 frequent concepts provided some additional information. Elaborate negotiation for five selected concepts mainly was about the topic 'flexible work', while minimal negotiation involved both topics equally often. There were differences between individual concepts with respect to the interaction between pronounced focus (concepts explicitly used: Sfard, 2001) and negotiation during the three phases of task execution. Minimally negotiated concepts mainly were proposed during the first phase. For elaborately negotiated concepts, the focus in respective phases was much less uniform. The five minimally negotiated concepts appeared to have a far greater chance of eventually appearing in the text than the five elaborately negotiated concepts. However, minimally negotiated concepts appear in the text during a later phase than when they were negotiated, or did not reappear at all. This may mean they needed to be reinstated in some way, from memory, by reading previous dialogue, or by explicitly proposing again in the final phase, and that some of them were forgotten. We even found cases where already written down concepts were reintroduced in the discussion. In contrast, elaborate negotiation leads to concepts either being written in the text immediately after negotiation, or not being used in the text at all.

Negotiation mainly serves to propose, inform, or explain (89.9%), rather than to argue. In this task, content is not discussed or negotiated to a great extent. More than two third of the dialogue patterns involve minimal negotiation. In the first phase, minimal negotiation serves to propose content for discussion, while in the last phase it serves to propose content for the text. Moderate negotiation, most frequent during the second phase, most frequently leads to explicit agreement. When we find elaborate negotiation, it is often argumentative. Argumentative negotiation relatively more often was about counterarguments and refutations of opposing points of view. While the participants did not explicitly acknowledge the results of elaborate negotiation most of the time, concepts raised during elaborate negotiation had a great chance of being included in the text during the same phase. In contrast, merely proposed concepts were often repeated between phases, even if they had already been written in the text.

## DISCUSSION

Some issues can be raised to explain the results. First, it seems that elaborate negotiation by these students in this task is quite a rare occasion. Although explicit agreement is rare, it seemed that students agree most of the time. The question is what they agree about. A pessimistic explanation is that they seem to be satisfied with any content, as long as it is plausible enough in terms of some liberal standard of minimal coherence with the proposed topic of the discussion. Participants seem to be keen at avoiding conflict, do not really discuss the plausibility and strength of produced information and are not much concerned with the argumentative quality of the resulting text. The social pressure to avoid conflict is stronger than the desire to challenge the partner (compare the chapters by Baker, and Veerman in this volume).

Another explanation could be that students agree because the issue is not enough discussible. There could be sufficient common ground available in relation to the topic, making more than minimal negotiation unnecessary. Grounding is assumed rather than acquired. The topic may not elicit enough doubt or conflict because participants basically agree on its implications and do not feel the need for elaborate discussion. However, we found a strong asymmetry between the two positions in terms of elaborate negotiation. Elaborate negotiation merely involved the *'flexible'* position, not the *'steady job'* position. If we suppose that, given the age of our participants, the first position is the preferred one, and the one with which they have most experience, it seems that the lack of elaborate negotiation could be in part ascribed to a lack of commitment to the *'steady job'* position. In other words, more involvement rather than more shared knowledge raises more negotiation. It is activated knowledge that is important, not available knowledge. In other words: the degree of activation in the landscape of concepts, rather than individual dispositions, is the trigger for negotiation. This idea is strengthened by the result that there was hardly any negotiation about experimentally provided reasons, even though half of these reasons reflected the opposite viewpoint. These reasons could have been taken as 'expert opinion' and hence, not as discussible, and hardly activated. The information source is significant here, and it puts some doubt on the educational value of expert information for negotiation in tasks such as these.

Thirdly, we can put forward the hypothesis that minimal negotiation serves many functions, often at the same time: proposing new information, proposing a debatable issue, explaining something by new information, checking mutual understanding, agreeing about task strategy, implicit agreement by changing focus to a next issue, and reinstating already proposed information. It is questionable whether this is the best way of serving all these functions. Quite obviously, some proposed concepts are forgotten, many debate opportunities are missed, and many misunderstandings may remain. An important conclusion is that participants should address all of these (and more) issues *explicitly* before we can expect any positive results from collaborative learning by negotiation. One option may be to explicitly splitting up a task in different phases (e.g. brainstorming, selecting content, formulating, linearising, etc), scripting collaboration according to different functionalities in different phases (van der Puil & Andriessen, 2002), or to construct different communication interfaces dedicated for specific functions in this task (Alamargot & Andriessen, 2002).

In the fourth place, writing down information in the *text* window is also a form of negotiation or serves as explicit sign of agreement. It seems that, in order to more precisely understand the negotiation of content in this task, one should include what is proposed at the level of the text. A related issue concerns our method of analysis, collapsing discourse patterns over individual cases. More closely examining task strategies at the individual level may reveal more subtle mechanisms for negotiation than currently reported.

Generally speaking, content in this collaborative writing task was not enough negotiated, and the elaborate negotiation that was observed did not lead to explicit acknowledgement of a result. It seems to us, that most participants did not explicitly discuss what they were doing and were not enough involved in a writing task in the sense of producing an argumentative *text*, as this text was hardly discussed at all. If there was no real writing, there may have been no good *communication*, at least in the sense of grounding mutual goals, task strategy, understanding of concepts, beliefs and attitudes, etc. In order to accomplish complicated assignments such as the current one, participants have to learn to be open about their goals and strategies. They should be explicit about the important decisions to be made, and at least indicate problems, agreement and disagreement. We do not think this is only a matter of task instruction, or lack of motivation. One factor is the unusual, and maybe impracticable interface for supporting these communication forms. Participants seemed to behave as if in an oral communication situation. There may be more to win in supporting communication itself. We should be careful in asking people to collaborate that are not enough aware of what it takes to collaborate. Supporting such a process by instruction and better interfaces is one thing, but schooling effective communication during collaboration in general may be needed for collaborative learning to be successful. An educational system, in which effective and explicit negotiation is not supported and rewarded, will never succeed in successfully implementing electronic collaboration tools.

What do the current results provide as additional information to the focus analysis and the metaphor of a collective landscape? If we distinguish between the three phases, we see different functions and forms of meaning negotiation. We propose to discuss our results in terms of the three processes distinguished above: content generation, text production, and task completion. Given the fact that processes in writing are known not to operate in strict a linear sequence of generation, formulation and revision (Coirier et al., 1999) we suppose that the three phases are heterogeneous with respect to the incidence of these processes, so what follows is an idealization.

During content generation (phase1), the landscape is constructed. Most concepts are produced during this phase; those that appear in minimal negotiation are generally kept in the landscape, albeit at a low level of activation, while those that appear in elaborate negotiation are written in the text. It seems that argumentation during content generation serves the important function of elaborating (or perhaps: constituting) concepts to the point of text formulation; of course only in the case participants decide the concept merits this status. Hence, during elaborate negotiation in content generation, concepts are constituted and evaluated. On the other hand, concepts merely being introduced during this phase (minimal negotiation), often have to be reinstated later, sometimes up to the point of being eventually written down in the text during text completion. In terms of a landscape, low hills often need to be reinstated later, while high mountains reflect concepts that are already in the text, and that serve as triggers for new concepts.

During text production (phase2), we observe moderate negotiation, that is, short explanatory sequences, during which information is mainly proposed, explained and often reinstated. Once a landscape has been formed, it is scanned rather than changed. The text completion phase (phase3) does not involve much explicit negotiation, and its duration is rather dependent on the time available for the subjects to complete the task. Ideally speaking, we would like to observe a revision phase, during which participants engage in reflective activities concerning text content and task goals. Perhaps we should have asked our subjects explicitly to revise the text during a later time, instead of requiring them to produce a text about a different topic.

To finish with a positive conclusion that these results give rise to: where we found elaborate negotiation, argumentation was the most important activity. While most of the time, negotiation served to back up the already agreed upon point of view, argumentation also involved developing and elaborating concepts serving as counterarguments (A+) and rebuttals (A-). The problem with argumentation is not that people cannot do it, but that they do not use it enough to understand it.

## AUTHOR'S CONTACT ADDRESS

*Jerry Andriessen*
*Dept. of Educational Sciences*
*FSS-IPEDON/ICO-ISOR*
*Utrecht University*
*Heidelberglaan 2*
*3484 CS Utrecht, the Netherlands*
*Telephone: +31 30 2534942; Fax: +31 30 2532352*
*Email: J.Andriessen@fss.uu.nl; Web: http://edu.fss.uu.nl/medewerkers/ja/home.htm*

## REFERENCES

Alamargot, D., & Andriessen, J.E.B. (2002). The "power" of text production activity in collaborative learning situations. In P. Brna, M. Baker, K. Stenning & A. Tiberghien (Eds.). *The role of communication in learning to model.* Mahwah, NJ: Erlbaum (pp. 212-229).

Alamargot, D., & Chanquoy, L. (2001). *Through the models of text production.* Dordrecht: Kluwer.

Anderson, J. R. (1988). The expert module. In M.C. Polson & J.J. Richardson (Eds.), *Foundations of Intelligent Tutoring Systems,* (pp 21-54). Hillsdale, NJ: Erlbaum.

Andriessen, J. E. B., Erkens. G., Overeem, E., & Jaspers, J. (1996, September). *Using complex information in argumentation for collaborative text production.* Paper presented at the UCIS '96 conference, Poitiers, France.

Bakhtine, M. (1981). La structure de l'énoncé [The structure of the utterance]. In T. Todorov (Ed.), *Bakhtine. Le principe dialogique.* Paris: Editions du Seuil.

Baker, M. (1996). Argumentation and cognitive change in collaborative problem-solving dialogues. *COAST Research Report Number CR-13/96,* University of Lyon, France.

Baker, M. (1999). Argumentation and Constructive Interaction. In J. E. B. Andriessen & P. Coirier (Eds.), *Foundations of argumentative text processing* (pp. 179-202). Amsterdam: Amsterdam University Press.

Bereiter, C., & Scardamalia, M. (1987). *The Psychology of Written Composition.* Hillsdale, NJ: Erlbaum.

Clark, H.H., & Brennan, S.E. (1991). Grounding in Communication. In L.B. Resnick, J.M. Levine & S.D. Teasley (Eds.), *Perspectives on socially shared cognition* (pp. 127-150). Washington: American Psychological Association.

Coirier, P., Andriessen, J.E.B., & Chanquoy, L. (1999). From planning to translating: The specificity of argumentative writing. In J.E.B. Andriessen & P. Coirier (Eds.), *Foundations of argumentative text processing.* Amsterdam: Amsterdam University Press.

Coirier, P., & Andriessen, J.E.B. (in press). Une approche fonctionnelle de la production des textes argumentatifs élaborés: une activité 'coopérante' ? In R. Bouchard, M. M. De Gaulmyn, & A. Rabatel (Eds.), *Actes de la Conférence: Le processus de rédaction (coopérative) - Des situations d'apprentissage aux situations professionnelles.* Université Lumière Lyon 2 & I.U.F.M. de Lyon.

Cooper, C.R., & Cooper, Jr. R.G., (1984). Skill in peer learning discourse: What develops? In S.A. Kuczaj II (Ed.), *Discourse development. Progress in cognitive development research* (pp. 77 - 97). New York: Springer.

Dillenbourg, P. (1999). Introduction: what do you mean by "Collaborative Learning"? In P. Dillenbourg (ed.), *Collaborative Learning: Cognitive and computational aspects* (pp. 1-19). New York: Pergamon.

Dillenbourg, P., & Baker, M. (1996, June). *Negotiation spaces in Human-Computer Collaborative Learning.* Proceedings of the International Conference on Cooperative Systems (COOP'96), Juan-Les-Pins (France).

Doise, W., & Mugny, G. (1984). *The social development of the intellect.* New York: Pergamon.

Erkens, G. (1997). *Cooperatief probleemoplossen met computers in het onderwijs: Het modelleren van cooperatieve dialogen voor de ontwikkeling van intelligente onderwijssystemen.* [Cooperative problem solving with computers in education: Modelling of cooperative dialogues for the the design of intelligent educational systems] Ph.D. thesis, Utrecht University, the Netherlands.

Erkens, G., Andriessen, J.E.B., & Peters, N. (in press). Interaction and performance in computer supported collaborative tasks. In: H. van Oostendorp (Ed.), *Cognition in a digital world.* Mahwah, NJ: Erlbaum.

Erkens, G., (Tabachneck-) Schijf, H., Jaspers, J. & van Berlo, J. (2000, September). *How does computer-supported collaboration influence argumentative writing?* Presented at the EARLI SIG-Writing conference, Verona, Italy.

Gere, A., & Stevens, R. S. (1989). The language of writing groups: How oral response shapes revision. In S. W. Freedman (Ed.), *The acquisition of written language : Response and revision* (pp. 85-105). Norwood, NJ : Ablex.

Giroud, A. (1999). Studying argumentative text processing through collaborative writing. In: J.E.B. Andriessen & P. Coirier (Eds.), *Foundations of argumentative text processing* (pp. 149-178). Amsterdam: Amsterdam University Press.

Hayes, J.R., & Flower, L.S. (1980). Identifying the organization of writing processes. In L.W. Gregg & E.R. Steinberg (Eds.), *Cognitive process in writing* (pp. 3-20). Hillsdale, N.J.: Lawrence Erlbaum.

Ingenluyff, E. (1999). *Coördinerende interactie. Een onderzoek naar de invloed van coördinerende interacties op een gezamenlijk geschreven tekst in een digitale leeromgeving.* [Coordinating interaction. A study about the effect of coordinating interactions on collaboratively written text in a digital learning environment.]. Masters Thesis, Utrecht University.

Johnson, D.W., & Johnson, R.T. (1975). *Learning together and alone.* Englewood Cliffs, NJ: Prentice-Hall.

Munneke, L. & Andriessen, J. E. B. (2000, September). *Learning through collaboratively writing an argumentative text.* Presented at the EARLI SIG-Writing conference, Verona, Italy.

Neuwirth, C. M., Kaufer, D. S., Chandhok, R., & Morris, J. H. (1994). Computer Support for Distributed Collaborative Writing: Defining Parameters of Interaction. In *Proceedings of the Conference on Computer-Supported Cooperative Work (CSCW'94)* (pp. 145-152). Chapel Hill, NC: Association for Computing Machinery.

Overeem, E. (2000). *Plaatjes als informatiebron bij het in samenwerking schrijven van argumentatieve teksten.* [Pictures as source of information during collaborative writing of argumentative texts.]. Masters Thesis, Utrecht University.

Peters, N. (1999). *Het collectieve conceptuele kennisnetwerk in constructie.* [The collective conceptual knowledge network under construction.]. Masters Thesis, Utrecht University.

Petraglia, J. (1998). *Reality by Design: the rhetoric and technology of authenticity in education.* Mahwah, NJ: Erlbaum.

Sfard, A. (2002). The Interplay of Intimations and Implementations: Generating New Discourse With New Symbolic Tools. *The Journal of the Learning Sciences, 11,* (2&3), 319–357

Sharan, S., & Sharan, Y. (1976). *Small-Group Teaching.* Englewood Cliffs, NJ: Educational Technology Publications.

Stalnaker, R. (1978). Assertion. In P. Cole (Ed.) *Syntax & Semantics 9: Pragmatics* (pp. 315-332). New York: Academic Press.

Teasley, S., & Roschelle, J. (1993). Constructing a joint problem space: The computer as tool for sharing knowledge. In S. P. Lajoie and S.J. Derry (Eds.) *Computers as Cognitive Tools* (pp. 229-257). Hillsdale, NJ: Lawrence Erlbaum Associates.

Thomason, R. H. (1990). Accommodation, Meaning and Implicature: Interdisciplinary foundations of Pragmatics. In P. R. Cohen, J. Morgan, & G. M. E. Pollack (Eds.) *Intentions in Communication* (pp. 325-365). Cambridge MA: The MIT Press.

Van de Laak, C. (2000). *Onderhandelen over conceptuele informatie.* [Negotiating about conceptual information.] Masters Thesis, Utrecht University.

Van den Bergh, H., & Rijlaarsdam, G. (1996). The dynamics of composing: modelling writing process data. In C.M. Levy & S. Ransdell (Eds.), *The Science of Writing* (pp.207-232). Mahwah, New Jersey: Erlbaum.

Van den Bergh, H., & Rijlaarsdam, G. (1999). The dynamics of idea generation during writing: an on-line study. In: M. Torrance & D. Galbraith (eds.), *Knowing what to write: conceptual processes in Text Production* (pp.99-120). Amsterdam: Amsterdam University Press.

Van den Broek, P. W., Risden, K., Fletcher, C. R., & Thurlow, R. (1996). A 'landscape' view of reading: Fluctuating patterns of activation and the construction of a stable memory representation. In: B.K. Britton & A.C. Graesser (eds.) *Models of understanding text* (pp. 165-187). Mahwah, NJ: Erlbaum.

Van den Broek, P. W., Young, M., Tzeng, Y., & Linderholm, T. (1999). The landscape model of reading: Inferences and the Online Construction of a memory representation. In: H. van Oostendorp & S. Goldman (eds.), *The construction of mental representations during reading* (pp. 71-98). Mahwah, NJ: Erlbaum.

Van der Puil, C. & Andriessen, J. E. B. (2002, January). Supporting the development of a working relation in a synchronous electronic collaborative writing environment. Proceedings of the workshop The role of AI in CSCL, CSCL2002, Boulder, Colorado.

Veerman, A.L. (2000). *Computer-supported collaborative learning through argumentation*. Enschede: Print Partners Ipskamp.

Veerman, A.L., Andriessen, J.E.B., & Kanselaar, G. (2000). Enhancing learning through synchronous electronic discussion. *Computers & Education 34* (2-3), 1-22.

# APPENDIX

*Examples of test questions*

- The number of people participating in labour in the age group of 55-64 in the Netherlands compared to other European countries is
  [ ] low
  [ ] high
  [ ] don't know
- The minimum wage for young people starts at the age of
  [ ] 15
  [ ] 16
  [ ] don't know
- The number of vacation days for the average worker is
  [ ] 32
  [ ] 26
  [ ] don't know

*General task instruction*

Welcome. I am going to give you a short introduction for the next three hours. Before I do this I would like to stress that you are not to touch the keyboard or the mouse before I tell you to.

This morning/afternoon you are going to cooperate in our research project about writing short argumentative texts. You are going to write a text on a particular topic with the help of a computer tool. You are going to write this text together with another person, who is sitting behind a different computer that is linked to your own by a network connection. The computer tool allows you to discuss the topic where you are to write about, and about the viewpoint that you have to argue for. It also allows you to work on the same text together.

The assignment and the instruction can be read in the assignment window. To read the complete text you have use the scrollbar by using your mouse. The scrollbar allows you to scroll the text up and down. Please read the instruction carefully and completely before you start to discuss and write the text.

To the right of the assignment window you can see the arguments window. Here you can find a number of possible reasons in favour or against the possible points of view with respect to the topic of discussion. It is possible, but not necessary, for you to use these reasons. You will receive three reasons, and your partner will be provided with three different reasons.

At the bottom-left you see three windows that you can use for negotiation and discussion with your writing partner. By clicking in your chat-box, you can type a message for your partner. While you are typing, your partner can read what you are writing, in the 'other's chat-box'. In the same way, you can read what you partner is writing by looking at the 'other's chat-box'. When your message is finished, you can send it to the chat-history box by pressing the enter key. In the chat-history you can read your previous discussions.

At the bottom-right you see the text-box, with two buttons. In the text-box you can write a text, after you have discussed in the chat-box what you want to be in this text. You and your partner can both work in the same text. If you want to add something to the text you click in the text box at the location where you want to write. This is only possible when your traffic lights are green. This means that at that moment, nobody else is writing in the text. If the traffic lights are red, then somebody else is writing. In that case you cannot write yourself, but you can read what the other is writing. When the other is writing you can signal that you want to write something by clicking on 'I want to write'. The other sees his traffic lights turning orange, indicating that maybe he/she should interrupt writing because you want to write. Only when the other has clicked on 'I am ready' your traffic lights turn to green and you can write in the text. If you are writing and the lights turn to orange than the other wants to write and you should consider concluding your writing. Remember at all times, when have finished you writing to press 'I am ready'. You can always chat, also when the other is writing in the text.

You are going to start reading the assignment and the introduction in the assignment window. Think about scrolling down to read all of the instruction text. Then you can start to negotiate with your partner about things that you would like to put into the text, and you can start writing the text. For all this you have 1 hour and 15 minutes. You should do your best to produce a complete and coherent text. I give a signal when 1 hour has passed.

When you both agree that your text really is ready and requires no changes whatsoever, you can both go to the grey task bar at the top of the screen, the menu has the option 'disconnect'. DO NOT PRESS EXIT. You should only do this if you both agree the text is absolutely finished, and when you have explicitly discussed this in the chat box.

Work accurately and seriously read the assignment. This is very important for our investigation and only then your work will be worth f 50, -

When you have finished writing your first text you are allowed a 10 minutes break before starting with the second assignment, in the same way as the first.

The main points of this instruction can also be found on your screen in the assignment window. Next to your computer you find a short manual for the program, including explanations about the functions of the different windows.

*Assignment instruction*

More and more companies use 'flexies' (flexible personnel) for performing structural tasks. So, this does not merely involve short-term tasks such as temporarily replacing ill personnel or holiday jobs. These flexible working forces are usually employed by a job agency and do not have a direct relationship with the organization where they are doing their work. At this moment there is a big debate, taking place within different societal groups, about the desirability of flexible job forces. Some are in favour of this trend towards flexibility, and they see big advantages, for the employers as well as for the employees. Others consider that a system with steady jobs provides both parties with many advantages. The government has assigned a project team to start a general debate about the desirability of a flexible job market.

We ask you for a constructive contribution to this debate by producing a text in which you argue in favour of a flexible organization of the labour market.

We ask you for a constructive contribution to this debate by producing a text in which you argue in favour of maintaining a system with fixed contracts.

*Protocol example phase 1*

| line | | Concept /mode | topic | action | utterance | | Dialogue pattern |
|------|---|---------------|-------|--------|-----------|---|------------------|
| 18 | 1 | CHAT | | DSC | Three is a split picture, on one half you see a number of desks with only one little man sitting behind them, on the other half many very busy desks… | | |
| | 2 | CHAT | | | let me think | | |
| 19 | 1 | CHAT | | DSC | next to the busy desks there are piles of work | DP9 | |
| 20 | 2 | flexible jobs | adapt | CHK | Do they mean that as a flex worker you can support where it is busy? Then you have all arguments in favor and mine must be against | | |
| 21 | 1 | flexible jobs | advantage | CHL | well, of course it is not all together in favor I think | | |

| 22 | 1 | flexible jobs | contacts | STM | because the split picture can also be taken as a how to put it … It shows that as a flex you can easily end up alone | | |
| 23 | 1 | flexible jobs | position | STM | ...a less responsible position | DP1 | |
| 24 | 1 | flexible jobs | contacts | STM | /no buildup of social contacts or so | | DP4 |
| 25 | 2 | flexible jobs | contacts | EVL | That's a good argument, which we can use, | | |

*Protocol example phase 2 (same protocol)*

| 86 | 2 | TEXT | | | (….and employer.) With a steady worker a stable working relationship between employer and employee is being created that concerns the terrains of working duties as well as that of social contacts and mutual commitment. (Another advantage..) | | |
| 87 | 2 | Steady jobs | | CHK | Agree? | DP6 | Dialogue pattern |
| 88 | 1 | Steady jobs | involvement | CHL | Well that's somewhat the same thing, twice involvement | | |
| 89 | 2 | TEXT | | | (revises) This involvement with the company leads a worker to qualitatively more committed to the production process. | | |
| | 1 | CHAT | | | Let me read….. | | |
| | 2 | CHAT | | | Or maybe connect the last sentence somewhat more wait, just write, this chatting takes too much time | | |

*Protocol example phase 3 (same protocol)*

| 95 | 1 | Steady jobs | Development | STM | individual development | DPI | |
|---|---|---|---|---|---|---|---|
| 96 | 1 | Steady jobs | Learning | STM | And study | DPI | |
| 97 | 1 | Steady jobs | Learning | EXP | Learning | DPI | |
| 98 | 1 | Steady jobs | Learning | EXP | Put it with learning | DPI | |
| 99 | 2 | TEXT | | | When the company employs flexible workers, every worker has to start anew within the company. When this worker has acquired the necessary experience he is bound to leave again.<br>This causes loss of knowledge for the company. Steady workers on the other hand accumulate knowledge and expertise within the company and will specialize in a specific facet of the work.<br>The employer can invest in this by allowing space for knowledge acquisition by offering time for study and visiting conferences, so that he can learn and develop his working skills | | *Dialogue pattern* |
| 100 | 2 | Steady jobs | income | STM | OK, now worker finance | DPI | |

# NOTES

[1] Some authors distinguish cooperation and collaboration; the first referring to situations in which there is role and task division, while second is reserved for participants together working on the task at the same time. We propose not to make this distinction, as it confounds task characteristics with task strategy. Participants' decisions about task division or working synchronously do not necessarily depend on the assignment.

[2] The dialogue actions within one dialogue pattern category (e.g. elicitation) add up to 100%.

[3] The 'rest' category concerns items that could not be classified because of the ambiguity of their argumentative orientation. They are included in table 6b for completing the score to 100%.

[4] The term 'allocation' is an inadequate translation of the Dutch 'afstemmen' which means that an employer has more flexibility in adapting the number of workers to the needs of a specific task.

ARJA VEERMAN

# CONSTRUCTIVE DISCUSSIONS THROUGH ELECTRONIC DIALOGUE

## INTRODUCTION

The research presented in this chapter is aimed at academic students in social sciences who have to deal with complex, ill-defined and not easily accessible knowledge, as well as with open-ended problems. To obtain insight and understanding in complex concepts or to solve open-ended problems, collaborative learning situations can be organised in which students are able to articulate and negotiate information, not only in relationship to fixed facts and figures but also to personal beliefs and values. Many studies have shown positive effects of collaborative learning in relation to factors such as group composition, task characteristics, forms of guidance and communication modes (Slavin, 1980; Johnson & Johnson, 1993, Webb & Palinscar, 1996; Erkens, 1997; Van Boxtel, 2000).

In collaborative learning situations, argumentation can be viewed as one of the main mechanisms for collaborative learning. (e.g. Piaget, 1977; Dillenbourg & Schneider, 1995; Baker, 1996; Savery & Duffy, 1996; Petraglia, 1997). Argumentation gives rise to conflict and negotiation processes in which students can critically discuss information, elaborate on arguments and explore multiple perspectives.

In this research, several collaborative learning situations are organised to trigger students' argumentation processes by the use of computer-mediated communication (CMC) systems. CMC systems are network-based computer systems offering opportunities for group communication. Examples are Internet relay chat, newsgroups and e-mail conferencing systems. CMC systems can support synchronous communication (same time, different place) as well as asynchronous communication (different time, different place). Currently, most CMC systems offer users text-based modes for communication only, due to the limitations in bandwidth (Collis, 1996). CMC systems offer new opportunities for students to actively participate in argumentative and constructive forms of interaction. Text-based and time-delayed communication may facilitate students to uncover contradictions, gaps and conflicts. Menu-based interfaces or graphical tools for organising arguments can be used to structure effective types of interactions. However, little is known about the effective use of electronic systems in order to support collaborative learning in academic education, particularly with respect to the role of argumentation.

*J. Andriessen, M. Baker, and D. Suthers (eds.), Arguing to Learn: Confronting Cognitions in Computer-Supported Collaborative Learning environments (117-143).*

In this chapter, three studies are reported that were conducted at the department of Educational Sciences at Utrecht University, The Netherlands. Undergraduate students were studied who engaged in several collaborative learning assignments in courses on Educational Technology and Computer-Based Learning. The research questions centre on the role of students' argumentative contributions in constructive discussions while learning together electronically. The investigation is aimed at discovering principles with regards to collaborative learning, argumentation and educational technology that can be framed and used as a vehicle for further studies in the field of computer support for collaborative learning and educational practice.

## ELECTRONIC DISCUSSIONS IN ACADEMIC EDUCATION

From a rhetorical perspective, academic education can be framed as an ongoing argumentative process (Petraglia, 1997). It is the process of discovering and generating acceptable arguments and lines of reasoning underlying scientific assumptions and bodies of knowledge. The purpose of collaborative discussion tasks is to have students externalise, articulate and negotiate alternative perspectives, inducing reflection on the meaning of arguments put forward by peers as well as experts.

It is believed that collaborative learning is particularly achieved when students are presented with conflicts, engage in argumentative processes and manage to produce a shared interpretation of information or arrive at a shared problem solution (e.g. Piaget, 1977; Doise & Mugny, 1984; Baker, 1996; Erkens, 1997; Savery & Duffy, 1996; Petraglia, 1997). In argumentation, students can give prominence to conflict and negotiation processes, critically discuss information, elaborate on arguments and explore multiple perspectives. Knowledge and opinions can be (re) constructed and co-constructed and expand students' understanding of specific concepts or problems. Thus, argumentation can be seen as an important mechanism for fruitful discussions and the production of constructive activities.

In effective collaborative argumentation students share a focus and negotiate about the meaning of each other's information. Incomplete, conflicting, doubted or disbelieved information is critically checked, challenged or countered on its strength (is the information true?) and its relevance (is the information appropriate?), until finally a shared answer, solution or concept arises. However, generating effective argumentation in educational situations is not always guaranteed. First of all, focusing is important for the interpretation and understanding of communication. Students have to initiate and maintain a shared focus of the task. They have to agree on the overall goal, descriptions of the current problem-state, and available problem-solving actions (Roschelle & Teasley, 1995). Failure to maintain a shared focus on themes and problems in the discussion results in a decrease of mutual problem solving (Baker & Bielaczyc, 1995; Erkens, 1997). Second, assessing information critically on its meaning, strength or relevance depends on many factors, such as the (peer) student, the role of the tutor, the type of task, the type of instruction and the selected medium (Veerman, Kanselaar & Andriessen, 2000; Baker, this volume). Key problems that can inhibit students to engage in critical argumentation are that students tend to believe in one overall correct solution or show difficulties with generating, identifying and comparing counter-arguments and with using strong, relevant and impersonalised justifications (Kuhn, 1991). In addition, students' exposure of a critical attitude can be inhibited because of socially biased behaviour. For example, students may fear to lose face (e.g. in front of the classmates), to go against dominant persons in status or behaviour (e.g. a tutor), or for what other people think (e.g. that you are not a nice person). Students may choose to avoid social positions by adopting non-implying positions or simply by ignoring the argumentative quality of utterances (see also Jermann & Dillenbourg, this volume; Andriessen, Erkens, Van de Laak, Peters & Coirier, this volume).

To support and optimise students' engagement in argumentative dialogues for collaborative learning purposes, computer-mediated communication (CMC) systems provide new educational opportunities. Text-based and time-delayed communication can be beneficial to keep track and keep an overview of complex questions or problems under discussion. Text-based discussion is by necessity explicit and articulated. In addition to the chat windows a history of the dialogue can be used to reflect over time on earlier stated information. Moreover, in CMC systems students lack physical and psychological cues such as physical appearance, intonation, eye-contact, group identity etc., which sometimes leads to democratising effects (Short, Willams & Christie, 1976; Kiesler 1986; Rutter, 1987; Spears & Lea, 1992; Smith, 1994; Steeples, Unsworth, Bryson, Goodyear, Riding, Fowell, Levy & Duffy, 1996). Critical behaviour, therefore, may be less biased towards a tutor or a dominant peer-student than in face-to-face discussion. However, it is unclear how the use of a CMC system, and which characteristics of such a system, relates to effective argumentation for collaborative learning purposes.

To assess students' discussions on collaborative learning results in open-ended knowledge domains, immediate challenges arises. Students need to develop understanding and insights into complex theories and concepts, which depend not only on facts and figures, but also on prior knowledge and experiences, beliefs and values, and expectations on what has to be learned. It is demanding to assess such knowledge beforehand and to relate this to collaborative learning processes. Because of the unpredictable nature of the unfolding discussions themselves, reliable post-tests are even more complicated to conceive. Instead of using pre- and post-tests, collaborative learning processes were assessed. The discussions were viewed as collective information networks in which content could grow and change dynamically by the production of *constructive activities:* messages in which content-related information was added, explained, evaluated, summarised or transformed. The production of constructive activities is regarded to signal collaborative learning-in-process and is related to the concept of knowledge-building discourse (Scardamalia & Bereiter, 1994). The notion of constructive activities can also be viewed in the light of Baker's description of constructive interaction (Baker, 1999). Although constructive activities are defined in a much more narrow way, Baker's principle that constructive interaction does not necessarily have to lead to representations that are accepted as correct from a normative point of view is kept high. Rather, they describe expressions of potential knowledge-building activities.

The purpose of this chapter is to analyse and compare students' discussions on the relations between focusing, argumentation and collaborative learning-in-process in different CMC systems, with and without forms of pedagogical support. The research questions are: (1) How can electronic dialogues, in synchronous and asynchronous CMC systems, be characterised in terms of focusing and argumentation and how does that relate to the production of constructive activities?, and (2) How does pedagogical support, provided by humans or the CMC system, relate to constructive discussions in collaborative learning situations?

## THREE STUDIES

In this section, three studies are described that involved different cohorts of undergraduate students who collaboratively worked on authentic discussion tasks in electronic environments as part of a two to three month course in Educational Technology and Computer-Based Learning at Utrecht University. In each task, students worked in pairs, trios or in small groups (eight to twelve students). With or without a (peer) coach present, they had to externalise (incomplete) knowledge, beliefs and values and to use each other as a source of knowledge and reflection in order to reach shared understanding or a (shared) solution. The tasks were aimed at the following goals:
1. Developing insight and understanding in a theoretical framework.
2. Co-constructing meaningful didactics for a computer-based training program.
3. Developing insight and understanding in educational theories in relation to technology.

*Table 1. Main entities of the three studies*

| Study | Task goal | CMC system | Additional features | Group | Time |
|-------|-----------|------------|---------------------|-------|------|
| Study 1 | Developing insight and understanding in a theoretical framework | NetMeeting (synchronous) | Text editor | 20 groups of 2 students | 45–60 minutes |
| Study 2 | Co-constructing meaningful didactics for a computer-based training program | Belvédère v2.0 (synchronous) | Graphical tool for argument construction | 13 groups of 2 or 3 students | 60-90 minutes |
| Study 3 | Developing insight and understanding in educational theories in relation to technology | Allaire Forums (asynchronous) | --- | 28 groups of 8-12 students | 2-week discussions |

The tasks were respectively conducted as a synchronous text-based discussion task, a synchronous text-based and graphical discussion task and an asynchronous text-based discussion task. Table 1 serves as an advanced organiser to provide a quick overview of the main differences between the three studies. Below Table 1, the three studies are described in more detail and in the sequence of data collection.

*Study 1: Netmeeting*

NetMeeting is a synchronous CMC system. Among other functions, NetMeeting can be used for text-based communication with groups of students of any number. The working screen of the program displays an unconstrained chat box. To communicate with a partner, messages can be created, sent and will be displayed in a shared chat-history. A history of the dialogue can be used to reflect over time on earlier stated information (see Figure 1).

The first study was integrated in an actual course on Educational Technology. One of the learning goals in this course was to reach insight and understanding in the 'Conversational Framework' (Laurillard, 1993; p.102), a model that one can use for analysing and categorising teacher-student interaction. The model is considered to be discutable and can be interpreted in many different ways (Bostock, 1996). A task was designed in which students had to use this framework in order to analyse and categorise sentences of a protocol of a teacher-student dialogue. First of all, students were instructed to categorise a couple of sentences on their own (in ten minutes of time). Then, they were randomly paired and confronted with their partners' categorisations. Subsequently, all pairs discussed their categorisations in a 45-60 minutes text-based discussion mode, facilitated by the NetMeeting system. The instruction was to finally reach shared answers.

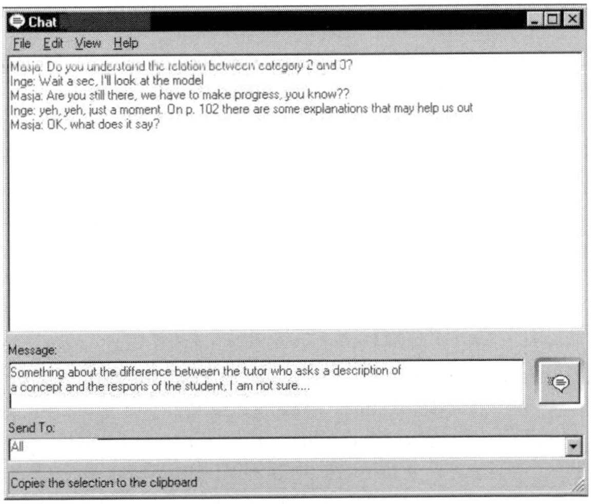

*Figure 1. Screendump of the NetMeeting system*

In sum, twenty student pairs engaged in the NetMeeting study. They were assigned to three different conditions: a 'structure' peer-coaching condition (five pairs), a 'reflective' peer coaching condition (four pairs) and a control group (no coaching; nine pairs). The 'structure' peer coach was trained to focus on argument building, particularly on generating and comparing alternative and contrasting statements, arguments and elaborations. In relation to features of the students' discussions the peer coach was instructed to ask questions such as: "What arguments can you give to support your choice/opinion?, "What counter-arguments can you think of ?", "Are there any other solutions...?", "Are there any arguments for or against other solutions?", "What conclusions can be drawn?" etc. The 'reflective' peer coach was trained to focus on discussing the meaning, strength and relevance of information and on challenging connections between claims and arguments. Dependent the state in the discussion, interventions included 'check' activities, such as checking arguments on the content, source, factual knowledge, logical reasoning chains etc. Questions that could be asked were aimed at explicitly linking claims to arguments and arguments to elaborations, for example: "Can you explain what you mean?", "What source have you used?", "Do you think this argument is strong or relevant?", "Why do think that?". The peer coaches were checked to act according to their roles. Peer-coached students were expected to focus more on the meaning of concepts than on the application of concepts compared to the control group. Student pairs guided by the 'reflective' peer coach were expected to produce particularly explanations through the mediation of checks; 'structure' coaches were expected to stimulate the production of evaluations through the mediation of challenges and counters. The discussions of student pairs in the three different conditions were analysed and compared on focus, argumentation and the production of constructive activities.

## Study 2: Belvédère (v2.0)

Belvédère is a synchronous network-tool developed by the Learning Research and Development Center at the University of Pittsburgh (Suthers, Toth & Weiner 1997; Suthers, this volume). Among many other applications, Belvédère can be used for constructing argumentative diagrams online with individuals or groups of students of any number (see Figure 2). The working screen of the program displays a communication and a diagram construction window. To communicate with a partner the student has a chat-box, which is similar to the NetMeeting system. Adding data into the diagram window is constrained; students must use the predefined set of boxes ('hypothesis', 'data', 'unspecified') and links ('for', 'against', 'and').

Belvédère provides students with a tool for non-linear argumentative diagram construction in addition to linear chat discussion. Since an argument is not linear by nature (e.g. Adam, 1992), Belvédère may enhance the process of collaborative learning through diagram-mediated argumentative discussion. The diagram construction tool may support students in organising their arguments and keeping track of the discussion by representing (discussed) information. This may trigger new discussion in the chat, about issues raised by the organised representation, maybe in the form of elaboration of discussed content or as arguments that have not

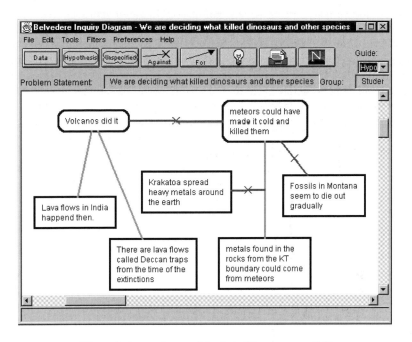

*Figure 2. Screendump of the Belvédère system, v2.0)*

yet been discussed or justified. This is expected to enhance the production of constructive activities

The Belvédère study was integrated in an actual course on Computer-Based Learning. Thirteen small student groups (two or three persons) were instructed to use the Belvédère system for 60 - 90 minute text-based discussions about learning goals and pedagogical aspects concerning their own design of a Computer-Based Learning program. They were asked to submit their constructed diagrams to the tutor. All thirteen discussions were analysed and compared on focus, argumentation and the production of constructive activities. The diagrams were analysed on the overlap of information between the chat and diagram boxes.

*Study 3: Allaire Forums*

Allaire Forums is an asynchronous network-tool that can be used for electronic group discussion. In Allaire Forums conferences can be created, which embody single or multiple 'threads' and 'branches'. In Figure 3, a thread is shown with several messages sent and 'branched'.

A study asynchronous Forum discussions was integrated in a three-month course on Educational Technology. Students' learning goals were to integrate personal experiences, theoretical knowledge and expert insights to reach conceptual understanding and new insights on the one hand, and to apply conceptual knowledge for educational problem solving on the other. Two conferences were created: one for discussing theoretical aspects of educational technology and one for discussing practical aspects. Every two weeks, in each conference two to three new threads were created by the tutor, which started with strong statements to provoke discussion. E.g. "simulation based learning fits the principles of a constructivist learning environment" or "human tutors adapt better to students' learning styles than intelligent tutoring systems". These statements were based upon what literature students had to study during the course.

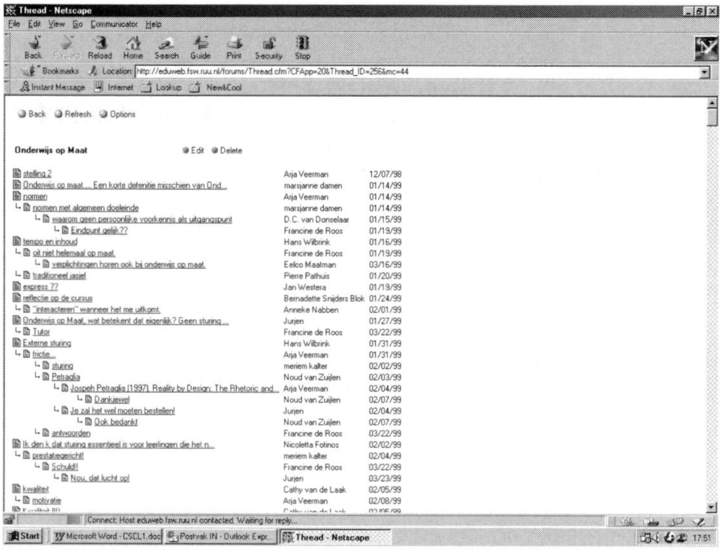

*Figure 3. Screendump of a discussion 'thread' in Allaire Forums*

Every two weeks, about 30 students were randomly assigned to different theoretical and practical discussion threads. In each thread, eight to twelve students participated. Students were instructed to make at least two short and readable contributions a week, per discussion (max. fifteen lines per message). A 'reflective' moderator supported some of these discussions by checking information on meaning, strength and relevance and on questioning connections between claims and arguments. Sometimes, the moderator also summarised information when the focus on the learning issues became lost. Moderated discussions were expected to contain more constructive activities through the mediation of checks and to be focused more strongly on the meaning of concepts than self-regulated discussions.

In sum, 28 discussions were collected: sixteen discussions were moderated, twelve were self-regulated. All discussions were analysed on focus, argumentation and the production of constructive activities. Thus, the effects of moderation interventions could be analysed in relation to students' focus, argumentation and constructive activities.

It is obvious that the three studies differ in many aspects, such as the CMC systems used and the assignments given to the students. In addition, the studies are not conducted within an experimental research design but in a temporal sequence. This means that no strict comparison of results can be allowed. However, across studies all discussions are analysed comparably on variables of focus, argumentation and the production of constructive activities. Therefore, a comparison among the three studies may reveal interesting findings for future research and discussion.

## DATA ANALYSES

All electronic discussions were automatically logged on the computer and screened on the presence of content-related messages. Content-related messages are defined as written contributions in which thematic information is expressed in relation to the task and learning goals. All content-related messages were subsequently analysed on three variables: (1) focus, (2) argumentation and (3) the production of constructive activities. These three variables were independently measured since different dimensions in the data defined them, respectively: task- and learning goals, argumentative dialogue moves and content. In the following paragraphs, the three variables and categories are first described and listed in Table 2. Then, an example is given of an electronic discussion in which messages are analysed on focusing, argumentation and the production of constructive activities.

*Table 2. Variables and categories to analyse content-related messages*

| Variables | Categories | |
|---|---|---|
| 1. Focus | a. | Meaning of concept |
| | b. | Application of concept |
| 2. Dialogue moves | a. | Statement |
| | b. | Acceptance |
| | c. | Conclusion |
| 3. Argumentative dialogue | d. | Check |
| moves | e. | Challenge |
| | f. | Counter-argument |
| 4. Constructive activities | a. | Adding information |
| | b. | Explaining information |
| | c. | Evaluating information |
| | d. | Transforming information |
| | e. | Summarising information |

*Focus*

Focusing is important for the interpretation and understanding of communication. In effective collaborative argumentation students initiate and maintain a shared focus on the task and learning goals. In this research two content-related focus categories reflect students' focus on the task and learning goals: (a) a focus on the meaning of concepts, (b) a focus on the application of concepts. In addition, students' focus could be on task strategy issues (planning how to start the task, time management, how to carry out the task), social issues, etc.

## Argumentation

Argumentation is considered to be an interactive process in which two or more participants express at least some doubt and/ or disagreement (Van Eemeren, Grootendorst & Snoeck Henkemans, 1995). Doubt or disagreement can be seen as starting points for elaborated discussions and constructive contributions. Expressions of doubt and disagreement can be operationalised in reference to several approaches on analysing Educational Dialogue, such as used in Dialogue Games, Exchange Structures and Communicative Acts, Argument and Rhetorical Structures (Pilkington, McKendree, Pain & Brna, 1999; Erkens, 1997). Such approaches indicate how argumentation is triggered, not what content is under discussion.

In this research, six types of dialogue moves are included in the analysing system: statements, acceptances, conclusions and checks, challenges and counter-arguments. Although all these categories may embody elements of argument, only check questions (e.g. "What do you mean by...."), challenges (e.g. "How can you justify that....") and counter-arguments (e.g. "I don't agree on the issue of...") are considered as *argumentative* dialogue moves.

In the Belvédère study, additional analyses are conducted to assess argumentative diagrams, which can include explicit claims and links to pro and con arguments. In Allaire Forums, further analyses are carried out with respect to the orientation of statements, which are positively, negatively or neutrally oriented towards strongly expressed and predefined claims.

## Constructive activities

Students' discussions can be viewed as collective information networks in which content can change dynamically and grow by the production of *constructive activities*: messages in which content-related information is added, explained, evaluated, summarised or transformed. Adding information means that an input of new information is linked to the discussion. Explaining information means that earlier stated information is for example differentiated, specified, categorised, or made clear by examples. Evaluations are (personally) justified considerations of the strength or relevance of already added or explained information. In transforming knowledge, already stated information is evaluated and integrated into the collective knowledge base in such a way that a new insight or a new direction transpires that can be used to answer questions or to solve problems. Summarising means that already given information is reorganised or restated in such a way that the main points or (sub) conclusions reflect the discussion. The production of constructive activities is regarded as to signal collaborative learning-in-process and is related to the concept of knowledge-building discourse (Scardamalia & Bereiter, 1994).

Discussion 1.3. THEORY "Phenomenography"

| Message subject | Participant | Date | Focus | Dialogue moves | Constructive activities |
|---|---|---|---|---|---|
| 1.  Claim | M1 | 06/01 | -- | [claim] | [claim] |
| 2.  -> response to the claim | S1 | 14/01 | | statement- | add |
| 3.  Phenomenography is about... | S2 | 09/01 | | statement- | add |
| 4.  Principles and first conclusion | S3 | 10/01 | shift | statement- | add |
| 5.  -> goals | M1 | 11/01 | | check | -- |
| 6.    -> it is about... | S4 | 11/01 | shift | statement- | explain |
| 7.    -> claim | S4 | 19/01 | | counter | evaluate |
| 8.  What's phenomenography? | S5 | 11/01 | shift | statement | add |
| 9.  Role of the individual | M1 | 12/01 | shift | check | -- |
| 10. Role of the individual | S5 | 12/01 | shift | statement | explain |

☐ Focus on the meaning of concepts      ▦ Focus on the application of concepts

| Msg | Text |
|---|---|
| 1 | "In phenomenography the role of the individual is insignificant." |
| 2 | Phenomenology: research about students' learning styles. Individuals are necessary. They are observed and questioned to define various learning styles. The individual is very important, not trivial! When various learning styles are developed, the individual becomes less important, attention shifts to groups of students with the same learning styles. |
| 3 | Phenomenography is about the way students learn and what they do with knowledge. Thus, the individual is not unimportant. |
| 4 | Principle (p. 34, 269; Laurillard): Phenomenography is about descriptions (graphy) of cases as they are (phenomena). Important is that different people describe (or conceptualise) in various ways the same (phenomenological) concept. Thus, I would say that the phenomenographical approach starts from the individual and does not suppress it. |
| 5 | Before we continue the discussion about the role of the individual, it may be useful to define phenomenography: is it a learning theory, a research method, a collection of ideas, what is it all about, what's it for? |
| 6 | **Phenomenography is about "descriptions of phenomena", especially about how students conceptualise important phenomena.** It is a research method, according to Laurillard. It can be used to find out which concepts of reality students already gained. *I don't see how the students can be insignificant. I don't think that is true.* |
| 7 | I'll take it back. I now think the individual is insignificant: it is all about concepts of the student population as a whole; no attention is paid to individual student concepts. To subscribe the claim: the individual is insignificant.... |
| 8 | Phenomenography is a research method. The method serves to analyse the descriptions of phenomena provided by students. This is what I think, because Laurillard states that some studies are phenomenographical because they describe the phenomena that students produce. On p. 43 Laurillard states: 'the methodology of phenomenography will tell us.' |
| 9 | The next question is about the role of the individual versus the meaning of groups in relationship to phenomenography. What is Laurillard's opinion? |
| 10 | I found something about the role of the individual on p. 36, third section. **"The goal of phenomenography is not about the student's conception but to study different conceptions of the population as a whole".** *Laurillard: "The analysis is not by individual therefore, but is carried out in terms of the meaning of the conceptions invoked in the course of a student's explanation".* |

*Figure 4. Example of a discussion fragment analysed on focus, (argumentative) dialogue moves and constructive activities.*

In this research, all content-related messages are analysed on types of constructive activities. Each message can be categorised once, as one of the following constructive activities: (a) addition, (b) explanation, (c) evaluation, (d) transformation, (e) summary.

*Example*

In Figure 4 an example is shown of an asynchronous discussion fragment of the study on Allaire Forums, which is analysed on focus, (argumentative) dialogue moves and the production of constructive activities. Since these discussions started with strongly predefined claims, additional analyses were carried out to categorise a statement's orientation towards the main claim (positive, negative or neutral). Explanations are given below Figure 4.

The discussion starts with Claim 3, which considers the subject of "phenomenography" in relation to the role of the individual. The discussion is moderated (M1) and the fragment involves five students (S1-S5). All messages (1-10) are organised by their 'message subject' and 'date'. In Allaire Forums these messages can be viewed full screen by clicking on the 'message subject'. The messages are shown as text in Figure 4.

Message nr. 1 includes a claim sent by the tutor ("In phenomenography the role of the individual is insignificant"). S2 and S3 respond to the claim (message nr. 3 and 4; notice the date!), and both apply this (conceptual) information against the claim. The moderator intervenes and asks the students to define the concept of phenomenography (message nr. 5). She tries to establish common ground but does not add her own statement or definition to the discussion. S4 reacts and gives an explanation (message nr. 6; underlined text) of earlier stated information (bold text) in direct relationship to the claim (focus on the application of concepts; italic text). S5 then defines the concept by specifically referring to literature. The moderator subsequently asks another check question: what do the students think about the role of the individual considering a phenomenographical approach (message nr. 9). S5 continues the discussion by explaining some earlier stated information (bold text) and referring to literature (italic text). The fragment shows that messages are not organised by date but by message replies. For example, S4 counters her own negative statement eight days later (message nr. 7); S1 replies to the first message at 14/01 (message nr. 2).

## RESULTS

In this section various types of results will be presented. First of all, the method of analyses will be discussed with respect to the inter-subject reliability rates of the variables of focus, argumentation and the production of constructive activities across studies. Second, results and interpretations will be presented and interpreted with respect to the first research question: how electronic discussions can be characterised in terms of focus, argumentation and constructive activities. Third, the effects of coaches, graphical support and human moderation are presented in relation to the second research question: how to support constructive discussions.

*Inter-subject reliability rates*

All electronic chat discussions were analysed on focus, (argumentative) dialogue moves and the production of constructive activities. Considering focus analysis, some difficulties occurred in the Belvédère study. In this study information overlapped between chat discussions and argumentative diagrams, which made it sometimes hard to define what students were focusing on. Thus, inter-subject reliability rates dipped to a Cohen's Kappa of .74., whereas a rate of .91. was reported in both the NetMeeting study and in Allaire Forums (Cohen, 1968). Considering (argumentative) dialogue moves, the analysing system proved to be straightforward to handle and inter-subject reliability rates were sufficiently high across the studies (Cohen's Kappa = .82 in NetMeeting; .83 in Belvédère and .89 in Allaire Forums). With respect to the production of constructive activities, extensive practice showed to be needed for reliable analysis. The highest inter-subject reliability rate was achieved in the study on Allaire Forums. In this study, two student assistants collaborated for two weeks to get a grip on the analysing system (Cohen's Kappa = .86). A Cohen's Kappa of .74 respectively .78 was measured in the NetMeeting and Belvédère study, in which less time was spent on practice (about a day). For qualitative data analysis that heavily depends on the interpretation of categories, these rates are still 'substantially' high and acceptable (Heuvelmans & Sanders, 1993).

*Chat discussions: focus, argumentation and constructive activities*

The first research question was how electronic dialogues in synchronous and asynchronous CMC systems can be characterised in terms of focusing and argumentation and how that relates to the production of constructive activities. To come to an answer to this question, all messages in the studies on NetMeeting, Belvédère and Allaire Forums are coded, counted and categorised on each of the three dimensions of focus, argumentation and constructive activities. In Table 3, all numbers and types of messages are presented. Table 3 can be read in the following way.

For example, in the NetMeeting study twenty discussions are gathered for analysis. On average, each of these discussions contains 102 messages. A message contains about ten words, on average. The total amount of messages is 2040.

Each chat discussion contains content-related and non content-related messages. On average, 61% of all NetMeeting messages is categorised as content-related. Subsequently, all content-related messages are analysed on focus, (argumentative) dialogue moves and constructive activities. In view of focus, in the NetMeeting study most content-related messages are focused on the application of concepts (80%). Taking into account argumentation, most content-related messages are categorised as information checks (22%). Considering the production of constructive activities, 33% of all content-related messages is categorised as being constructive. Most constructive messages are categorised as additions (40%) and evaluations (45%).

*Table 3. Number and type of chat messages across the three studies*

|  | NetMeeting | Belvédère | Allaire Forums |
|---|---|---|---|
| Sum of discussions analysed | 20 | 13 | 28 |
| Average number of messages; per discussion | 102 | 99 | 34 |
| Average number of words; per message | 10 | 11 | 120 |
| Sum of messages analysed | 2040 | 1287 | 952 |
| | | | |
| Messages on average; per discussion (100%): | | | |
| - Non content-related messages (focused on task strategy, social issues etc.) | 40 (39%) | 57 (58%) | 4 (12%) |
| - Content-related messages | 62 (61%) | 42 (42%) | 30 (88%) |
| | | | |
| Content-related messages on average; per discussion (100%): | | | |
| - Focused on the meaning of concepts | 12 (20%) | 24 (57%) | 14 (47%) |
| - Focused on the application of concepts | 50 (80%) | 18 (43%) | 16 (53%) |
| | | | |
| Content-related messages on average; per discussion (100%): | | | |
| - Not argumentative (statements, accepts etc.) | 36 (58%) | 21 (50%) | 21 (71%) |
| - Checking information | 14 (22%) | 9 (21%) | 7 (23%) |
| - Challenging information | 7 (12%) | 4 (10%) | 1 (3%) |
| - Countering information | 5 (8%) | 8 (19%) | 1 (3%) |
| | | | |
| Content-related messages on average; per discussion (100%): | | | |
| - Not constructive messages | 42 (67%) | 22 (52%) | 8 (27%) |
| - Constructive messages | 20 (33%) | 20 (48%) | 22 (73%) |
| | | | |
| Constructive messages, on average; per discussion (100%) | | | |
| - Additions | 8 (40%) | 9 (45%) | 7 (30%)[*] |
| - Explanations | 3 (15%) | 3 (15%) | 11 (50%) |
| - Evaluations | 9 (45%) | 8 (40%) | 2 (10%) |
| - Summaries | 0% | 0% | 1 (5%) |
| - Transformations | 0% | 0% | 1 (5%) |

[*] *Figures are rounded off to whole numbers*

*Number of messages*

The NetMeeting and Belvédère systems were used to carry out short, synchronous discussion tasks in pairs or triples. In Belvédère, students were instructed to conduct the task in 60 - 90 minutes. In NetMeeting, students got about 45 to 60 minutes. However, the mean number of messages is comparable (99 versus 102), as well as the mean number of words (ten versus eleven). In Allaire Forums, students had two weeks to discuss claims asynchronously. Compared to the synchronous discussions, the mean number of messages per discussion is low (34), however, the number of words per message is about twelve times as high (120).

These differences characterise the different types of collaboration and communication processes in synchronous and asynchronous CMC systems. Synchronous collaboration has to be fast, due to a high psychological pressure to respond as soon as possible (Moore, 1993). The communication process can often be viewed as 'talking in text'. In general, asynchronous collaboration goes at a slow pace and written messages are more cautiously composed and elaborated. Processes are often more similar to writing a letter than to talking to a friend.

*Content-related versus non content-related messages*

Figure 5 shows an overview of content-related versus non content-related messages sent across the three studies. Remarkable is the high percentage of content-related messages in the asynchronous system Allaire Forums (88%). The percentages of content-related messages in the synchronous systems NetMeeting and Belvédère are much lower (61% resp. 42%).

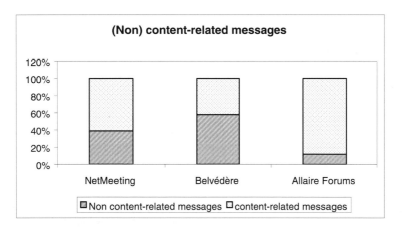

*Figure 5. Percentages of (non) content-related messages*

One of the explanations for this result is that despite instruction and hands-on-experience, students had lots of technical trouble to use the NetMeeting system. They sometimes even broke down their full network connection. The Belvédère study did not cause this kind of trouble, although students now had to split their attention between chat discussion and diagram construction. This forced them to engage in a serious amount of planning and technical talk. In Allaire Forum students were able to use the system straightforwardly. They were also not bothered by having to split their attention between windows or part-tasks. Thus, they could keep their concentration high and their discussions highly content-related.

*Focus*

Figure 6 shows an overview of all content-related messages sent across the three studies that were focused on the meaning of concepts or on the application of concepts. In the NetMeeting study, most content-related messages were focused on the application of concepts (80%). In the Belvédère study most content-related messages were focused on the meaning of concepts (57%). In the study on Allaire Forums about half of the messages was focused on the meaning of concepts (47%), the other half was focused on the application of concepts (53%).

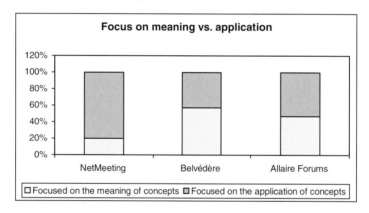

*Figure 6. Percentages of messages focused on meaning versus application of concepts*

An explanation of this result is that in NetMeeting students had to carry out a discussion task in order to solve a problem. Solving the problem was not the main learning goal, but meant as a method to engage students in deep conceptual discussion. However, time restrictions and technical trouble pressed the students to hurry on and to focus more on the application of concepts than on discussing meaning. Solving the problem seems to have become more important than engaging in deep discussion, without a clear end-goal or fast result. In Belvédère, students also had to engage in discussion through a set of questions that had to be answered at the end. However, students had more time on task, which was also less constrained. In Allaire Forums, students' discussion topics were aimed at both theoretical and practical issues of educational technology. The topics were thought to trigger differences among discussions, but they were all comparably focused on a mix of foci on the meaning and application of concepts. No need for a definite end-product, problem solution or clear answer together with long time delays between messages may have triggered students not to focus that strongly on the application of concepts but to shift focus back and forth between application and meaning.

*Argumentation*

Figure 7 shows an overview of all content-related messages across the three studies, divided among general types of dialogue moves and the following types of argumentative dialogue moves: checks, challenges and counter-arguments. Most argumentative dialogue moves were produced in the Belvédère study. Every second content-related message was an argumentative dialogue move (50%). The NetMeeting discussions were also quite argumentative. Of all content-related messages, 42% were coded as an argumentative dialogue move. Fewest argumentative dialogue moves were produced in the study on Allaire Forums (29%). In all three studies, a comparable percentage of check messages was produced: between 21-23% of all content-related messages. In the NetMeeting and Belvédère study, respectively 12% and 10% of all content-related messages were coded as a challenge. In Allaire Forums hardly any challenges could be found (3%). In the Belvédère study, most counter-arguments were produced (19%). Compared to the countering percentages in the NetMeeting study (8%) and in Allaire Forums (3%), this is quite a high percentage.

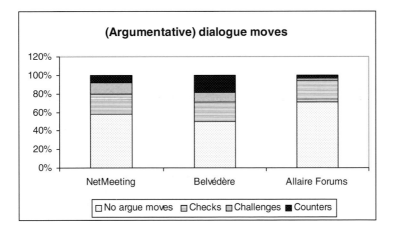

*Figure 7. Percentages of (argumentative) dialogue moves*

The results show that the synchronous discussions in NetMeeting and Belvédère are much more argumentative than the asynchronous discussions in Allaire Forums. Although the number of checks is comparable across the three studies, in NetMeeting and Belvédère the number of challenges is three to four times as high. Counter-arguments were mainly produced during the Belvédère discussions, probably stimulated by the graphical diagram window (see Suthers & Hundhausen, 1997; Veerman & Treasure-Jones, 1999; Suthers, this volume). Also, the mode of communication seems to be of influence with respect to the production of 'direct' forms of argumentation (challenges and counter-arguments) and 'indirect' forms (checks). Synchronous communication has to be fast, students have less time to ask elaborate questions, to show their doubts and to explain their problems. They rather step into direct forms of communication, sometimes jumping to conclusions. Asynchronous communication provides students with more opportunities to aim at a real understanding of the problem.

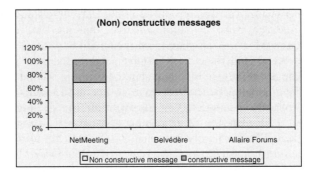

*Figure 8. Percentages of (non) constructive messages*

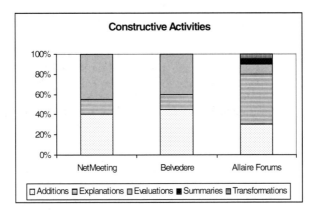

*Figure 9. Types of constructive messages*

*Constructive messages*

In Figure 8 it is shown that most constructive messages were produced in the study on Allaire Forums. From all content-related messages, 73% were coded as one of the constructive activities. In the Belvédère study, almost half of the content-related messages were coded as a constructive activity: 48%. In NetMeeting, the percentages were lowest: 33%. Figure 9 shows the various types of constructive messages across the three studies. Remarkably, in the synchronous studies NetMeeting and Belvédère almost half of all constructive messages were coded as Evaluation, which is in contrast to the low percentage of Evaluations in the asynchronous study on Allaire Forums. Regarding the percentage of Explanations, it is just the other way around.

The results show that most constructive messages were produced in Allaire Forums. The lowest number of constructive activities was found in the NetMeeting discussions whereas in Belvédère half of the content-related messages was coded as being constructive. Remarkably, most constructive messages in NetMeeting and Belvédère were additions and evaluations whereas in Allaire Forums most constructive messages were coded as explanations. Yet again, this can be due to the mode of communication. Synchronous communication is fast, students do not have many opportunities to produce extended explanations and are swayed to jump to evaluations and conclusions.

*Support for constructive discussions*

The second research question was about how to provide pedagogical support by humans or electronically to enhance constructive discussions. Results and interpretations are presented from respectively different types of peer-coaching, graphical support and reflective moderation. The chapter is then closed with a section for conclusion and discussion.

*'Reflective' coaching versus 'structure' coaching*

In the NetMeeting study, the two coaching conditions and the control group were tested on differences in focus, argumentation and the production of constructive activities. It was expected that peer-coached discussions would trigger either indirect or direct forms of argumentation, thus, stimulating the production of constructive activities. However, analysis of variance (MANOVA) only showed two small differences with respect to challenging information and adding activities were found (see Table 4). Challenges were mostly made by the peer coaches in the 'structure' and 'reflective' condition; most additions were produced in the control group. Although the actions of the coaches were checked and it was concluded that they accomplished their roles correctly, it show that the number of challenges somewhat increased without having a further effect on the production of constructive activities. Thus, no relation was found between challenging information and the production of constructive activities.

*Table 4. Comparison between the number of messages of coached student groups and a control group in NetMeeting*

|  | 'structure' coach | | 'reflective' coach | | Control group | | | |
|---|---|---|---|---|---|---|---|---|
|  | *mean* | *s.d.* | *mean* | *s.d.* | *mean* | *s.d.* | *F-value* | *P-value* |
| Focus |  |  |  |  |  |  |  |  |
| - meaning | 8 | 3 | 17 | 11 | 18 | 13 | 1.50 | 0.25 |
| - application | 73 | 12 | 58 | 13 | 60 | 21 | 1.57 | 0.24 |
|  |  |  |  |  |  |  |  |  |
| Argumentation |  |  |  |  |  |  |  |  |
| - check | 18 | 8 | 25 | 5 | 23 | 5 | 2.12 | 0.15 |
| - challenge | 15 | 2 | 12 | 5 | 8 | 6 | 3.19 | *0.07* |
| - counter | 9 | 3 | 8 | 4 | 7 | 8 | 0.08 | 0.93 |
|  |  |  |  |  |  |  |  |  |
| Constructive activities |  |  |  |  |  |  |  |  |
| - addition | 12 | 4 | 9 | 2 | 16 | 7 | 3.41 | *0.06* |
| - explanation | 4 | 3 | 9 | 12 | 10 | 4 | 0.97 | 0.40 |
| - evaluation | 13 | 7 | 13 | 5 | 18 | 11 | 0.73 | 0.50 |
| - transformation* |  |  |  |  |  |  |  |  |
| - summary* |  |  |  |  |  |  |  |  |

*hardly or not found at all*

## Graphical support

In the Belvédère study, all thirteen chats and diagrams were additionally analysed on the overlap of information. The idea was that the diagram construction tool could support students in organising arguments and keeping track of the discussion by representing information that students agreed upon or that served to trigger 'new' discussion in the chat. This was thought to enhance the production of constructive activities. To assess the overlap of information, information was traced from the diagram boxes back into the chat discussions and explored on also being stated or argued about.

In sum, 195 diagram boxes were put into the Belvédère diagram windows (mean per diagram = 15; s.d. = 10). It showed that 42 of these boxes contained information that was also stated or discussed somewhere in the related chat discussion. Correlation measurements showed that the number of overlapping diagram boxes related significantly to the number of constructive activities produced in the chat discussion ($r = 0.63$; $p < 0.05$). Apparently, the diagram construction tool could support students' constructive discussions as long as they used their chat and diagram in an integral manner.

*'Reflective' moderation*

In the study on Allaire Forums, sixteen asynchronous discussions were moderated and compared to twelve self-regulated discussions on focus, argumentation and the production of constructive activities (see Table 5). Moderated discussions were expected to include more constructive activities through the mediation of checks and to be more conceptually oriented than self-regulated discussions.

Due to a very low number of challenges and counter-arguments (see Table 3), only one category of argumentation was used for analyses, which includes all types of argumentative dialogue moves. The various types of constructive activities were also summed up in order to have enough data to run a T-test. Although self-regulated discussions were slightly less focused on the meaning of concepts, no significant differences were found.

*Table 5. Comparison between moderated versus self-regulated discussions in Allaire Forums*

|  | Moderated (n=16) | | Self-regulated (n=12) | | | |
|---|---|---|---|---|---|---|
|  | *Mean* | *s.d.* | *mean* | *s.d.* | *T* $(df = 26)$ | *p-value* |
| Focus |  |  |  |  |  |  |
| - meaning | 15 | 6 | 12 | 6 | 1.05 | 0.30 |
| - application | 15 | 5 | 16 | 6 | 0.51 | 0.62 |
| Argumentation: - Σ(checks, challenges, counters) | 9 | 3 | 9 | 2 | 0.66 | 0.51 |
| Constructive activities: - Σ (additions, explanation, evaluations etc. ) | 22 | 7 | 21 | 6 | 0.30 | 0.77 |

Thus, against expectations but in line with the NetMeeting study, a similar lack of results was found in the study on Allaire Forums. The 'reflective' moderators acted according to their roles, but no effects were found with respect to the quality of the discussions. Yet, in Allaire Forums the moderators were instructed to scaffold students' asynchronous discussions. This meant that they had to provide the students with a maximum of pedagogical support in the first week of discussions and then gradually fade away in later discussions. Students were expected to progressively move to self-regulated discussions in which they applied 'reflective' actions to their own discussions. Beyond expectations, further analyses showed that the moderator's modelling actions appeared to affect students' behaviour immediately in the first two weeks. This caused a fast change in students' behaviour that overruled any possible overall effects of the moderator's interventions (see for detailed analyses Veerman, 2000).

## DISCUSSION AND CONCLUSIONS

This chapter reports on three studies that involved undergraduate students collaboratively working on authentic discussion tasks in synchronous and asynchronous computer-mediated communication (CMC) systems (Netmeeting, Belvédère, Allaire Forums). To examine whether the use of CMC systems could facilitate students' collaborative learning-in-process, their electronic discussions are characterised in terms of constructive and argumentative contributions. In addition, effects of different forms of support are compared: from peer-coaching synchronous discussions and offering graphical support at the interface to reflective moderation in asynchronous discussions. The first research question was aimed at characterising the electronic discussions in terms of focus and argumentation and in relation to the production of constructive activities, a measurement used to define collaborative learning-in-process. The idea was that different CMC systems would have different effects on the characteristics of the electronic discussions. Besides, argumentation was assumed to trigger learning-in-process. The second research question considered the role of support, provided by a human coach, the electronic system or a human moderator. In relation to these main research questions, the results of the three studies will be discussed below.

The NetMeeting and Belvédère system were used to carry out short, synchronous discussion tasks. In Allaire Forums, students had two weeks to discuss claims in asynchronous discussions. In NetMeeting and Belvédère, a high frequency of short messages was sent to the discussions whereas in Allaire Forums, frequencies were less high but messages were much longer. In addition, messages in Allaire Forums were 1,5 to two times more often content-related than in the Belvédère and NetMeeting discussions. These differences characterise the different types of collaboration and communication processes in synchronous and asynchronous CMC systems. In synchronous discussions students engage in a fast flow of communication. Real-time pressures them (psychologically) to read and respond to each other's contributions within seconds or at most minutes. Focus shifts to non-content related aspects or technical issues easily cause students to lose track of an argument or to lose the overview of the issues under discussion. In asynchronous discussions students may take hours, days, weeks, and sometimes even longer to read, write and think about contributions that triggered their interest, instead of seconds or minutes. More time may afford re-reading and reflection, keeping track of the line of discussion and treating non content-related interactions or technical disturbances as they are: temporary interruptions.

With respect to focusing, in the NetMeeting study most content-related messages were focused on the application of concepts whereas in Belvédère and Allaire Forums about half of the messages was focused on the meaning of concepts; the other half was focused on the application of concepts. A possible explanation of this result is that in the NetMeeting study solving the problem became more important than engaging in deep discussion. In Belvédère, students had more time on task and could work less problem-oriented. In Allaire Forums, long time delays and less clear end-goals may have triggered the students not to focus too strongly on the application of concepts but to shift back and forth between application and meaning. Considering Laurillard's theory of academic learning, this process may have been especially productive (Laurillard, 1993). She argues that academic learning cannot be directly experienced. Students have to work on both descriptions of the world (theories, concepts etc.) and act within this world (apply knowledge and concepts to tasks). Shifting focus between meaning and application, therefore, may have been particularly fruitful.

Taking argumentation into account, the results show that the synchronous discussions in NetMeeting and Belvédère are much more argumentative than the asynchronous discussions in Allaire Forums. Again, the mode of communication seems to be of influence with respect to the production of 'direct' forms of argumentation (challenges and counter-arguments) and 'indirect' forms (checks). Synchronous communication has to be fast, students have less time to ask elaborated questions, to show their doubts and to explain their problems. They rather step in direct forms of communication, sometimes jumping right into conclusions. In general, asynchronous communication is much slower, often more relaxed and provides students with much more opportunities to aim at a real understanding of the problem. Indeed, time on task and students' personal characteristics (prior knowledge, attitude, beliefs and values etc.) also play a role in this story. Interesting studies about such issues can be found in Stein, Calicchia & Bernas (1996) and Krosnick & Petty (1995).

With respect to the production of constructive activities, most constructive messages were produced in Allaire Forums. Remarkably, in NetMeeting and Belvédère, most constructive messages were additions and evaluations whereas in Allaire Forums most constructive messages were coded as explanations. Yet again, this can be due to the mode of communication. Synchronous communication is fast, students don't have many opportunities to produce extended explanations and are swayed to jump right into evaluations and conclusions.

Considering the relation between focus and argumentation on the one hand and the production of constructive activities on the other, some results are presented in Table 6.

What can be inferred from these simplified and qualitatively presented results in Table 6, is that argumentation does not play a clear, single or major role in the production of constructive activities. Although check questions are important, challenges and counters do not necessarily lead to more constructive discussions. For instance, in the NetMeeting study more challenges in the 'structure' peer coach condition did not have an effect on the number or type of constructive activities produced. In addition, in Belvédère most counter-arguments were stated without having an effect on the production of constructive activities. The use of the chat discussion in close relation to the diagram window appeared to be much more important, as well as a content-related focus.

*Table 6. Focus, argumentation and constructive activities across the three studies*

|                       | NetMeeting   | Belvédère            | Allaire Forums |
|-----------------------|--------------|----------------------|----------------|
| Focus                 |              |                      |                |
| - Content-related mess. | Medium       | Low                  | High           |
| - Type                | Application  | Application / meaning | Application / meaning |
|                       |              |                      |                |
| Argumentation         |              |                      |                |
| - Number              | Medium       | High                 | Low            |
| - Type                | Checks, challenges | Checks, challenges, counters | Checks |
| Constructive activities | Low        | Medium               | High           |
| - Number              | Evaluation   | Evaluation           | Explanation    |
| - Type                |              |                      |                |

Remarkably, in neither asynchronous nor synchronous discussions are students driven to produce summaries or information transformation. This may be due to the required cognitive effort but also to an incomplete, intuitive and personalised understanding of the information under discussion (Kuhn, 1991). Students need sufficient understanding of a topic and a mutual framework for interpreting each other's information before they can state firm positions and stick to a position (Coirier, Andriessen & Chanquoy, 1999). To reach new insights, there must be a certain level of (shared) understanding. In the three studies, considering task characteristics, students' preparation time, prior knowledge and time available for discussion, reaching (deeper) understanding may have been the highest goal attainable, especially through the use of asynchronous CMC systems. Reaching new insights may be just the next step, for instance, when students are sufficiently prepared to take firm positions to engage in critical, strong and hefty argumentation (triggered best by synchronous CMC systems?).

In discussing the characteristics and relations between the variables of focus, argumentation and the production of constructive activities, some effects of human support and electronic facilitation have already come forward. First of all, hardly any effects were found of the peer-coaching conditions in the NetMeeting study. At first sight, similar results were found in the study on Allaire Forums. Yet, in Allaire Forums the moderator's strategy was to model and scaffold the students to progressively move from guided discussions to self-regulated critical discussions in which they could apply their own 'reflective' actions to their discussions. Beyond expectations, the moderator's modelling actions appeared to affect students' behaviour immediately in the first two weeks. This caused a fast change in students' behaviour that overruled the possible overall effects of the moderator's interventions. Nevertheless, it appears that task characteristics (open-ended, conceptual discussion task, flexible time constraints), interface affordances (to keep an overview, to organise discussions graphically) and the mode of communication (with opportunities for explanation and reflection) interact and determine to a much greater extent the constructiveness of a discussion than a human coach or moderator.

To conclude, the role of argumentation in collaborative learning situations has to be reconsidered. Triggering students to critically check each other's information in order to maintain shared levels of understanding is useful and can be effectively provoked through task design, interface characteristics and the mode of communication. However, stimulating 'direct' forms of argumentation appears to be effective only then when students are well prepared and have a substantial knowledge base. In CMC situations, support is desirable to co-ordinate communication and to establish and maintain a conceptually oriented focus. More studies are required to assess human support, especially considering the role of an effective coach or moderator, which is still unclear. In addition, experimental studies are required to research the effects of interface design and modes of communication in order to support students' collaborative learning in computerised environments.

## AUTHOR'S CONTACT ADDRESS

*Arja L. Veerman, Ph.D.*
*TNO - Human Factors, Dep. of Training & Instruction*
*Kampweg 5, 3769 ZG Soesterberg*
*The Netherlands*
*tel.: ++31 – (0)346 – 356 454*
*fax.: ++31 – (0)346 – 353 977*
*e-mail: veerman@tm.tno.nl*

## ACKNOWLEDGMENT

Thanks to the support and input from Jerry Andriessen, Gellof Kanselaar, Gijsbert Erkens, Jos Jaspers and other colleagues from Utrecht University, my work on CSCL and argumentation could be converted into a thesis, which serve as the basis for this chapter. Pierre Dillenbourg and Michael Baker gave me ideas and revisions several times, for which I am grateful. Dan Jones and Dan Suthers have to be thanked for their extensive support on the Belvédère computer system throughout the years.

## REFERENCES

Adam, J. M. (1992). *Les textes: Types et prototypes - Récit, description, argumentation et dialogue* [The texts: Types and prototypes- Story, description, argumentation and dialogue]. Paris: Nathan.

Andriessen, J.E.B. Erkens, G. Van de Laak, C. Peters, N. & Coirier, P. (this volume). Argumentation as negotiation in electronic collaborative writing. In J. Andriessen, M. Baker & D. Suthers. *Arguing to learn.* The Netherlands: Kluwer Academic Publishers.

Baker, M. (1996). Argumentation and cognitive change in collaborative problem-solving dialogues. *COAST Research Report Number CR-13/96*, France.

Baker, M., & Bielaczyc, K. (1995). Missed opportunities for learning in collaborative problem-solving interactions. In J. Greer (Ed.), *Proceedings of AI-ED 95 - 7th World Conference on Artificial Intelligence in Education* (pp. 210-218). Charlottesville: Association for the Advancement of Computing in Education (AACE).

Baker, M. (1999). Argumentation and constructive interaction. In P. Coirier & J. E. B. Andriessen (Eds.), *Foundations of argumentative text processing* (pp. 179-202) Amsterdam: Amsterdam University Press.

Baker, M. (this volume). Computer-mediated interactions for the co-elaboration of scientific notions. In J. Andriessen, M. Baker & D. Suthers. *Arguing to learn*. The Netherlands: Kluwer Academic Publishers.

Bostock, A.J. (1996). A critical review of Laurillard's classification of educational media. *Instructional Science* (24), 71-88.

Cohen, J. (1968). Weighted kappa: nominal scale agreement with provisions for scales disagreement of partial credit. *Psychological Bulletin 70*, 213-220.

Coirier, P., Andriessen, J.E.B., & Chanquoy, L. (1999). From planning to translating: The specificity of argumentative writing. In P. Coirier & J.E.B.Andriessen (Eds.) *Foundations of argumentative text processing*. Amsterdam: Amsterdam University Press.

Collis, B. (1996). *Tele-learning in a digital world: The future of distance learning*. London: International Thomson Computer Press.

Dillenbourg, P., & Schneider, D. (1995). Mediating the mechanisms which make collaborative learning sometimes effective. *International Journal of Educational Telecommunications, 1*(2-3), 131-146.

Doise, W. & Mugny, G. (1984). *The social development of the intellect*. Oxford: Pergamon Press.

Erkens, G. (1997). *Cooperatief probleemoplossen met computers in het onderwijs: Het modelleren van cooperatieve dialogen voor de ontwikkeling van intelligente onderwijssystemen* [Cooperative problem solving with computers in education: Modelling of cooperative dialogues for the design of intelligent educational systems]. Ph.D. thesis, Utrecht University, the Netherlands.

Heuvelmans, A. P. J. M. & Sanders, P. F. (1993). Beoordelaarsoverstemming [Inter-subject reliability measurement]. In Eggen, T. J. H. M. & P. F. Sanders (Eds.), *Psychometrie in de praktijk* (pp. 443-469). Arnhem, The Netherlands: CITO.

Jermann, P. & Dillenbourg, P. (this volume). Elaborating new arguments through a CSCL scenario. In J. Andriessen, M. Baker & D. Suthers. *Arguing to learn*. The Netherlands: Kluwer Academic Publishers.

Johnson, D. W., & Johnson, R. T. (1993). Creative and critical thinking through academic controversy. *American Behavioural Scientist, 37*(1), 40-53.

Kiesler, S. (1986). The hidden message in computer networks. *Harvard Business Review, 64* (1), 46-58.

Krosnick, J. A. & Petty, R. E. (1995). *Attitude strength: Antecedents and consequences*. New Jersey: Lawrence Erlbaum.

Kuhn, D. (1991). *The Skills of Argument*. Cambridge: University Press.

Laurillard, D. (1993). *Rethinking university teaching: a framework for the effective use of educational technology*. Routledge, London.

Moore, M. G. (1993). Theory of transactional distance. In D. Keegan (Ed.), *Theoretical principles of distance education* (pp. 22-38). London: Routledge.

Piaget, J. (1977). *The development of thought: Equilibration of cognitive structures*. New York: Viking Penguin.

Petraglia, J. (1997). *The rhetoric and technology of authenticity in education*. Mahwah, NJ: Lawrence Erlbaum.

Pilkington, R., McKendree, J., Pain, H., Brna, P. (1999). *Analysing educational dialogue interaction: towards models that support learning*. 'A One day Workshop at AI-Ed '99', 9th International Conference on Artificial Intelligence in Education, Le Mans, France. July 19-22, 1999.

Roschelle, J. & Teasley, S.D. (1995). Construction of shared knowledge in collaborative problem solving. In C. O'Malley (Ed.), *Computer-supported collaborative learning*. New York: Springer-Verlag.

Rutter, D. R. (1987). *Communicating by Telephone*. Oxford: Pergamon Press.

Savery J. & Duffy, T. M. (1996). Problem based learning: An instructional model and its constructivist framework. In B. Wilson (Ed.), *Constructivist learning environments: Case studies in instructional design* (pp. 135-148). Englewood Cliffs, NJ: Educational Technology Publications.

Scardamalia, M., & Bereiter, C. (1994). Computer support for knowledge-building communities. *The Journal of the learning sciences, 3*(3), 265-283.

Slavin, R.E. (1980). *Co-operative learning: theory, research and practice.* Prentice-Hall: Englewood Cliffs, NJ.

Short, J., E. Williams, and B. Christie (1976). *The social psychology of telecommunications.* New York: Wiley.

Spears, R. & Lea, M. (1992) Social influence and the influence of the social in computer mediated communication In: *Context of computer mediated communication.* Ed: Martin Lea, Bodmin, Great Brittain.

Steeples, C., Unsworth, C., Bryson, M., Goodyear, P., Riding, P., Fowell, S., Levy, P., & Duffy, C. (1996). Technological support for teaching and learning: Computer-mediated communications in higher education (CMC in HE). *Computers & Education, 26* (1-3), 71-80.

Stein, N. L., Calicchia, D. J,. & Bernas, R. S. (1996). Conflict talk. Understanding and resolving arguments. In T. Givon (Ed.), *Typological studies in language: Conversational analysis* (pp. 233-267). Amsterdam: John Benjamins.

Suthers, D., Toth, E. and Weiner, A. (1997). An Integrated Approach to Implementing Collaborative Inquiry in the Classroom. *Proceedings of the conference on Computer Supported Collaborative Learning: CSCL'97* (pp.272-279).

Suthers, D. & Hundhausen, C. (2001). Learning by Constructing Collaborative Representations: An Empirical Comparison of Three Alternatives. In P. Dillenbourg, A. Eurelings & K. Hakkarainen (Eds.), *European Perspectives on Computer-Supported Collaborative Learning: Proceedings of the First European Conference on Computer-Supported Collaborative Learning* (pp.577-584). Maastricht, The Netherlands: Universiteit Maastricht.

Suthers, D. (this volume). Studies of representational support for collaborative inquiry with Belvedere. In J. Andriessen, M. Baker & D. Suthers. *Arguing to learn.* The Netherlands: Kluwer Academic Publishers.

Van Boxtel, C. A. M. (2000). *Collaborative concept learning. Student interaction, collaborative learning tasks and physic concepts.* Enschede, The Netherlands: Print Partners Ipskamp.

Van Eemeren, F. H, Grootendorst, R., & Snoeck Henkemans, A.F. (1995) *Argumentatie* [Argumentation]. Groningen, The Netherlands: Woltersgroep.

Veerman, A. L., & Treasure-Jones, T. (1999). Software for problem solving through collaborative argumentation. In P. Coirier & J. E. B. Andriessen (Eds.), *Foundations of argumentative text processing* (pp. 203-230). Amsterdam: Amsterdam University Press.

Veerman, A.L., Andriessen, J.E.B. & Kanselaar, G. (2000) Enhancing learning through synchronous discussion. *Computers & Education, 34*(2-3), 1-22.

Veerman, A.L. (2000). Computer-supported collaborative learning through argumentation. Enschede: Print Partners Ipskamp. (Thesis, to download at: http:// eduweb.fss.uu.nl/arja/).

Webb, N. & Palinscar, A. (1996). Group processes in the classroom. In D. Bermler & R. Calfee (Eds.), *Handbook of educational psychology.* Simon & Schuster Macmillian: New York.

RACHEL PILKINGTON AND AISHA WALKER


# USING CMC TO DEVELOP ARGUMENTATION SKILLS IN CHILDRE WITH A 'LITERACY DEFICIT'


## INTRODUCTION

Constructive argumentation is a process of confronting cognitions – it is a process of deliberating between participants' diverse positions and reasons for believing in them (see Andriessen, Baker & Suthers, this volume). This chapter is concerned with how we create learning communities that enable children to express and confront their cognitions. In particular, how we create a climate in which children are encouraged to reason about the evidential support for, and consequences of their beliefs. The chapter will focus on a project aimed at facilitating a learning culture in which children can develop argumentation skills necessary to demonstrate "knowledge transformation" as opposed to "knowledge telling" (Bereiter & Scardamalia, 1987). The work described here forms part of a project in progress at the Chapeltown and Harehills Assisted Learning Computer School (CHALCS) with the wider aim of improving children's literacy.

There are many young people who do not reach their educational potential because of a "literacy deficit", in which reading comprehension and written communication skills lag behind the development of other skills. CHALCS is a community centre with charitable status created to enable such children to study out of school hours. The CHALCS literacy programme achieves good results with young children.

However, some children (in the 13-15 age group) continue to fall further behind. One reason may be that in addition to basic literacy, for older children the curriculum increasingly demands "knowledge transformation" rather than "knowledge telling" (Bereiter & Scardamalia, 1987). Children of this age must learn not only to form and articulate their opinions but also to justify them and to select what is relevant to the context.

This chapter addresses the question of whether synchronous text-based Computer Mediated Communication (CMC) can enhance these students' skills by motivating them to practice constructing such justifications through written debate.

*J. Andriessen, M. Baker, and D. Suthers (eds.), Arguing to Learn: Confronting Cognitions in Computer-Supported Collaborative Learning environments (144-175).*
© *2003 Kluwer Academic Publishers. Printed in the Netherlands*

Recent research has suggested that online synchronous text-based discussion (e.g. Chat) can motivate children to write (Warschauer, 1999). However, if Chat is to help students develop argumentation skills it is first necessary for students to develop a culture of interaction in which constructive debate *is possible*. For this, children first need to learn to focus on the topic to be discussed, to listen to, engage with and respond sociably and constructively to each other's contributions. This makes considerable demands on the attention and concentration of children. These basic collaborative skills may be considered pre-requisite to improving and developing debating skills and, perhaps, some aspects of skilled writing such as: an awareness of audience, the ability to see things from another person's point of view, to put oneself in the place of the reader and to imagine and sustain alternative and contrasting perspectives or "voices".

## THE RESEARCH CONTEXT

The study to be reported here investigates whether using CMC Chat to debate topics (which the children choose) improves the quality of written argumentation within this medium (for children in the 10-15 age group). On-going research will investigate whether there is a commensurate improvement in face-to-face debate and argumentation in individual students' extended written compositions. The context for this research is the Chapeltown and Harehills Assisted Learning Computer School (CHALCS). CHALCS is not a school as such, but a community centre that provides an environment for children to study out of school hours. CHALCS is located in one of the poorest areas of Leeds and aims to combat the high disaffection and low expectation that can further undermine educational goals and the individual achievements of children living in the area (http://www.chalcs.org.uk).

Most students at CHALCS are of African-Caribbean or South Asian ethnic origin. For many students, English is an additional language. The majority of students hear about CHALCS by "word of mouth" but teachers also occasionally refer students to CHALCS. Attendance is voluntary and both paid and volunteer tutors provide tuition. CHALCS provides timetabled classes with formal tuition (not tied to the National Curriculum), and open access sessions. The average CHALCS class contains 14-18 students. The main fields of study are maths, science and IT - primarily for students aged 11-18 years. However, the literacy programme is aimed at children from 8-15 years. Classes take place in the evenings (6-8 p.m.) and on Saturday mornings. There is a separate project in the same building that runs daytime "Exclusion Programmes" for children who are excluded from school; some of these students also sometimes attend the twilight classes. Open access sessions take place between 4-6 p.m. In these sessions pupils come to use the computers for homework or other educational activities.

Computers are integral to the work of CHALCS and computing facilities are provided both in order to enable students to develop the IT skills they need to be competitive in the modern job market but also to enhance student motivation. The centre offers PCs on a Novell network running either Windows 95 or 98. A range of software is available including Microsoft Office; Internet access is also provided.

The CHALCS literacy programme has proved successful with younger children. However, some children may fall behind again later. Their basic skills may limit their confidence when writing essays and so prevent them from "moving on" to develop critical essay writing skills. In designing a new programme (targeted at children aged 10-15 years), the aim was to liberate children from the limitations of their basic skills (spelling and grammar) whilst encouraging them to articulate and justify their opinions in writing. Having built confidence through practice in written debate, it was hoped that newly acquired argumentation skills could be built upon when scaffolding the writing of longer and more formal pieces of non-fictional writing following the Chat programme. Since this case-study was to form a small-scale evaluation of an authentic classroom environment in which the researcher worked with the tutor to support him in the design and delivery of the new programme, an experimental approach was not appropriate. Instead the approach was to study the progress of individual children and the quality of their group interaction through the Chat medium over time.

## RELATED RESEARCH: TOWARD A MODEL OF WRITING PROCESS

*Towards Knowledge Transformation*

Bereiter & Scardamalia (1987) distinguish between "knowledge transformation" and "knowledge telling". Knowledge telling may be defined as the simple disgorging of everything a writer knows about a topic whereas knowledge transformation is the process of converting content into a text that is appropriate to the context and audience, by selecting and justifying relevant material, genre and structures. Bereiter and Scardamalia suggest Knowledge in this context is composed of structural knowledge (of linguistic structures and strategies) and world knowledge (what is known about the subject). When the essay demands a critical discussion rather than a narrative, relevant structural knowledge must include knowledge of what makes a weak or a strong argument and the ability to apply this knowledge when reasoning about the selection and manipulation of content material.

Theories of scaffolding (for example, Bruner 1978; Vygotsky, 1978) suggest that developing writers can learn to solve problems involved in transforming knowledge into text more easily when working with a peer than when working alone. The exposure to the different experiences and approaches of peers may help students to assimilate new writing schemata or accommodate existing ones. Flower (1994) shows how structured collaborative planning of written work can enable students to "construct a robust strategy for being a constructive planner" (p143). Through collaboration, students can also learn to use writing strategies that are more mature than those they are currently able to use on their own. However, Burnett (1993) argues that collaboration in writing is only effective when the co-authors engage in "substantive conflict" rather than consensus. The concept of substantive conflict and its possible relationship to the development of writing is discussed further in section 3.2 below.

*Argument*

When children first start writing at school they are largely expected to write narrative, whether factual or fictional (Andrews, 1995). As their writing develops, they are expected to extend their skills to argumentative writing. However, there is no clear progression from narrative to argument and, as Andrews demonstrates, children (and many adults) often require scaffolding to develop augmentative writing skills. Argumentation is seen as a complex of Speech Acts (Searle, 1969) performed by advancing a series of statements linked to an expressed opinion with the intention of convincing someone of your point of view (Tindale, 1999). The series of statements may be thought of as the premises of argument, and the expressed opinion the conclusion (see e.g. Toulmin, 1958). However to deserve the name argument either the premises or the link between premises and conclusion must be challenged in some way: arguments are oriented towards the resolution of dispute or conflict (Tindale, 1999). The notion that conflict (inconsistency) and argument (rational dialectic as a mechanism for resolving inconsistency) develop our understanding is central to both Piaget's theory of learning and also to attempts by philosophers to define "rules of engagement" or "dialogue games" that facilitate the pursuit of knowledge by eliminating weak arguments. Instances of weak arguments (or fallacies as they are sometimes called) might include those that rely on appeals to authority "it is so because x (or I) say it is so", are circular[1] or question begging.[2] (See e.g. Walton (1984) for a review of dialogue games aimed at avoiding such weak arguments). When asked to debate an issue, children (and many adults) may:

- Advance statements without filtering those statements for relevance to the particular discussion question;
- Repeat statements that have already either been accepted or are currently disputed;
- Advance statements without checking first that they are consistent with their own statements;
- Fail to deny or infer valid conclusions from premises or infer invalid conclusions from them;
- Fail to recognise and/or explicitly challenge such inconsistency;
- Fail to advance statements that are known to support counter-arguments;
- Deny earlier acceptance of a premise when an unwanted conclusion is inferred from it.

For this reason it has been suggested that opportunities to learn the skills of argument "learning to argue" as opposed to "arguing to learn", should be provided within the curriculum. In other words, there should be structured opportunities within the curriculum where the central aim is not to learn about X (the laws of physics, or a turning point in history), but rather, to learn how to argue (see, for example, Veerman, 2000).

Kuhn et al (1997) showed that people were better able to justify their opinions after discussing opposing views with others in pairs. This supports Burnett's findings that collaborative discussion that involves "substantive conflict" improves writing quality. Burnett identifies four types of decision-making:

> "(1) immediate agreement; that is, making an unelaborated decision about a single point, (2) deferring consensus by elaborating a single point, (3) deferring consensus by considering alternatives, which is one kind of substantive conflict, and (4) deferring consensus by voicing explicit disagreement, which is another kind of substantive conflict" (p.134).

Burnett claims that co-authors who engaged in (3) and (4) produced better quality writing than those who did not. However, Burnett also says that (2) can be constructive. It follows from this that simple agreement between co-authors is less likely to produce the type of collaboration that yields good quality writing.

Learning to engage in such processes is not easy. As Schwartz & Glassner (this volume) point out, students don't know how to link natural arguments to beliefs and knowledge. They can also tend to take on board arguments from sources they regard as authoritative without questioning them. However when they do question alternative cognitions, more elaborate arguments are likely to be expressed and these can help to break through entrenched positions (see also Andriessen & Erkens, et al., this volume; Jermann & Dillenbourg, this volume).

Mercer & Wegerif (1999) make a similar distinction to Burnett concerning children's talk. They categorised talk as exploratory, disputational or cumulative, where exploratory talk comes closest to satisfying Burnett's conditions for deferment of consensus. Mercer & Wegerif concluded that practice in engaging in "exploratory talk" improved children's reasoning skills on independent reasoning tests.

An important research question is whether learning to engage in debate-style "substantive conflict", in which students learn to address each other's points by responding to them and reinitiating discussion on them (in ways that move beyond simple disputative forms of dialogue to forms characterised by relatively high levels of inquiring, challenging clarifying and justifying), can lead to an improvement in the quality of argument in other non-interactive individual compositions of written argument. A related point is whether the use of electronic Chat, which shares some characteristics of debate through its synchronous, interactive nature, can form a more effective bridge between media to support such transfer. The longer-term goals of our on-going programme of research also include an examination of the effect of face-to-face discussion on argumentative writing, which may provide some insight into these questions.

However, in order to test whether such effects can be found it is first necessary for students to develop a culture in which constructive debate can take place. For this children need to learn to focus on the topic to be discussed, to discriminate between what is relevant and what is not, to engage with each other's comments – to listen to each other's points of view, reflect upon them and respond to them. This demands focused attention from children. Developing such basic social collaborative skills may be thought of as "pre-requisite" for any programme aimed at improving the quality of debate. In the work presented here we test whether electronic Chat is a suitable medium for developing the necessary collaborative culture and examine any concurrent effect on the quality of children's' written arguments within the Chat medium.

*Computer Mediated Communication Supporting Writing and Argument*

Studies on the use of computers in writing have demonstrated that that their use can reduce writing apprehension and increase fluency (for example: Neu and Scarcella, 1990; Pennington, 1996; Phinney, 1990; Warschauer, 1999). Most of the studies into computers and writing have been carried out using word processing tools. Some studies have, however, made similar claims for synchronous Computer Mediated Communication (e.g. Sullivan & Pratt, 1996; Beauvois, 1997; Warschauer, 1999).

We believe that a synchronous text-based CMC tool such as Chat can provide a rich context for "exploratory talk" and "substantive conflict" (as identified by Mercer & Wegerif, 1999 and Burnett, 1993). When used to practice debate such tools should also lead to an improvement in children's argumentation and reasoning skills as well as the benefits to writing identified by Pennington and others.

Another claim made for CMC is that it enables people to participate more equally in a discussion (Sullivan and Pratt, 1996; Warschauer, 1996). In particular, Warschauer (1996) compared face-to-face and electronic discussion with racially mixed groups and found that ethnicity was a factor in limiting a student's face-to-face participation but did not restrict participation in CMC. In a mixed group such as a CHALCS class, this could be very beneficial.

## FRAMEWORK FOR THE LITERACY PROGRAMME

The CHALCS literacy programme was designed to target 10-15 year olds, as that is the group that appears to benefit least from existing provision. Following the hypothesis that online synchronous text-based discussion and computer-assisted writing will provide effective scaffolding of non-fictional writing, the new programme, called Discussion and Reporting Electronically (DaRE) is following a writing process model (as described by Flower and Hayes, 1981) that consists of the following phases:
- Group-based brain-storming of content ideas;
- Focused document structure planning; individual and group composition;
- Individual and group reflection on the process and product of writing;
- Synthesis of group ideas and the integration of critical feedback;
- Presentation of work to an identified audience.

Within DaRE these phases are incorporated into the following elements:

- Generation of topic themes via an asynchronous bulletin board;
- Synchronous text-based discussion of a topic;
- Collaborative planning and writing of a summary report;
- Presentation of the report to the group;
- Receiving critical feedback from tutor and peers through an online bulletin board;
- Collaborative compilation of the discussion summaries into a class 'webzine' to be published on the CHALCS public web site for other CHALCS pupils, parents and friends of the project to read.

## PILOT STUDY

The study reported here concentrates on the results of phase 1 – synchronous text-based discussion of topics. The literature reviewed above suggests that regular use of text-based synchronous Computer Mediated Communication for debate might reasonably be expected to lead to:

- An increased fluency and ability to express on-topic opinions in writing (e.g. Phinney, 1990; Pennington, 1996);
- An enhanced awareness of context including greater awareness of what is relevant and what is irrelevant (Veerman, 2000);
- A greater willingness to listen to others including responding to the points made by others (e.g. Warschauer, 1999);
- An increased ability to develop and support arguments (in similar ways as described by Burnett, 1993; Kuhn et al, 1997; Veerman, 2000);
- A greater willingness to include and affirm others (e.g. Sullivan and Pratt, 1996).

Therefore a small-scale study was devised to test the value of synchronous CMC tools within the DaRE context in order to determine the extent to which such benefits accrue within the quality of transcripts over time. The study used a synchronous bulletin board to start and conclude the discussions with the main debate being conducted through the medium of synchronous online Chat.

*Method*

*Materials*

The classroom is arranged with the computers in a double horseshoe formation with the teacher's computer at the head of the class. Figure 1 shows the layout of the CHALCS classroom. WebCT®, a web-based virtual learning environment, has been installed at CHALCS. WebCT combines a range of tools for managing courses and course materials including the facility to display and link lecture notes; a student project presentation area; e-mail; bulletin boards and Chat, although for this study only the Chat and bulletin board features were used. These are illustrated in figures 2 and 3.

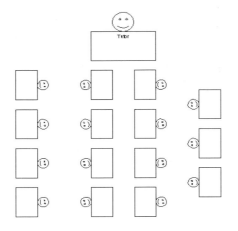

*Figure 1. The CHALCS classroom.*

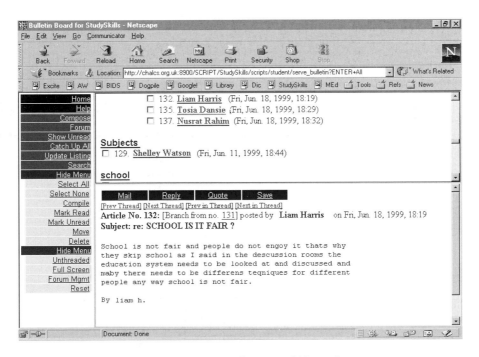

*Figure 2. The Bulletin Board 'Starter'.*

*Procedure*

Each class lasted for two hours and was led by a tutor from the CHALCS literacy team. In the early weeks of the study, a researcher was also present.

Although the intention of the researcher was to make observations, in practice the children needed considerable support with managing the technology. Occasionally the researcher also joined the discussions, taking the role of a second tutor. The first part of the session (usually one hour but occasionally longer) was given to the study tasks. The teacher posted the discussion topic to the bulletin board (see figure 2) before the start of the session. Topics were drawn from the children's suggestions based on the work of the previous week. The children read the posted question and used the Chat rooms to discuss the topic (see figure 3). At the end of the session each child composed and posted a reply to the bulletin board.

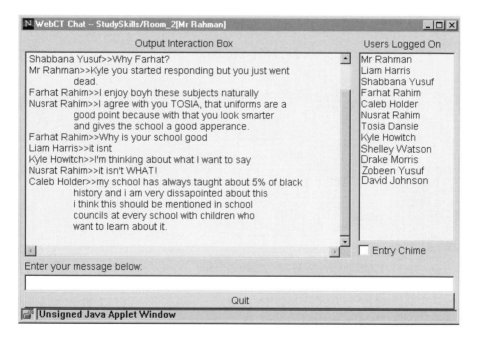

*Figure 3. The Chat Tool in Use.*

After the session, the tutor read the Chat logs and bulletin board postings before formulating a new discussion topic. The remainder of the class was used for other activities, which were not part of the study, such as reading comprehension, homework and practice for Key Stage 3 Assessments. These types of activity would have filled the entire session had the CMC discussions not been introduced.

Figures 3 illustrate the Chat tool in use. Please note that in these figures, and in all the Chat examples in subsequent tables, the children's names have been changed in order to maintain anonymity. Nineteen children took part: Tables 1 and 2 show the composition of the group.

The children were drawn from eleven local schools with one child who had been permanently excluded from school. There were 12 logged Chat sessions in all. Of these, six sessions (three from before mid-term and three from after mid-term) were taken for analysis.

*Table 1: Children in the study cohort by sex and ethnic group.*

|                    | Girls | Boys |
|--------------------|-------|------|
| **Asian (Pakistani)** | 5     | -    |
| **West Indian**    | 4     | 5    |
| **African**        | 1     | -    |
| **Arabic**         | -     | 1    |
| **Arab/Asian**     | -     | 1    |
| **African/White**  | -     | 1    |
| **White**          | 1     | -    |
| **Total**          | 11    | 8    |

*Table 2: Ages of the children in the study cohort.*

| School year (age) | Number of children |
|-------------------|--------------------|
| **6 (10-11)**     | 1                  |
| **7 (11-12)**     | 4                  |
| **8 (12-13)**     | 6                  |
| **9 (13-14)**     | 7                  |
| **10 (14-15)**    | 1                  |

*Results – Overall Impressions*

This section presents some general impressions based on frequency count data. Six of the twelve Chat sessions were analysed. These six sessions are felt to be representative - half the total number of Chat sessions were analysed and they are selected at roughly equal intervals throughout the programme. Data are presented on the number of words, turns, turns on-task, and the number of turns containing reason moves for these six sessions (Walker & Pilkington, 2001). This is supplemented by a more detailed look at just the first and last of the sessions based on applying the

DISCOUNT scheme's (Pilkington, 1999) Exchange Structure Analysis and Move analysis. In the first session only, participants split into two sub-groups in two different Chat rooms instead of staying in one Chat room. Where tables include data relating to session one the two sub-groups are shown as group 1 and group 2. In all subsequent sessions children used the same Chat room. Tables 6-9 show the number of reasoning moves in relation to the numbers of other kinds of move for the first and last Chat sessions. Impressions gained from these analyses are discussed more closely in section 5.4, which looks qualitatively at data from the six analysed sessions and provides illustrations of the dialogue. Examples illustrating the coding of turns (for Exchange Structure, Moves and whether on or off task) are given in the appendix.

*Increasing Fluency and Ability to Express Opinions*

Table 3 suggests that children's turns increased in length and complexity during the study programme (see also Walker and Pilkington, 2001). However, although the number of words increased over time, there was a trend towards fewer longer and more thoughtful turns. The table also suggests children became more focused on the task over time with a shift towards fewer off-task turns. The topics chosen by the children also change over time.

*Table 3. Overall Results: Increasing fluency, complexity, and ability to discriminate what is relevant*

|  | Topic | Words | Turns | Mean turn length | Turns on task |
|---|---|---|---|---|---|
| 30th April | Aliens | 2021 | 373 | 5.42 | 25.2% |
| 7th May | Pop Music | 1880 | 323 | 5.82 | 44.0% |
| 14th May | TV | 831 | 219 | 3.79 | 78.0% |
| 18th June | Is School Fair? | 1127 | 76 | 14.83 | 78.9% |
| 2nd July | Women in Sport | 883 | 75 | 11.77 | 93.3% |
| 9th July | Family Roles | 1549 | 187 | 8.28 | 80.7% |

In later sessions the topics are more likely to prompt an interesting debate. Taken together these results seem to suggest an increased awareness of appropriate content and audience. However, in order to see if this is the case a more detailed look at changes in contributions over time is necessary. In the early sessions, there were more turns in a discussion but the turns were significantly shorter than in later weeks. On 30th April only 6.9% of turns were more than 10 words long including only 0.5% more than 20 words long. By 9th July, 23% contained more than 10 words with 10.6% more than 20 words long. The analysis of moves (speech acts) per turn (see section 5.2.4) further supports this view that the number of moves per turn increased. As students' turns became more complex they became longer and tended to consist of more than one move per turn.

*Increasing Awareness of Context and Relevance*

Accompanied by the changes described above, a more striking change was taking place in the degree to which the children focused on the topic or question to be debated. Turns were designated on task, off task or social/organising (relating to managing the dialogue and its participants).

*Table 4. Turns on-topic, comparing the first and last Chat sessions.*

| First Session, 30th April, Aliens: Turns on task by Group | | | | | |
|---|---|---|---|---|---|
| | **Disruptive** | **Off task** | **On task** | **Social/ Organising** | **Total** |
| **Group 1** | 51 | 18 | 30 | 42 | 141 |
| **% of total** | 36.2 | 12.8 | 21.3 | 29.8 | - |
| **Group 2** | 40 | 22 | 64 | 112 | 238 |
| **% of total** | 16.8 | 9.2 | 26.9 | 47.1 | - |
| | | | | | |
| **Total 1 & 2** | 91 | 40 | 94 | 154 | 379 |
| **% of total** | 24 | 10.6 | 24.8 | 40.6 | - |
| **Last Session, 9th July, Family Roles: Turns on task** | | | | | |
| | **Disruptive** | **Off task** | **On task** | **Social/ Organising** | **Total** |
| | 2 | 0 | 151 | 47 | 200 |
| | | | | | |
| **% of total** | 1 | - | 75.5 | 23.5 | - |

Turns were marked disruptive if they were judged to be very distracting or involved behaviour such as insulting another participant. (Marked up examples are illustrated in the appendix.) From Table 4 it can be seen that there was a marked decrease in the amount of disruptive and off-task behaviour between the first and last session. Group 1 in session 1 showed a particularly high instance of trading insults as a form of social interaction. This behaviour had declined to near zero by the last session. This was accompanied by a large increase in on-topic talk – an increase from around ¼ to ¾ of the dialogue turns. Some of this increase resulted from a decrease in the need for students to try to regulate the participation of other students – indicated by a decrease in the number of social and organising turns. Thus, over time, students were less likely to need to ask each other to "shut up", remind each other to talk about the topic, or ask each other to respond to what they had previously said. This analysis is supported by the more detailed move (speech act) analysis presented in section 5.2.4 and in the qualitative discussion of results (section 5.3). This increase in "focus on task" may be seen as indicative of "having a more interesting debate", certainly of being more engaged in the debate and this may relate to the children's choice of topic – children tended to propose topics that had greater potential for rich debate later in the programme. This may itself reflect development of structural knowledge or "learning what makes an interesting topic for debate".

*Addressing the Points of Others – Exchange Structure Analysis*

The first session (30th April – Aliens) and the last session (9th July – Family Roles) were analysed in more detail using the DISCOUNT scheme (Pilkington, 1999).

*Table 5. Exchange Structure Analysis of first and last Chat Sessions showing extent of participant'.*

| First Session, 30th April, Aliens: Exchange Roles by Group | | | | |
|---|---|---|---|---|
| | **(I)** | **(R)** | **(RI)** | **(R->I)** |
| **Group 1** | 87 | 41 | 9 | 2 |
| % of total | 62.6 | 29.5 | 6.5 | 1.4 |
| | | | | |
| **Group 2** | 126 | 69 | 33 | 2 |
| % of total | 54.8 | 30 | 14.3 | 0.87 |
| | | | | |
| **Total 1 & 2** | 213 | 110 | 42 | 4 |
| % of total | 57.7 | 29.8 | 11.4 | 1.1 |
| Last Session, 9th July, Family Roles: Exchange Roles | | | | |
| | I | R | RI | R->I |
| **Total** | **86** | 76 | 33 | 0 |
| % of total | **44.1** | 39 | 16.9 | - |

Two levels of the DISCOUNT analysis scheme were used: Exchange Structure Analysis (ESA) and move analysis. The results of the ESA analysis are reported here whilst the results of the move analysis are discussed in section 5.2.4. ESA compares the rate of Initiating (I) with Responding (R) and Reinitiating (RI). Reinitiating involves not providing an expected responding turn but instead producing a new turn within the same exchange that requires resolution before the previous exchange can be closed. The most usual instance of this is when seeking clarification or when challenging the previous turn. This is distinguished from Responding (closing a previous exchange) and then Initiating (beginning a new exchange) within the same turn. The latter is called role swapping as it serves to change who holds the initiative in dialogue from one participant to the other (marked R->I).

In the first session only (as explained earlier) participants used two different Chat rooms instead of one Chat room. This is shown as group 1 and group 2 for session one but in both groups there was a relatively high rate of initiating compared with responding and reinitiating. Particularly, in group 1, turns did not tend to involve the challenges and clarifications typical of reinitiating. Overall this pattern suggests dialogue that is only loosely coherent in the sense of participants engaging with each other's points and a dialogue low in substantive conflict. Overall, early dialogue was characterised by individuals stating their opinions rather than responding to those of others. The dialogue in the last session shows a relative improvement with a better balance between initiating and responding turns and with higher levels of reinitiating. The move analysis presented in section 5.2.4 further supports this impression.

*Developing and Supporting Arguments*

The analysis of moves (speech acts) per turn (total number of moves in the dialogue session divided by the total number of turns in the dialogue session) indicated an increase from 1.1 moves per turn on 30th April to 1.6 moves per turn by 9th July. It seems that as students' turns became longer they tended to consist of more than one move per turn. This appears to be due to an increase in the number of reasons supporting opinions since the proportion of these types of moves tended to increase whilst the proportion of other kinds of move tended to decrease or stay about the same (though there was a much more modest increase in justifications than in reasons). Types of reasoning move include reasons offered to support a statement within an initiating turn (Reason in Table 6), and reasons offered in response to a challenge by way of justification (Justify in Table 6). The combined total for informative, comparative and narrative moves was 3 times the total of justifications and reasons on 30th April but only 1 ½ times that of justifications and reasons on 9th July. This indicates that many more agreements and disagreements were supported with reasons than had been previously.

*Table 6. Comparison of reasoning and justification moves for first and last Chat.*

| First Session, 30th April, Aliens: Reasoning Moves by Group | | |
|---|---|---|
|  | **Justify** | **Reason** |
| **Group 1** | 1 | 0 |
| **% moves 1** | 0.7 | - |
| **Group 2** | 4 | 7 |
| **% moves 2** | 1.5 | 2.6 |
|  |  |  |
| **Total 1 & 2** | 5 | 7 |
| **% of total** | 1.2 | 1.7 |
| **Last Session, 9th July, Family Roles: Reasoning Moves** | | |
|  | 7 | 38 |
| **% moves** | 2.4 | 13.1 |

Table 7. Comparison statement moves for first and last Chat.

| First Session, 30th April, Aliens: Statement Moves by Group | | | | |
|---|---|---|---|---|
| | Agree | Disagree & No-commitment | Inform & Compare | Narrate |
| Group 1 | 7 | 3 | 49 | 4 |
| % moves 1 | 5.0 | 2.2 | 35.3 | 2.9 |
| Group 2 | 12 | 18 | 45 | 0 |
| % moves 2 | 4.4 | 6.6 | 16.5 | - |
| | | | | |
| Total 1 & 2 | 19 | 21 | 94 | 4 |
| % of total | 4.6 | 5.1 | 22.8 | 1.0 |
| Last Session, 9th July, Family Roles: Statement Moves | | | | |
| | 30 | 16 | 73 | 0 |
| % moves | 10.3 | 5.5 | 25.2 | - |

Table 8. Comparison of questioning moves for first and last Chat.

| First Session, 30th April, Aliens: Questioning Moves by Group | | | | |
|---|---|---|---|---|
| | Challenge | Clarify | Explore (What if?) | Inquire/Request |
| Group 1 | 9 | 0 | 0 | 19 |
| % moves 1 | 6.5 | - | - | 13.7 |
| Group 2 | 27 | 2 | 2 | 42 |
| % moves 2 | 9.9 | 0.7 | 0.7 | 15.4 |
| | | | | |
| Total 1 & 2 | 36 | 2 | 2 | 61 |
| % of total | 8.7 | 0.5 | 0.5 | 14.8 |
| Last Session, 9th July, Family Roles: Questioning Moves | | | | |
| | 21 | 9 | 1 | 31 |
| % moves | 7.2 | 3.1 | 0.3 | 10.7 |

Table 7 shows that the number of informative statements stayed about the same though the number of agreements increased whilst the number of disagreements did not. This difference is probably accounted for by changes in behaviour towards more affirming and encouraging remarks (including telling others when you agree with their position). On-task disagreements may have increased but are likely to have been compensated for by a fall in off-task and disruptive disagreements.

Overall there was no increase in the amount of questioning indicated in Table 8, particularly the types of questioning indicative of substantive conflict. There was a moderate increase in the proportion of clarification questions but the number of challenges (principally 'why?' type questions which ask for justification) was not higher in the last session. This can probably be accounted for by a large fall in off-topic and disruptive challenges, counteracted incompletely by an increase in on-topic challenging. On 30th April the combined total of off-topic disruptive or social challenges was twice that of on-topic challenges whilst on 9th July all the challenges were on-topic.

*Creating an Inclusive and Safe Learning Culture*

That conflict was not substantially reduced over time but rather changed from less productive and supportive types of off-topic challenging to more productive on-topic challenging is further supported by evidence of a fall in the number of moves in the categories "instruct", "feedback" (principally negative feedback) and "meta & nominates" (moves about the dialogue itself and turns directed at an individual child). See Table 9. As children became more focused on the discussion they had less need to remind each other to talk about the topic. This is consistent with an improvement in willingness to listen to each other's points of view.

In general it seems that the discussion became "safer" and more "affirming" for children to take part in over time as the amount of disruptive behaviour and negative feedback decreased whilst positive feedback increased. According to Tuckman's (1965) developmental sequence of group development, we would expect to see this happen as the group moved from the 'storming' to 'performing' phases. However, to see if this is really the case, it is necessary to look at the content of these moves in context and this is explored further in the next section.

*Table 9. Comparison of organising moves for first and last Chat.*

| First Session, 30th April, Aliens, Organising Moves by Group | | | | | |
|---|---|---|---|---|---|
| | Instruct/ Suggest | Meta & Nominates | Close | Open | Feedback |
| **Group 1** | 18 | 16 | 6 | 7 | 0 |
| **% moves 1** | 12.9 | 11.5 | 4.3 | 5.0 | - |
| **Group 2** | 29 | 47 | 3 | 20 | 15 |
| **% moves 2** | 10.62 | 17.2 | 1.1 | 7.3 | 5.5 |
| | | | | | |
| **Total 1& 2** | 47 | 63 | 9 | 27 | 15 |
| **% of total** | 11.4 | 15.3 | 2.2 | 6.6 | 3.6 |
| Last Session, 9th July, Family Roles: Organising Moves | | | | | |
| | 10 | 30 | 2 | 10 | 12 |
| **% moves 6** | 3.4 | 10.3 | 0.7 | 3.4 | 4.1 |

The fall in the number of opening and closing moves shown in Table 10 is an artefact of children swapping between groups in session one. In the last session (as in all other sessions bar the first session) children entered one room and tended to stay there giving approx. one opening "Hi!" and one closing "Bye" move per child as they entered or left the Chat.

*Table 10. Simple agreement and disagreement from 30/4*

| 16 | Paula | I think that there is no such thing as aliens, Sahmeena |
|----|-------|----------------------------------------------------------|
| 17 | Farhat | same here |
| 18 | Farhat | whats up with you nusrat |
| 19 | Sahmeena | Puala- I think they do |
| 20 | Farhat | both the sisters have the same view |
| 21 | Paula | Well I don't think so |

*Qualitative Discussion of Results*

*Increasing Fluency and Ability to Express Opinions*

Over time on-task contributions became longer, more complex and more articulate in expressing a point of view. Thus, Table 10 illustrates that in the first session many turns involved only a few words and often tended to involve simple agreement and disagreement. By the last session, multi-sentential on-topic turns like those in Table 11 were much more common.

*Table 11. More complex and articulate expression of opinions from 9/7.*

| 37 | Sahmeena | Some religions says that the farther has to work and the mother look after the house and children. But some mothers work as well. |
|----|----------|----------------------------------------------------------------------------------------------------------------------------------|
| 38 | David | I think that in the home the jobs between men and women should be equal, because I think that for too many years in the past not enough work has been done by men in the house, and also recently there has been quite alot of programmes on televison about househusbands. I also definitely disagree with Shabbana |

*Discriminating What is Relevant - Topic Selection and Focus*

In the earliest session, there were many more off-task turns. In the example in Table 12 (which continues the dialogue in Table 10), the children are not seriously addressing the question and seem more interested in social banter.

*Table 12. Poorly Focused Discussion from 30/4.*

|      | Sahmeena | Puala I may have seen one[3] ....you |
|------|----------|--------------------------------------|
| 22.  | Paula    | You must be joking                   |
| 23.  | Sahmeena | Puala I'm not joking                 |
| 24.  | Paula    | Whatever                             |
| 25.  | Paula    | Sahmeena you must be mental          |

*Table 13. More highly focused discussion from 9/7.*

| 12 | Sahmeena | The question that has to be answered is 'who should look after the family'? What do you think faz? |
|----|----------|---------------------------------------------------------------------------------------------------|
| 13 | Liam     | the babiesitter                                                                                   |
| 14 | Farhat   | both mother and father should look after the family                                               |
| 15 | Shabbana | No Zobeen because our mum works and so does our dad. Also everone does the house work in the house not only mum |
| 16 | Mustafa  | hello                                                                                             |
| 17 | Sahmeena | I think both the parents hold the responsibility of organising the house.                         |
| 18 | Zobeen   | Liam what if there are no babysitters???                                                          |
| 19 | Farhat   | thats true shabbana                                                                               |

In contrast by 9th July (Table 13) the children are giving the topic much more focused attention. There is also a marked difference in the nature of off-task turns when the early and later sessions are compared. In the early sessions, prolonged off-task exchanges are commonplace. The content of the exchange in Table 14 has no relevance to the topic (aliens). In the later sessions, however, off-task exchanges like this are rare.

*Table 14. Typical off-task exchange on 30/4.*

| 29 | Jabir  | SO YOU THINK YOU ARE A RICK MAN                    |
|----|--------|----------------------------------------------------|
| 30 | Elodie | drake your sad MAN!                                 |
| 31 | Drake  | Nuff respect to DMX Ruff Ryders                    |
| 32 | Tosia  | What the heck is a rick man                         |
| 33 | Drake  | Wobble Wobble                                       |
| 34 | Elodie | easi drake ruff ryders are RUFF. p.s your lip drake |

*Addressing the Points Made by Others – Being Prepared to Listen*

In earlier sessions much of the dialogue tended to consist of individuals talking without engaging with each other, see Table 15.

*Table 15. Each individual initiating without responding to each other. 30/4.*

| 26. | Paula | Planet Earth what about you |
|-----|-------|------------------------------|
| 27. | Shabbana | NUSRAT TALK |
| 28. | Paula | what happend to Nusrat |
| 29. | Shabbana | WHAT DO YOU THINK PAULA |
| 30. | Paula | Get lost shel |
| 31. | Zobeen | Farhat talk |
| 32. | Shabbana | HI ZOBEEN# |
| 33. | Sahmeena | EARTH CALLING PUALA ANYONE HOME? |
| 34. | Zobeen | Hi Shabbana can YOU talk to me? |
| 35. | Shabbana | ZOBEEN ZEENAT LOVES YOU# |

*Table 16. Each individual addressing each other. (9/7).*

| 42 | Shabbana | no if you are referring to Islam that is not true because mums and dads bothe should have the right to work |
|----|----------|-------------------------------------------------------------------------------------------------------------|
| 43 | Mustafa | I agreeyes |
| 44 | Liam | why did Islam come into it |
| 45 | Mustafa | because it did |
| 46 | Liam | why though |
| 47 | Shabbana | because it did Liam |
| 48 | Drake | because it did |
| 49 | Sahmeena | Becuse In that religion the farther has to work |
| 50 | Liam | yes but why |
| 51 | Mustafa | because it came up |
| 52 | Liam | what |
| 53 | David | Why |
| 54 | Zobeen | Religion is religion Liam! |

In later sessions participants responded directly to each other and challenged each other as the discussion became more focused and more on-topic. Although, as the example in Table 16 shows, it does not follow that the children are adept at providing non-circular justifications in response to such challenges.

*Developing and Supporting Argument - Towards a more Reasoned Debate*

In addition to evidence that children acquired the prerequisites for reasoned debate, such as being able to focus on the topic, address each other's contributions and avoid disruptive and offensive behaviour, there was also evidence that over time children produced stronger arguments. As the example in Table 16 illustrates, over time children learnt to challenge repetitive statements (though this could still be circular). In Table 16 Liam repeatedly challenges repetitive statements and, although not receiving a completely satisfactory explanation in the end nevertheless his persistent challenging is rewarded with two alternative statements "because in that religion the father has to work" and (finally) a link back to Sahmeena's original statement to which this extract refers (see Sahmeena in Table 11). Thus, Zobeen's last comment "religion is religion!" presumably means something like 'it came up because Islam is an example of a religion and Sahmeena mentioned some religions'.

The ability to generate challenges thus represents progress towards substantive conflict and (potentially) ultimately towards knowledge transformation. Note: it does not follow from evidence of constructive argument in written Chat debate that individual children writing on their own outside the Chat situation will show evidence of constructive argumentative writing. However, it is argued that engaging constructively with the points of others through the production of justifications in response to challenges is evidence of a progression towards an awareness of audience and the selection and manipulation of knowledge to "persuade" that audience through writing. Challenging others viewpoints was also evident in Table 13 this time Shabbana uses a 'disagree' move ("No Zobeen...") followed by a 'justify' move ("because our Mum works and so does our Dad"). Later, Zobeen uses a 'what if' style 'explore' question to expose the limitations of Liam's solution (to get a baby-sitter).

*Table 17. On topic but not advancing the debate (30/4.)*

| 11 | Drake | I would stab it,shoot it, blow it up, and then bun a big fat juicy spliff |
|----|-------|------------------------------------------------------------------------|

*Table 18. Justifying and reasoning on-topic (9/7).*

| 85 | Drake | Not always in some families the feminine gender works and the father sstays home and works! |
|----|-------|---------------------------------------------------------------------------------------------|

| 184 | Drake | Men and women should be treated equally because it takes them both to make a waaaaaaaa! |
|-----|-------|----------------------------------------------------------------------------------------|

As already illustrated in Table 14, Drake could be particularly disruptive in earlier sessions. In Table 17, Drake (30th April) is describing what he would do if he met an alien. Although he is technically on-task, his creative/narrative remark is not appropriate for a debate. In Table 18 on the other hand, Drake both responds and initiates in the discussion with two contributions that show that he has thought about what other people have said, can evaluate their comments and can put forward reasoned opinions.

*Table 19. Unelaborated opinion (30/4)*

| 206 | Shabbana | OF COURSE ALIENS EXIST |
|-----|----------|------------------------|

*Table 20. Elaborated opinion on (7/9)*

| 188 | Shabbana | Men and women all have equal rights to anything done in a family house - hold. People say that a father is the head of the house but to me I think that the person who wrote that is not clever. This is because I feel that anyones mum and dad is the head of the house. I feel that mums and dads and children shoulld all become a team and do all the house work together. Not just the mum doing all the work. |
|-----|----------|---|

A similar development can be seen in Shabbana's contributions on 30th April and 9th July (Table 19 and Table 20). In the earlier session Shabbana expresses an opinion but gives no further elaboration, when asked 'why?' she replies that she doesn't know. Her contribution on 9th July on the other hand is well elaborated; she explains the context of her opinion and shows willingness to argue even if the reasons why she holds this particular position are not fully articulated.

Zobeen found it difficult to justify her opinions in the first week of the programme as Table 21 demonstrates. As can be seen from the turn numbers in the left hand column this thread of the conversation was distributed over a much longer section of dialogue in which a lot of distracting off-topic talk was also taking place.

Sahmeena and Farhat are quite persistent in trying to get Zobeen to support her opinion. Eventually she states that the evidence for aliens is faked but finds it difficult to substantiate this view and she includes circular arguments – simple repetition of her already stated position. This is contrasted with her turns in the last session where although the number of her turns is fewer the turns she produces provide comparative statements to support her argument concerning inequality (see Table 22).

*Table 21. Zobeens reasoned opinions (30/4).*

| 188 | Sahmeena | ZObeen - Well if you think aliens do'nt exist YOU tell me why? |
|-----|----------|---------------------------------------------------------------|
| 190 | Zobeen   | Its hard to explain Sahmeena                                  |
| 192 | Sahmeena | Zobeen try to explain                                         |
| 205 | Sahmeena | Zobeen I'm asking for an explation- Why do'nt you belevie in aliens |
| 214 | Zobeen   | The evidence is made up Sahmeena                              |
| 216 | Farhat   | HOW DO YOU KNOW THE EVIDENCE IS NOT FAKE?                     |
| 220 | Zobeen   | Because Farhat I KNOW!                                        |
| 225 | Zobeen   | They are fake Sam                                             |
| 230 | Zobeen   | Aliens aren't true                                           |
| 233 | Zobeen   | They aren't true                                             |
| 235 | Zobeen   | You belive in SPACESHIPS sahmeena                             |
| 236 | Zobeen   | I ts FAKE                                                     |

*Table 22. Zobeens reasoned opinions (9/7).*

| 8   | Zobeen | The father of the house earns money along with the mother. The mothers in some familys work and do housework! |
|-----|--------|---------------------------------------------------------------------------------------------------------------|
| 95  | Zobeen | Women stay at home for their children but some fathers, its always this and that at work!                      |
| 170 | Zobeen | Mostapha if you think it is alright for both the mother and father to work in the house, then shouldn't you spare a thought on how the mother isn't told but she still gives her full attention to the child? |
| 192 | Zobeen | It is also quite unfair on the women that in some cases, have the responsibility of ALL the housework! That is TIGHT! |

*Changes in Attitude - Becoming More Constructive and Less Destructive*

Before the programme the tutor rated Drake as unmotivated and childish in class. Afterwards the tutor remarked on the apparent increase in maturity. In the early weeks Drake's behaviour in the discussions rarely advanced the debate and could be destructive, even offensive. In the later sessions, however, Drake's behaviour was generally much more constructive.

*Table 23. Consecutive disruptive/offensive turns on 30/4.*

| 75 | Drake | Liam has only got a Barbie Doll |
|----|-------|--------------------------------|
| 76 | Drake | With a hole |

| 80 | Drake | I'll do to you what they did to JFK JABIR |
|----|-------|-------------------------------------------|

*Table 24. Socially constructive turn on 2/7.*

| 25 | Drake | Sahmeena talk to everybody else not just Faz! |
|----|-------|-----------------------------------------------|

*Table 25. disruptive/offensive turns 30/4.*

| 41 | Sahmeena | Puala I'll talk to you, you loner |
|----|----------|-----------------------------------|
| 42 | Zobeen | Paula I guess you want someone to talk to! |
| 49 | Paula | I'm not a loner infact everyone is talking to me |

| 57 | Paula | If enybody talks to Sahmeena I'm going to beat them up really badly |
|----|-------|--------------------------------------------------------------------|

Table 18 also shows that in later sessions when Drake made joky contributions e.g. "Men and women should be treated equally because it takes them both to make a waaaaaaaa!" they were within the framework of the debate and contributed to the discussion. However, it was not just the boys who could be aggressive in early sessions, 'the girls' produced some disruptive behaviour too, as table 25 illustrates.

*Inclusiveness of Discussion*

One of the striking features of the online debates in the first week was the way children divided themselves into two different Chat rooms. One group tended to consist of boys with the Black and White girls whilst the other group tended to contain girls, mainly Asian. The girls, especially Farhat, Sahmeena, Zobeen and

Shabbana (these four children share a family relationship) seemed quite possessive of their 'space'.

*Table 26. Examples of 'exclusive' communication from 18/6.*

| 119 | Shabbana | FARHAT 2 SISTERS ARE TALKING DON'T BUT IN |
| 120 | Zobeen | Well you talk to us |
| 121 | Farhat | IT IS OKAY THAT MY STYLE |
| 122 | Sahmeena | FARHAT WAKE UP CALL WERE TALKING ABOUT ALIENS NOT JUST SAYING 'HI' |
| 123 | Paula | What do you want to talk about shel |
| 124 | Shelley | anything |
| 125 | Zobeen | Nusrat who are you talking to |
| 126 | Shabbana | PAULA SHUT UP |

*Table 27. Frustration at non-inclusive talk from 9/7.*

| 21 | Farhat | I agree sahmeena |
| 22 | Shabbana | thank you Faz |
| 23 | Mustafa | yougetone |
| 24 | Farhat | anytime |
| 25 | Drake | Sahmeena talk to everybody else not just Faz! |
| 26 | Liam | yes |
| 27 | Mustafa | yes |
| 28 | Zobeen | yes |
| 29 | Mustafa | yes |

For example, in Tables 26 and 27, they talk mainly to each other and can appear to exclude others. Table 27 shows that this could at times frustrate some of the children. Nevertheless, in the later sessions, there are also far more examples of 'inclusive' talk, where children respond to each other, either commenting on opinions or asking each other's views, see Table 28.

*Table 27. More inclusive talk from 9/7.*

| 57 | Aliza | Mostafa do you think that men and women should do things equal |
| 58 | Mustafa | you can say that again |

| 66 | Aliza | tosia I agree |
| 67 | Mustafa | I don't. Women should be at home for the men |

| 92 | Tosia | I partly agree with Shelley… |

*Affirming and Encouraging Others*

As the discussion programme progressed the children appeared to have greater respect for other people and their opinions. In the earlier sessions the children tended to berate each other or ignore each other's contributions if they did not agree with them (see for example Paula Table 12 "Sahmeena you must be mental"). In the later sessions, as the primary mode of discussion was debate and not banter, disagreement seemed to occur less often, but when it did happen was more likely to be expressed explicitly and with a considered challenge to the other person's statement.

On 9th July Mustafa remarked, "Women should be at home for the men". As Table 29 shows, this provoked considerable disagreement. However, there are no unreasoned insults such as those that appeared in earlier sessions. Instead the children produce a variety of arguments - mainly functional arguments as classified by Kuhn et al., op cit. (see also Walker and Pilkington, 2001).

*Table 29: Disagreement 9/7.*

| 78 | Tosia | Mustafa is living in the past. Things have changed Mustafa. Wake Up!!! |
|---|---|---|
| 88 | Liam | womenand men should be equal and should not be (at home waiting for the man) as Mustafa said |
| 101 | David | Mustafa do you intend to have a job and a wife when you're older or are you going to carry on being sexist? |
| 128 | David | Mustafa do you live in the kind of family you are advertising "Where the women cleans the house and the man goes out to work". |

*Table 30. Social/organisational intervention with negative feedback (30/4).*

| 112 | Farhat | BABY ZOBEEN |
|---|---|---|
| 113 | Shabbana | I HATE YOU TO ZOBEEN |
| 114 | Farhat | BABY ZOBEEN |
| 115 | Zobeen | Thanks Farhat! |
| 116 | Farhat | BIG BABY SHABBANA |
| 117 | Zobeen | Thats good Farhat! |
| 118 | Paula | Shut up shabbana and zobeen you are giving me a headache |

As the debate became more focused and on-topic the need to give others negative feedback and/or the need for explicit attempts to manage the contributions of others decreased. In Table 30 Paula intervenes to stop the others from continuing to banter.

In contrast by the last session (Table 31) there were several examples of positive feedback and explicit validation.

*Table 31. Positive feedback (9/7).*

| 19 | Farhat | thats true shabbana |
|----|--------|---------------------|
| 22 | Shabbana | thank you Faz |

| 189 | Sahmeena | good point shabanna |
|-----|----------|---------------------|

*Summary of Results*

Children's turns in the Chat were found to increase in length and complexity during the study programme. However, although the number of words increased over time, there was a trend towards fewer longer turns. As students' turns became more complex they became longer and tended to consist of more than one move per turn.

There was a marked decrease in the amount of disruptive and off-task behaviour between early and late sessions. Group 1 in session 1 showed a particularly high instance of trading insults as a form of social interaction. This behaviour had declined to near zero by the last session. This was accompanied by a large increase in on-topic talk.

The large fall in off-topic and disruptive challenges appeared to be counteracted incompletely by an increase in on-topic challenging. In the first session the combined total of off-topic disruptive or social challenges was twice that of on-topic challenges whilst in the last session all the challenges were on-topic. This suggests a shift from disputive talk towards more exploratory forms of argument indicative of Burnett's "substantive conflict". This is further supported by an increase in the number of reasons and justifications offered from the first to the last session. Many more agreements and disagreements were supported with reasons than was the case previously.

The exchange analysis showed a relatively high rate of initiating compared with responding and reinitiating in the first session. Turns did not tend to involve the challenges and clarifications typical of reinitiating. Overall this pattern suggested early dialogue was characterised by individuals stating their opinions rather than responding to those of others, creating a dialogue that was only loosely coherent. The dialogue in the last session showed a better balance between initiating and responding turns with higher levels of reinitiating. In addition it seems that the discussion became "safer" and more "affirming" for children to take part in as the amount of disruptive behaviour and negative feedback decreased whilst positive feedback increased.

*Discussion of Results*

This chapter focused on a project aimed at facilitating a learning culture in which children could develop argumentation skills. The study addressed the question of whether synchronous text-based Chat could motivate children to extend and develop their written debating skills. For this, children needed to learn to focus on the discussion topic, to discriminate between what was relevant and what was not, to engage with each other's comments, listen to each other's points of view and respond to them appropriately.

Much of the benefit of the programme so far seems to lie with children having learnt through practice in discussing topics of their own choosing, not only what makes a good topic for debate but also basic collaborative skills that are pre-requisite to improving the quality of argument. Thus, children learnt to:

- Focus on the discussion question and not disrupt the debate with off-task banter of an offensive nature;
- Advance statements that represented their own position but also to respond to those advanced by others;
- Encourage the participation of all members of the group and not talk exclusively to those in their friendship group;
- Provide explicit validation and encouragement when they agreed with points made.

In addition to these changes, which might be thought of as basic collaborative pre-requisites for argumentation rather than argumentation skills in their own right, the analysis suggested that children also improved their argumentation skills by:

- Reducing the number of times they simply repeated their conclusion;
- Reducing the number of times they resorted to personal attacks on others when they disagreed with a point of view;
- Producing fewer longer and more thoughtful turns that more clearly linked their opinions to supporting statements;
- Challenging unsupported statements and providing justifications for their own unsupported statements when challenged;
- Discriminating between relevant and irrelevant statements, challenging irrelevant or repetitious statements;
- Explicitly agreeing as well as disagreeing with statements;
- Providing examples that supported alternative viewpoints.

*Limitations of the Study*

The extent to which conclusions from this study can be generalised is limited. The study is a small one carried out with a single group of students. Moreover, because of the voluntary nature of children's attendance at CHALCS, the children did not all attend classes regularly. This means that the performances of some children did not change to the same extent as those of the children who attended more regularly. Thus, although the online *behaviour* of regular attendees changed as the study progressed, irregular attendees tended to exhibit the same behaviour patterns in later sessions as they had done in earlier ones. This was potentially disruptive to the group as a whole.

The computer-based Chat programme was an addition to an existing course and was intended to provide an opportunity for children to develop the skills of argument rather than teach any particular subject – "learning to argue" as opposed to "arguing to learn". One consequence was that the tutor did not attempt to correct factual errors in children's contributions. In another setting, with more focus on content, the teacher could have spent more time collecting web sites (or other resources) for children to study before the discussion, ensuring a more knowledge-rich debate. The teacher might also have given feedback to the children on their bulletin board contributions or taken examples from the children's writing for the teaching of language points. The roles the tutor might take, as a facilitating participant or as a manager of learning tasks and online environment, have by no means been fully explored. Preliminary work with the same tutor in face-to face discussion suggests that in keeping with the findings of Sullivan and Pratt (1996), the percentage of the dialogue accounted for by students as opposed to the tutor is far greater in the electronic Chat than in the face-to-face classroom and this is likely to be an important factor (if not the most important factor) in the success of the programme. As Veerman (this volume) also suggests, the role of the tutor requires further investigation. Initial impressions suggest that it is particularly difficult for the tutor to steer discussion in synchronous Chat environments because everyone is able to participate at once. However, with scaffolding, participants may learn to take greater individual responsibility for focusing the debate. The principal role for the tutor may be to facilitate this process.

The WebCT environment was originally created for college students and the designers had not considered that younger teenagers might abuse the facility that exists to send private messages. WebCT does not even record the fact that a private message has been sent, and this makes it difficult for the teacher to control or prevent the sending of abusive or inappropriate messages. This point has been put to the WebCT designers but it seems there are no plans to address this in the immediate future. The content of the first session, when the children had not all realised that the discussions were logged (although they had been informed of this), showed that some group members will send offensive messages to each other if they think that they can get away with it. For this reason the tutor prohibited the sending of private messages and enforced this by occasionally patrolling the classroom. However, the fact that the sending of private messages was possible (and did happen, especially in the early stages) means that some of the Chat logs may not be complete and this is unfortunate.

*Conclusions and Future Work*

Within the context of an out of school programme for disadvantaged pupils a study was carried out using CMC Chat with 10-15 year-old children as part of a wider programme to improve literacy. The aim was to try to motivate children to develop their written argumentation skills through this medium. This pilot programme seemed to be successful in that over time children:

- Increased the fluency and complexity of their writing;
- Became more focussed on-topic, addressing the discussion question more closely;
- Became more responsive to each other's contributions;
- Became more adept at making, backing and challenging arguments;
- Created a more inclusive and 'safer' learning culture in which children were less likely to be berated and more likely to be validated and encouraged to participate.

Although these results are highly encouraging and, if sustained, are likely to impact on children's critical thinking abilities, it has not yet been demonstrated that these effects can be transferred to face-to-face discussions or course-work in other subject lessons nor that they will impact upon children's extended writing outside the online Chat situation. Data related to these points is in the process of being analysed.

Extended writing tends to be discouraged by other participants in synchronous Chat since it takes too much time to read and digest. Therefore the continuing DaRE programme is aimed at achieving the transfer of these newly acquired skills to extended writing contexts through bridging tasks and tools (including collaborative report writing using a word processor and document sharing through applications such as NetMeeting). This will not only enable longer pieces of writing to be constructed but will also enable children to learn to structure arguments and to learn and check grammar and spelling.

In this study the participation of the tutor was minimal and interventions tended to concentrate on curbing the worse excesses of disruptive behaviour. It may be that this hands-off approach is ideal to encourage students to "learn by doing". Alternatively students may benefit from the modelling of appropriate roles by the tutor or peers. Appropriate roles for the tutor to take within the debate need further research. In particular, the positive effect that the tutor's behaviour might have upon the debate is the subject of further investigation. Ways of providing scaffolding, by which the tutor models desired behaviour and gradually fades from the process, are being tried and investigated (Kuminek and Pilkington, 2001).

## AFFILIATIONS AND ACKNOWLEDGEMENTS

The authors Rachel Pilkington and Aisha Walker are from the Computer Based Learning Unit, The University of Leeds, U.K. The work reported here was part funded by an ESRC CASE Research

Studentship in collaboration with Chapeltown and Harehills Assisted Learning Computer School (CHALCS), Leeds, U.K. The authors particularly thank Mr Brainard Braimah (Director CHALCS), Mr Abdul Jalloh (Literacy Tutor CHALCS) and the children who participated in this research.

# REFERENCES

Andrews, R. (1995). *Teaching and Learning Argument*. London: Cassell.

Beauvois, M. H. (1997). High-Tech, high-touch: from discussion to composition in the networked classroom, *Computer-Assisted Language Learning*, 10 (1), 57-69.

Bereiter, C., & Scardamalia, M. (1987). *The Pyschology of Written Composition*. Hillsdale, New Jersey: Lawrence Erlbaum and Associates.

Burnett, R. E. (1993). Decision-making during the collaborative planning of co-authors. In A. Penrose & B. Sitko (Eds.), *Hearing Ourselves Think: Cognitive Research in the College Writing Classroom*. Oxford: Oxford University Press, pp.125-146.

Flower, L. (1994). *The Construction of Negotiated Meaning: A Social Cognitive Theory of Writing*. Carbondale, Illinois: Southern Illinois University Press.

Flower, L. S. & Hayes, J. R. (1980). The dynamics of composing: making plans and juggling constraints. In L. Gregg & R. Steinberg (Eds.), *Cognitive Processes in Writing*. Hillsdale, New Jersey: Lawrence Erlbaum, pp 31-50.

Flower, L. S. & Hayes, J. R. (1981). A cognitive process theory of writing. *College Composition and Communication*, 32, 365-387.

Harwood, D. (1995). The pedagogy of the world studies 8-13 project: the influence of the presence/absence of the teacher upon primary children's collaborative group work. *British Educational Research Journal*, 21 (5), 587-611.

Kuhn, D., Shaw, V. and Felton, M. (1997). Effects of dyadic interaction on argumentative reasoning. *Cognition and Instruction*, 15 (3), 287-315.

Kuminek, P.A. & Pilkington, R.M. (2001). Helping the tutor facilitate debate to improve literacy using CMC. *Proceedings of IEEE International Conference on Advanced Learning Technologies* (pp. 261-263), Madison, USA. 6-8th August.

Mercer, N & Wegerif, R. (1999). Children's talk and the development of reasoning in the classroom. *British Educational Research Journal*, 25 (1), 95-111.

Neu, J. & Scarcella, R. (1990). Word processing in the ESL writing classroom: a survey of student attitudes. In P. Dunkel (Ed.), *Computer Assisted Language Learning and Testing*. New York: Newbury House.

Pilkington, R. M. (1999). *Analyzing Educational Discourse: The DISCOUNT Scheme. CBL Technical Report No. 99/2*. Computer Based Learning Unit, The University of Leeds, Leeds LS2 9JT, UK.

Pennington, M. (1996). Writing the natural way: on computer. *Computer Assisted Language Learning, 9* (2-3), 125-142.

Phinney, M. (1990). Computer-Assisted Writing and Writing Apprehension in ESL Students. In P. Dunkel (Ed.), *Computer Assisted Language Learning and Testing*. New York: Newbury House.

Searle, J. (1969). *Speech Acts: An Essay on the Philosophy of Language*. Cambridge: Cambridge University Press.

Sullivan, N., & Pratt, E. (1996). A comparative study of two ESL writing environments: a computer-assisted classroom and a traditional oral classroom. *System, 24* (4), 491-501.

Tindale, C. W. (1999). *Acts of Arguing: A Rhetorical Model of Argument*. New York: State University of New York Press.

Toulmin, S. (1958). *The Uses of Argument*. Cambridge: Cambridge University press.

Tuckman, B. W. (1965). Developmental sequence in small groups. *Psychological Bulletin, 63, 6, 384-399*.

Veerman, A. (2000). *Computer-Supported Collaborative Learning through Argumentation*. Utrecht: ICO.

Vygotsky, L. S. (1978). *Mind in Society: The Development of Higher Psychological Processes*. Cambridge, Mass: Harvard University Press.

Walker, S. A., & Pilkington, R. M. (2000). Networked communication and the collaborative development of written expression at key stage three. *Proceedings of the Second International Conference on Networked Learning 2000* (pp.28-37). Lancaster, UK. 17th-19th April.

Walker, S. A., & Pilkington, R. M. (2001). Facilitating computer-mediated discussion classes: a study of teacher intervention strategies. *Proceedings of IEEE International Conference on Advanced Learning Technologies* (253-257). Madison, USA. 6-8th August.

Walton, D. N. (1984). *Logical Dialogue Games and Fallacies*. Lanham: University Press of America. (Published Ph.D. thesis).

Warschauer, M. (1996). Comparing Face-to-Face and Electronic Discussion in the Second Language Classroom in CALICO Journal 13 (2): 7-26.

Warschauer, M. (1999). *Electronic Literacies*. Mahwah, New Jersey, Erlbaum.

Warschauer, M., Turbee, L., & Roberts, B. (1996). Computer Learning Network and Student Empowerment. *System, 24* (1), 1-14.

*World Wide Web*

**CHALCS** http://www.chalcs.org.uk
**TeenChat** http://www.teenchat.com
**WebCT** http://www.webct.com/

## NOTES

[1] For example, 'x because y', 'why x?', 'because y'.
[2] For example, 'have you stopped beating your wife?' which contains the premise that you were beating your wife; whether you answer 'yes' or 'no', both answers suggest acceptance of this premise – no suggests you are still beating your wife whilst yes suggests that you were but have now stopped.
[3] Here 'one' means 'an alien'.

## APPENDIX

*Example 1. from Group 1, 30th April, Aliens*

| Turn | Student | Contribution | Exchange Role | Move | Task |
|------|---------|--------------|---------------|------|------|
| 104. | Drake | Elodie your more like SKUNK ANANSI | I | inform | Off-disrup |
| 105. | Dexter | I'don't believe in aliens | R | inform | on |
| 106. | Elodie | were's my | I | ? | ? |
| 107. | Jabir | Ufo are fun | I | inform | on |
| 108. | Elodie | you look like and smell like scunk anasi | I | inform | Off - disrup |
| 109. | Elodie | reply drake | I | instruct | social |
| 110. | Tosia | you know this! | R | meta | social |
| 111. | Drake | ELODIE IS THE NEW G. GLITTER | I | inform | Off-disrup |

*Example 2. from Group 2, 30ᵗʰ April, Aliens*

| Turn | Student | Contribution | Exchange Role | Move | Task |
|------|---------|--------------|---------------|------|------|
| 181. | Paula | Adam is the nutty professor | I | inform | off |
| 182. | Farhat | OOH YEH!!!!!!!!!!!!!!!!!!!!!!!!!!!!!!!!!!!!!!! | R | inform | off |
| 183. | Shabbana | FARHAT THE BABY | I | inform | disrup |
| 184. | Zobeen | Yeah Shabs! | R | agree | disrup |
| 185. | Farhat | WELL DONE 100% | R | agree | disrup |
| 186. | Sahmeena | ZObeen - Well if you think aliens do'nt exist YOU tell me why? | I | challenge | on |
| 187. | Nusrat | ALIENS AND BABIES DON'T MIX! | I | inform | disrup |

*Example 3, from 9ᵗʰ July, Family Roles*

| Turn | Student | Contribution | Exchange Role | Move | Task |
|------|---------|--------------|---------------|------|------|
|  | Liam | hello | R | Open | social |
| 10 | Shelley | Hi what do you think. | I | Open Inquire | Social on |
| 11 | Drake | man and woman is both equal! | R | inform | on |
| 12 | Sahmeena | The question that has to be answered is 'who should look after the family'? What do you think faz? | I | Meta Reason Inquire nominate | On social |
| 13 | Liam | the babiesitter | R | inform | on |
| 14 | Farhat | both mother and father should look after the family | R | inform | on |
| 15 | Shabbana | No Zobeen because our mum works and so does our dad. Also everone does the house work in the house not only mum | RI | Nominate disagree justify justify | on |

# JAN M. VAN BRUGGEN & PAUL A. KIRSCHNER

# DESIGNING EXTERNAL REPRESENTATIONS TO SUPPORT SOLVING WICKED PROBLEMS

## INTRODUCTION

In this chapter we consider the use of external representations in a CSCL-environment in which learners collaboratively solve 'wicked' problems (e.g. how can we reduce school drop-out?) or analyze proposed solutions to these problems (did this anti-corruption program work?). Solving these problems or analyzing proposed solutions obviously requires analysis of the causes of the problem as well as considerations about which actions are likely to be successful and acceptable. The nature of these ill-structured problems is such that neither analysis nor solutions are 'true or 'false': they are the result of an argumentative process in which participants eventually reach an agreement on a common analysis and a solution, that may be 'good' or 'bad'.

The question that we try to answer in this chapter is how external representations may facilitate this problem-solving process and what characteristics of external representations are important to consider. We draw on various backgrounds to provide initial answers to this question. After a discussion of wicked problems we present a number of characteristics of external representations, and how these characteristics may be related to the problem-solving process. One of the core notions here, brought forward by Suthers (this volume, 2001) is that characteristics of external representations, he uses the term 'representational notation', have a direct bearing on the contents of the discourse of collaborating learners. Thus, external representations seem to offer opportunities to guide learners. There are reasons to assume that external representations not only offer profits, but also have associated cognitive costs. We will discuss results in CSCL research that suggest load-adding effects and offer evidence that higher levels of specificity of external representations are accompanied by higher levels of cognitive load.

To develop a 'representational notation' to support collaborative solving of wicked problems we draw on different backgrounds. In the first place we draw from computer-supported collaborative learning (CSCL), where environments were developed that use external representations to express explanations of phenomena together with consistent or inconsistent evidence. Belvedere (Suthers & Weiner, 1995) and Sensemaker (Bell, 1997) are two well-known examples of such systems.

*J. Andriessen, M. Baker, and D. Suthers (eds.), Arguing to Learn: Confronting Cognitions in Computer-Supported Collaborative Learning environments (177-203).*

These are environments developed for a particular domain, namely scientific inquiry, and their external representations limit learners to expressing arguments related to theories, hypotheses and data and the evidential relationships between them. Solving wicked problems requires these and other objects to support argumentation regarding goals, criteria and constraints that any solution has to meet. There is a correspondence to design problems, which are often ill-structured and characterized by high levels of uncertainty about the actual goals, criteria and stop-rules that can be applied (Goel & Pirolli, 1992). In fact, design problems have been typified as 'wicked problems' by Rittel and Webber (1984). We will in particular look at a number of methods and tools that help to explicate the reasoning behind particular designs. Finally, we draw from work on logical framework analysis (Sartorius, 1996) and theory-driven evaluation, in particular the notion of program theory (Chen, 1990) that demands that the assumptions behind a program are made explicit, i.e. assumptions regarding program implementation and short-term effects as well as to intermediate processes and their role in producing long-term outcomes.

All this may lead to a representational notation, but will the external representations produced by using this notation facilitate collaborative solving of wicked problems or collaborative analysis of proposed solutions? In this chapter we will not try to answer that question, but concentrate on a more modest question, namely whether the objects used in this representational notation help us to understand the *content* of the discourse of students trying to solve a wicked problem.

## WICKED PROBLEMS

According to Rittel and Webber the kind of problems that "planners deal with - societal problems - are inherently different from the problems with which scientists and perhaps some classes of engineers deal. Planning problems are inherently wicked" (Rittel & Webber, 1984, p. 135-136). Rittel and Webber give a number of characteristics of 'wicked problems': they have no definitive formulation – the information needed to understand the problem depends on one's idea for solving it and they have no stopping rule – "the planner terminates work on a wicked problem, not for reasons inherent in the 'logic' of the problem. He stops for considerations that are external to the problem: he runs out of time, or money, or patience". "Solutions to wicked problems are not true-or-false, but good or bad." (op. cit., pp. 136-139).

Conklin and Weil (1997) describe a "subtle and pervasive pain in organizations", caused by a misunderstanding of the nature of the problems that organizations face. Organizations are, according to them, trying "to solve a new class of problems - wicked problems - using thinking, tools, and methods that are only useful for simpler problems" (p. 1). In other words it is becoming increasingly difficult to tackle problems and projects in a linear way in solitude. Problems have become so complex (poorly defined or even wicked) and projects have become so complex and multifaceted that they can only be approached through multidisciplinary teams consisting of a number of experts with different backgrounds. Consider the following description by Conklin and Weil (1997) of a wicked problem within the car industry, i.e. determining the features of a new car.

1. The actual problem is not understood until a solution has been developed. In the design of a car, some features interact with others. Adding structural support in the doors, for example, makes the car safer from side impact, but the added weight increases the cost, changes the fuel economy and ride, and requires adjustment to suspension and braking systems. Making the car safer also impacts marketing, raising issues such as pricing and demand-"How much do people really care about side-impact survivability?" And all these problems interact.

2. There are different stakeholders in how the problem is resolved. There are two clearly defined and opposing camps: the people who know what is needed (Marketing or Sales) and the people who know what can be done (Engineering or Manufacturing). Virtually all product features and design problems fall squarely into both camps. One side argues that there is no point building the product if it doesn't have Feature X; the other argues that Feature X is so expensive, complex, time consuming, untested, or otherwise impossible that it should not be tackled on this project. Management has its own stake in these decisions, as do many others in the organization. Some key stakeholders, such as customers and regulatory bodies, are generally not even represented in the design meetings.

3. The constraints change over time. Almost all solutions have the constraints of time (the problem must be solved before some critical date, condition, or event) and money (the solution must be cost effective). Quality is usually another key constraint. In the case of car design, some decisions, such as the addition of side-impact reinforcements, might be forced by unpredictable constraints, such as the need to impress a politician or a Wall Street analyst with the company's commitment to safety.

4. The problem-solving process ends when resources run out. Whatever is finally decided, it will be hard to claim that it was the right answer. No amount of study, laboratory experiments, or market surveys will indicate the ideal solution. At some point, the design team will have to make a decision. Inevitably, once the car is produced, critics will point out that the doors are heavy and difficult to open, while people injured in side-impact accidents will file law suits against the company.

As can be seen in the example:

- Wicked problems are composed of an interlocking set of issues and constraints, rather than a definitive statement of the problem itself. These problems are often not fully understood until a solution has been developed.

- There are many stakeholders who have expertise in different aspects of the problem to be solved, making effective problem solving more a social process than a cognitive one. Obtaining the right answer is less important than having the stakeholders accept the solution that emerges.

- The constraints on the solution change over time because everything one does is done at a faster pace in a changing world. Stakeholders come and go, communication is often incomplete and rules invariably change.

'Wicked problems' are formally a subset of ill-structured problems: their goals are unclear (the problem is ill-defined), their search space is not well defined (and ill-structured) and neither the applicable operators nor the constraints are given. There seem to be some unique features to wicked problems however. In the first place, possible solutions cannot be tested and revised (one obviously cannot 'try out' a trajectory for a freeway). Secondly, not even the description of a 'wicked problem' is without implicit, often political, assumptions. Is the trajectory of the freeway a problem of creating a transport infrastructure, an economic problem, or an ecological problem? Thus, wicked problems are social problems involving many stakeholders each of whom may bring different problem representations and solution strategies to the scene.

Consider the following example, taken from a small set of protocols that were made available to us by Tom Duffy. Participants were instructed to prepare recommendations to reduce school drop-out and present those to the US Governors within a month. Participants were further instructed that they would only have one second meeting shortly before their presentation to the Governors and that they could compile a list of research questions to be answered before their second meeting.

Given this task, what can we tell about the contents of argumentation that we have to support? We assume that there will be a process during which the problem will be analyzed, which requires negotiation on a number of hypotheses about the causes of drop-out and data to support these hypotheses, but as the example above shows, there may be widely differing views on the nature of the problem. Before offering any solution (recommendations) one has to consider the constraints that the recommendations have to fit in: e.g., time, money as well as the acceptability (social, political etcetera) of any recommendation. Often, as is the case here, the constraints are not given but have to be negotiated by the problem solvers themselves. When the problem solvers specify their recommendations - any policies or interventions that the Governors have to implement - we expect arguments that corroborate that the interventions will ultimately lead to the stated goal and how they do so, i.e. what the intervening processes or assumptions are and how likely they are to materialize. Finally, all this has to be wrapped up in a presentation that has to convince the Governors, which is a demand that will act as a constraint for all interventions considered.

As this example shows, the type of reasoning involved is not only of the 'why'-type of scientific inquiry, but is also in the area of 'how'-questions related to design (how can we create something that will achieve X) and program planning and evaluation (what interventions may change a problematic social situation?). Moreover, there are no certitudes in these domains: all statements can be considered claims that one might question, qualify or refute and therefore the argumentation may become complex. External representations to support this process require an underlying representational notation with elements (objects and relations) drawn from a number of different domains, and possibly a complex set of rules to represent (if we wish our learners to do so) the argumentation. Such a complex representational notation may have drawbacks, however, which we discuss from the perspective of cognitive load theory. We will first discuss a number of general characteristics of external representations to lay out some vocabulary for this chapter.

## CHARACTERISTICS OF EXTERNAL REPRESENTATIONS

Suthers' (this volume, 2001) makes a distinction between the *representational notation*, (the primitives: concepts, relations and rules for their use), the implementation of the formalism in *representational tools* (the software interfaces used to construct and work with external representations) and the *representational artifacts* that the learner constructs using the tools. According to him each representational notation (and its associated implementation and resulting artifacts) guides the learners by constraining what knowledge can be expressed and by making some of that knowledge more salient.

The concept of representational notation entails a number of characteristics presented by De Jong et al (1998):

A first characteristic is that of the *ontology*, which is used here in the HCI meaning and not in its original philosophical meaning "refers to the *content*, to the objects and relations one uses to represent a domain, not so much to the symbols by which objects and relations are denoted" (de Jong et al., 1998, p. 11). Any ontology will offer a restricted view on a domain and will make it easier to express certain aspects of the domain. An ontology not only defines the primitives by which the domain may be represented, it also restricts the type of argument that can be expressed. In Belvedere, for instance, data in support of a hypothesis is linked by an evidential 'pro' link. Other evidence may be entered as direct evidence against the hypothesis, or undercutting the relation between the former data and the hypothesis, but there is no way in which data can *refute* other data or a hypothesis. One may criticize the Belvedere coach for not correctly handling refuting relations (eg Chryssafidou, 1999), but that misses the point: the problem, if it is any at all, is not with the implementation, but with the underlying ontology. The Toulmin model of argumentation shows a similar complexity: there is no way to discuss the validity of data other than by transforming a data object into a claim (Lee & Lai, 1991; Van Eemeren, Grootendorst & Henkemans, 1996). Ontology is the first characteristic we are concerned with: what objects and relations do we need in a representational notation that supports the solving of wicked problems?

A second characteristic of external representations is *specificity*, defined by Stenning and Oberlander (1995, p. 98) as "the demand of a system of representation that information in some class be specified in any interpretable representation". The specificity of a representation may require disambiguation: in a semantic net representation we may have a vague relation stating that "Object A is_next_to Object B". Now assume we need to represent this information in a diagram. Using this representation we have to picture A and B at particular localities, disambiguating the vague 'next_to'. Thus, graphical representations may limit abstraction and aid processability of the information. Cox formulates a design guideline: "select a representation with sufficient expressive power to capture the indeterminacy in the problem, but no more than is needed" (Cox, 1999, p.350). Specificity can be used to constrain what can be expressed in an external representation, and can be used to force categorical choices. The evolution of Belvedere offers interesting examples of the role of the *specificity* of the representational scheme and the effects it may have on the interaction between learners. Suthers (1995) notes that Belvedere forces learners to indicate which type of object they add (the specificity of the representation forces disambiguation). This often led to epistemological discussions between learners (that would not be represented in the evidence maps however). Suthers points out that a weaker representational structure could have evaded the issue, but that this would also have obscured the need to discuss these important points. In terms of *specificity*, a weaker representation would leave room for different (implicit) interpretations of the representation. However, it was also noted that the rich set of objects and relations available in one of the first versions of Belvedere would lure learners into discussions on subtle differences that were hardly relevant to the task. One of the lessons that we may learn from this research thus seems to be that it is of critical importance to offer learners a view on the domain, possibly a restricted ontology, that focuses them on the objects and relations they should learn about, which is not necessarily a high fidelity domain representation.

A third characteristic of external representations discussed by de Jong et al. is the *modality* of a representation, described as the form of expression used for displaying information: text, animations, graphs, et cetera. Thus, notational systems with the same set of underlying concepts and relations (the ontology) may express these objects and relations differently, for instance as graphs, hypertexts or feature-comparison matrices. Suthers (1999, 2001) has drawn attention to the effects that these different notations may have on the discourse of the learners and ultimately on learning outcomes.

An ontology should consider the prior knowledge of the learners, but we might go one step further and question the one-to-one correspondence between the ontology to represent the domain and the objects and relations presented to the learner to represent the domain. An ontology for a domain can use a fine-grained set of concepts and relations, yet only a subset of it could be used in the (initial) learning environment, i.e. the *specificity* of the external representation need not necessarily be maximized. The Belvedere research clearly underlines the idea that maximizing specificity may have counterproductive effects, whereas forcing certain (but not all) categorical choices may evoke important epistemological discussions between learners. Offering a richer ontology and a higher specificity than the tasks requires will, in terms of cognitive load theory, increase the extraneous cognitive load. When developing a representational notation these are potential drawbacks that we have to consider.

## PROFITS AND COSTS OF THE USE OF EXTERNAL REPRESENTATIONS

We will now turn to the use of external representations and the implications from a cognitive load perspective. The basic questions here are whether the use of an external representation may lead to a change in extraneous cognitive load and whether it will lead to a change in germane cognitive load. Consider the use of an external representation by a person who is using this scheme individually. Such a scheme may act as an external memory, and subjectively, may function properly, even though from an outsider's viewpoint the representation does not look adequate. Now turn to a collaborative setting in which the representation will have to be shared by another person. As long as the symbol system and what it expresses are well known to the participants, say a simple calculation, sharing the representation may be relatively easy, although one might spend more time on making the representation readable and understandable to others (Cox, 1999). Sharing a representation may thus bring additional (cognitive) costs.

The question is thus, what are the benefits and what are the costs (in psychological terms) involved in using external representations for collaboratively solving problems. We will discuss these in terms of Cognitive Load Theory (CLT). Cognitive Load Theory (Chandler & Sweller, 1991; Sweller, 1988; Sweller, van Merriënboer & Paas, 1998) distinguishes three forms of cognitive load that together determine the total cognitive load.

Information varies on a continuum from low to high in element interactivity (Paas, Renkl, & Sweller, in press). Each element of low element interactivity material can be understood and learned individually without consideration of any other elements. Elements of high element interactivity material can be learned individually, but cannot be understood until all of the elements and their interactions are processed simultaneously. Compare, for example, learning the operations of the 12 function keys in a photo-editing-suite and learning to manipulate a photo with that suite. In *intrinsic cognitive load* the demands on working memory capacity imposed by element interactivity are intrinsic to the material being learned, and cannot be altered by instructional manipulations.

The manner in which information is presented to learners and the learning activities required of learners can also impose a cognitive load. Where that load is unnecessary and interferes with learning, it is referred to as an *extraneous* or *ineffective cognitive load*. Much instructional material imposes extraneous cognitive load because it was developed without functionally considering the structure of information or cognitive architecture of the learner.

The last form of cognitive load is *germane* or *effective cognitive load*. As is the case with extraneous cognitive load and unlike intrinsic cognitive load, germane cognitive load is influenced by instructional design. The manner in which information is presented to learners and the learning activities required of learners are factors relevant to levels of germane cognitive load. Whereas extraneous cognitive load interferes with learning, germane cognitive load enhances learning. Instead of working memory resources being used to engage in search, for example, as occurs when dealing with extraneous cognitive load, germane cognitive load results in those resources being devoted to relevant processes, such as schema acquisition and automation.

Intrinsic, extraneous and germane cognitive load are additive in that together, the total load cannot exceed the working memory resources available if learning is to occur. Thus, with a given intrinsic cognitive load, the extraneous cognitive load should be minimized and the germane cognitive load should be optimized by instructional design (Sweller et al., 1998). According to CLT the cognitive load in complex tasks, where the learner has to maintain several information items in working memory, may become so high that it will prevent knowledge formation.

As pointed out by Duffy and Cunningham (1996) one impact of external representations is that 'off-loading' basic cognitive demands may permit the learner to attend to higher-level representations. There have been a number of different explanations given for this cognitive facilitation, namely:

- diagrams require less representation than a verbal representation and they are easier to interpret (Larkin & Simon, 1995).

- alternative representations are computationally simpler and can be carried out more easily. Roman numerals are less suitable for mathematical operations than Arabic (Zhang & Norman, 1994).

- perceptual characteristics of representations can induce a 'cognitive bias' (Zhang, 1997) that facilitates problem solving.

- the specificity of an external representation can force the disambiguation of information that supports making inferences (Stenning & Oberlander, 1995)

In the CSCL-literature other benefits are also discussed: external representations are promoted in CSCL as 'augmenting' cognitive activity, e.g. Pea (1993), and as offering new views, for instance by visualization, e.g. Jonassen, Peck & Wilson (1999). External representations can also help to maintain the focus in discussion and argumentation (Veerman, 2000), forcing explicitation and possibly producing a self-explanation effect.

There are good reasons to accept that, apart from the already named 'off-loading' effects that Duffy en Cunningham discuss, there can also be what we will call 'load-adding effects' to the use of external representations. Introduction of a number of external representations in CSCL-environments requires integration of representations and coordination between participants. Both the integration (Schijf & Simon, 1998) and the coordination is problematic (Lesgold, 1998; Boshuizen & Schijf, 1998). It does not take much imagination to envision that some of the already discussed aspects of representations can have load-adding effects: the richer the ontology of the representational system the more difficult it will be to use (at least for beginners). Specificity is a quality of a representational schema that promises profits (inferences are facilitated), but may also introduce costs (the processing necessary for disambiguation). By limiting categorical choice in the representational notation to only those objects and relations that correspond to learning goals, extraneous cognitive load is decreased and germane cognitive load increased.

In other words, we need to be cognisant of the possible introduction of cognitive load when external representations are used. For this reason we have carried out a small-scale experiment to determine the effects of external representations on cognitive load (Van Bruggen & Kirschner, 2000). Participants were ten paid student volunteers from the University of Maastricht, eight female, two male. Eight participants were in their second year, two female participants were in their 5th year (one of whom was left out of the analyses because she failed to comply with the instructions). Students came from different study majors (International Economic Studies, International Affairs, Health Sciences, Medicine) and their age ranged from 19 to 24.

Participants were instructed to analyse a Worldbank program using a system for external representation. Two versions of representational scheme were employed, one with high detail (HD condition) and one with low detail (LD condition). In both conditions the representational scheme expressed the information about the program in terms of program STRUCTURE, FACTS about the program, and relevant BACKGROUND information. In the HD condition the *type* of facts and background information had to be specified in greater detail and the *relations* to other objects in the representation were more detailed. Figure 1 gives the HD scheme with the subcategories of FACTS and BACKGROUND, the LD version had no subcategories.. The HD scheme used *support, denies, qualifies* and *assumes* as relations, the LD scheme only used *for* and *against* relations.

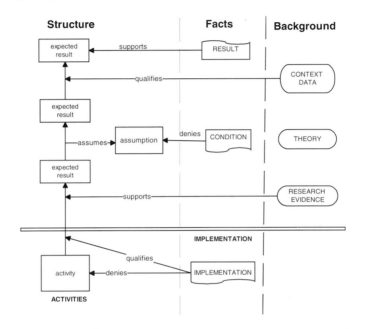

*Figure 1. HD representational scheme*

In the written instructions for using the representational system, measures of cognitive load were included. Cognitive load can be assessed by determining the amount of mental effort spent by a person involved in carrying out a (cognitive) task (Paas, Renkl, & Sweller, in press; Paas & van Merriënboer, 1994). The cognitive load was measured on a 9-point rating-scale (Paas, 1992; Paas, Van Merriënboer & Adam, 1994), which measured the invested mental effort perceived by the participants. The mental effort measures ranged from very, very low mental effort to very, very high mental effort. The first part of the instructions on the program structure (containing cognitive load measures 1-2) were identical, the second part (with measures 3 through 6) varied greatly with respect to the specificity.

We found two important results. First, we found a negative correlation between prior knowledge and average cognitive load experienced ($r = -.82$). The second interesting result is presented in table 1, where the averages of the cognitive load have been corrected for prior knowledge.

*Table 1: Average cognitive load corrected for prior knowledge*

|  | high specificity | low specificity |
|---|---|---|
| measures 1-2 | 3.48 | 4.65 |
| measures 3-6 | 5.23 | 4.96 |

Although the number of participants is too small to draw statistical conclusions, the results do point in the direction that we need to consider the possible load-adding effects of such characteristics as specificity when designing and working with external representations. The question of whether this load-adding effect would be compensated by facilitating inferences is beyond the scope of the experiment.

Apart from the possible increase in cognitive load, there are other boundary conditions that we also need to take into account in interpreting these data. In the first place, we are discussing representational systems with a complex set of objects and relations and we thus need to consider that the users will need time to learn and master working with the notation. In the second place, as already stated, in this individual paper-and-pencil design users can and will create their own (idiosyncratic) representations and use representational notations that are congruent with their own way of thinking. Such a representation, if meant for another person, needs to be more detailed and provided with richer (an)notations than one that is meant for the user him/herself. (Cox, 1999). This is probably less a problem in a computerised environment, where the interface can more or less force conformity to the representational notation.

## REPRESENTION AND SUPPORT FOR ARGUMENTATION

In the remainder of this chapter we will draw from two distinct research traditions: CSCL and design argumentation. Both struggle with questions of how best to represent and support argumentation, albeit in quite different domains. Many CSCL systems have addressed scientific inquiry as a domain and a number of specialised environments for this domain have been developed. Design argumentation has used (and sometimes specialised) general argumentation tools to support the specific needs of maintaining a rationale behind the design. For our purposes we seem to need contributions from both sides. The kind of problems that we are considering requires argumentation similar to scientific inquiry to support analysis and reasoning about causes found in CSCL systems. Furthermore, we will need an environment that not only allows one to express argumentation, but also supports the argumentation process of *learners* as CSCL environments try to do. On the other hand, we need a representational notation that allows to express reasoning in terms of goals, constraints, feasibility et cetera, the realm of tools used in design argumentation.

*Representation of argumentation*

Bell (1997) makes a distinction between discussion-based tools and knowledge representation tools in CSCL. Discussion-based tools support dialogical argumentation in a group. Examples are CSILE (Scardamalia, Bereiter, Maclean, Swallow & Woodruff, 1989; Scardamalia & Bereiter, 1994) and the Collaboratory Notebook (Edelson, Gomez, Polman, Gordin & Fishman, 1994; Edelson, O'Neill, Gomez & D'Amico, 1995). Knowledge representation tools not only support the dialogical argumentation of the participants, but also support the representation of the argumentation by the individuals. Furthermore, the tools have to support argumentation, whose structure and content correspond to, in this case, a valid scientific argumentation. Examples of this can be found in systems such as SenseMaker (Bell, 1997) and Belvedere (Paolucci, Suthers & Weiner, 1995; Suthers & Weiner, 1995; Suthers, Toth & Weiner, 1997).

The Knowledge Integration Environment (Bell, 1997) allows learners to investigate rival hypotheses by guiding them to claims and evidence. The Sensemaker subsystem collects a hypothesis and its supporting or refuting evidence in a so-called 'claim frame'. Conflicting evidence that supports one explanation while refuting another is not explicitly signalled. The Belvedere environment offers a chat window, and a shared visual workspace where learners construct scientific explanations in so-called 'evidence maps'. The environment has a coach that comments on the structure of the evidence maps and makes suggestions for improvements. The characteristics of the notation of the evidence maps are what we concentrate on here. The *ontology* of the evidence maps in Belvedere is defined in the objects and relations that students may use when they create evidence maps. In the current version of Belvedere, these are 'principle', 'hypothesis', 'data' and 'unspecified'. The relations are reduced to a basic set of 'for', 'against' and 'and'. Students can express the strength of their beliefs in the objects and relations. Belvedere supports discussion of rival hypotheses by linking evidence (data) or by undercutting the link. It does not support direct refutation of data.

Suthers (1995) notes that the representational system forces learners to indicate which type of object they add (the *specificity* of the representation forces disambiguation). This often led to epistemological discussions between learners that will not, however, be represented in the evidence maps. Suthers notes that a weaker representational structure could evade the issue, but that this would also obscure the need to discuss these important points. A weaker representation would leave room for different interpretations of the representation. There were a number of drawbacks associated with the earlier representational scheme of Belvedere. The early versions of Belvedere had more objects and relations and offered a very explicit Toulminian perspective on argumentation. In subsequent versions of Belvedere, the number of objects and especially the different types of relations (*precision* of the representation) were reduced. The reduction in the number of objects and relations was logically motivated because they were considered redundant. It was also noted, however, that the detailed level at which relations could be presented could lead to interference with the task. It seemed to cause students to deal with non-goal tasks (Suthers et al., 1997).

Discussion-based tools offer students an asynchronous environment in which they can exchange arguments. The structure of the argumentation is not explicitly represented, i.e. it may be embedded in the threads of an electronic discussion. One of the best known discussion-based environments is CSILE (Scardamalia et al., 1989; Scardamalia & Bereiter, 1994), now commercially available as Knowledge Forum. In Knowledge Forum students use a communal database of interrelated text and graphic notes. When working with a recognized problem, students are required to enter notes with an identified type of content: "My Theory", "I Need To Understand", "New Information", "Comment". Notes are related by links like 'References', 'Build-On', and 'Quotes'. A special note is the 'Rise-Above' note that subsumes a number of nodes. All notes are entered in the communal database and are available to other students for search and comment. Knowledge Forum offers a number of views (diagrams, maps) to which a network of related notes can be attached.

The Collaboratory Notebook (Edelson & O'Neill, 1994; Edelson et al., 1995) is a shared workspace in which learners can enter pages and relate them to each other through the use of hyperlinks. There are several types of pages, including questions, conjectures, evidence for, and evidence against. In the table of contents for a Collaboratory notebook the icons represent different types of nodes and the indentation represents the threads in the discussion. The discussion in the Collaboratory Notebook is scaffolded by an interface that monitors the semantic links between nodes. Scaffolds suggest particular follow-up pages (e.g. an 'evidence for' page as a follow-up to a 'conjecture page'). In this way the structure of the argumentation is modelled to the students.

Belvedere and Knowledge Forum provide us with interesting contrasts as far as ontology and specificity of the representations are concerned. In the Belvedere environment there is a close correspondence between ontology and specificity: the set of objects and relations is limited and the user is forced to choose a particular object (hypothesis, data, principle) and a particular relation (consistent/inconsistent). It is this specificity of the representation that enables the coaching component found in Belvedere. The notes in the Collaboratory Notebook are typified in a similar way. The relations between nodes are indicated in the indentation in the table of contents and by textual description in the notes. Knowledge Forum, on the other hand, does not use different types of notes to indicate the function in the argument or discussion and the relations used are referential (build-ons, quotes). The exact functions of the notes and the referential links in the discussion have to be determined from their textual specification.

Although there is ample research on the individual systems (and others not reviewed here) for computer-supported collaborative learning, there is very little research that compares the effects of the different representational schemes used. Admittedly, direct comparison of complete systems will not suffice: they are not only different in the external representations used but also in other aspects: scaffolding, coaching, support of coordination processes. Suthers (1999) has drawn attention to the lack of comparative studies in the area and his results (Suthers, this volume; 2001) indicate that characteristics of external representations can be linked to the content of learner's discourse.

The ontology of the representational schemes share a core of concepts and relations to discuss scientific explanations and evidence. The Collaboratory Notebook and Knowledge Forum embed dialogue management and scaffolding within the nodes the students can create. For our purposes, these representational systems are usable starting points to represent the 'why'-part of a wicked problem, although we may have to consider that structuring a wicked problem involves many viewpoints and its value is not decided solely by scientific criteria; acceptability of a corresponding solution to the stakeholders plays an important role as well.

A number of systems used to represent design argumentation, in particular design rationale, are interesting for our purposes. Design rationale is a systematic approach to lay out the reasons for and the reasoning behind the decisions that lead to the design of an artifact (Shum & Hammond, 1994; Carroll & Moran, 1991) although the term design rationale is used in other senses as well (Moran & Carroll, 1996). We will not deal with any domain-specific design tools, but will only consider general tools to support the kind of design deliberations where alternatives are evaluated against criteria and constraints, decisions have to be made to select those alternatives that will reach the goals given the constraints in which the designer has to operate. In order to graphically represent these topics, as well as the argumentation for or against their (partial) solutions, a number of representational schemes were developed. We will only present a limited number of systems and refer the reader to Shum & Hammond (1994) for an in-depth review of the domain.

IBIS (Issue-Based Information System) was introduced by Rittel, who also originated the term wicked problems, as a method to deal with the diverse interlocking issues brought forward in planning and design deliberations (Rittel & Webber, 1984). IBIS supports deliberations on the pros and cons (**Arguments**) of alternative answers (**Positions**) to questions raised (**Issues**). Decisions as to which answers are accepted or rejected are called **Resolutions**. IBIS uses several types of links between the nodes, such as responds-to, questions, supports, specialises, generalises. A first software implementation of the method was gIBIS (Conklin & Begeman, 1988) leading to the now commercially available QuestMap system.

The type of discussion in IBIS is issue-based: there is no top-down refinement involved in the way that arguments are represented, nor are the issues themselves structured. Using IBIS we can represent the deliberations present in, say, our school drop-out example. The question regarding the causes of drop-out is represented as an Issue. Several hypotheses regarding the causes can be formulated (Positions) and data (Arguments) can be added to support or attack these hypotheses. Using the questions relation in IBIS we may add an Issue to, for instance, discuss the validity of certain Arguments. In a similar way an Issue object can be formulated to start a discussion of the constraints or criteria that any solution has to meet. IBIS was developed to help explicate the complexities of 'wicked' problems and for that end the ontology may be sufficient, but there are drawbacks, especially when we consider use in educational settings: the issue structure is weak and the representational notation does not force important categorical choices (for instance between alternatives, constraints, interventions).

We intend to use external representations to facilitate problem-solving, but as we have seen, there is evidence that external representations may interfere with the task. In the design rationale literature there are several reports of interference of capturing design rationale with design and construction tasks. Fischer, Lemke, McCall and Morch (1996) report experiences with PHI (Procedural Hierarchy of Issues), a representational scheme developed to overcome some of the weaknesses of IBIS. PHI tries to ensure that all design questions are represented (not only the issues raised) and have a clearly stated function in design. The integration of PHI with construction activities led to disappointing results: students failed to relate construction and argumentation. Design deliberations left out issues relating to construction and discussed topics with questionable impact on actual design (Fischer, Nakakoji, Ostwald, Stahl & Sumner, 1993). Gruber and Russell (1996) mention a similar interference effect in the use of the Instructional Design Environment (Pirolli & Russell, 1990; Russell, Moran & Jordan, 1988), one of the first environments that captured design rationale during construction. There have been various explanations for this interference effect. We present one that has a direct bearing on the design of external representations. Shum et al. (1997) have pointed to a possible mismatch between task demands and the ontology of their representational scheme QOC (Questions, Options, Criteria). Shum noticed an interference effect when a designer who had used QOC profitably in an earlier session ran into trouble using the notation when engaged in a design process that consisted of a series of design refinements to satisfy multiple constraints (Shum, MacLean, Bellotti & Hammond, 1997). These results were attributed to the different approaches required by the task (meet constraints, top-down, depth-first) and the method: raise Questions, Options and Criteria (formulate alternatives, breadth first).

The final system to be discussed is Decision Representation Language (DRL) which offers a set of objects and relations that closely match the argumentation in solving the kind of problems that we are interested in and seems to overcome most of the weaknesses of IBIS. Originally developed to support decision management, Lee and Lai (1991) present DRL as a means of formal notation of design rationale, and show how DRL can represent several "spaces" of design rationale (argument, alternative, evaluation, criteria and issue space). This layered view is interesting because in solving wicked problems the problem solvers themselves have to define (and review) the goals, alternatives and constraints.

The most important objects in DRL are **alternatives**, **goals** and **claims**. **Alternatives** are the options between which a decision has to be made. **Goals** specify the desirable properties of an option. The top-level node of the goal hierarchy is a **Decision Problem**. In DRL **Claims** are used to represent arguments that are relevant to a decision between alternatives, and all relations in DRL are specialisations of the claim object. A claim is related to another claim by a **support**, **denies** or **qualifies** relation. Thus, all objects and relations in DRL are refutable. Figure 2 represents the main elements of the DRL notation.

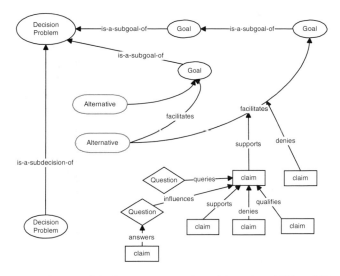

*Figure 2: part of the DRL notation adapted from Lee, 1990 p. 112)*

We have used DRL as our starting point to develop a representational notation to support solving or analyzing wicked problems in the area of social science. We will present this scheme and our first results below. First, however we will shift our focus from the contents of the representational notation to the way external representation can support the argumentation process.

*Supporting the argumentation process*

In CSCL environments, integration or at least coordination, of multiple representations is necessary. Students have to somehow reconcile their individual representations. Several stakeholders may be involved in design deliberations. In collaborative settings, multiple agents may have to coordinate multiple representations (conceptual and surface). Although it may not be necessary that they (completely) integrate their individual representations, they have to at least establish a partially shared representation. The collaborative use of external representations of argumentation involves participants in a complex process of knowledge sharing and grounding, in particular when the participants are from different backgrounds (Boshuizen & Schijf, 1998; Alpay, Giboin & Dieng, 1998). In this section we will briefly review means by which CSCL-environments have sought to support (or provoke) argumentation, maintaining coherence and focus and knowledge negotiation. In doing so these environments assume that the learner brings certain skills and attitudes to the collaborative tasks. We will not go into the details of these assumptions to which Pilkington and Walker (this volume) offer some sobering thoughts.

*Task characteristics*

Veerman and Treasure-Jones (1999) in reviewing a number of systems that intended at least to support and coordinate argumentation between learners, also considered task characteristics. They concluded that tasks that provoke argumentation by learners have at least some of the following characteristics: multiple acceptable solutions exist; competitive instructions are given; role-playing or predefined conflicting stances are used; required information is distributed among the members of the group; students with conflicting original beliefs are grouped together; there is an initial individual work stage in which students construct there own stance or solution, and a joint product is required. Support by the system, according to Veerman and Treasure-Jones (1999), can be offered by structured interaction at the interface, preferably without restrictions on turn-taking in the communication window or on the use of dialogue moves. Veerman (2000) has explored how task and software characteristics for a range of computer tools may provoke and support argumentation by students. Although the interplay among task, software environment and task approaches by (groups of) students showed complex patterns, she found some evidence that the Belvedere environment helped students to maintain focus and seemed to stimulate the production of constructive activities (add, explain, evaluate, transform or summarise information).

*Coherence and focus*

CSCL environments like Knowledge Forum and the Collaboratory Notebook allow students to add notes to a shared environment. The structure of the notes can become complex and additional help may be needed to keep students focused on the ongoing deliberations and to offer them adequate overviews. Maintaining coherence and focus in computer-mediated conferencing systems is problematic: discussions tend to lose coherence (Herring, 1999). CMC systems, according to Hewitt (1997), discourage convergent discourse (forcing a reply to a single contribution), and stimulate the discourse becoming more diffuse (branching), eventually leading to a situation in which participants only address sub-branches ignoring other topics altogether. Hewitt, Scardamalia and Webb (1997) implemented the 'Knowledge Map': a tool that allows CSILE notes to be related to more than one other node and offers several views on the relations between nodes, like history, refers-to and referred-by.

Synchronous environments like Belvedere offer students a chat box where they can exchange their ideas about the current state of the evidence maps and the actions to be undertaken. It has been noted that the relation, if any, between the contents of the chat box discussions and the evidence maps is not very clear (Veerman, 2000) and that synchronicity may have a strong interfering effect on interaction and outcomes (Veerman, this volume). One way to strengthen the link between the interaction and the shared artifact is to structure the dialogue between participants. Baker and Lund (1997) offered learners a structured communication interface where learners characterised the type of interaction they were pursuing by selecting appropriate screen buttons. Baker and Lund found that students working with the structured interface produced more task focused and reflective interactions (explanation, justification, evaluation) than students working with a chat-box interface. However, the amount of argumentative interactions was very low in both groups and they did not differ in the quality of the solutions they produced (See Baker, this volume for a more successful attempt to stimulate argumentation).

In the Belvedere environment the coach can help students to *focus* on parts of the evidence diagram that need further attention. Once invoked, the coach scrutinises the structure of the argument in the evidence map for a number of known weaknesses. The coach recognizes a number of patterns, e.g. 'confirmation bias', where the evidence map contains only data in favour of a particular hypothesis, non-discriminating data, data not accounted for by a hypothesis, et cetera. The coach highlights the elements in the evidence map and presents its diagnosis with suggestions.

## Knowledge negotiation

In collaborative situations participants have to maintain a common ground and negotiate about conflicting knowledge. Obviously, all systems discussed offer at least a minimum functionality to support negotiation: chat boxes, discussion notes and similar devices, however here we will consider how conflict can be represented and how knowledge negotiation and conflict resolution are supported. There are two levels of representation of conflict involved: representation of conflicting views of learners ("This is a principle". "No, it is a warrant") as well as representation of conflicting information. Belvedere assumes that learners reach an agreement on the applicable type of object before it is entered in the shared workspace. It does not support representation of conflict between learners. In the evidence map explicit labelling of conflicting information (e.g. between data and hypothesis) is supported. SenseMaker represents theories in separate 'claim frames' but it cannot express inconsistencies between information held in separate frames..

Miao, Holst, Holmer, Fleschutz and Zentel (2000) state the following requirements for knowledge negotiations in CSCL: (a) detect conflict, i.e. visual indications of places where conflicts occur, and support the negotiation process; (b) support expressing (individual) opinions; (c) support representing confidence in the knowledge about information represented in a shared artifact; (d) initiate a negotiation process; (e) support conflict resolution. Miao et al. point out that in many CMC-based systems the information needed to spot the location of conflicts, individual comments or opinions is hidden in textual descriptions. This means that, in general, there is no way for the system to know where a conflict exists, let alone offer support to resolve it. The CROCODILE environment (Pfister, Wessner, Holmer & Steinmetz, 1999) contains a number of facilities to detect and represent conflict and to support knowledge negotiation. The content in this environment is represented at two layers: a hypermedia document structure and the so-called *learning net* that represents the main topics in the domain as a graph. The learning net represents shared knowledge, and for each topic in the learning net the 'degreement' (degree of agreement) is visually represented. The environment has a number of communication scripts or learning protocols (Miao, Holst, Haake & Steinmetz, 2000), some of which are specialised in collecting data and calculating 'degreement', others are envisaged that guide the negotiation process.

A pragma-dialectical approach to computer support of conflict resolution is prototyped in the DIALECTIC system (Chryssafidou, 2000). Pragma-dialectics approaches argumentation as part of a critical discussion governed by valid dialectical procedures for resolving differences of opinion between two individuals, a "protagonist" and an "antagonist" (Van Eemeren, Grootendorst & Henkemans, 1996). DIALECTIC is a tool that supports writing argumentative text. It represents argumentation visually as a set of rival standpoints and arguments. Arguments support or refute a standpoint or other arguments. A coach inspects this 'argument map' and can apply a number of pragma-dialectical heuristics to offer support to the learner, for instance by indicating where attacking and defensive moves are needed.

SIBYL, a prototype of a qualitative decision management system (Lee, 1990) is an implementation of DRL. SIBYL performs a number of services, of which we only present plausibility management, because it is a more general approach to conflict detection than described above. In plausibility management the system updates the a-priori plausibility of a claim if other claims are added that support, qualify or deny the claim. Plausibility management is a special form of dependency management that maintains a consistent state in the knowledge base when changes are introduced. In SIBYL users can be associated with a claim, and the number of associated users can be used as a parameter in the procedures that update plausibilities (cf CROCODILE's 'degreement'). Consider an example of SIBYL's services applied to the arena of scientific inquiry. Here one might qualify the claim that data D supports hypothesis H by pointing out that D is measured using an unreliable instrument. If the plausibility of this statement surpasses a certain threshold, plausibility management will set the plausibility of the claim **supports**(D,H) to zero. On the larger scale of dependency management the effects may be further propagated. Assume that H is supported by other claims, but already has a low plausibility. The refutation of **supports**(D,H) may now have the effect that the plausibility of H is falling below a critical threshold, so that the claim that H is a valid explanation of a phenomenon has to be retracted. SIBYL offers rich support in expressing conflicting arguments and keeping trace of the plausibility of claims. It's modelling capacities for expressing *individual* opinions and remarks (i.e. expressing different views of individuals on the same topic) are limited.

From the CSCL-literature we may learn that supporting argumentation by external representations (and solving wicked problems is very much an argumentative process) requires more from a representational formalism than the textual expression of an argument. In discussion-based tools, conflict will be hard to detect by a computer and may stay unnoticed by the learner in the threads of a discussion. Knowledge representation tools offer better opportunities for computer-based support, but as we have seen, it depends on their representational formalisms whether arguments can be formulated (are all objects and relations debatable?) and whether they will support detection of conflict between learners and information in the shared workspace. SIBYL demonstrates an approach to conflict detection that also points to another problem we may have to deal with: conflicts and conflict resolution may have propagating effects beyond the local conflict topic.

## EXTERNAL REPRESENTATIONS FOR WICKED PROBLEMS

In this final section we will discuss how we are trying to develop external representations to support problem solving of wicked problems, drawing from CSCL and studies in design rationale. We will present some very premature results from an analysis of discussion protocols in which we have tried to analyze the contents in terms of a DRL-based category system. A wicked problem like 'how can we reduce school drop-out?', will engage participants in a process where they structure the problem, define constraints and features, return to problem structuring et cetera, thus moving through the several 'spaces of design rationale' mentioned above. Our hunch here is that laying out these spaces in an external representation will help participants to maintain focus and coherence.

We have taken DRL as our starting point in describing the concepts and relations (i.e. the ontology) of a system for external representation to support solving the type of wicked problems we mentioned, or analyzing proposed solutions. The 'spaces' concept of DRL is important here, because we cannot assume a linearly progressing problem-solving process. Rather, subjects may become entangled in partial solutions, return to a redefinition of constraints or criteria, restate the problem, et cetera. Furthermore, what we are describing is a system to capture the content of the argumentation, not the process or communicative functions involved. We used DRL to reformulate Logical Framework (Sartorius, 1996) representations of programs, and amended it with concepts taken from theory-driven evaluation theory (Chen, 1990; Rossi, Freeman & Lipsey, 1999). In Logical Framework Analysis (LFA) a project is decomposed into several layers starting from input through immediate outcomes to long-term effects. At each level performance indicators and means to verify them are defined and important assumptions spelled out, requiring intense discussion and argumentation between the stakeholders of the program. We added elements from theory-driven evaluation in order to represent intervening mechanisms that link the actual intervention to the expected short-term and long-term results. This is basically a set of assumptions about the effects that the intervention will have on the target population.

Figure 3 gives an impression of the objects and relations in the representation. As in DRL, all relations are to be considered claims. Here the relation between Authority data and Hypothesis is interpreted as a claim that the following data supports the hypothesis. All claims may be challenged or queried as is indicated by the question related to the data and the claim that denies the claim that the intervention will lead to the outcomes. Other DRL relations (facilitates, qualifies) are used as well. The oval figures to the right represent elements of the Logical Framework Approach.

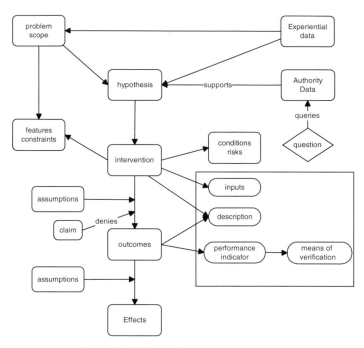

*Figure 3: DRL-based representation system*

As a first check on the usability of this representation system, we used it to analyse a small set of discussion protocols of students[1] trying to find a solution to the increase of school drop-out. The participants, American students with different educational backgrounds (debaters, philosophers, education majors), were confronted with the following problem: the annual meeting of the Board of State Governors has asked a team of experts, the participants, to prepare recommendations to reduce school drop-out and to present those recommendations within a month to the Board. Participants were further instructed that they would have one other meeting shortly before the presentation to the Board of Governors, and that they could compile a list of research questions to be answered before that meeting.

We prepared a content analysis schema to study the typed written protocols of the first 90-minute sessions. The scheme uses the following major categories: *Analysis* (statements dealing with problem definition, delineation, hypotheses on causal factors and data to corroborate the analysis) *Constraints* (statements on constraints that the solutions must meet, desirable features and associated risks) *Interventions* (statements regarding the intervention logic: planned interventions, their expected short-term outcomes, assumptions that relate the actions to the long-term effects) and *Presentation* (statements dealing with the preparation of the

---

[1] We acknowledge the assistance of Tom Duffy, who made available the protocols.

presentation of the recommendations). This analysis focuses on the major content categories. It does not deal with the relations between these objects and it does not deal with process characteristics.

Three coders each coded two complete protocols[2]. The protocols were segmented on the basis of the turns in the dialogue; the coders were instructed to code for the main idea expressed in the turn. Agreements on the main categories were 72%, 77% and 79% for respectively the Philosophers (P), Educators (E) and Debaters (D) protocols. Kappa's for the protocols ranged from 0.59 (P), through 0,66 (E) to 0,69. Although these kappa's are rather low, we think they may be improved by segmenting on a lower level than the turn. Table 2 presents the percentage of coded segments in the main categories:

*Table 2: main categories (percentages)*

|  | *P* | *E* | *D* |
|---|---|---|---|
| *Analysis* | 13.1 | 20.6 | 25'.8 |
| *Constraints* | 10.1 | 4.6 | 1.9 |
| *Interventions* | 24.9 | 11.0 | 23.5 |
| *Presentation* | 6.2 | 14.7 | 3.1 |
| *Other* | 45.5 | 48.7 | 46.0 |

In the first place the table shows that these content categories can cater for a substantial amount of the turns in the dialogues. Secondly, table 2 shows a number of remarkable differences among the three groups: only the educators paid considerable attention to the preparation of the presentation. The proportion of turns on Analysis of the educators and debaters is almost twice that of the philosophers. Philosophers, on the other hand, expend far more dialogue on Constraints and Features. Closer inspection of the protocols seems to indicate different approaches to the task. The debaters identify a number of *separate* causes (drugs, gangs, pregnancy and others), adding some experiential data to support these claims. They then systematically work down the list of these causes trying to define an intervention that will eliminate the cause or reduce its effects. Their score on analysis and interventions is produced by enumerating (and repeating) their list of causes, and their dialogue on the details of the problems they encounter when they consider how to implement the interventions for each of the separate causes.

The discussion of the philosophers takes a completely different route. After delineating the problem (what is drop-out), and without any discussion of the possible causes of drop-out, they discuss features and constraints of possible recommendations, which leads them to define a general intervention method ('carrot

---

[2] Coding and analysis of the protocols were done with the MEPA program made available to us by Gijsbert Erkens of the Utrecht University.

and stick') and some important constraints, which they call a meta-recommendation (no intervention shall violate the integrity or quality of education). A substantial amount of their dialogue on interventions seems produced by 'Gedankenexperimenten' in which they test whether a particular implementation is feasible. This approach breaks down when they come to the conclusion that the general 'carrot and stick' approach is incompatible with their meta-recommendation, because the social pressure on teachers and schools will prevent them from withholding incentives as well as from punishing students. The philosophers then retract to an approach similar to that of the debaters.

The education majors obviously have more background knowledge to substantiate their analysis and recommendations and their protocol has lengthy passages in which research data are summarised. The analysis of the problem is very short, or even shallow, and very early on in the protocol their recommendation – stimulate charter schools – is formulated. There is some sort of 'confirmation bias' in the protocol: no alternative causes or interventions receive substantial attention and the participant who questions whether the recommendation would reduce drop-out is mostly ignored. The educators seem to test their recommendation not on whether it will actually reduce drop-out but on whether it will fit stated policies of the Governors.

These results show resemblance to the analysis of social science problem-solving by James Voss and his colleagues (Voss, 1991; Voss, Greene, Post & Penner, 1983; Voss, Tyler & Yengo, 1983). Voss, Greene, Post & Penner (1983) had experts, novices and beginning experts solve the problem of how to increase Soviet agricultural production. Analysis of the protocols showed that experts identified more abstract problems as the factors producing the problem, and they stated more general abstract solutions to which lower-level problems were subordinate. Novices decomposed the problem into low-level subproblems to which solutions where proposed. They failed to evaluate solutions in terms of constraints and they did not specifiy subproblems that could be encountered when proposed solutions were implemented.

We of course need further analysis to go beyond these impressions. It seems however that our categories can account for a major part of the *content* of the dialogues. Thus, these categories may prove a usable starting point for the further development of a system using external representations to offer guidance to learners in solving these types of problems: the different approaches that we found all have sufficient important weaknesses to allow improvement. This first analysis also shows a major weakness: the representation is biased towards formulation (and argumentation) of a number of (rival) hypotheses and linked interventions: it offers insufficient support to a description in terms of abstract causes and solutions and their decomposition.

We have concentrated on the major content of the representational notation, but we have to go beyond that in order to use the notation to facilitate collaborative problem solving. In the first place we have to research its use in settings in which learners construct and share the external representations during problem solving. That implies, as far as the content is concerned, that decisions have to be made about the ontology (how to represent abstract causes, for instance) and an appropriate level of specificity of the representational notation. It also implies that we have to go beyond an analysis of the content of the discourse and address processes of knowledge sharing, negotiation and coordination in the collaborative solving of wicked problems.

## CONCLUSIONS

Developing a representational notation for a CSCL-environment in which learners try to solve wicked problems is a challenging task, some might say a wicked problem by itself:

First, the objects and relations needed for the representational notation have to be taken from different domains including scientific inquiry, design argumentation and program planning and evaluation, each domain rich enough to contribute to a very complex notation. The CSCL research teaches us however, that rich ontologies and high levels of specificity can interfere with the problem-solving process and Cognitive Load Theory hints in the same direction.

Second, we have to cater for different representations of the problem: what some represent as a technical problem is a marketing problem to others. This not only poses problems to the notation, but also to support of knowledge sharing, conflict detection and resolution and coordination.

Third, the argumentation in solving wicked problems is such that all statements should be considered debatable claims that may be questioned, supported, denied, or qualified. As we have pointed out, this is not a matter of local conflict resolution alone: results may propagate.

Fourth, there is no clear-cut order in the problem solving process that we could use to sequentially focus learners to particular aspects of the representation. They seem to move back and forth between the layers identified by Lee and Lai: for example, partial solutions are not only tested against constraints and features, they are also used to refine these criteria.

The results we have presented are modest and only deal with the minimal content of a representational notation. As described above, enough problems remain to warrant further research.

## AFFILIATION

*Jan M. van Bruggen & Paul A. Kirschner*
*Educational Technology Expertise Center Open University of the Netherlands.*
*P.O. Box 2960, 6401 DL Heerlen, The Netherlands*
*Telephone: +31.45.5762754; Fax: +31.45.5762802*

*Email: jan.vanbruggen@ou.nl*

# REFERENCES

Alpay, L., Giboin, A., & Dieng, R. (1998). Accidentology: an example of problem solving by multiple agents with multiple representations. In M. W. Van Someren, P. Reimann, H. P. A. Boshuizen, & T. de Jong (Eds.), *Learning with multiple representations* (pp. 152-174). Amsterdam: Pergamon.

Baker, M., & Lund, K. (1997). Promoting reflective interactions in a CSCL environment. *Journal of Computer Assisted Learning, 13,* 175-193.

Bell, P. (1997). Using argument representations to make thinking visible for individuals and groups. In R. Hall, N. Miyake, & N. Enyedy (Eds.), *Proceedings of CSCL '97: The Second International Conference on Computer Support for Collaborative Learning* (pp. 10-19). Toronto: University of Toronto Press.

Boshuizen, H. P. A., & Schijf, H. J. M. (1998). Problem solving with multiple representations by multiple and single agents: an analysis of the issues involved. In M. W. Van Someren, P. Reimann, H. P. A. Boshuizen, & T. de Jong (Eds.), *Learning with multiple representations* (pp. 137-151). Amsterdam: Pergamon.

Carroll, J. M., & Moran, T. P. (1991). Introduction to this special issue on design rationale. *Human-Computer Interaction, 6,* 197-200.

Chandler, P., & Sweller, J. (1991). Cognitive load theory and the format of instruction. *Cognition and instruction, 8,* 293-332.

Chen, H.-C. (1990). *Theory-driven evaluations.* Newbury Park, CA: Sage Publications.

Chryssafidou, E. (1999). Computer-supported formulation of argumentation: a dialectical approach. *presentation at the symposium 'Belvedere: review and new applications',* Heerlen, 29-9-1999.

Chryssafidou, E. (2000). DIALECTIC: Enhancing essay writing skills with computer-supported formulation of argumentation. *Workshop on Interactive Learning Environments for Children,* Athens, 3-3-2000.

Conklin, E. J., & Begeman, M. L. (1988). gIBIS: A hypertext tool for the exploratory policy discussion. *ACM Transactions on Office Information Systems, 6,* 303-331.

Conklin, E. J., & Weil, W. (1997) *Wicked problems: naming the pain in organizations.* http://www.gdss.com/wp/wicked.htm. Accessed: 05-06-2001.

Cox, R. (1999). Representation construction, externalised cognition and individual differences. *Learning and Instruction, 9,* 343-363.

de Jong, T., Ainsworth, S., Dobson, M., van der Hulst, A., Levonen, J., Reimann, P., Sime, J.-A., Van Someren, M. W., Spada, H., & Swaak, J. (1998). Acquiring knowledge in science and mathematics: the use of multiple representations in technology-based learning environments. In M. W. Van Someren, P. Reimann, H. P. A. Boshuizen, & T. de Jong (Eds.), *Learning with multiple representations* (pp. 9-40). Amsterdam: Pergamon.

Duffy, T. M., & Cunningham, D. J. (1996). Constructivism: implications for the design and delivery of instruction. In D. H. Jonassen (Ed.), *Handbook of research for educational communications and technology* (pp. 170-198). New York: Macmillan Library Reference USA.

Edelson, D. C., Gomez, L. M., Polman, J., Gordin, D., & Fishman, B. (1994). Scaffolding student inquiry with collaborative visualization tools. *paper presented at the Annual Meeting of the American Educational Research Association,* New Orleans, LA.

Edelson, D. C., O'Neill, D. K., Gomez, L. M., & D'Amico, L. (1995). A design for effective support of inquiry and collaboration. In J. L. Schnase & E. L. Cunnius (Eds.), *Proceedings of CSCL '95 : the first international conference on computer support for collaborative learning : October 17-2, 1995 . Indiana University . Bloomington, Indiana, USA* (CSCL 95 ed., pp. 107-111). Mahwah, NJ: Lawrence Erlbaum.

Fischer, G., Nakakoji, K., Ostwald, J., Stahl, G., & Sumner, T. (1993). Embedding critics in design environments. *Knowledge Engineering Review, 8,* 285-307.

Fischer, G., Lemke, A. C., McCall, R., & Morch, A. I. (1996). Making argumentation serve design. In T. P. Moran & J. M. Carroll (Eds.), *Design Rationale: Concepts, Techniques, and Use* (6 ed., pp. 267-293). Hillsdale, NJ: Lawrence Erlbaum Associates. (Originally published in Human-Computer Interaction, 1991, vol 6, 3+4, 393-419)

Goel, V., & Pirolli, P. (1992). The structure of design problem spaces. *Cognitive Science, 16,* 395-429.

Gruber, Th. R., & Russell, D. M. (1996). Generative design rationale: beyond the record and replay paradigm. In T. P. Moran & J. M. Carroll (Eds.), *Design Rationale: Concepts, Techniques, and Use* (pp. 323-349). Hillsdale, NJ: Lawrence Erlbaum Associates.

Herring, S. (1999) *Interactional coherence in CMC.* Journal of Computer-Mediated Communication. 4. Accessed: 28-07-2000.

Hewitt, J. (1997). Beyond threaded discourse. *WebNet '97.*

Hewitt, J., Scardamalia, M., & Webb, J. (1997). Situative design issues for interactive learning environments: the problem of group coherence. *Paper presented at the Annual Meeting of the American Educational Association,* Chicago.

Jonassen, D. H., Peck, K. L., & Wilson, B. G. (1999). *Learning with technology: a constructivist perspective.* Upper Saddle River, NJ: Prentice Hall.

Larkin, J. H., & Simon, H. A. (1995). Why a diagram is (sometimes) worth ten thousand words. In J. Glasgow, N. N. Narayanan, & B. Chandrasekaran (Eds.), *Diagrammatic reasoning; cognitive and computational perspectives* (pp. 69-109). Menlo Park, CA: AAAI Press/MIT Press. (originally published in Cognitive Science, 11, 1987, pp 65-99)

Lee, J. (1990). SIBYL: a qualitative decision management system. In P. H. Winston & S. A. Shellard (Eds.), *Artificial Intelligence at MIT; expanding horizons* (pp. 105-133). Cambridge, MA: MIT Press.

Lee, J., & Lai, K.-Y. (1991). What's in design rationale? *Human-Computer Interaction, 6,* 251-280.

Lesgold, A. (1998). Multiple representations and their implications for learning. In M. W. Van Someren, P. Reimann, H. P. A. Boshuizen, & T. de Jong (Eds.), *Learning with multiple representations* (pp. 307-319). Amsterdam: Pergamon.

Miao, Y., Holst, S., Haake, J. M., & Steinmetz, R. (2000). PBL-protocols: guiding and controlling problem based learning processes in virtual learning environments. *Proceedings of the Fourth International Conference of the Learning Sciences (ICLS2000), Ann Arbor, MI, June 14-17.*

Miao, Y., Holst, S., Holmer, T., Fleschutz, J., & Zentel, P. (2000). An activity-oriented approach to visually structured knowledge representation for problem-based learning in virtual learning environments. *paper presented at Fourth International Conference on the Design of Cooperative Systems (COOP 2000),* Sophia Antipolis, France, 23-5-2000.

Moran, T. P., & Carroll, J. M. (Eds.). (1996). *Design rationale :concepts, techniques, and use.* Mahwah, N.J.: L. Erlbaum Associates.

Paas, F. (1992). Training strategies for attaining transfer of problem-solving skill in statistics: A cognitive-load approach. *Journal of Educational Psychology, 84,* 429-434.

Paas, F., Renkl, A., & Sweller, J. (in press). Cognitive Load Theory. *Educational Psychologist.*

Paas, F,. Tuovinen, J. E., Tabbers, H., & Van Gerven, P. (in press). Cognitive Load Measurement as a Means to Advance Cognitive Load Theory. *Educational Psychologist.*

Paas, F., Van Merriënboer, J. J. G., & Adam, J. J. (1994). Measurement of cognitive load in instructional research. *Perceptual and Motor Skills, 79,* 419-430.

Paolucci, M., Suthers, D., & Weiner, A. (1995). Belvedere: stimulating students' critical discussion. *CHI95 conference companion, interactive posters, May 7-11, Denver CO* (pp. 123-124).

Pea, R. D. (1993). Practices of distributed intelligence and designs for education. In G. Salomon (Ed.), *Distributed cognition: psychological and educational considerations* (pp. 47-87). Cambridge: Cambridge University Press.

Pfister, H.-R., Wessner, M., Holmer, T., & Steinmetz, R. (1999). Negotiating about shared knowledge in a cooperative learning environment. In C. Hoadley & J. Roschelle (Eds.), *Computer Support for Collaborative Learning; designing new media for a new millennium: collaborative technology for learning, education and training, Palo Alto, California, December 12-15, 1999* (pp. 454-457). Palo Alto: Stanford University, CA.

Pirolli, P., & Russell, D. M. (1990). The instructional design environment: Technology to support design problem solving. *Instructional Science, 19,* 121-144.

Rittel, H. W. J., & Webber, M. M. (1984). Planning problems are wicked problems. In N. Cross (Ed.), *Developments in design methodology* (pp. 135-144). Chichester: John Wiley & Sons. (published earlier as part of 'Dilemmas in a general theory of planning', Policy Sciences,4, 1973, 155-169)

Rossi, P. H., Freeman, H. E., & Lipsey, M. W. (1999). *Evaluation: a systematic approach* (6th ed.). Thousand Oaks: Sage Publications.

Russell, D. M., Moran, Th. P., & Jordan, D. S. (1988). The instructional-design environment. In J. Psotka, L. D. Massey, & S. A. Mutter (Eds.), *Intelligent Tutoring Systems: lessons learned* (pp. 203-228). Hillsdale: Lawrence Erlbaum Associates.

Sartorius, R. (1996). The third generation logical framework approach: dynamic management for agricultural research in projects. *European Journal of Agricultural Education and Extension, 2,* 49-62.

Scardamalia, M., Bereiter, C., Maclean, R. S., Swallow, J., & Woodruff, E. (1989). Computer-supported intentional learning environments. *Journal of Educational Computing Research, 5,* 51-68.

Scardamalia, M. A., & Bereiter, C. (1994). Computer support for knowledge building communities. *The Journal of the Learning Sciences, 3,* 265-283.

Schijf, H. J. M., & Simon, H. A. (1998). One person: multiple representations: an analysis of a simple, realistic multiple representation learning task. In M. W. Van Someren, P. Reimann, H. P. A. Boshuizen, & T. de Jong (Eds.), *Learning with multiple representations* (pp. 197-236). Amsterdam: Pergamon.

Shum, S., & Hammond, N. (1994). Argumentation-based design rationale: what use at what cost? *International Journal of Human-Computer Studies, 40,* 603-652.

Shum, S. J., MacLean, A., Bellotti, V. M. E., & Hammond, N. V. (1997). Graphical argumentation and design cognition. *Human-Computer Interaction, 12,* 267-300.

Stenning, K., & Oberlander, J. (1995). A Cognitive Theory of Graphical and Linguistic Reasoning: Logic and Implementation. *Cognitive Science, 19,* 97-140.

Suthers, D. (1995). *Designing for internal vs external discourse in groupware for developing critical discussion skills.* CHI' 95 research symposium, Denver.

Suthers, D. (2001). Towards a systematic study of representational guidance for collaborative learning discourse. *Journal of Universal Computer Sciences, 7,* 254-277.

Suthers, D., & Weiner, A. (1995) *Groupware for developing critical discussion skills.* http://www-cscl95.indiana.edu/cscl95/suthers.html. Accessed: 14-07-1998.

Suthers, D. D. (1999). Effects of alternate representations of evidential relations on collaborative learning discourse. In C. Hoadley & J. Roschelle (Eds.), *Computer Support for Collaborative Learning; designing new media for a new millenium: collaborative technology for learning, education, and training. CSCL 99, December 12-15, Palo Alto, CA* (pp. 611-620). Palo Alto, CA: Stanford University.

Suthers, D. D., Toth, E. E., & Weiner, A. (1997). An integrated approach to implementing collaborative inquiry in the classroom. In R. Hall, N. Miyake, & N. Enyedy (Eds.), *Proceedings of CSCL '97: The Second International Conference on Computer Support for Collaborative Learning* (pp. 272-279). Toronto: University of Toronto Press.

Sweller, J. (1988). Cognitive load during problem solving: Effects on learning. *Cognitive Science, 12,* 257-285.

Sweller, J., van Merriënboer, J. J. G., & Paas, F. G. W. C. (1998). Cognitive architecture and instructional design. *Educational Psychology Review, 10,* 251-296.

Van Bruggen, J. M., & Kirschner, P. A. (2000). *Usability of a representational scheme for expressing program theory.* Heerlen: Open Universiteit Nederland, Otec.

Van Eemeren, F. H., Grootendorst, R., & Henkemans, F. S. (1996). *Fundamentals of argumentation theory; a handbook of historical backgrounds and contemporary developments.* Mahwah, N.J: L. Erlbaum.

Veerman, A. (2000). Computer-supported collaborative learning through argumentation. PhD dissertation University of Utrecht

Veerman, A. L., & Treasure-Jones, T. (1999). Software for problem solving through collaborative argumentation. In J. Andriessen & P. Coirier (Eds.), *Foundations of argumentative text processing* (pp. 203-229). Amsterdam: University of Amsterdam Press.

Voss, J. F., Greene, T. R., Post, T. A., & Penner, C. (1983). Problem-solving skill in the social sciences. In G. H. Bower (Ed.), *The psychology of learning and motivation: Vol. 17. Advances in research and theory* (pp. 165-213).

Voss, J. F., Tyler, S. W., & Yengo, L. A. (1983). Individual differences in the solving of social science problems. In R. F. Dillon & R. R. Schmeck (Eds.), *Individual differences in cognition (vol 1)* (pp. 205-232).

Voss, J. F. (1991). Informal reasoning and international relations. In J. F. Voss & D. N. Perkins (Eds.), *Informal reasoning and education* (pp. 37-58). Hillsdale, NJ, US: Lawrence Erlbaum Associates, Inc.

Zhang, J. (1997). The nature of external representations in problem solving. *Cognitive Science, 21,* 179-217.

Zhang, J., & Norman, D. A. (1994). Representations in distributed cognitive tasks. *Cognitive Science, 18,* 87-122.

P. JERMANN & P. DILLENBOURG

# ELABORATING NEW ARGUMENTS THROUGH A CSCL SCRIPT

## INTRODUCTION

The CSCL community faces two main challenges with respect to learning and argumentation. The scientific challenge is to understand how argumentation produces learning, that is to discover which cognitive mechanisms, triggered by argumentative interactions, generate new knowledge and in which conditions. The engineering challenge is to determine how to trigger productive argumentation among students. These two challenges are often investigated in parallel, but this contribution focuses on the latter.

There are two ways to favour the emergence of argumentation, either pro-actively, by structuring collaboration, or retroactively, by regulating interactions (e.g. a tutor monitors the pair dialogues). Structuring collaboration either means scripting collaborative activities or designing a dedicated communication tool. The features of such argumentation tools constitute a central concern of this book. This contribution addresses both forms of structuring. We describe ArgueGraph, a CSCL script encompassed in a web-based environment, and then compare two different interfaces for this environment.

The notion of script enables us to formalize the educational context in which argumentation is expected to appear. A script is a story or scenario that students and tutors have to play as actors play a movie script. Most scripts are sequential: students go through a linear sequence of phases. Each phase specifies how students should collaborate and solve the problem. A phase is described by five attributes: the task that students have to perform, the composition of the group, the way that the task is distributed within and among groups, the mode of interaction and the timing of the phase (Dillenbourg, 2002). The ArgueGraph script fosters argumentation by forming pairs of students with conflicting opinions. Conflicting situations are of particular interest with respect to collaborative interaction because they enable socio-cognitive conflict (Doise & Mugny, 1981): a social conflict (having a different perspective) has to be solved through a cognitive coordination of the points of view. However, further studies showed that conflict is neither a necessary, nor a sufficient condition for cognitive change. Beyond the intensity of conflict, it is the verbalization necessary to solve the conflict, which seems related to learning effects (Blaye, 1988; Butterworth, 1982).

*J. Andriessen, M. Baker, and D. Suthers (eds.), Arguing to Learn: Confronting Cognitions in Computer-Supported Collaborative Learning environments (205-226).*
© *2003 Kluwer Academic Publishers. Printed in the Netherlands.*

This chapter reports two experiments based on the same script but using different environments. These experiments confirmed what Suthers (this volume), Baker (this volume) and Veerman (this volume) found in different contexts: the ergonomic features of the communication tool influence argumentation. Some features obviously have a strong impact: audio versus text-based communication, synchronous versus asynchronous, etc. What this book shows is that argumentation is also influenced by more subtle features of the medium. Our experiments revealed some of these features.

Similar experiments are described in Schwarz & al. (2001). The authors are interested in the effect of argumentation on collective and individual arguments. They have their students produce arguments about animal experimentation. They show that students produce more complex and elaborated individual arguments as they interact with other students. They also compare two tools used to construct collective arguments. One is inspired by Belvedere (Suthers, this volume) and graphically represents the relations between pros and contras as well as the conclusion of argumentation. The other is a simple table that holds pros and contras and doesn't explicitly show relations between arguments. The collective arguments are more elaborated when using the argumentative map than when using the table. However, this advantage doesn't show up in the final individual arguments.

This chapter is organized as follows. First we describe the learning activity that was used in the two experiments we made. Then, we present the details of each experiment in two separate sections. Then we compare the results from the two experiments and finally we abstract design factors that have an impact on argumentation.


## THE ARGUEGRAPH SCRIPT

The ArgueGraph script is used in the beginning of a master course on the design of educational software. The two reported experiments were run in the normal course settings that combine co-present interactions and distant learning. The environment was part of Tecfa Virtual Campus, used by our students on a daily basis. The learning objectives are to make students understand the relationship between learning theories and design choices in courseware development. For instance, the students have to learn that the notion of immediate feedback is related to the behaviourist framework and is especially relevant some types of procedural sills acquisition or for rote learning.

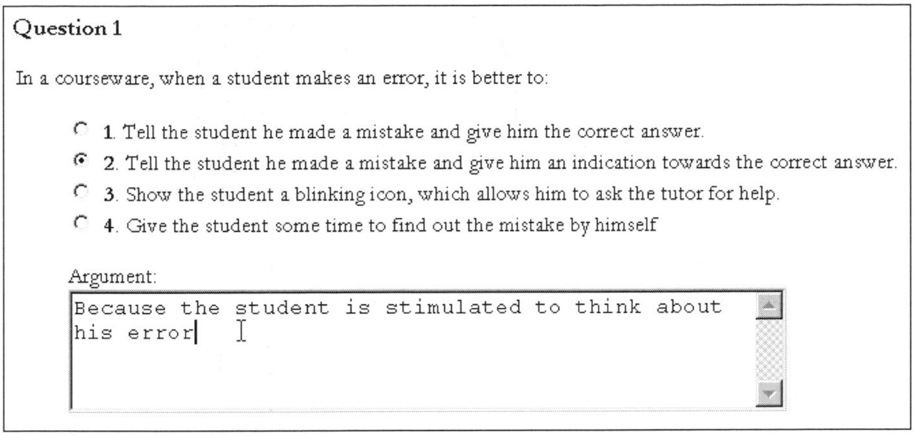

---

**Question 1**

In a courseware, when a student makes an error, it is better to:

     ◯  1. Tell the student he made a mistake and give him the correct answer.

     ◉  2. Tell the student he made a mistake and give him an indication towards the correct answer.

     ◯  3. Show the student a blinking icon, which allows him to ask the tutor for help.

     ◯  4. Give the student some time to find out the mistake by himself

Argument:

```
Because the student is stimulated to think about
his error|   I
```

---

*Figure 1: Question display in version 1. Students use the radio button to make an exclusive choice. They provide a written argument for their choice.*

The script for the activity consists of five phases:

1. **Solo phase**: Students fill in a questionnaire about design principles in courseware development. Questions measure opinions and students provide a short written argument for each of their choices (figure 1). The proposed answers are not correct or incorrect but reflect different pedagogical styles and are grounded in different learning theories to be addressed in this course.

2. **Display phase**: The choices made at phase 1 are then transformed into two scores reflecting whether students privilege system- vs. user-driven interactions on the one hand and a discovery vs. teaching based pedagogy on the other hand. The system draws a scatter plot on the basis of these scores and represents each student's position (figure 2). The choice of scores for each answer was done in a rather arbitrary way. The final sum of scores collected by a student is not a scientific estimate of his pedagogical style. It is only a very rough approximation. The goal is not to produce a very exact value but to use the distances between students to create pairs for the third phase of the script.

3. **Duo phase**: Students fill in the same questionnaire in pairs. Pairs are formed so as to maximize differences within a pair according to the answers the students gave to the individual questionnaire. While filling in the questionnaire the students see the arguments they gave to support their answers in the individual phase. They have to agree on a common choice and provide a common argument.

4. **Debriefing phase**: The system produces a synthesis and a scatter plot representing the "migration" of each student from his initial position to the

common position. The synthesis lists the individual and common arguments given for each question and draws a pie chart with the distribution of answers. Finally, a brief statement presents the relationship between underlying theories and the options the students can select in a question. During this debriefing phase, the teacher reviews all arguments produced by individuals and pairs and relates them to the various theoretical frameworks in the domain (behaviorist, constructivist, socio-cultural, ...). Most pieces of information used in the debriefing have been mentionned in the arguments provided by the students. The teacher's role is to structure this mountain of information into a more coherent framework.

5   **Homework phase**: Finally, students get some homework. They have to analyze the answers to one of the questions including thereby theoretical stakes and their own opinion

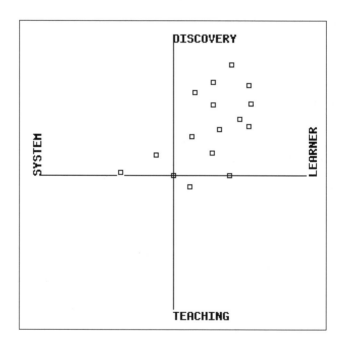

*Figure 2: Scatter plot of individual answers. Each square corresponds to a student's opinion. The horizontal axis opposes system vs. learner driven interaction. The vertical axis opposes discovery-based learning vs. teaching. Names of students have been removed from the figure for confidentiality.*

This script, as many others (Dillenbourg, 2002) is not purely collaborative, as it includes also individual phases (1 and 5) and collective phases (2 & 4). Only phase 3 is really collaborative. "Collective" differs from "collaborative" due to the fact that it does not necessarily imply rich interactions among students. Simply, the system collects individual productions or data and makes them available to the whole group (Jermann & Dillenbourg, 1999).

This activity was run twice with different timing of the phases and tool features. In the first experiment, the whole script was held in a four-hour session. Students had to make an exclusive choice in favour of a particular answer and provide a written argument supporting their choice (figure 1). Making an exclusive choice means that students were able to choose only one of the possible answers to the question asked.

In the second experiment, the script span over three weeks, the first three phases taking place at the student's home. Once they completed phase 1, students were told by email who their partner would be for phase 3. They set up a date and a time with their partner and would both dial up to the network at that time and answer the questionnaire together. Students had to make a non-exclusive choice by rating their level of acceptance for each possible answer through the use of a five-point slider. Labels for the sliders were 'Never', 'Rarely', 'Sometimes', 'Often', and 'Always' (figure 3).

## EXPERIMENT 1

*Research question*

Intuitively, the Argue & Graph activity worked very well, as indicated by the high degree of learner involvement during all phases. However, the tool was not subject to a formal evaluation procedure. Nevertheless, we collected all answers and arguments in order to grasp learning mechanisms. Namely, we investigate the differences between individual answers and pairs' answers.

*Subjects*

We ran two pre-experiments, with 15 students in 1997 and 17 students in 1998 respectively, after which the system was improved with regard to various functionalities. The experiment reported in this section was run on October 22nd 1998 with 18 students. Most students were located in the same quarter of the graph (Figure 1). This phenomenon is probably due to the fact that the questions did too clearly reflect the pedagogical values sponsored at TECFA and did not take into account the technical or financial dimensions of courseware development.

*Variables*

The pairing method used in phase 2 aimed at creating conflictual situations, i.e. make pairs answer a question to which individuals gave different answers. Hence, our first variable is the actual frequency of conflict, i.e. the number of times pair members had given different individual answers in solo. For 52% of the answers there was a conflict between the two solos answers. In other words, the method used to form pairs was rather effective. There is some relation between the distance in the graph and the frequency of conflict (the five pairs with a distance of 1 have a disagreement rate of 38%, while the pairs with a larger distance have a disagreement rate of 52.5%), but the size of the sample is not sufficient to compute a correlation rate.

Since students answer twice to the same questionnaire, we have the opportunity to examine what differentiates answers given alone and in pairs. In this experiment, subjects sit next to each other in front of the machine. We did not record their discussion. Hence, the analysis is restricted to their answers, i.e. the options selected and the arguments introduced in the system to justify this choice. We describe these answers with three variables:

*Type of argument (solo and duo)*

- Accept: the argument provided supports the option selected, e.g. "I choose option 2 because it makes the learner autonomous".
- Discard: the argument rejects another option, e.g. "I choose option 2 because option 3 is too heavy to implement".
- Condition: the argument states some conditions for the option selected, e.g. "I choose option 2 if the learner is very young". Conditions can be imposed onto a certain category of learners (children, adolescents, adults, novices, experts...), or specific task domains (mathematics, verbal communication, procedural versus declarative knowledge...), or onto specific learning goals (consolidation, discovery...) or material settings (screen size, computer power...).

*Style of argument (solo and duo)*

- Justification: the argument contains at least one idea not present in the phrasing of the selected option
- Reformulation: the argument does not contain any idea different from those present in the selected option.

*Semantic relation between solo arguments and duo argument:*

- Union: the duo argument contains the ideas stated by both solo arguments
- Victory: the duo argument contains the ideas of one of the solo arguments
- New: the duo argument contains an idea, which is not present in either solo arguments

Table 1 illustrates the usage of this coding scheme for the solo and duo answers of one pair at question 1 (see figure 1 for the wording of the question). Subject1 solo argument shows a combination of several types of arguments: options 1 and 4 are discarded while option 3 is accepted conditionally. Notice that option 2, which is the actual choice of the student, is not addressed explicitly by the corresponding argument. Arguments with this level of complexity are quite rare, for most of the arguments were coded with a single type and style, like it is the case for subject2 solo argument. All three arguments were considered as 'Justifications' because they contain new ideas with regard to the option stated in the question. The duo argument is 'New' with respect to the content, because it introduces the idea of the learner's autonomy, which was not stated as such in the solo arguments. This examples illustrates what we call a conflict in this paper as the subjects gave different answers in the solo phase.

*Table 1. Coding example*

| Subject | Answer | Phase | Argument (we translate) | Coding |
|---------|--------|-------|-------------------------|--------|
| 1 | Option 2 | SOLO | If he is directly given the correct answer, he might not remember it, if we don't say anything, he might not be aware of his error... The help icon is certainly a good solution, if one can see clearly that it gives help and that it appears only on errors. | Discard option 1, justification <br><br> Discard option 4, justification <br><br> Condition for option 3, justification |
| 2 | Option 3 | SOLO | trade-off between paternalism and neo liberalism | Accept option 2, justification |
| 1 & 2 | Option 3 | DUO | It allows him to ask for help when he needs it. | Accept option 2, justification <br><br> New Content |

*Results*

The system collected 180 solo answers and 90 duo answers to the questionnaire respectively. Some answers were incomplete, for instance when a student made a choice without providing an argument. The valid cases remaining for the analysis are 166 solo arguments and 67 duo arguments. The two authors of this chapter coded the arguments once and did not use a second judge to validate the coding. Yet, most of the coding was straightforward.

*The type of arguments varies between solo and duo phases*

Table 2 presents types of arguments for the solo and duo phases. We computed three proportion tests to compare the solo and duo phases. The proportion of 'Accept' arguments is similar in both phases even if significantly higher in the solo phase ($U=0.048$, $p<.05$). It appears that the proportion of 'Discard' arguments in the solo phase is higher than in the duo phase ($U=0.037$, $p<.05$). The proportion of 'Condition' arguments is higher in the duo phase than it is in the solo phase

(U=0.034, p<.05). We will comment on the 'Condition' arguments when examining the effect of conflict on duo arguments.

*Table 2.   Type of arguments across solo and duo phases*

|  |  | Phase | | | | |
|---|---|---|---|---|---|---|
|  |  | SOLO | | DUO | | Difference |
|  |  | Count | % | Count | % | % |
| Type of | Accept | 136 | 82 | 51 | 76 | - 6 |
| argument | Condition | 8 | 5 | 12 | 18 | + 13 |
|  | Discard | 22 | 13 | 4 | 6 | - 7 |
|  | Total | 166 | 100 | 67 | 100 |  |

*The style of arguments varies between solo and duo phases*

Table 3 presents styles of arguments for the solo and duo phases. The proportion of 'Reformulation' is very high in the solo phase (more than half of the answers are simple reformulations of the choices proposed in the question). This proportion is much lower in the duo phase (U=0.06, p<.05). We interpret this difference as follows. When answering alone, students had no reason to make the effort to justify their choice with an elaborated argument even if they elaborated one in their head. In pairs, the discussion that was necessary to agree on an argument seems to force students to make it explicit and to elaborate it. This interesting observation confirms the usefulness of this method. The difference could however also be due to a simpler mechanism: the fact that the students have to answer twice to the same question might let them feel obliged to be produce a more elaborated answer on the second time.

*Table 3.   Style of arguments across solo and duo phases*

|  |  | Phase | | | | |
|---|---|---|---|---|---|---|
|  |  | SOLO | | DUO | | Difference |
|  |  | Count | % | Count | % | % |
| Style of | Justification | 72 | 43 | 57 | 85 | + 42 |
| argument |  |  |  |  |  |  |
|  | Reformulation | 94 | 57 | 15 | 15 | - 42 |
|  | Total | 166 | 100 | 67 | 100 |  |

*The type of duo arguments varies according to conflict*

Let us now look at the duo arguments. Since we designed the learning activity in order to create conflicts, we will focus the analysis around this variable to see if it has an influence on the type and style of arguments.

Sometimes the AB pair chooses the answer given by A in the solo phase; sometime it chooses B's answer. We counted the pair symmetry, i.e. whether the pair chooses systematically the answers of the same peer. Data revealed that all pairs but 2 were rather symmetrical, the difference between the number 'wins' of A and B ranging from zero to two (out of ten answers). .

Table 4 presents the type of arguments for situations with and without conflict. In both cases 'Accept' arguments are predominant, students give an argument, which directly supports their common choice. 'Condition' arguments are interesting because they violate the instructions given to the students: they were asked to choose only one possible option and to give an argument supporting it. This way of proceeding would correspond to the production of 'Accept' arguments. Paradoxally, the 'Condition' arguments match the underlying pedagogical goals of the activity better than the 'Accept' type. We want to show the students that there is not one correct theory in courseware design but that each design choice depends on specific contextual features.

All but one 'Condition' arguments were given in a conflictual situation where students have to defend their choice against another's opinions. This type of argument is a way to solve the conflict by complexifying the argument. Indeed, establishing 'if..then..else' constructions allows to make concessions to the loser of the conflict. Unfortunately 2 cells from table 4 have expected count less than 5 so we cannot compute a reliable Chi-square test to validate these observations. Nevertheless, we modified the instructions given for the production of arguments and implemented a semi-structured interface to foster the production of 'Condition' arguments. The section about Experiment 2 reports the results we obtained.

*Table 4.  Type of arguments across conflict*

|  |  | Conflict |  |  |
| --- | --- | --- | --- | --- |
|  |  | NO | YES | Total |
| Type of argument | Accept | 28 | 23 | 51 |
|  | Condition | 1 | 11 | 12 |
|  | Discard | 3 | 1 | 4 |
|  | Total | 32 | 35 | 67 |

*The semantic relation between solo and duo arguments varies according to conflict*

The semantic relation between solo and duo arguments is related to conflict as can be seen in Table 5. When there is no conflict, students often take the arguments they gave in the solo phase and put them together to produce a 'Union' argument. Since there is no conflict, 'Victory' arguments correspond to the pair choosing one of the two arguments and use it as duo argument. When there is a conflict between the choices students made in the solo phase, the 'New' and 'Victory' arguments are more numerous. A 'Victory' in this context corresponds to one student winning the conflict on both aspects of the answer: the choice and the argument. A 'New' argument reflects a compromise, even if the pair chooses the choice of one student, the argument they provide contains a new idea. 9 out of 12 'Condition' arguments given in the duo phase are at the same time 'New' arguments.

*Table 5.   Semantic relation between solo and duo arguments across conflict*

| $(X^2 = 6.136, p = .047)$ | | Conflict | | |
| --- | --- | --- | --- | --- |
| | | NO | YES | Total |
| Semantic relation | New | 6 | 14 | 20 |
| | Union | 16 | 8 | 24 |
| | Victory | 10 | 13 | 23 |
| | Total | 32 | 35 | 67 |

## Discussion

Answering together to the questionnaire had an impact on the style of arguments (Reformulation vs. Justification) produced by the students. The duo arguments are more elaborated than the solo arguments. We propose that the reason for this change is that students make their opinions explicit and thereby more elaborated during the discussion. The type of arguments (Accept vs. Discard vs. Condition) also varies across solo and duo phases. 'Discard' arguments are more frequent in the solo phase while 'Condition' arguments are more frequent in the duo phase.

In the duo phase, half of the cases are conflictual, i.e. students did not make the same choice in the solo phase. 'Condition' arguments appear mostly in a conflictual situation. We have interpreted the production of this type of argument as resulting from a strategy intended to solve the conflict more fairly than by a 'Victory' of one of the students.

## EXPERIMENT 2

### Design and Research Question

Some students felt uncomfortable in having to make only one choice in experiment 1 and we noticed that forcing them to do so was in contradiction with the goal of the learning activity. With the version of the tool used in this experiment, students can accept or reject all alternatives by setting sliders to identical values.

The first experiment led to interesting results. Particularly, students accommodated to the conflict imposed to them by complexifying their arguments about design choices. This phenomenon met our pedagogical goals and thus, we wanted to further increase the production of conditional arguments. It lead us to a implement a modified answering modality that consists in rating possible choices on a five point lickert scale. Labels for this scale were 'Never', 'Rarely', 'Sometimes', 'Often' and 'Always' (See figure 3).

We were also interested in the argumentation going on during the duo phase. In order to record discussions we implemented a JAVA application that enables students to share a questionnaire and discuss through a chat tool while filling in the common choices and arguments. Whenever a student moves a slider or writes an argument into a text area, his or her partner immediately gets to see it. Having implemented that facility, it was possible to program the activity in a distance learning setting. Students were asked to do the solo phase at home during week 1. The system collected their choices and we run a pairing algorithm to match students with different opinions. Students then had to contact their designated partner and do the duo phase at their convenience during week 2. Finally, the debriefing took place during week 3 at the university.

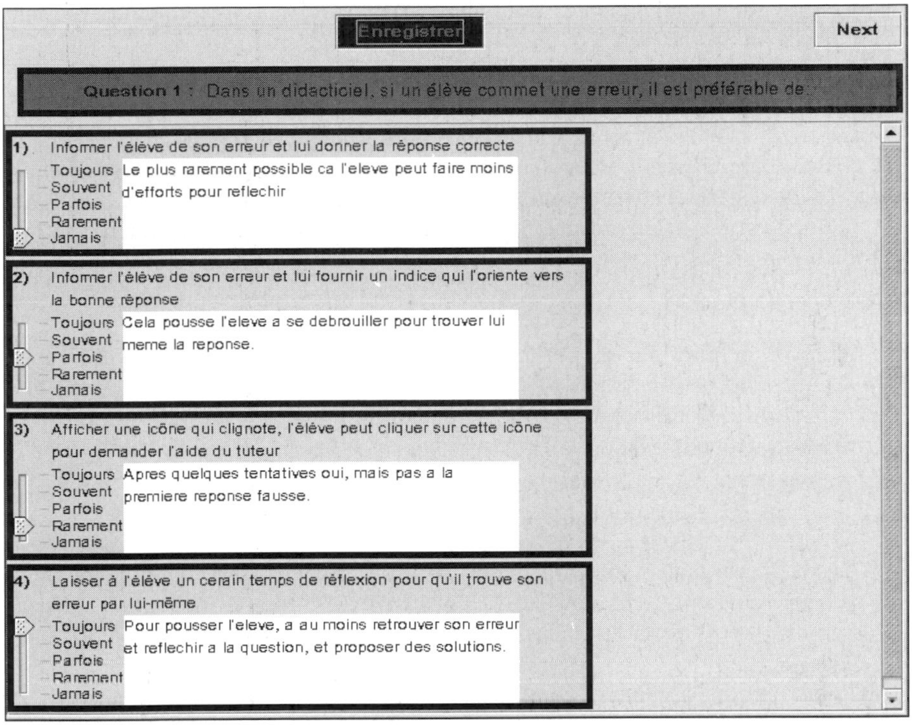

*Figure 3: Question display in version 2. Students use the sliders to make a choice for each of the possible answers. They provide a written argument for each of their choices. The question and the options displayed are the same as the English version displayed in figure 1.The labels next to the sliders correspond to the scale ranging from 'Always' to 'Never'.*

*Subjects*

This experiment was run in 1999 between November 4th and November 30th. The participants were 16 students attending to the postgraduate diploma in educational technologies delivered by TECFA.

*Variables*

Due to the new features of the tool, the variables used to code the arguments provided by the students differ from those used in experiment 1. Choices among alternative answers to the questions are not exclusive: it is possible to agree or to disagree with several alternatives by setting their respective sliders to the same value. The distinction between acceptance and rejection of an answer can be expressed by the manipulation of the sliders. Also, conflict is a continuous variable that depends on the difference of choices made by students.

*Choice (solo and duo)*

The choice score reflects wether students select Never, Rarely, Sometimes, Often or Always. The distance between each label on this scale corresponds to one point. We use a numeric scale ranging from 0 to 4 to represent the selections of students.

*Level of conflict (duo)*

The level of conflict for a particular alternative corresponds to the difference between the solo choice scores of the two learners. For a particular question, the level of conflict corresponds to the sum of differences over all the possible alternatives to that question.

*Type of arguments (solo and duo)*

- Causal: the argument states a reason in favor or against the alternative. This category covers the Accept and Reject categories from experiment 1. Causal arguments are answers to the question 'why' and are represented by 'because' clauses.
- Condition: the argument states some conditions for the option selected by restricting its validity, e.g. "after some trials, yes, but not at the first error". Conditional arguments are answers to the question 'when?' and are represented by 'if' clauses.
- Other: there is no argument provided, the argument states subjective preferences for an alternative, e.g. "I like it better", non-arguments e.g. "I don't know, understand, ...".

Causal and Conditional categories might co-exist in a single argument. In those cases we assigned a Conditional code to the argument.

*Semantic relation between solo arguments and duo argument:*

- Union: the duo argument contains the ideas stated by both solo arguments
- Victory: the duo argument contains the ideas of only one of the solo arguments

- New: the duo argument contains an idea which is not present in either solo arguments

*Results*

There were 26 alternative answers distributed over 9 questions. With 16 students this gives us 416 potential solo arguments and 208 potential duo arguments. Only one student out of 16 did not manage to fill out the solo questionnaire completely. She answered to the 3 first questions, totalising 9 choices out of 29 possible. Thus, the total number of solo answers collected by the system is 399. We had a big dropout rate in the duo session due to technical problems with the software and absenteeism. Three pairs did not manage to take the duo phase at all. Only five pairs remain in the analysis. Those pairs did not provide arguments for all the possible answers and skipped some questions. In the analyses concerning choices, we will use all the choices made by those five pairs, even if there was no argument provided. This corresponds to 260 solo arguments and 96 duo arguments. In the analyses concerning the arguments, we will eliminate the cases where there was no argument provided. This corresponds to 220 solo arguments and 88 duo arguments.

*The level of conflict is low*

The level of conflict across pairs is very low (M=1.04, s=0.79). Overall, on one particular duo choice, students were confronted with answers differing by only one point on the answer scale. The lowest mean of conflict for a pair was 0.6 and the highest was 1.4. These values are rather small and this is due to our pairing method, which gave the advantage to an even distribution of conflict over the intensity of the conflict. The distribution of level of conflicts is illustrated by figure 4.

*The distribution of choices varies between solo and duo*

The choices students made when evaluating alternatives range from 'Never' to 'Always' on a scale from 0 to 4. The mean value of choices in the solo phase is M=2.35 (s= 0.98). For the duo phase the mean is very similar (M=2.12) but the standard deviation (s=0.48) is half as big. This gives us a first indication about the choices in the duo phase, namely that the choices are centred around 'Sometimes' and that the extreme choices ('Never' and 'Always') are less present than in the solo phase. A test of variance confirms that the variance of the solo choices is bigger than the variances of the duo choices (F=4.47, p<0.05).

Table 6 shows that the proportion of 'Sometimes' doubled in the duo phase (U=6.36, p<.05) and that the proportion of 'Always' (U=.94, p<0.05), 'Rarely' (U=.87, p<0.05) and 'Often' (U=1.61, p<.05) decreased. 'Never' choices disappeared from the duo phase. A chi-square test confirms that Phase and Choice are dependant ($X2$=49.897, p=.000). Figure 5 illustrates this change in the distribution of choices very clearly.

At first glance, we interpret this move towards 'Sometimes' as a result of discussion taking place. Students would agree on choosing 'Sometimes' to handle conflictual situations. We will look later at the conflict variable to see if this is the case.

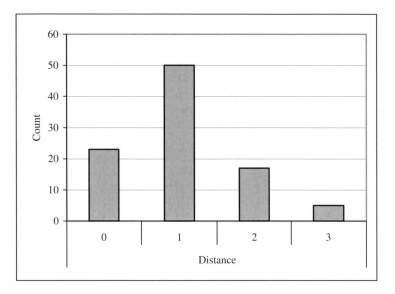

*Figure 4: Distribution of Conflict levels (M=1.04, s=0.79).*

*Table 6.   Choice across solo and duo phases*

| (X2= 49.897, p = .000) | | Phase | | | | |
| --- | --- | --- | --- | --- | --- | --- |
| | | SOLO | | DUO | | Difference |
| | | Count | % | Count | % | % |
| Choice | Never | 8 | 3 | 0 | 0 | 3 |
| | Rarely | 37 | 14 | 4 | 4 | 10 |
| | Sometimes | 103 | 40 | 78 | 81 | 41 |
| | Often | 78 | 30 | 12 | 13 | 17 |
| | Always | 34 | 13 | 2 | 2 | 11 |
| | Total | 260 | 100 | 96 | 100 | |

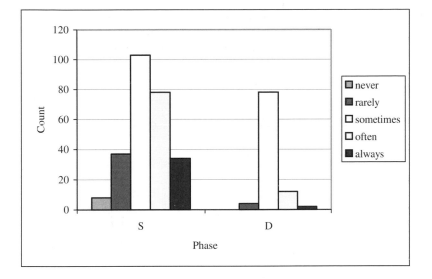

*Figure 5: Distribution of choices in solo and duo phases*

### Type of arguments does not vary between solo and duo

Student's answers not only consist in setting the sliders but also in providing written arguments. Table 7 presents the type of arguments across the phases of the script. A chi-square test ($X2=2.246$, NS) tells us that the type of argument is independent from the phase in which they were produced. When taking a closer look, it appears that the proportions of Causal, Condition and Other arguments do not change from the solo phase to the duo phase (all $p>.05$). We expected an increase of 'Condition' arguments in the duo phase because in experiment 1 we considered them a privileged way to handle conflicts. However, in table 7, not all cases in the duo phase are conflictual and the increase of 'Condition' arguments might become apparent when opposing conflictual and non-conflictual situations.

*Table 7.  Type of argument across solo and duo phases*

| ($X^2 = 2.246$, NS) | | Phase | | | | |
|---|---|---|---|---|---|---|
| | | SOLO | | DUO | | Difference |
| | | Count | % | Count | % | % |
| *Type of argument* | *Causal* | 161 | 73 | 62 | 70 | 11 |
| | *Condition* | 41 | 19 | 14 | 16 | 3 |
| | *Other* | 18 | 8 | 12 | 14 | 6 |
| | *Total* | 220 | 100 | 88 | 100 | |

*Choosing 'Sometimes' is not related to conflict*

Do students use 'Sometimes' as a way to solve conflict? Examining the relationship between conflict level and choices will tell us more. As previously said, the level of conflict was rather low and because there are only few cases where the conflict level is greater than 1, we will aggregate the data and compare the cases where there is no conflict with the cases where there is conflict. In experiment 1, the definition of conflict was straightforward: students who chose a different alternative were in a conflictual situation. In this experiment, conflict is a continuous variable. Is a difference of 1 on the scale of choices perceived as conflictual by students? We propose two alternate definitions of conflict. We define weak conflict as follows: situations where the difference between students' choices is equal to 0 are non-conflictual and situations where the difference is higher than 0 are conflictual. Strong conflict is defined as follows: situations where the difference between students' choices is equal to 0 or 1 are non-conflictual and situations where the difference is higher than 1 are conflictual.

Table 8 shows the count and proportions of choices according to weak conflict. There are too many cells with expected frequency lower than 5 to compute a reliable chi-square test. The proportion of 'Sometimes' answers is not higher in the conflictual situations (p>.05).

*Table 8.   Choice across weak conflict (levels 0 versus 1,2,3)*

| ($X^2 = 2.246$, NS) | | Weak conflict | | | | |
|---|---|---|---|---|---|---|
| | | NO | | YES | | Difference |
| | | Count | % | Count | % | % |
| Choice | Never | 0 | 0 | 0 | 0 | 0 |
| | Rarely | 1 | 5 | 3 | 5 | 0 |
| | Sometimes | 15 | 71 | 55 | 82 | 11 |
| | Often | 5 | 23 | 7 | 10 | 13 |
| | Always | 0 | 0 | 2 | 3 | 3 |
| | Total | 21 | 100 | 67 | 100 | |

When using strong conflict we get the same configuration of proportions. Table 9 shows that the total of cases with and without conflict is the opposite with this definition of conflict, we have more non-conflictual cases than conflictual cases. Again, the number of cells with expected frequencies lower than 5 prevents us from using a chi-square statistic. When using a proportion tests, there is no difference between conflictual and non-conflictual situations regarding the 'Sometimes' choices (p>.05).

*Table 9. Choice across strong conflict (levels 0,1 versus 2, 3)*

| | | Strong conflict | | | | Difference |
|---|---|---|---|---|---|---|
| | | NO | | YES | | |
| | | Count | % | Count | % | % |
| Choice | Never | 0 | 0 | 0 | 0 | 0 |
| | Rarely | 3 | 4 | 1 | 5 | 1 |
| | Sometimes | 54 | 80 | 16 | 80 | 0 |
| | Often | 9 | 13 | 3 | 15 | 2 |
| | Always | 2 | 3 | 0 | 0 | 3 |
| | Total | 68 | 100 | 20 | 100 | |

We can now negatively answer to the question if the increase of 'Sometimes' choices in the duo phase results from the resolution of conflictual situations.

*Type of arguments does not vary according to Conflict*

Table 10 and table 11 show the type of argument across weak conflict and strong conflict respectively. In both cases, it is not possible to compute reliable chi-square statistics. Proportion tests comparing the frequency of 'Condition' arguments in conflictual and non-conflictual situations are not statistically significant (p>.05). The difference of 12% for the proportion of 'Condition' arguments in table 11 is statistically not significant due to the small size of the sample. It nevertheless indicates a higher proportion of 'Condition' arguments in conflictual situations similarly to what was found in experiment 1.

*Table 10. Type of argument across weak conflict (levels 0 versus 1, 2, 3)*

| | | Weak conflict | | | | Difference |
|---|---|---|---|---|---|---|
| | | NO | | YES | | |
| | | Count | % | Count | % | % |
| Type of argument | Causal | 16 | 76 | 46 | 69 | 7 |
| | Condition | 4 | 19 | 10 | 15 | 4 |
| | Others | 1 | 5 | 11 | 16 | 11 |
| | Total | 21 | 100 | 67 | 100 | |

*Table 11. Type of argument across strong conflict (levels 0,1 versus 2, 3)*

| | | Strong conflict | | | | Difference |
|---|---|---|---|---|---|---|
| | | NO | | YES | | |
| | | Count | % | Count | % | % |
| Type of argument | Causal | 53 | 78 | 9 | 45 | 32 |
| | Condition | 9 | 13 | 5 | 25 | 12 |
| | Others | 6 | 9 | 6 | 30 | 21 |
| | Total | 68 | 100 | 20 | 100 | |

*More New arguments and less Union arguments are produced in conflictual situations.*

Table 12 and table 13 present the semantic relation between solo and duo arguments according to weak and strong conflict respectively. With both weak and strong definitions of conflict, chi-square tests tell us that the semantic relation and conflict are dependant (weak conflict, $X2= 8.496$, p=.014 and strong conflict, $X2= 6.558$, p=.038). When looking closer at the proportions for the weak conflict we see a greater proportion of 'New' arguments (U=1.3674, p<.05) and a lower proportion of 'Union' arguments (U=1.5404, p<.05) in conflictual situations. With strong conflict, only the difference for 'New' arguments remains significative (U=2.0468, p<.05). There is no statistically significant difference concerning 'Victory' arguments with either definitions of conflict.

*Table 12. Semantic relation across weak conflict (levels 0 versus 1, 2, 3)*

| $(X^2= 8.496, p=.014)$ | | Weak conflict | | | | |
|---|---|---|---|---|---|---|
| | | NO | | YES | | Difference |
| | | Count | % | Count | % | % |
| Semantic relation | New | 5 | 24 | 35 | 52 | 26 |
| | Union | 10 | 48 | 12 | 18 | 30 |
| | Victory | 6 | 28 | 20 | 30 | 2 |
| | Total | 21 | 100 | 67 | 100 | |

*Table 13. Semantic relation across strong conflict (levels 0, 1 versus 2, 3)*

| $(X^2= 6.558, p=.038)$ | | Strong conflict | | | | |
|---|---|---|---|---|---|---|
| | | NO | | YES | | Diffenrece |
| | | Count | % | Count | % | % |
| Semantic relation | New | 26 | 38 | 14 | 70 | 32 |
| | Union | 20 | 29 | 2 | 10 | 19 |
| | Victory | 22 | 22 | 4 | 20 | 2 |
| | Total | 68 | 100 | 20 | 100 | |

*Discussion*

From the results we described, conflict seems to have had no statistically significant effect on the type of arguments provided by the students. We did not find evidence for an increased production of 'Condition' arguments in conflictual situations. Conflict had an effect though, as is shown by the increasing proportion of 'New' arguments and the decrease of 'Union' arguments in conflictual situations.

Few choices in the solo phase and almost no choices in the duo phase were labelled 'Never' and 'Always'. Students didn't take extreme positions, staying to the less implying 'Rarely', 'Sometimes' and 'Often'. This seems to be a general phenomenon that is at work every time somebody has to answer to a Likert scale.

Whatever the labels attached to the extremes, people tend to answer in the proximity of the centre of the scale. But here, this tendency to have moderate public opinions had a positive implication on the type of arguments. Half of the 'Condition' arguments were produced next to a 'Sometimes' choice.

## GENERAL DISCUSSION

### Conflict works

Doise and Mugny (1981) proposed a theory of knowledge development rooted in an extension of the piagetian developmental psychology. They illustrated it by a series of experiments on socio-cognitive conflict. The basic idea of this theory is that social and cognitive factors are interdependent and both responsible for the development of knowledge. Also, there are two ways to handle a conflictual situation. A social resolution consists in conforming to the others' opinion to reduce the discrepancy. A cognitive resolution consists in taking the position of the other party and adapting one's own with respect to the other's. The cognitive change then, results from the reduction of a social tension through perspective taking and accommodation of one's own cognitive structures.

In our case, learning takes place as students evaluate alternative answers to a questionnaire. We want students to think about design choices by evaluating the characteristics of the situation that present those choices. This means that we expect them to be able to justify any answer to the questionnaire without an important theoretical background. This approach works in this domain since questions are about educational choices and everybody has ideas about education; it would not apply to all domains.

When answering in pairs to the questionnaire, there were questions where students gave different answers and were de facto in a conflictual situation. The students use several strategies to handle this situation, each of which has implications for potential learning outcomes. The strategy closest to a social resolution of the conflict consists in taking both arguments and putting them side-by-side. There is no content-related discussion necessary to produce those type of answers. We described those cases as a 'Union' of solo arguments. Following a 'Victory' strategy, the pair takes one of the individual arguments and uses it for the pair. If the loser gives up without argumentation, this case corresponds to a social resolution as well. If the victory is the result of one student convincing the other and changing his beliefs, we are closer to a cognitive resolution. However, with this strategy, only one student changed his mind. Finally, producing a 'New' argument is closest to a cognitive resolution because the pair creates an argument that possibly matches both positions.

In both the first and the second experiment the proportion of 'New' arguments is higher in conflictual situations than it is in non-conflictual situations. The opposite is true concerning the 'Union' arguments; they are less frequent in conflictual situations than in non-conflictual situations. This result indicates that conflict is a useful mechanism to trigger deeper exploration of the domain. Students produce more new ideas when solving conflicting viewpoints.

Handling disagreement is a delicate matter especially when disagreement is imposed by an external means. As a matter of fact, our students did not choose to be in a conflictual situation. The resolution of conflicting opinions sometimes happens with a reference to justice. Students don't want to hurt each other and will make efforts to give the same amount of credit to each other. In some pairs' dialogues, the students manage to take answers from each other in an equilibrated manner. Other pairs, more comfortable with differences of opinions argue about the meaning they confer to concepts they used in the solo phase to find a common position. They also make the difference of opinions explicit in the discussion.

We should not over-generalize these results, which occurred on a very specific learning script. This script has been purposely designed for scaffolding rich interactions from conflicts. The necessity to be careful in generalizing these results is illustrated by their sensitivity to interface features, as explained in the next point.

### The characteristics of the tool matter

Concerning the type of arguments, we were particularly interested in 'Condition' arguments. These arguments contain conditions and restrictions concerning the validity of a statement. For instance, a student might choose, "it is good to provide an animation feed-back on a correct answer" and, instead of providing an argument, adds the condition "IF the learner is a child". We saw that 'Condition' arguments appeared in experiment 1 mostly as a way to solve the opinion conflict. In experiment 2, the proportion of 'Condition' arguments was similar in the solo and the duo phase. And in the duo phase itself, there was no difference between conflictual and non-conflictual cases with this regard.

Even if the two experiments are presenting important differences, the questions and alternatives were the same. It is striking to see that in experiment 2 the conditional arguments are as numerous in the solo phase as they were in the experiment 1 duo phase.

We think that the sliders students use to make choices change the way they evaluate the options and provide arguments. For example, the labels 'Never' and 'Always' are adverbs with an absolute meaning. 'Never' and 'Always' imply a causal explanation, which we coded as either Reject or Accept in the first experiment and Causal in the second experiment. On the other hand, 'Sometimes' so to say 'calls' for a conditional argument stating the conditions in which the answer is true and the conditions that make it false.

For instance, it is grammatically more accurate to say "[Rarely or Sometimes] use video animations, they are distracting, except for young children" than to say "[Never] use video animations, they are distracting, except for young children". Never is never is... Even if less accurate from a grammatical point of view, arguments like the second example appeared in the data. Nevertheless, we think that the possibility to answer 'Sometimes' increases the number of Condition arguments as well in the solo as in the duo phase.

But why didn't the proportion of 'Condition' increase even more with conflict? An important difference between the experiments is that in the first one, students had to choose only one alternative while they had to evaluate all of them in the second experiment. In experiment 1, 'Condition' arguments also are a strategy to refer to other alternatives than the one chosen. Implicitly, saying A if X, can mean B if not X. Solving the conflict needed one student to change his or her choice. Considering that this was the only choice the pair could make, this change was an important concession. The pair would then set up an argument that compensates for the change made by one student by incorporating his or her previous choice as a 'Condition' in the new argument. In experiment 2, the production of several 'Causal' arguments can replace this need to refine the conditions for one choice This would explain why 'Condition' arguments do not serve conflict resolution in experiment 2.

*The timing matters*

The two experiments also were differing with respect to the timing. Experiment 1 took place during a four-hour period with only 20 minutes separating the solo and the duo phases. During the debriefing, students were actively participating and justifying their arguments. Experiment 2 took place over a period of three weeks with one week between each main phase of the script. The participation during the debriefing was much less intensive than in experiment 1. The students didn't feel nor act accountable for the choices they made and the arguments they provided. Past opinions were not strong enough to trigger another round of argumentation during the debriefing.

## CONCLUSION

This chapter presents an analysis of arguments produced by students in a learning activity entitled "Argue Graph" where students twice answer to a questionnaire, a first time alone and then in pairs. We observed that answering in pairs had a positive impact on the elaboration of arguments provided to justify a choice in the questionnaire. We interpreted the improvement of arguments as stemming from the discussion necessary to give a common answer. Students make their opinions explicit and thereby more elaborated during the discussion. The tools' features orient the way students perceive the task. The social implication of expressing opinions in these experiments may explain the differences in the type of arguments that were produced. We argue for a social psychological interpretation of the context of CSCL activities. Usually people tend to avoid social positioning by adopting non-implying positions. When a tool or a script allows them to stay 'pat' they will use this opportunity.

## ACKNOWLEDGMENTS

TECFA Virtual Campus has been developed with the collaboration of Cyril Roiron, David Ott, Jean-Chirstophe Brouze, Daniel Schneider, Daniel Peraya, Patrick Mendelsohn, Philippe Lemay and Didier Strasser.

## AFFILIATION

*Patrick Jermann (Patrick.Jermann@epfl.ch);*
*Pierre Dillenbourg (pierre.dillenbourg@epfl.ch);*
*Ecole Polytechnique Fédérale de Lausanne (EPFL); CH-1015 Lausanne,*
*Switzerland*

## REFERENCES

Blaye, A. (1988). Confrontation socio-cognitive et résolution de problème (A propos du produit de deux sous-ensembles). Doctorat de l'Université de Provence.

Brown, A.L. & Palincsar, A.S. (1989). Guided cooperative learning and individual knowledge acquisition. In L.B. Resnick (Ed). Knowling, learning and instruction, essays in honor of Robert Glaser. Hillsdale, NJ: Lawrence Erlbaum Publisher.

Butterworth, G. (1982). A brief account of the conflict between the individual & the social in models of cognitive growth. In G. Butterworth & P. Light (Eds) Social Cognition (pp. 3-16). Brighton, Sussex: Harvester Press.

Chi M.T.H., Bassok, M., Lewis, M.W., Reimann, P. & Glaser, R. (1989). Self-Explanations: How Students Study and Use Examples in Learning to Solve Problems. Cognitive Science, 13,145-182.

Doise, W. & Mugny, G. (1981). Le développement social de l'intelligence. Paris: InterEditions.

Dillenbourg, P., Jermann, P., Schneider, D., Traum, D. and Buiu, C. (1997). The design of MOO agents: Implications from a study on multi-modal collaborative problem solving. In Proceedings of AI&ED'97 Conference. B. du Boulay and R. Mizoguchi (Eds.). IOS Press.

Dillenbourg, P. (2002) Over-scripting CSCL: The risks of blending collaborative learning with instructional design. In W. Jochens & P. A. Kirschner (Eds) Three worlds of CSCL: Can we support CSCL? Heerlen, The Netherlands: Open Universiteit Nederland.

Hutchins, E. (1991). The social organization of distributed cognition. In L. B. Resnick , J. M. Levine & S.D. Teasley (Eds.), Perspectives on Socially Shared Cognition.

Hutchins (1995). How a Cockpit Remembers Its Speeds. Cognitive Science 19, 265-288.

Jermann, P. & Dillenbourg, P. (1999). Dialectics for collective activities: an approach to virtual campus design. In Proceedings of AI&ED'99 Conference.

Nickerson, R.S. (1993). On the distribution of cognition: some reflections. In G. Salomon (Ed) Distributed Cognition (pp. 229-261). Cambridge University Press, New York.

Schoenfeld, A. H. (1987). What's All the Fuss About Metacognition ? In Cognitive Science and Mathematics Education. Ed: Alan H. Schoenfeld. London: Lawrence Erlbaum Associates.

Smith, J.B. (1994). Collective Intelligence in Computer-Based Collaboration. Hillsdale, NJ: Lawrence Erlbaum.

Schwarz, B. B., Neuman, Y., Gil, J. & Ilya, M. (2001) Effects of argumentative activities on collective and individual arguments. Proceedings of ECSCL 2001, Maastricht, Netherlands.

BARUCH. B. SCHWARZ AND AMNON GLASSNER

# THE BLIND AND THE PARALYTIC:

*Supporting argumentation in Everyday and Scientific Issues*

## INTRODUCTION: ARGUMENTATION AS A CENTRAL FORM OF LITERACY

Traditionally, we define a literate person as somebody who knows how to read, write and calculate. In other words, the literate person is able to handle the signs and symbols used by the society in which she lives. However, this definition is fuzzy. What do we mean by knowing how to read? Do we mean knowing how to decipher the meaning of canonical texts that teachers have themselves constructed or accepted from people who have been invested the authority to give the exact meaning of texts (writers of teaching materials for example)? Indeed, teachers' written guides often give pedagogical advice how to analyze texts, to extract the main idea: the role of the reader is then to reconstruct a meaning (see Kintsch's situation model, 1986). Also, when students analyze a text, their objective is generally not more than to comply with the demands of a curriculum, that is (in general) to master skills. However, while literacy definitely involves analytical skills, confining it to a series of skills is far too restricted, and puts aside contextual factors in literacy. As noticed by Olson (1994), in opposition to children's oral propensity to identify speech acts in conversation, when interpreting written signs they have difficulties to identify their illocutionary force. In other words, children may have difficulties in reading partly because they don't know for which purpose the texts with which they are presented with were written. The approach to literacy we adopt here conveys the versatility that any literate human must exhibit, to be able to communicate actions through different modes and to negotiate them. This practically means that the literate human should express actions in various modes such as reading or writing, with flexible motives such as clarifying an issue, presenting, demonstrating, defending, or convincing.

The literate child would possibly read a text and interpret it in order to defend his or her point of view, or write an essay to convince peers, etc. Such an approach gives a central role to orality in literacy. As stated by Kuhn (1962), "to be literate is not

227

*J. Andriessen, M. Baker, and D. Suthers (eds.), Arguing to Learn: Confronting Cognitions in Computer-Supported Collaborative Learning environments (227-260).*
© *2003 Kluwer Academic Publishers. Printed in the Netherlands.*

enough to know the words; one must learn how to participate in the discourse of some textual community". And that implies knowing which texts are important, how they are to be read and interpreted, and how they are to be applied in talk and action.

Such a view of literacy invites then to design activities in which oral, reading, and writing practices are integrated in activities in which the participants are aware of a common motive and goals going beyond the compliance with mastery of skills. But how is it possible to integrate among these practices? The issue is not a simple one, as it is critical for students to fulfill goals they set up by themselves, or to which they adhere. We claim that the integration of multi-modal activities can be organized through argumentative practices. Argumentation may foster children's engagement in verbal, reading and writing practices. To elaborate an educational program based on this new approach of literacy, we first briefly review how people function in argumentative activities. We discern between everyday argumentation and scientific argumentation, which is a central representative of educated argumentation. We show that human have strengths and weaknesses in these two kinds of argumentative activities. The new approach to literacy we propose incorporates both everyday and scientific argumentation. We propose principles for this approach and describe an environment designed according to these principles. Finally, we show how children could construct good arguments through dialectical activities with this environment

## STRENGTHS AND WEAKNESSES IN "EVERYDAY ARGUMENTATION"

Numerous studies have shown the natural propensity of children to participate in verbal argumentative activities. They play social games such as pretending, or when they want to hide their motives to other participants. For example, Orsolini (1993) has shown that toddlers are able to use justifications in disputes. The child then adapts his or her argumentative moves to the motives he or she wants to fulfill. In many contexts, children know to justify, to defend or to attack views because such functions are vital in everyday activity. They help them to win, or to be accepted socially. More generally, argumentation serves people as a kind of social exoneration or as a social account (Antaki, 1994). Studies of argumentation during conversation show that students are extremely skillful at (counter-)challenging, conceding, etc., during conversation (e.g. Resnick, Salmon, Zeitz, Wathen, & Holowchak, 1993; Pontecorvo & Girardet, 1993; Stein & Miller, 1993, Baker, this volume), when discussing everyday issues. When the group of students is taken as an entity, Resnick and colleagues (Resnick et al. 1993) have shown that the elaboration of the argument through conversation is extremely coherent. The analysis of the structure of the conversation (turn taking, reference to previous turns) reveals that participants consider the elaboration of the argument both locally and globally. However, in spite of the dexterity people show when discussing everyday issues, it appears that good argumentative processes (e.g., challenges) do not necessarily lead to final good arguments according to analytical criteria. Also, the arguments elaborated (even if they are formally acceptable) are often not acceptable in communities for which educational institutions must account (scientific community, cultural accepted values). Finally, even when the arguments elaborated are good and normative, their authorship is not clear in discussions among several participants. These problems are serious. They question the link between "good" argumentative activity (or "good" arguments-processes) and "good" arguments-products. This lack of match is at the root of what we call the blind and the paralytic paradox.

To convey this paradox, we first explain what specialists define as good arguments-products. Since the antiquity, arguments have been considered as structures consisting of premises and a conclusion deriving from the premises. The goodness of an argument depends on the nature of the link between premises and conclusion that needs to comply with formal rules. Toulmin (1958) extended the Aristotelian structure of arguments to add warrants and datum as two different kinds of premises. These warrants represent the connection between the evidence and the conclusion. Arguments are "good" if premises are grounded and if the conclusion can be drawn from the premises according to formal rules.

According to the criteria set above, arguments-products collected in individual interviews or written questionnaires are quite often mediocre. For example, in her pioneering study on argumentative skills, Kuhn (1991) asked various populations ranging from adolescence to advanced adulthood about everyday issues through the use of an interview that always contained the same template of questions. Roughly, individuals were asked to express a standpoint concerning a social issue (e.g., "What causes prisoners to return to crime?"), reasons corroborating this standpoint, alternative arguments and how to refute these arguments. Kuhn used this interview template to ask subjects of various ages and level of instruction. She found that adolescents as well as adults rely more on non-justified beliefs, than on an articulated theory. Their arguments often consist of discrete reasons disconnected from each other (this finding may be imputed to the method of structured interview, though). Another result of Kuhn's study is the almost total inaptitude in considering alternative arguments or theories, and the impossibility of defending one own argument against a specific opposing argument, or to rebut it. Kuhn found that this state of things recurs across everyday topics, and does not depend on age. These results fit research on informal reasoning (which is equated to the production and the evaluation of arguments) in other domains such as political relations (Voss, 1991) or medical science (Christiensen & Elstein, 1991), in which it was shown that reasoning relies on deeply rooted beliefs and is biased. In all these domains, people do not change or learn arguments. Rather, they rationalize; that is, they appropriate any assertion or data that reinforces their own argument-product, and discard any data or evidence that contradicts it.

A study by Means and Voss (1996) that measured arguments-products as a function of grade, ability and knowledge on everyday issues found that high-ability students (according to Wechsler-Binet tests) were distinctly superior to average and low-ability students. This study extended the Kuhn study, and showed that arguments-products are generally one-sided, and acceptability of reasons invoked is often quite low. In other words, arguments-products are biased, and reasons invoked are generally not acceptable. Moreover, it was found that the interaction between ability level and grade does not lead to significant differences. This finding has important educational outcomes: It is generally the ability level that accounts for performance regardless of the grade. In particular, there are young high-level students who perform better than older average or low-level students, and *schooling does not bridge the gaps.*

From these results, Means and Voss elaborated a two-component model of informal reasoning. One component is informal reasoning <u>skill,</u> which is the ability to generate and to evaluate arguments, to use counter-arguments, to use qualifiers and meta-statements effectively. This skill may be seen as language structures that allow one to store, retrieve and evaluate information. The second component is topic knowledge, which includes both subject knowledge and personal experience. Informal reasoning is attained through the acquisition of language structures (especially argumentation) that facilitate storing and accessing of knowledge and the development of differentiated situation models. Means and Voss claimed that the content-independent skill is often not mastered, and affects the development of topic knowledge. Argumentation plays then two roles: the first one is epistemological, the arguer asking about the certainty, the validity or the quality of new knowledge in general; the second is ontological, the object of argumentation being richer, as more knowledge is gradually integrated in arguments.

The Means and Voss interpretation that the content-independent skill was not mastered was based on the analysis of arguments-products collected in written questionnaires according to criteria for formally good arguments. This claim is not compatible with the propensity to participate in everyday argumentative activities, or in other words with the goodness of arguments-processes. Rather, we suggest that argumentative skills can be differently activated in different contexts. In the case where students participate in everyday argumentative activities, they are more inclined to (counter)challenge or to give reasons for their viewpoints. However, they are not able to bridge between their natural propensity to participate in argumentative activities and their personal experience to elaborate new arguments. In other words, they may raise personal knowledge, but this bridge between argumentative moves and personal knowledge is sterile. It is as if, when dealing with everyday issues, people know how to "move forward in their argumentation", but they often do not know where to go, how to elaborate any new knowledge. They are somehow "blind" although they are swift in their argumentative moves.

## STRENGTHS AND WEAKNESSES IN SCIENTIFIC ARGUMENTATION

At a first glance, "Argumentation in Science" sounds an oxymoron, at least when speaking about scientists. It has been believed for a long time that scientists progress in their field according to deductive processes, naive inductivism and modelization according to abstract templates, and that they design experiments systematically and rationally. However, naturalistic descriptions of the activity of some scientists have shown a totally different picture. For example, the study of Faraday's notebooks has demonstrated that the design of his experiments was driven by hypotheses grounded on intuitions, not by a systematic rationalized program of research (Tweney, 1991). Dunbar (1993) went further in the study of the reasoning processes of scientists and observed the *on-line process of scientific discovery.* He found that the goals scientists set affect all aspects of discovery: for example, the generation of hypotheses or the strategies for constructing experiments. From a deductive point of view such heuristics are invalid, but they fit "good" informal reasoning.

Research on students' scientific reasoning showed that, like scientists, students' generation of hypotheses or theories is grounded in beliefs. But this bias affects not only the construction of hypotheses or theories, but also their validation: When confronted with data inconsistent with their beliefs, students do not tend to evaluate their current hypotheses. Rather, they tend to ignore the problematic data and often do not consider alternatives. For example, in a study about how Grade 5 and Grade 6 children plan, perform and interpret experiments to learn about the relations between design features and speed of race cars in a computerized microworld, Schauble (1990) showed that, by the end of the experiment, students did not fully understand those features that disconfirmed their initial beliefs. Invalid heuristics that preserved children's favored theories about cars were evident throughout.

The serious limitations on belief revision and strategies for evaluating arguments in children are not, after all, very surprising. What is presented in schools is not the reconstitution of a process of apprehending scientific theories such as Faraday's electromagnetic theory, but rather, a presentation of knowledge such as Maxwell's posterior mathematization of Faraday's theory of electromagnetism. There is then a gap between scientific knowledge as it is presented in schools and the origin of this knowledge. And indeed, Perry and Kitchener (1992) have characterized the beliefs of many as either "dualist" or "multiplicist". That is, a large proportion of the students believed that knowledge claims can be classified either as proven fact or as unproved opinion, and on the other hand a large proportion believed that knowledge claims are opinions, equally good, "because everything's relative". It is worth noticing, though, that the kind of scientific knowledge developed in classes follows partly from the difficulty of coping with a simulation of a dynamic flux of information progressively stored from experiments, and the subsequent construction of competing theories: so far, most educational environments fail to provide students with conditions comparable to those encountered by Faraday at Davy's laboratory. Rather, secondary science textbooks and teachers often promote belief in science as naive inductivism and an idealized view of processes and products of science (Pomeroy, 1993; Duschl, 1990).

To sum up, although the importance of education to scientific argumentation has been recognized (Duschl, 1990; Kuhn, 1991, 1993; Ohlsson, 1992), serious difficulties of implementation need to be overcome. The first one concerns the creation of environments in which resources support discussion about hypotheses/theories and possible alternatives. This is a serious difficulty in teacher-led discussions as well as in peer discussions. On the one hand teacher-led discussions are tightly controlled, thus may not fully engage all students, and may fall into the mode of teacher-initiation, student-response, teacher-evaluation (Cazden, 1988). On the other hand, in peer discussions, participants often focus on "action talk" directed to the immediate task rather than to reflecting on the task. They then tend to suppress conflict rather than bringing it to the surface it and resolving it (Baker, 1999). Another difficulty is that scientific argumentation has a set of constraints, conventions and criteria that are an artificial imposition in everyday argumentation. For example criteria for acceptability in scientific issues rely either on controlled experiences or on formal proofs, while in everyday issues, they rely on a "makes sense" epistemology (Perkins, Farady, & Bushey, 1991).

For all the reasons raised above, students accept scientific arguments as such because persons identified with the scientific community transmit them (Meichtry, 1993; Songer & Linn, 1991; Kedem, 1999). They "see" them because they are provided with indisputable evidence of their truth (through both peremptory affirmations of the teacher and demonstrations in the laboratory). However, they don't know how to relate to these arguments, to check or to challenge them, and to use them in further activities. In other words, in science, children "see" arguments. However, they are "paralytic" concerning argumentative activities of which these scientific arguments may be the subject (e.g., "Are there competing arguments?" or "Can I conciliate these arguments with facts I know from my personal experience that apparently contradict these arguments?"). Had we claimed that the picture we have drawn is general, we would have been unjust towards several leading programs recently committed to foster argumentation. Instead of reviewing some of them and forgetting others, we prefer listing some of the design principles we claim to be necessary for the elaboration of learning environments for argumentative activity. These principles rely on general research findings and specific findings with some of the pioneering learning environments dedicated to the fostering of argumentation.

We conclude from the two last sections that in everyday issues, we are generally highly skillful in challenging, counterchallenging, justifying or agreeing during conversation but the arguments we hold are often mediocre according to analytical criteria. We know to "move forward" but we don't know very well "where to go", how to construct and evaluate arguments; we are "swift but blind". In contrast, in scientific domains we are used to accept well-made arguments, but generally do not use them in further activities to convince, challenge or justify our viewpoints. We "see the point" but "cannot move forward"; we are paralytic. In the rest of the chapter we propose an approach to education to argumentation in which the blind and the paralytic help each other. We propose principles for this approach and describe an environment designed according to these principles.

## DESIGN PRINCIPLES FOR "ARGUMENTATIVE" EDUCATIONAL PROGRAMS

The ubiquity of argumentation in human social activity and the natural propensity children have in participating in argumentation led us to elaborate an educational program based on argumentation as a form of literacy. As any educational program, this program must not only propose activities for gains at a microgenetic level (during problem-solving sessions for example), but at a meso-genetic level, to give participants the opportunity to capitalize on outcomes of previous activities in further ones. It is then not only its ubiquity but its versatility that turns argumentation to particularly adequate for education. Children can participate in successive argumentative activities in which they fulfill different motives, and the design of the educational program relies on this crucial feature.

Of course, any educational program is specific. It focuses on a target population and on tools at one's disposal or that can possibly be designed. The design of an educational program based on argumentation is different though. Although, it has been an inherent part of education for thousands of years, it has little didactical modern tradition for guiding its elaboration[1]. The Kishurim project team at the Hebrew University bases the development of the program on experience and the empirical research conducted in classes for three years, and on results of empirical research on collaborative learning already known. The conclusions of the empirical research are expressed here as design principles for educational programs based on argumentation. We list now these principles and present further on the theoretical tenets and experimental findings from which they stem. he first is *chaining of different activities*, that is, we organized series of argumentative activities around the same theme, but proposed different motives to the participants in each of the activities. The second principle concerns the fact that this chaining should comply with the *alternation of dialectical and synthetic activities*. The third one is that *the tools should enable sharing the display of different arguments in the same space*, importing them from one activity to another one and transforming these arguments. The fourth principle concerns the domains of argumentative activity, the *"decentration" of argumentative activities from one exclusive domain*. Practically, we alternated argumentative series activities around moral dilemmas and around more scientific issues. The last principle is about content: we stipulate that *the issues should lead to account for multiple perspectives*. Each of the principles is presented here as well as its theoretical and/or empirical grounds.

## Chaining of activities

Although it has been shown that dyadic interaction to work out an issue is generally beneficial for individuals, several studies have shown that this tendency is not general. For example, it appears that too much engagement in one single argumentative activity may lead to undesirable effects such as polarization (Lord, Ross, & Lepper, 1979) and on the other hand, too much engagement in individual synthesis may lead to lack of accuracy (Wilson & Schooler, 1991). Also, studies showed that the effects of collaborations are considerably tempered if the activity is a problem-solving session in which one of the participants (tutor or peer) takes the role of boosting understanding. As shown by Davenport and Howe (1999), children obtain partial benefits from peer interaction, receiving support from either problem solving or strategic understanding but not from both. In contrast, in a recent study, Davenport, Howe, & Noble (2000) showed that collaborative problem solving in dyadic interaction when followed by a tutoring session in which tutors prompt understanding of the problem solving, leads to more accentuated gains than in dyadic interaction alone. The same beneficial effect of chaining activities was identified by Staudinger and Joos (2000) when they showed that adults engaged in "wisdom" issues, gain more from discussions with peers and "individual appraisal" than from social interaction only. This is because individuals engaged in discussions do not have enough opportunities to integrate ideas raised during discussion. These findings are in line with research on the effect of collaboration on cognitive development in childhood and adolescence (e.g., Azmitia, 1996; Rogoff & Chavajay, 1995). These studies show that it is not during the interaction between peers or between adult and child that improvements in cognitive performance are observed, but rather improvements are observed subsequently, during the child's individual performance. We suggest that this is not a matter of observation but concerns the timing of the internalization of social interaction. This internalization seems to occur aftermath: When chaining activities on the same theme, students actualize outcomes (methods, strategies, etc.) in successive activities in which they take a new perspective relative to the same theme.

*The contiguity of dialectical activity with synthesis*

If chaining is an important design principle, it seems that empirical research has also something to tell about the nature of the successive activities in the chain. It seems that not any chaining of activities is beneficial, but rather, the alternation of the social with the more individual activities. For example, a growing number of studies shows that the chaining of dialectical activity followed by a synthesis is particularly beneficial for learning. We have already mentioned the studies by Davenport, Howe, & Noble (2000) and by Staudinger & Joos (2000). Studies by Woodruff and Meyer (Woodruff & Meyer, 1997; Meyer & Woodruff, 1997) show that the succession of critical argumentation with consensual argumentation allows students to "internalize social interactions". Hershkowitz and Schwarz (1999) studied argumentative activities in which small groups of students solved mathematical problems followed by the writing of a collective report and by a synthesis orchestrated by the teacher in a whole class forum. They traced the transformations hypotheses underwent during the different stages. Hypotheses improved. These improvements were attributed not to the succession of activities but to the proximity of collaborative problem solving, reporting and synthesis. For example, hypotheses solely relying on previous experience or on intuition in problem solving were reformulated in the synthesis accompanied with evaluative comments, that were only implicit in the collaborative problem-solving. Also, in the synthesis, students compared their hypotheses (outcomes of their previous collaboration) with hypotheses elaborated by other groups, and this comparison led students to adopt different perspectives, more principled. Similarly, in a recent study performed within the Kishurim environment (Schwarz, Neuman, Gil, & Ilya, 2002), solipsistic activities alternated with communal ones. This alternation led to the constant improvement of arguments-products according to criteria such as type of argument (one-sided, two-sided, compounded), acceptability, and quality (abstractedness, etc.).

*Tools for sharing, transforming and importing arguments*

As people often do not know to construct "good" arguments in informal conversation, and to use scientific arguments in formal or informal conversations, researchers decided to introduce another "player" in this kind of activity. These are tools mediating argumentation. Among the first and the most prominent, Lesgold, Suthers and colleagues (see the chapter by Suthers in this volume) designed a computerized tool for fostering scientific argumentation, the Belvedere system. The Belvedere system was designed to support argumentative talk between peers. It directed peers toward considerations of evaluation, construction, and revision of scientific theories and concepts, by putting scientific controversies in the center of action. This software package is designed to facilitate students' analysis of argumentation elements embedded in varying media sources, enables the construction of a graphical representation of the elements – an Argumentative Map using text boxes of various shapes to represent the different elements (hypotheses, conclusions, illustrations etc.), and links between them by arrows between the boxes. The home screen enables students to create a map of all the assertions presented in the various sources in the conflict. The working environment of this screen provides simultaneous work with a text source (or multiple text sources), and the map which is being constructed. It is possible to "copy and paste" from the sources to the map. Also, easy access to the different texts and media sources is provided. The classical link subject-object with such a tool is all but simple, as the object (goal) of the student is generally not explicitly an argument, but a justification, a presentation, a defense, etc. As people generally do not construct proper arguments, the role of the tool should be first to mediate the elaboration of proper arguments simply to happen. The Belvedere software with its ontology, may play this mediating role by providing one with terms such as "reasons", or "experiments" that are embedded in the system itself. This ontological characteristic is shared by other systems fostering argumentation, the question in each case remaining whether the mediating tools mediate activities of argumentation and how.

A second potential role of tools is that, as they can represent several arguments, they may be a space for sharing, evaluating and discussing several arguments. In other words, Argumentative Maps are important first because they provide ontology for dealing with arguments and second because they provide a space for sharing and discussing alternative arguments.

*Alternation between social and scientific themes*

The succession of activities and the contiguity of dialectical and reflective activities insure in principle the improvement of arguments as products. But our educational purpose is also more general; it concerns giving students opportunities to learn to participate in argumentative activities properly. The role of the teacher in such a process is not simple, as her interventions may easily "impair" an engagement that must flow. Therefore, teaching directly what is a good argument or good argumentation is not practical. Rather, the teacher must instill argumentative norms such as "what counts as an argument", "what is an acceptable reason", or "whether a specific argumentative move is desirable/acceptable". The pedagogical principles involved here are complex. Their elaboration depends on empirical studies we presently conduct. The pedagogical principles will be expressed in a further publication. In addition to the central role of the teacher in instilling argumentative norms, our program capitalized on "the blind and the paralytic paradox": We took advantage of children's natural propensity to participate in argumentation, and on our natural tendency to accept scientific arguments. We helped the paralytic to walk and then let the blind to find his way. In more specific terms, we alternated scientific themes in which we coached students in argumentative activities and everyday themes in which the students used the same tools and the organization of tasks was similar to the scientific ones. Norms accepted in scientific themes were accounted for in everyday themes and vice-versa. Of course, some of the argumentation norms in everyday themes were unacceptable in science (for example what counts as a good reason in everyday issues, which is often grounded on accepted truisms). The contrary was also true. But the setting of the structure of themes and activities implicitly invited students to compare, capitalize on, or differentiate between the two themes. Through this alternation, the argumentative activities (their actions, rules, norms, etc) were contextualized, either because they were general (when common to both themes), or because they were specific.

*Tasks based on wicked problems possibly leading to different perspectives.*

The last design principle concerns the very content of the argumentative activities. There is a consensus that argumentative activities should be organized around wicked problems (see van Bruggen & Kirshner, this volume) in which argumentation should lead to cope with oppositions. While dilemmas such as capital punishment_ or experiments on animals_ have been reported as inducing argumentative activity, and argumentative functions helped students coping with oppositions, there are cases in which participants express their agreement on an issue but engage in argumentative activity to reinforce their arguments. For example, in a recent study (Schwarz, Benaya, & Shmaya, 2001) we found that the issue of the use of mild drugs was not seen as a real dilemma in a Grade 9 class in which we introduced this issue as a part of our program. Virtually everybody in the class expressed his/her opposition to the use of drugs before and during the successive activities. Consequently, the use of mild drugs was not a dilemma for these students. However, we showed that they actively engaged in argumentative activity to reinforce their arguments through considering multiple perspectives (Schwarz et al., 2001). Thus, we suggest that, although perspectives may be raised when engaging in a dilemma where standpoints are generally diverse, there are other activities in which conflicts between standpoints are not necessary to lead to the improvement of arguments. Rather, the design of the task should account for the potential of the issue chosen to lead to multiple perspectives.

We describe now the Kishurim program, a learning environment that fulfills these five design principles.

## THE DESCRIPTION OF THE ENVIRONMENT

The program described here, the Kishurim project, was developed and is currently implemented in Israel. It has been adapted to various grades from Grade 2 to Grade 10. The Israeli educational system was not ready to allot time for fostering argumentation. We guess that most national educational systems would not reserve hours for teaching argumentation for its own sake. In many classes however, schools decide to dedicate hours for the teaching of computer literacy (the teaching to master the use of common technological tools such as Word Office, databases or Internet tools). To master these tools, students gain at being engaged in meaningful tasks. The Kishurim program was "marketed" to schools and institutions as a product intended to familiarize students with various technological tools, an objective reached indeed along the Kishurim project although this mastery was only one of its by-products. The description of the environment is done here according to its implementation in Grade 9 heterogeneous classes representing the 60% upper level of the general population. The tools we used were:

- An Argumentative Map (AM). A key feature of AMs is that they are used to represent both evidence for and evidence against each assertion. Assertions are evaluated/criticized/ rebutted by an opponent of the author of the assertion. AMs thus capture (counter-)arguments and their mutual evaluation.
- Databases providing textual sources (for example, cases, examples, or data) for use against or for different viewpoints.
- A presentation program to make public arguments. Students could create screens integrating text, sound, graphics, animation, and video snapshots (generally the PowerPoint software was chosen, but more sophisticated programs were sometimes preferred).

The databases and their use are not presented here for the sake of brevity, as their use imply various practices that are different from those adopted with the two other tools. Argumentative Maps and the presentation program were designed to allow sharing arguments and to demand the use of an argumentative ontology (argument, reason, evidence, refutation, etc.). These tools then comply with the principle concerning tools for sharing and transforming arguments.

To further describe the environment, we list here the common practices in the Kishurim project through the "Tattletale", a task examined further on. This task concerns an everyday issue. It is typical regarding the multiple phases and their structure. We describe here their succession.

(1) *Presentation of a dilemma*: The teacher tells the class that there has been a problem of thefts in one school. John, one of the students, caught one of his best friends, Ron, with the purse and the money of their common best friend, Steve. Ron implores John not to tell. His family has a very low income and he is in a great trouble. He promises he will not do it again. Should John tell about the theft?

(2) *Individual argumentation*: Students fill a questionnaire individually. They are asked (Q1) whether they think it is preferable to tell who stole the purse and why, (Q2) which reasons an opponent to their viewpoint should bring forward, and (Q3) what to answer such an opponent.

(3) *Planning a presentation*: At this phase, small groups of students discuss how to plan a multimedia presentation. In the "Tattletale", this phase was spontaneously decided by students and not by the teacher. This decision is natural having in mind that students experienced previous tasks in which the final goal was to defend their viewpoint with a multimedia presentation.

(4) *Brainstorm argumentation*. The teacher gathers all the students and asks them for their viewpoint. In this free conversation, students decide when to participate. They often react to opinions raised by their peers, and sometimes interrupt them.

(5) *Round of turns argumentation*. The teacher controls a pre-established order of asking for arguments. All students have time to express their viewpoint.

(6) *Round of turns counter-argumentation*. The teacher orchestrates another controlled round of turns to figure out the reasons an opponent could raise. Each student attacks his or her previous argument.

(7) *Small group dialectical argumentation*: Small groups of students collaborate to construct their arguments, and display them in the argumentative map.

(8) *Preparing the defense of an argument*: Students collaborate to design a multimedia representation based on their argumentative map.

(9) *Defending an argument*: Students use their presentation to convince their audience (the whole classroom) that they are right.

The Tattletale task exemplifies several characteristics of activities of the Kishurim project. First, the context for each of the phases is quite different and students must cope with new goals. In each phase, students are led to contextualize arguments already expressed in previous phases. For example, in the round of turns counter-argumentation, the student may use other perspectives or arguments (e.g., previously uttered by other students in the round of turns argumentation or in brainstorm argumentation). In the preparation of the defense, students may capitalize on the way arguments and reasons were accepted or rejected in previous stages. Each stage has a quite different character. Stages (2), (7) and (8) are reflective, while stages (4) and (9) are truly dialectical. Stages (3), (5) and (6) are hybrid as they invite activities that are dialectical and reflective at the same time. The Tattletale was typical, and as such it complied with the chaining of activities and with the alternation between dialectical and reflective activities. It is of course a wicked problem for which several perspectives, all of them legitimate, may be raised: the social concern about thefts, the psychological harm, allegiance to friends (to the victim and to the thief) and the background for the act (distress, poverty, etc.).

The alternation of everyday and scientific themes will be shown in the two next sections through the description of the succession of the activities "Does vacuum exist?" and "The Tattletale".

Thus the Kishurim project, as exemplified in the Tattletale (and later on in "Does vacuum exist?") complies with the design principles for environments fostering argumentation, enunciated above. The rest of this paper is on the description of the implementation of Tattletale and on the impact of the "Does vacuum exist?" task on the Tattletale. These activities were experienced in a Grade 9 class in which two hours per week were allotted for "computer literacy". The class was heterogeneous regarding reading and writing skills. The school valued collaborative problem solving among students with different levels and backgrounds. In order to give all students the opportunity to experience the use of technological tools, the class was split into two groups of sixteen students, and in each of these groups, students organized themselves in small groups of three to five students. We give a general description of the scientific activity ("Does vacuum exist?"), and examine products of small groups in the class. In the task around an everyday issue (the Tattletale), we analyze the work of one small group. We focus on the transformations an argument raised by one student at the beginning of the Tattletale task underwent along its different stages. We also try to identify traces of her previous participation in "Does vacuum exist?" in the Tattletale.

## HELPING THE PARALYTIC TO GROPE: MODELING ARGUMENTATION IN SCIENTIFIC ISSUES

For modeling argumentation is scientific issues, we decided to choose issues on which students' misconceptions do not hinder the engagement in the activity, as we did not want to focus on the final argument to adopt but rather to focus on (a process of) argumentation. The issue "Does vacuum exist?" is a good choice. There are some misconceptions linked to vacuum. However, the topic "vacuum" is not very much experienced and discussed in everyday experience. Hence, appropriating or abandoning an argument on this issue is not too problematic a move, being more related to argumentation than to rooted beliefs. This issue was then a good choice for modeling scientific argumentation.

*The description of the task " Does vacuum exist?"*

The issue "Does vacuum exist?" is a celebrated debate pursued during thousands of years. Thinkers from different disciplines such as philosophy, theology, mystics, and physics were engaged in a vivid debate on the existence of vacuum. This debate has been reconstructed by the Israeli Educational Broadcast (Kedem, 1999). The production sacrifices historical facts for the sake of presenting the issue as a coherent dialogic debate. For example, Figure 1 shows a discussion between Democritus (6th century BC) and Aristotle (4th century BC)! Other participants in this debate are a medieval monk, and four Renaissance scientists, Galileo, Boyle, Torricelli, and Von Guericke.

Figure 1 shows that Democritus and Aristotle first present their arguments. The arguments (assertions, theories and evidence that support their key assertion) can be summarized as such:

For Democritus, the vacuum issue is linked to the theory of atoms: If this theory is right, then between atoms there exists vacuum. The theory is illustrated by the fact that it is impossible to cut a stick of wood in two indefinitely.

For Aristotle, the vacuum issue is also linked to a theory. The world is a world of matter, and not of "nothing." Aristotle makes it clear that this assertion-premise is central for understanding a multitude of physical phenomena. Negating it implies negating a whole coherent theory for explaining the world.

Democritus opposes Aristotle's key assertion by adopting it first (a rhetorical action). He infers (as does it Aristotle, but in the opposite direction), that the world is full of matter. He then deduces that this premise negates any kind of motion. This assertion obtained by inference is in opposition to the assertion that bodies move in the world, a statement of fact Aristotle himself absolutely believes to be true. This opposition constitutes a rebuttal for Aristotle's key assertion of his argument.

*[Democritus and Aristotle walk together in the streets of classical Athens, 5th century B.C.]*

De:   Vacuum exists, for sure!

Aris: No way!

De:   The issue of the existence of vacuum is a very important and basic one. Based on the assumption that vacuum exists, I elaborated a whole theory according to which matter is built of atoms, and between them it's empty. The proof of the existence of vacuum is halfway to the proof that my theory about atoms is correct.

You see this stick? I can split it in two? And split it again in two? And so on... Can I continue indefinitely? No! Only to the point I'll reach the atom. The atom, it's impossible to split! And what stands between atoms? Vacuum!

Aris: Negating the existence of vacuum is for me very central for understanding many phenomena in the world. I don't believe in something that does not exist. And the vacuum is the crystallization of nothing. Our world is a world of matter; it has no vacuum in it!

De:   Let's assume that vacuum does not exist. In this case, he world is plenty of matter. How motion can then be possible in such a world? Motion is possible only if there is some place free to move there. And in the world, bodies are in motion; even the air is in motion. So there must be a plenty space in which the primitive motion began.

Aris: Your argument that vacuum is necessary for the existence of motion is not logical. I argue not only that vacuum is not necessary motion, but that it is the enemy of motion! Why? Because in vacuum, no motion is possible! The runnier a liquid is, the faster bodies will fall in it! For example, if I throw a stone into oil, it will fall slower than into water. And in vacuum where there is nothing? Where there is no friction at all that disturbs motion? If nothing disturbs, the speed of the stone will be infinite! And there is nothing like infinite speed! So, no motion can exist in vacuum, and a place where no motion is possible does no exist. There is no infinity and there is no vacuum!

De:   Really! And if the world is full of matter, how things can move?

Aris: Bodies move together, I tell you, they move in harmony

Anim:   Mr. Aristotle, is it possible to ask something? You both sound so right that it's confounding. But why only opinions? You say "To my opinion" or "I think that". But why don't you try to prove your statement that vacuum exists or does not exist?

*Figure 1. An excerpt of a (fictitious) dialogue between Aristotle and Democritus*

Aristotle counter-opposes Democritus' rebuttal. He asserts that vacuum is not necessary for motion. On the contrary, it opposes motion. This assertion is supported by experience (the runnier a liquid is, the faster bodies fall into it), and he infers that were vacuum to exist, bodies would "fall" into it at an infinite speed. And, as he asserts it, there is nothing such as infinite speed (or infinity in general). As shown here, the debate is exemplary in the sense that:

- each of the opponents clearly exposes his argument (key assertion, evidence, supporting assertions), including epistemological considerations
- each antagonist challenges his opponent on his supporting assertions

Such an exemplary debate is a way to model argumentative thinking. One may argue that it lacks the vividness of true debates and this may be right. However, true engagement was sacrificed for the sake of clarity. We wanted to show and analyze an idealized debate, and true engagement, especially when mixed with enthusiasm, risked blurring the clear boundaries of the components of the respective arguments of the antagonists. The different phases of this activity as they occurred in classroom are described here: the phase of engagement, the phase of argumentation analysis, the phase of synthesis, and the phase of preparing a presentation.

*The phase of engagement*

The phase of engagement consists first in watching a movie of the Israeli Educational Broadcast. The teacher also shows the students a number of texts written on the issue (embedded in an Internet site, but not inserted in the production[2]). Of course the texts are simplified and adapted to junior high-school level. Last, and not least, the phase of engagement ends by the teacher's clear announcement of the ultimate goal of the activity: to prepare a multimedia presentation reflecting the historical debate. In summary, the phase of engagement exposes students to the ontogenesis of an exemplary debate and shows that the debate on vacuum was not created out of nothing.

*Argumentation analysis*

Small groups of three to five students receive the protocol excerpts of the debate on vacuum shown in Figure 1, and are asked to progressively construct an AM. Figure 2 displays two AMs constructed by two different groups. The two maps are two acceptable ways to represent the two arguments in Figure 1. Differences between maps mainly came from the identification of explanations, or illustrations of theories/reasons as being the theories/reasons themselves. For example, the proposition "There is no such thing as infinite speed" in Map 1 illustrates the theory that infinity does not exist. There is no doubt that this phase is constraining as students analyze a debate that is not theirs. They must identify each component of the argumentative talk, categorize it (justification, proof, evidence from experience or from an experiment, appeal to a theory), and link it with the appropriate key assertion or with competing assertions.

*Synthesis*

We exemplified in Figure 2 that there is no such thing as <u>the</u> correct AM, even in a scientific discussion. This plurality is beneficial inasmuch the teacher can initiate a discussion on the respective maps of the small groups. Students were invited to present and justify their AMs, and to criticize or evaluate the AMs of the other groups. Some elements in the maps were rectified because some links or categories were unjustifiable. This phase was the real argumentative phase in the task, at the end of which teacher and students negotiated an agreement on a collective AM that was based on several maps. Figure 3 shows this collective map.

*Preparing a presentation*

At this phase students worked again in small groups. A producer (in fact a multimedia advisor) assisted them and invited all small groups to design and produce a presentation of the vacuum issue according to several criteria. The criteria were that the design of the presentation must (1) be based on the AM, (2) contain arguments and counter-arguments in a way that makes visible reasons or supporting evidence for all the arguments, (3) show objections or rebuttals, (4) contain some evaluation of the whole argumentation. The producer proposed these criteria as a way to convince others of the correctness of arguments advanced. Students were encouraged to use sources such as the video, the text file of the video protocol, text and graphical files from the database on the vacuum (on the Internet site), and any other source they wished. We present here one of the presentations, as it was developed by one of the groups, in collaboration the producer. The home page of the presentation contains two buttons for the key assertions "Vacuum exists" and "Vacuum does not exist". Pressing on one of these buttons, for example "Vacuum exists", displays a screen with the first assertion expressed by Democritus (Fig. 4a). This assertion is supported by a video demonstration accessible by pressing on the corresponding key (Fig. 4b). The next supporting assertion (expressed by Democritus) can be obtained from this screen, as well as Aristotle's objection to this specific assertion (not inserted in the present article). Also, it is possible to reach the AM (Figure 3) from any screen, and to jump from any element of this map to its content. The home page also contains an historical outlook that shows the succession of actors with the principal supporting evidence they provided to the whole issue. In some sense, this is a kind of evaluation of the arguments. More substantial evaluation can pop up from any of the forms in the Argumentative Map. For example, clicking on the experience recalled by Aristotle according to which "the less dense matter is, the quicker the fall into it" opens the following window: "This is his life experience. Aristotle relies on his experience, and it is a problem that Greek scientists did not support their hypotheses with real experiments with exact measures". This evaluation was already raised during the synthesis phase, thus only "imported" by the students in their presentation.

**Map 1:**

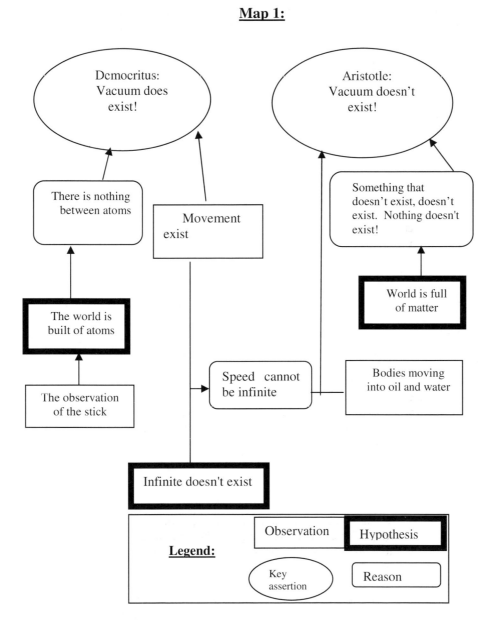

*Figure 2a. Two Argumentative Maps of the dialogue between Aristotle and Democritus (part1)*

## Map 2:

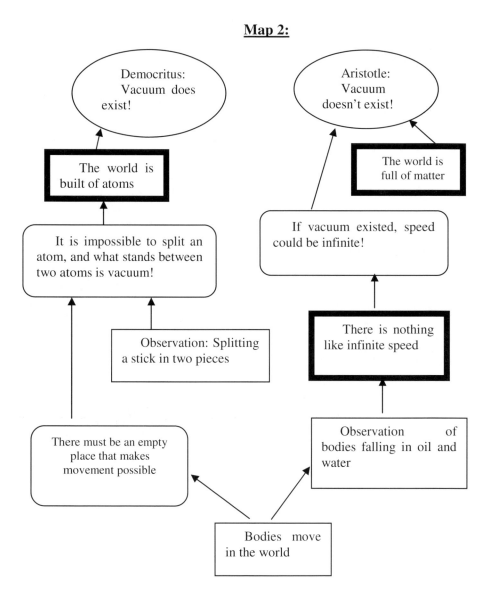

*Figure 2b. Two Argumentative Maps of the dialogue between Aristotle and Democritus (part2)*

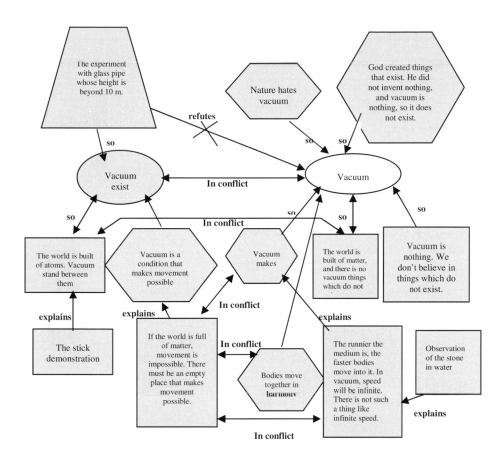

*Figure 3. The collective AM elaborated by the students and the teacher*

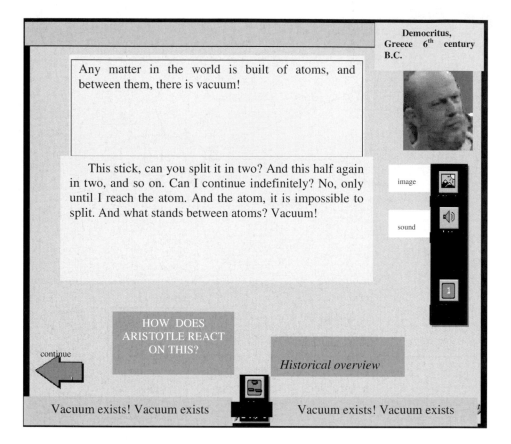

*Figure 4a. The first assertion expressed by Democritus in presentation of debate among them*

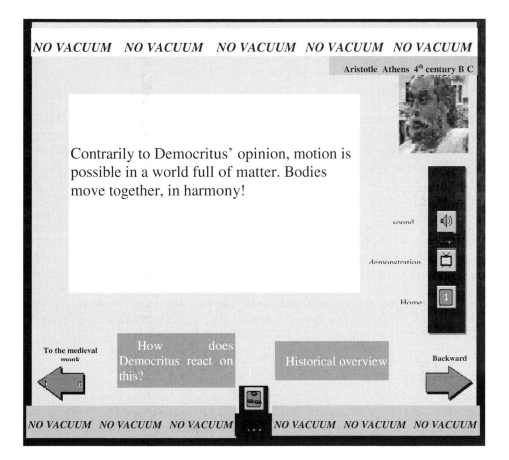

*Figure 4b. The first assertion expressed by Aristotle*

As alluded to in Figure 4, the presentation complied with the four criteria, namely, it relied on the collective AM, displayed reasons supporting arguments on separate screens, but yet buttons could link these screens to objections or rebuttals, and was evaluative. The processes undergone by students during the different phases of the

"Does vacuum exist?" task are not described. We only described a few products suggesting that the program was viable, as the "existence of such products" showed that groups of students evolving in this environment could actively engage in analyzing a scientific controversial issue. Moreover, in spite of the constraining character of the scientific task, students did not comply only with the strict fulfillment of criteria. They used various sources in order to enrich the background on the scientists, or to import pictures of the milieu in which they evolved. They used the additional texts we provided when they wished so, in order to make a show, and an interesting one.

## THE FATE OF ONE ARGUMENT THROUGH MULTIPLE CONTEXTS

The task in which students engage right after "Does vacuum exist?" is the "Tattletale". Our approach in the description of this task is more analytic and we focus here on the fate of one argument that emerged at the beginning of the "Tattletale" and underwent modifications through it. There are nine activities in the Tattletale (see the list above), but in the first one, the presentation of the dilemma, students do not externalize any action. The history begins then with the second one, the individual argumentation, during which each student fills a questionnaire. The history of this argument originates in the individual argument expressed by one girl, Ori, who eventually collaborated with another girl, Carmel, and one boy, Tom who collaborated in some stages of the task. At the time Ori raises her argument, Tom is absent. We consequently trace the changes in Ori's argument along all activities of the Tattletale mainly when she interacts with Carmel. We present here the answers given by the two girls to the questions Q1, Q2, and Q3, formulated above. The two individual arguments (Q1) are quite different. It appears that Ori and Carmel could imagine alternative arguments (in Q2), and rebut them (Q3).

| Ori | Carmel |
|---|---|
| 1: We shouldn't tell because he did it because he was in big trouble, and there are other ways to deal with the situation. Also, it will get him into big trouble, and will lead him to other bad things. | Q1: Yes, we should tell, because although he did it because of hardship, he did something wrong. Victims have the right to know, and this will convince Ron to stop stealing. |
| Q2: If he's not accused (if they hide the robbery), others will learn from it (that one can steal). | Q2: Ron did it because of hardship, and now that John knows it, he can help him to stop, and then Ron will stop. |
| Q3: Nobody will know that the thief was caught. The thief will stop and will return the money and will find work. Rehabilitation! That's what we want, and to be rehabilitated you have to stop the vicious cycle that the thief got stuck in. If others will find out, they'll hurt him, and won't forgive him | Q3: If one reveals that Ron did it, many more people will help Ron. |

The motive in this activity is to *potentially* convince others. The artifacts at Ori's disposal are the story, the structured questionnaire, and the social norms relevant to the dilemma. Some norms Ori relies on include avoiding sneaking, and giving a second chance to delinquents rather than punishment.

The next (third) phase, planning a presentation, was spontaneously decided by Ori, Carmel, and other students in other groups. Ori and Carmel, who sat around the same table while filling the questionnaire, initiated the following dialogue:

Ori: We'll do it in a presentation? We'll do a sad boy left alone, while all the others buy things [pause] But we have a kind of problem, we don't agree [they probably looked at each other's questionnaire].

Carmel:       It's not a problem, because we have to present the second side!

Ori:  Oh right! [The two girls lift their hands and make a gesture of "take five"]

This spontaneous phase happened in two other groups. It is reasonable to suggest that while engaged in this new task, the groups recognized the same frame as for "Does vacuum exist?". They then appropriated the overall objective "to prepare a presentation" in the new activity. But in fact, it seems that there is more than a mere appropriation of the motive of the activity. When Ori declares "we have a kind of a problem, we don't agree" and Carmel replies, "We don't have any problem because we have to present the second side", collaboration in an argumentative activity seems to them normative although they do not share the same key assertion. The conflicting arguments of Aristotle and Democritus and their respective camps displayed in the presentations of the scientific activity were used there to convey a controversy between others. It seems that when Carmel declares, *we don't have any problem, because we have to present the second side!*, she appropriates the possibility of presenting both sides. At this point, it is not clear whether this appropriation only reflects Ori's and Carmel's willing to succeed in their common task (as appears in the "take five" gesture), or a deeper understanding of the advantage of presenting both sides. The following activities will clarify the issue. The above excerpt shows also two changes in Ori's argument. First, she plans the addition of an example, the picture of a sad boy left alone that supports her supporting assertion (*he did it because he was in big trouble*). Secondly, she clearly states her argument as a scenario, and as such she adapts it to the goal (Ori and Carmel) assigned (to themselves), presenting the dilemma with a multimedia tool.

In the fourth phase, the brainstorm argumentation, students try again to state personal arguments, and Ori expresses her standpoint publicly. We bring here the relevant excerpt. It also includes Carmel's reaction.

Teacher: Which kind of dilemma must John decide on?

Dana:         That somebody should tell to someone else.

Carmel:       It's better to leave it between them, and not to spread it around. The problem is whether to tell to everybody or to secretly help Ron.

Teacher:      What do you call it? To tattle I think.

Carmel:         It's not to tattle
T:    Tattletale or not, this is the dilemma. Do you know what that means?
Ori:  That he won't have a chance to get out of it.
Carmel:         It's not true.
Ori:  He'll have a stigma. Also, Steve will be offended.
Dana:            But he has a problem, and that way, the guys will help him. It's for his own good!
Ori:  But nobody will want to help him. He won't do it again.
Carmel:         Who knows if he won't do it again?
Ori:  I do! And also, Ron won't tell other people that he's in big trouble at home. He should get a second chance.

In this brainstorm argumentation, the motive of the students changed again. As they do not have time to develop ideas, they want to be accepted and to win, so that they present short arguments without using terms such as "because", "although", etc. for supporting their key assertions, nor meta-statements such as "I think" or "probably". Rather, all arguments are one-sided. Ori's argument is fragmented in four parts. In the second one, she transforms the reason that supported her argument in her questionnaire, rehabilitation, into a more direct assertion that speaks to the audience (He'll get a stigma). She also adds a reason (Steve will be offended) she did not include in the individual argumentation, after Carmel's opposition. Such a reason has more chances to gain the empathy of the audience. Acceptability is also very important for Carmel who opposes the teacher when she affirms that telling the others means tattling. She knows that tattling violates rules of behavior in schools, so she denies that her telling is really tattling. Another change is Ori's argumentation is quite telling: she does not evoke the reason "He did it because he was in big trouble". A reasonable possibility for this omission is that Dana evokes the same reason but to support a conflicting argument when she declares *But he is in hardship, and that way, the guys will help him. It's for his own good*! Therefore the force of the reason "He did it because he was in big trouble" becomes weaker in the debate. To summarize, all changes we noticed reflect the norms and goals in brainstorm argumentation: students need to defend their position, to win in a "real" debate. The artifacts they capitalize on are not only the arguments they already expressed or heard in former activities but also arguments or reasons raised during the brainstorming.

In the fifth activity, the round of turns argumentation, the teacher systematically controls the enunciation of arguments, as appears in the following excerpt:

Carmel: We have to tell, because victims of thefts have the right to know, and in that way, it's possible to help the thief. Because then, it will shock him.
Ori:  It will only hurt him. He will not have a chance. He'll have a stigma for the rest of his life. We should give him a chance to repent and to do what is right. If you don't tell, you give a chance both to return the money and for a better life.
Adam:            One has to tell on Ron because otherwise, he may do it again. And besides, people should be punished for what they do.

Sivan:          This is someone who stole from others. People should know what he did, maybe in the future, people won't want to get close to him. Still, he deserves a second chance.

Dana:          I wouldn't tell everybody. Maybe his friends, to help him.

Maya:          You have to tell, but only to friends that can help him.

Noa: Like Ori said, the punishment is worse than what he did. He won't do it again. He got his punishment that his friend saw him. If we tell, it won't help. It will cause him injustice. If he does it again, it's clear that he will be a suspect.

This stage also shows numerous changes in arguments. First, they are more complete in the sense that they contain a standpoint and one or two reasons for supporting it. Also, there is an effort to *integrate* contradicting assertions in the course of the turns of arguments. After Carmel and Ori present their contradicting arguments, Sivan "blends" *people have the right to know* (argued by Carmel) with *you give a second chance* (argued by Ori) to argue *People should know what he did, perhaps in the future, people won't want to come close to him. However, he deserves a second chance*, which is not yet very coherent but that clearly includes Carmel and Ori assertions. The same happens with Maya (Of course, this tendency to integrate cannot include Carmel and Ori, who opened the round of turns). Also, there is a general tendency to reduce the volume of arguments by deleting assertions, and by generalizing. Examples of deleted assertions are *he did it because he was in big trouble* and *Steve will be offended* that Ori expressed at previous stages, which disappear here. These deletions are not surprising, as they came as reactions to short objections. Here, in the round of turns argumentation, children are not limited by time. They can use more reasons; they can avoid the use of authority too. We are far from Ori's reaction *I do!* to Carmel's query *Who can be sure he won't do it again?* in the brainstorm argumentation.

The round of turns counter-argumentation was extremely challenging. We already mentioned Kuhn's finding according to which large parts of the general population fail to defend opinions that are opposed to the ones they hold. The teacher invited students to imagine what could be the reaction of people who don't agree with their argument. Many students did not take their turn. This is what Ori's counter-argument:

Ori: We should tell because otherwise John will think that he can keep on stealing and that he got off clean. He must be punished otherwise he will do more bad things, not only stealing. If a person doesn't learn from his mistakes, this is what happens.

The reasons Ori invokes here are new. It seems that Ori appropriated in her counter-argument reasons she heard previously. For example, the truism *If one doesn't learn from his mistakes, this is what happens* seems a generalization of Carmel's statement in the last activity *in that way, it's possible to help the thief. Because then, this will shock him* and perhaps of what Adam said in the same activity (*otherwise, he may do it again. And besides, one has to be punished for one's acts*). Therefore, a cognitive argumentive skill (in Kuhn's terms), which is rare in adolescents, is exploited here in an adequate social setting.

In the seventh phase, the small group dialectical argumentation, the teacher asked Ori and Carmel to construct together an argumentative map. He also asked to indicate on the map to which extent they were confident that their reasons supported their standpoint. Ori and Carmel collaborated during this phase to articulate together each of their conflicting arguments. They decided to use darker background colors for indicating confidence. It seems that the practices in which they participated in the scientific task were directly transposed in this activity, as Ori and Carmel also added examples to illustrate their reasons. The AM is displayed in Figure 5.

Ori and Carmel drew lines between the ellipses (standpoints) and the rectangles (reasons) in order to point at support (in black) or a conflict (in red). Here also, arguments change. The most salient one concerns their abstractedness stemming from more specific reasons raised in previous phases. For example, the reason *There are better ways to repent than causing more injustice* is abstract. It seems to stem from reasons such as *We should give him a chance to repent and to do what is right. If you don't tell, you give a chance both to return the money and for a better life* given by Ori herself in the round of turns argumentation. Also, it seems to integrate Noa's turn in the same activity *It will cause him injustice. If he does it again, it's clear that he will be a suspect* This argument seems to have been abstracted in *His deeds will haunt him all his life* in the map. These changes in all reasons brought forward in the AM emerged from sheer collaboration between Ori and Carmel:

Carmel:        Let's begin with your side [Carmel draws a circle in which she writes "Shouldn't tell"]

Ori:  He did what he did because of hardship [Carmel types into a new rectangle]

Carmel:        Anything else?

Ori:  Yeah. If one tells, Ah... one second I would like to tell

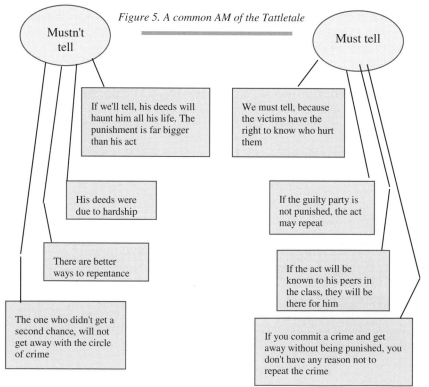

*Figure 5. A common AM of the Tattletale*

Constructing counter-arguments that was so difficult in the round of turns counter-argumentation is done here by the dyad quite easily, as Ori and Carmel aim to succeed in the construction of a multimedia presentation. Also, the AM serves as a common space to share arguments (see Carmel's statement *Let's begin with your side*) and to express arguments according to an appropriate ontology (standpoints, reasons, examples, conflicting reasons).

At the eighth phase, preparing the defense, Ori, Carmel and Tom try to "market" the example Ori gave in the previous activity on their AM, a man who did not get a second chance and who could not get out of crime. The triad prepares a common multimedia presentation. This presentation is linked to all components of the AM. The following excerpt exemplifies the collaboration in the triad:

Ori:       Let's move to the next slide. We'll combine the buttons, we'll draw a man, we'll draw the examples (Ori intends to link between examples on the AM and additional slides illustrating them.) [Ori and Tom search in the graphical database for a picture illustrating Ori's example -- a man who did not have a second chance].
Ori:       We need to find the picture of a man. Not the thinker [a ready-made animation on the head of which there are "thought balloons"]. We can maybe draw lines with the brush?
Carmel: You want to do a man?
Ori:       Maybe we should draw an arrow and a circle, and then he has to get out of the circle (pause). Let's show a circle that the thief cannot get out of.
Tom:      We can draw on another computer
Ori:       Maybe we could take the smiley from the database and we'll draw a sad man near to it?
Carmel: [imports the thinker] But in fact he doesn't have any choice
Ori:       Maybe we should put an X on the second side (on one group of balloons) [No reaction].
Carmel: Which title should we choose?
Ori:       He didn't get the opportunity to think a different way
Carmel: To behave and think a different way
Ori:       We'll put him inside a circle with arrows. Outside there is the smiley but he can't reach him [No reaction].

Figure 6 shows two screens of the presentation.

It is interesting to notice the degree of engagement of the participants in marketing Ori's argument. The degree of engagement was so high that although Carmel thinks "one should tell", she controls the use of the multimedia tool to market Ori's argument to which she personally opposes.

The last activity, defending the argument, was less vivid than previous activities. The group chose Ori to defend the argument embodied in the multimedia presentation. Ori just read the text written in the presentation without using rhetorical moves to convince her audience. The same happened with the other groups. We suggest that this "failure" is due to two factors. First, the teacher and our team were not clear about how to present the argument of a group in which there is disagreement. Secondly, defending an argument before an audience is a rhetorical activity to which junior high-school students are totally unprepared: children and most of adults generally do not practice argumentative defense before an audience, in and out of school.

*Figure 6. A presentation staging the Tattletale*

## DISCUSSION: MECHANISMS OF CHANGE

The nine successive activities in which Ori and her peers participated led to a deep change in the form and content of her arguments. We showed that, unsurprisingly, these changes are modeled by the norms, artifacts at disposal and motives in the successive activities. The specific changes that occurred are of interest, though. For example, we saw that in the round of turns argumentation, students aim at integrating or contrasting arguments through the mediation of arguments expressed previously (in a questionnaire or a debate). We also saw that at that stage authority does not play the same role as in brainstorm argumentation. Students use meta-statements to evaluate their assertions, or those expressed by others. They also try to generalize assertions. In contrast, during the brainstorming argumentation, arguments are dominated by the appeal to personal authority as source of knowledge. As the motive is to win the debate, and to defend arguments from attacks, students suppress non-normative assertions (such as "We have to tattle") and meta-statements (such as "I think that" "probably", or "it depends") and are more assertive. Also, the addition of visual examples matched the motive to convince other people through the mediation of a multimedia presentation. The insertion of counter-arguments in the presentation was led by the same motive. Table 1 displays the motives, artifacts, and norms at each of the activities.

An important phenomenon visible in Table 1 is the transformatory character of artifacts through the successive stages of the Tattletale task. Reasons used in previous stages (by the arguer or other participants) for a specific goal are used and transformed according to other goals and motives. For example, some counter-arguments uttered in the round of turns counter-argumentation, were used to construct the argumentative map in order to convince people with different opinions. At least for the case of Ori, this transformatory character also led to a sensible improvement in her argument, from a one-sided statement to a more poised and two-sided argument.

To a certain extent, Table 1 suggests that the design principles for educational programs based on argumentation were legitimate. Of course, our suggestion here is not based on an experimental design. But as these principles are rooted on other experimental studies and theoretical considerations, Ori's case illustrates them. (1) The chaining of argumentative activities led Ori to capitalize on previous activities in order to improve her basic argument. (2) The alternation between dialectical and synthesis activities was beneficial: for example, reasons uttered (by proponents or opponents) in brainstorm argumentation were incorporated in further activities without really being discussed. The case of round of turns of (counter-)argumentation was quite interesting as the last speakers incorporated reasons uttered by the first ones. So these activities elicited both appropriation and assimilation. (3) Students shared arguments with the AM. The map was a space in which Ori and her group could represent respective arguments, discuss, evaluate and market them per se even when one of the participants did not adhere to the argument she sought to strengthen. (4) As for the alternation between scientific and social themes, it appears that after participating in "Does vacuum exist?", Ori and Carmel deliberately decided to use the framework presented to them for this activity in the Tattletale. We are aware that this flexibility reflected an attraction to the manipulation of multimedia devices. But this is not the whole story. They explicitly referred to norms of scientific argumentation ("looking at the two sides", or evaluating reasons for their own sake). We know and have reported that in everyday conversations people generally do not adopt this critical epistemology. Here, they easily transposed a series of practices learned by a scientific issue (for which

*Table 1. The motives, artifacts and norms at each of the activities*

| Activity | Motive | Artifacts (moral norms not included) | Social Interactions and Argumentative Norms | Change of form |
|---|---|---|---|---|
| Presentation of a dilemma | See the issue | | | – |
| Individual argumentation | To express personal opinions To convince "potential" others | Details of the story Structured questionnaire | Solipsistic Personal arguments are one-sided | – |
| Planning a presentation | Common success | Details in the story Individual arguments in Q1 Presentation software | Collaborative work Legitimacy of contradictory arguments | Addition of examples (in a visual form) |
| Brainstorm argumentation | To win the debate or to be accepted | Individual arguments in Q1 Arguments expressed previously in the debate | Initiative for turn-taking Argumentation based on authority | Deletion of non-normative or brittle assertions and of meta-statements Addition of agreed upon arguments |
| Round of turns argumentation | Express personal argument | Individual arguments in Q1 Arguments expressed previously in the debate | Control by teacher Waiting for turn Arguments must be justified | Deletion of non-normative or brittle assertions. Use of meta-statements. Generalization of assertions. Reinsertion of previous arguments. Addition of agreed upon arguments |
| Round of turns argument play | Promote counter-arguments | Individual counter-arguments in questionnaire. Counter-arguments expressed previously in the debate. | Control by teacher Waiting for turn Contradictory viewpoints in arguments may be acceptable. | Use of meta-statements |
| Small group dialectical argumentation | Common success | (Counter) arguments expressed in previous stages. Argumentative map | Collaborative work Legitimacy of contradictory arguments | Reinsertion of previous arguments |
| Preparing a defense | Common success | (Counter)-arguments expressed in previous stages. Argumentative map. Presentation software tool. | Collaborative work Legitimacy of contradictory arguments | Reinsertion of previous arguments Arguments integrate contradictory arguments |
| Defending an argument | Convince large audience | | Obligation to cope with alternative arguments. | |

opting for an argument over another one did not involve much belief, but rather was accepted) onto a social issue. (5) At last, the importance of the final principle concerning the multiple perspectives the task should engender, is evident: students dealt about friendship, social order, justice and folk psychology, and interwove them rather than opposed them and chose one.

## COULD THE BLIND AND THE PARALYTIC HELP EACH OTHER?

The current program does not pretend to change students' "scientific epistemology" from being absolutist, skeptical, or relativist, to scientific. Nor does this program aim to improve some aspects of scientific reasoning. Similarly, it does not pretend to improve general reasoning capabilities in a social domain. The aim is paradoxically both more limited and more general. We suggest that this environment engages students in activities in which action and talk are intertwined; the objects talked about are own or others' changing arguments. Similar tools and kinds of activities are recurrently presented to students. They are first engaged in an issue, possibly express personal argument, collaboratively construct an argumentative map, participate in structured or unstructured public debates, prepare a presentation or defend it publicly. The Argumentative Maps they produce must fulfill several criteria that are in accordance with argumentative standards.

It is still premature to speak about "Kishurim" as a well-structured project in which the effects of the environment on students' argumentative thinking can be clearly analyzed. However, there are already promising directions that can be followed. The first direction is methodological. The tools used for staging and composing a presentation allow the teacher-researcher to trace products (maps, screens and links between them) that are collected chronologically. We used this approach in a recent study (Schwarz et al., 2002) to analyze what we called migration of knowledge across participants, and along activities. Pushing more in such a direction is necessary for experimentally comparing the effects of different kinds of argumentative activities and for testing the validity of the argumentative principles. Another direction oriented on the analysis of argumentative processes and the construction of knowledge should be also developed. Research is presently conducted to understand the role of AMs in argumentative activities (dialectical evaluative, etc.). We ask how AMs support the articulation of arguments, and of argumentative moves (challenges, counterchallenges, refutations, concessions, etc.). We also ask about the status of AMs in argumentative activities, for example: Do they help elaborating mental tools or rather, are the argumentative functions facilitated by the argumentative map not internalized? The same questions can be addressed for the presentation tools in relation to the activity of defending. Such a program of research is a new endeavor as only a few studies have concentrated on argumentative/reasoning processes in conversation (e.g., Pontecorvo & Girardet, 1993; Resnick et al., 1993; Schwarz & Hershkowitz, 1995; Schwarz et al., 2000), and in these studies, no technological devices were included. A technologically based environment seems, at first glance, to complicate a situation that is anyway complex. Anyway, as argumentative maps and sources of information such as databases are quite common cultural tools used with some dexterity by a growing number of students, this program of research is a must.

We saw that conventional education fails to provide students with appropriate environments for fostering argumentation. While most questions about the "couple" technology-argumentation are quite open, the primary results obtained in this experiment suggest that we probably made that a good match. However, the status of our claim in not more than a hypothesis rooted in previous experimental findings (that supported the design principles) and on our pedagogical experience. Systematic research is needed to warrant this hypothesis. Blinds and paralytics may help together at integrating the natural propensity to argue ("move in our opinions") – but to which direction, and the tendency to accept ("to see") well-established knowledge in school activities.

## AFFILIATION

*Baruch B. Schwarz and Amnon Glassner,*
*School of Education, The Hebrew University*
*Mount Scopus, Jerusalem, 91905, ISRAEL*
*msschwar@mscc.huji.ac.il*

## REFERENCES

Andriessen, J. & Coirier P. (1999). *Foundations of Argumentative Text Processing* (pp. 179-202). Amsterdam University Press.

Azmitia, M. (1996). Peer interactive minds: Developmental, theoretical, and methodological issues. In Baltes, P. B., Staudinger, U. M., & et al. (Eds.), *Interactive minds: Life-span perspectives on the social foundation of cognition* (pp. 133-162). New York, NY, USA: Cambridge University Press.

Antaki, C. (1994). Explaining and Arguing. The social Organization of Accounts. Sage Publication.

Baker, M. (1999). Argumentation and constructive interaction. In J. Andriessen, P. Coirier (Eds.), *Foundations of Argumentative Text Processing* (pp. 179-202). Amsterdam University Press.

Baker, M. (2002). Computer-Mediated Argumentative Interactions for the co-elaboration of scientific notions. This volume.

Cazden, C. B. (1988). *Classroom discourse*. Portsmouth, NH: Heinemann Educational Books.

Christensen C., & Elstein, S. (1991). Informal Reasoning in the Medical Profession. In J. F. Voss, D. N. Perkins, & J. W. Segal (Eds.), *Informal Reasoning and Education* (pp.17-35). Hillsdale, N.J.: Lawrence Erlbaum Associates.

Coirier, P., Andriessen, J. & Chanquoy, L. (1999). From Planning to Translating the Specificity of Argumentative Writing. In J. Andriessen, P. Coirier (Eds.), *Foundations of Argumentative Text Processing* (pp. 1-28). Amsterdam University Press.

Davenport, P. & Howe, C. (1999). Conceptual gain and successful problem-solving in primary school mathematics. Educational Studies, 25, 55-78.

Davenport, P., Howe, C., & Noble, A. (2000). Peer interaction and the coordination of knowledge. *Swiss Journal of Educational Sciences, 22*(3), 481-508.

Dunbar, K. (1993). Concept Discovery in a Scientific Domain. *Cognitive Science, 17*(3), 397-435.

Duschl, R. A. (1990). Restructuring Science education: The importance of theories and their development. New York, Columbia University: Teachers College Press

Duschl, R. A., & Gitomer, D.H. (1991). Epistemological perspectives on conceptual change: Implications for educational practice. *Journal of Research in Science Teaching, 28*, 839-858.

Duschl, R. A., & Hamilton, R. (1992). Philosophy of Science, Cognitive Psychology, and Educational Theory and Practice. Suny Series in Science Education. Albany: State University of New York Press.

Hershkowitz, R., & Schwarz, B. B. (1999). Reflective processes in a technology-based mathematics classroom. *Cognition and Instruction*, 17, 66-91.

Kedem, O. (1999). "Temporarily Definitive". The planning, development, production and educational implementation of a series of films and its effects on Students' conceptions and views regarding the Nature of Science. Doctoral Dissertation. University of Salford, Salford, UK.

Kintsch, W. (1986). Learning >From Text. In L.B. Resnick (Ed.). *Knowing, Learning, and Instruction* pp(25-46). Hillsdale, N.J.: Lawrence Erlbaum Associates.

Kuhn, T. (1962). The structure of scientific revolutions. Chicago: The University of Chicago Press.

Kuhn, D. (1991). *The skills of argument.* Cambridge: Cambridge University Press.

Kuhn, D (1993). Science as argument: Implication for teaching and learning scientific thinking skills. *Scientific Education, 77*, 319-337.

Lord, C., Ross, L., & Lepper, M. (1979). Biased assimilation and attitude polarization: The effect of prior theories on subsequently considered evidence. *Journal of Personality and Social Psychology, 37*, 2098-2109.

Means, M. L. & Voss, J. F. (1996). Who reasons well? Two studies of informal reasoning among children of different grade, ability and knowledge levels. *Cognition and Instruction, 14*(2), 139-179.

Meichtry, Y. .J. (1993). The Impact of Science Curricula on Students Views About the Nature of Science. *Journal of Research in Science Teaching, 30*(4), 429-443.

Meyer, K. & Woodruff, E. (1997). Consensually driven explanation in science teaching. *Science Education, 81*, 173-92.

Ohlsson. S. (1992). The cognitive skill of theory articulation: A neglected aspect of science education. *Science & Education, 1*, 181-189.

Olson, D. (1996). *The World on paper.* Cambridge University Press.

Orsolini, M., (1993). "Dwarfs do not shoot": An Analysis of Children's Justifications. *Cognition and Instruction, 11*(3 & 4), 281-297.

Orsolini, M., & Pontecorvo, C. (1992). Children's talk in classroom discussion. *Cognition and Instruction, 9*, 113-136.

Perkins, D. N., Farady, M., & Bushey, B. (1991). Everyday reasoning and the roots of intelligence. In J. F. Voss, D. N. Perkins, & J. W. Segal (Eds.), *Informal Reasoning and Education* (pp. 83-105). Hillsdale, N.J.: Lawrence Erlbaum Associates.

Pomeroy, D. (1993). Implications of teachers' beliefs about the nature of science: Comparisons of the beliefs of scientists, secondary science teachers, and elementary teachers. *Science Education, 77*, 261-278.

Pontecorvo, C. & Girardet, H., (1993). Arguing and reasoning in understanding historical topics. *Cognition and instruction, 11*(3 & 4), 365-395.

Resnick, L. B., Salmon, M., Zeitz, C. M., Wathen, S. H., & Holowchak, M. (1993). Reasoning in conversation. *Cognition and instruction, 11*(3 & 4), 347-364.

Rogoff, B., & Chavajay, P. (1995). What's become of research on the cultural basis of cognitive development? *American Psychologist, 50*(10) 859-877.

Roschelle, J. (1992). Learning by collaboration: convergent conceptual change. *The Journal of the Learning Sciences, 3*, 235-276.

Schauble, L. (1990). Belief revision in children: The role of prior knowledge and strategies for generating evidence. *Journal of Experimental Child Psychology, 49*, 31-57.

Schwarz, B. B., Benaya, L. & Shemaya, H. (2001). Symmetry and Learning in Argumentation Among Peers. Paper presented at the First International Conference on Communication, Problem-Solving and Learning, University of Strathclyde, Glasgow.

Schwarz, B. B., & Hershkowitz, R. (1995). Argumentation and reasoning in a technology-based class. *Proceedings of the Seventeenth Annual Meeting of the Cognitive Science Society*, 731-735, Pittsburgh, PA.

Schwarz, B. B., Neuman, Y. & Biezuner, S. (2000). Two "wrongs" may make a right...If they argue together! *Cognition & Instruction, 18*(4), 461-494.

Schwarz, B. B., Neuman, Y. & Gil, J., & Ilya, M. (2002). Construction of collective and individual knowledge in argumentative activity: An empirical study. *The Journal of the Learning Sciences, 12*(2).

Songer N., & Linn, M. (1991). How Do Student's Views of Science Influence Knowledge Integration? *Journal of Research in Science Teaching, 28*(9), 761-796.

Staudinger, U. M., & Joos, M. (2000). Interactive Minds – A paradigm for the study of the social-interactive nature of human cognition and its life-span development. *Swiss Journal of Educational Sciences, 22(3)*, 559-574.

Stein, N., & Miller, C.A. (1991). I win... you lose: the development of argumentative thinking. In J. F. Voss, D.N. Perkins & J. Segal (Eds.), *Informal reasoning and Instruction* (pp.265-290). Hillsdale, N.J.: Lawrence Erlbaum.

Stein, N., & Miller, C.A. (1993). The development of memory and reasoning skill in argumentative contexts: evaluating, explaining, and generating evidence. In R. Glaser (Ed.), *Advances in instructional psychology, Vol. 4* (pp. 235-285). Hillsdale, N.J.: Lawrence Erlbaum Associates.

Suthers. D. (2002). This volume.

Toulmin, S.E. (1958). *The uses of argument*. Cambridge: Cambridge University Press.

Tweney (1991). In J. Voss, D Perkins, & J. Segal (Eds.), *Informal Reasoning and Education*. Hillsdale, N.J.: Lawrence Erlbaum Associates.

Van Bruggen, J. M. & Kirschner, P. A. (2002). Designing external representations to support solving wicked problems. This volume.

Voss, J. F. (1991). Informal Reasoning and International Relations.. In J. F. Voss, D. N. Perkins, & J. W. Segal (Eds.), *Informal Reasoning and Education* (pp.37-58). Hillsdale, N.J.: Lawrence Erlbaum Associates.

Wilson, T. & Schooler, J. (1991). Thinking too much: Introspection can reduce the quality of preferences and decisions. *Journal of Personality and Social Psychology, 60*, 181-192.

Woodruff, E. & Meyer, K. (1997). Explanations from intra- and inter-group discourse: students building knowledge in the science classroom. *Research in Science Education, 27*(1), 25-39.

## NOTES

[1]There have been pioneering studies in which students were prompted to an argumentative talk in classrooms, in order to investigate the development of reasoning. Studies on Italian children's classroom discussions in history (Pontecorvo & Girardet, 1993; Orsolini & Pontecorvo, 1992) indicate that, with appropriate interventions from a teacher, even very young students can produce substantial explanatory and argumentative discourse, that lead to historical analysis and synthesis.

[2] Examples are texts written by the Stoics (Greek philosophical school) that infer from their atomistic views that the universe has no center (a heresy in Christian medieval theology). Or texts written by Maimonides (medieval Aristotelian philosopher) who proves that an atomistic view of matter entails an atomistic view of time and space (!), something which is inconceivable for Aristotelians. Or a modern physics text in which it is noticed that, at the present stage of technological development, it is impossible to obtain absolute vacuum.

TIMOTHY KOSCHMANN

# CSCL, ARGUMENTATION, AND DEWEYAN INQUIRY

## Argumentation *is* Learning

Speaking generally the fact of inference may be identified with the phenomenon of *evidence*. Wherever anything is discovered and used as evidence there, and only there, is inference. Now the hunting for, the weighing and sifting, the determination of force of evidence, is something which takes place in public, in *plein air*. That which is done in the courtroom with the participation of witnesses, court officials, jury, etc., and in consequence of which a man is hung, is not anything which can profitably be termed psychical. It belongs in the category where plowing, assembling the parts of a machine, digging and smelting ore belong—namely, behavior, which lays hold of and handles and rearranges physical things.

(Dewey, 1985, MW10:90-91)[1]

## INTRODUCTION

This collection represents something of a departure from prior work on argumentation. There is, for example, an established literature concerned with how argumentation is structured (cf., Anderson, et al., 1997; Eemeren et al., 1996). There are related research traditions devoted to developmental aspects of argumentation (e.g., Felton & Kuhn, 2001; Stein & Bernas, 1999) and exploring the relationship between argumentation and abstract reasoning skills (e.g., Chinn & Anderson, 1998; Kuhn, Shaw, & Felton, 1997; Stein & Miller, 1993). Research on argumentation within the CSCL community, however, has had a somewhat different orientation. As reflected in the chapters here and elsewhere,[2] CSCL researchers have focused on (1) how argumentation can be exploited as a site for learning generally and (2) how learning accomplished in this way might be augmented using technology. The goal, therefore, is one of fostering productive argumentation in instructional settings. Several of the chapters, however, testify to the difficulties attendant to facilitating such forms of argumentation among learners.

It appears, from the findings reported here, to be difficult to get learners to produce well-elaborated arguments in instructional settings, that is the actual arguments produced tend to be sparse and the quality of the argumentation low. In the corpus of CMC interaction compiled by Baker (this volume) only a quarter of the accumulated interaction was coded as argumentative, though the task was constructed in such a way as to foreground disagreements. Veerman (this volume) studied effects of different

261

J. Andriessen, M. Baker, & D. Suthers (eds.), *Arguing to Learn: Confronting Cognitions in Computer-Supported Collaborative Learning Environments (pp. 261-269).*
© 2003 Kluwer Academic Publishers. Printed in the Netherlands.

forms of computer-mediation on class discussions in different university courses and, again, she reported that roughly only a quarter of the postings in any of the mediation conditions (42% of 61% in Netmeeting, 50% of 42% in Belvedere, 29% of 88% in Allaire Forums) constituted "argumentative dialogue moves." Whether this is a high or low proportion of argumentation is difficult to say—purely argumentative discourse would be difficult to sustain in any situation, instructional or otherwise. Jermann and Dillenbourg (this volume) pre-tested student volunteers and paired them in such a way as to promote conflict. They found, however, that the level of conflict among the students' expressed positions was low. Andriessen, Erkens, Laak, Peters, and Coirier (this volume) rated 71% of the chat exchanges that occurred during their collaborative writing task as involving only "minimal" negotiation. The title of Schwarz and Glassner's chapter highlights problems of quality. It suggests that children (and possibly many adults) are disabled with respect to argumentation—they argue volubly but "blindly," that is with insufficient regard for the organization of their everyday arguments and they find themselves "paralyzed" when called upon to appraise the arguments put forward by scientists and other authorities. As Andriessen et al. summarized, "Participants seem to be keen at avoiding conflict, do not really discuss the plausibility and strength of produced information and are not much concerned with the argumentative quality of the resulting text" (p. 107). Furthermore, interventions designed to stimulate and support argumentation in instructional settings seem to produce mixed results. Several chapters discussed the issue of representational guidance. Suthers (this volume), however, found no significant differences in learning outcomes when subjects used different tools for representing and managing arguments. Teachers' effectiveness at facilitating argumentation also came under question. Veerman, in her study of different forms of computer-mediation on class discussions, reported that faculty coaching had no discernable effect on the proportion of argumentation moves produced by students.

These findings attesting to the difficulties in fostering argumentation in instructional settings would seem to run counter to our intuitions. Observe interaction on any school playground and you will find argumentation aplenty. As Schwarz and Glassner observed in their chapter, even young children would appear to be both able and willing to engage in elaborate argumentative dialog. Why the difference between the playground and the classroom? Apparently the difficult part is not fostering argumentation per se, but rather fostering the right kind of argumentation—argumentation that is conducive to learning. But what is the relationship of argumentation to learning? That would seem to be the crucial theoretical issue.

## THEORIZING THE RELATION BETWEEN
## ARGUMENTATION AND LEARNING

The chapters of this volume do not seem to take a unified position with regard to the question of how argumentation is related to learning. They begin with different assumptions about what needs to be learned, about where learning occurs, and, more fundamentally, what it means to learn in the first place. Because of this, the ways in which argumentation is linked theoretically with learning plays out differently in different chapters.

The very idea of "confronting cognitions" suggests a particular theory about what constitutes learning. It is a theory with strong connections to the neo-Piagetian notion of social conflict as a stimulus for learning (Doise & Mugny, 1984; Perret-Clermont & Schubauer-Leoni, 1981). The connection between argumentation and social conflict seems a natural one (What *is* argumentation if not social conflict?). The goal for the design of interaction, then, becomes one of making disagreement visible. This can be seen most clearly in the Baker and the Jermann and Dillenbourg chapters and the specific interventions they describe. This form of theorizing, however, arises in other chapters as well. Veerman (this volume), for example, writes:

> In argumentation, students can [give] prominence to conflict and negotiation processes, critically discuss information, elaborate on arguments and explore multiple perspectives. Knowledge and opinions can be (re)constructed and co-constructed and expand students' understanding of specific concepts or problems. Thus, argumentation can be seen as an important mechanism for fruitful discussions and the production of constructive activities. (p. 118)

"Constructive" interaction, therefore, is dialog that promotes conflict[3] and part of Veerman's study was to determine the proportion of constructive dialog that occurred with different forms of mediation. The Andriessen et al. and Pilkington and Walker chapters differ from the others in that both are concerned with the processes of collaborative composition rather than conceptual change. Both employ a form of discourse analysis in which textually-mediated exchanges are broken down into isolated moves or speech acts. Both also presume that social conflict serves as a precursor to learning and in this way embrace conflict theory as an underlying framework. Social conflict theory appeals to a grain-in-the-oyster model of learning. Learning (the pearl) occurs through a process of conceptual adaptation or accommodation in response to an intrusion or disruption (the grain of sand). It describes, therefore, a fundamentally psychological process, albeit one influenced by social factors. But, therein lies the rub. As Andriessen et al. conceded, "The relationship between argumentation and learning by collaboration is not direct" (p. 85). How is it precisely that we link a social cause to a cognitive/psychological effect? It is this dualism that makes the relation between argumentation and learning problematic for social conflict theory.

Social conflict theory is not the sole means of theorizing learning and its relation to argumentation employed in this volume, however. Schwarz and Glassner in their discussion of literacy seem to employ a quite different way of theorizing learning.

They quote Kuhn (1962) as observing, "to be literate [it] is not enough to know the words, one must learn how to participate in the discourse of some textual community" (p. 230). Becoming literate in this sense has strong connections to Bruffee's (1993) definition of collaborative learning, Gee's (1992) description of entering into a Discourse (with a big "D"), and Lave and Wenger's (1991) description of legitimate peripheral participation in a community of practice. By this perspective, which might be termed a "social practice" view (Lave & Wenger, 1991, p. 31), learning is treated not as an occult, psychological phenomenon but rather as a social one involving transformations in community membership and social identity. But this leads to a fundamentally different way of theorizing the relation between argumentation and learning. If participating in argumentation is seen as one part of being a full-fledged member of some discourse community, then joining the community must entail learning how to argue competently within it. The shift from arguing to learn to learning to argue marks a more profound shift in underlying metaphor, from viewing learning as a process of *acquisition* to a change in *participation* (Sfard, 1998). A participatory view of learning avoids the dualism of social conflict theory, but does so at a cost. What is lost is the attention to content that comes along with a focus on arguing as a means to learning.

There is yet another theoretical approach to understanding the relation between argumentation and learning and evidence of its influence can be seen in some of the chapters. This alternative approach has its roots in the theory of distributed cognition based on the assumption that cognition is not an individual psychological matter but instead distributed across multiple members of a team performing a collaborative activity. As Hutchins (1995) described it:

> The proper unit of analysis for talking about cognitive change includes the socio-material environment of thinking. *Learning is adaptive reorganization in a complex system.* (p. 289, author's italics)

Hutchins' (1995) classic example of adaptive reorganization involves the collaborative task of navigating a large naval vessel down a channel. Argumentation could be conceptualised as navigating through a problem space.[4] The complex system that carries out the activity consists not only of the participants, but also the artefacts employed in carrying out the activity. "Representational tools," as described in Suthers' chapter and the chapter by Bruggen and Kirschner, are one part of the socio-material environment and are designed to support productive argumentation. From the perspective of distributed cognition, learning is a "sociogenetic" rather than a "microgenetic" process, using a distinction borrowed from Saxe (2002). It includes not only the participants' appropriation of the culturally-provided tools and practices for argumentation, but also the evolution of these very same tools and practices over time. As was the case for social practice theory, the theory of distributed cognition treats learning as a process of restructuring a socially-organized activity. But, like social conflict theory, learning by the theory of distributed cognition is seen as a process of acquisition, albeit one in which the learning so acquired accrues to a complex socio-material system rather than an individual psychological agent.

There is nothing inherently wrong with employing different theories of learning when talking about argumentation. It is, in fact, common in new areas of inquiry to have some contention with regard to foundational theory (Kuhn, 1962). This kind of diversity, however, does introduce certain problems. First, each of these theories (i.e., social conflict, social practice, and distributed cognition) seems to only provide a partial account of the phenomena of interest—social conflict theory attends to content, but neglects social consequences; social practice theory, on the other hand, attends exclusively to social consequences and thereby neglects content; an analysis based on distributed cognition highlights change at a cultural (anthropological) level, but does not address change at an individual (psychological) level. Second, we have no theoretically-grounded way of combining these accounts, since they arise from different traditions and lack a shared conceptual foundation. In order to found a science of argumentation and learning, therefore, one in which diverse contributions can hope to build upon one another, there needs to be a convergence in goals and research questions.[5] Such a convergence can only take place, however, when there is concurrence with regard to underlying theories and assumptions. But if existing theories of learning do not seem to provide the basis for such a convergence, where are we to turn for alternatives?

## ARGUMENTATION AS JOINT INQUIRY

In earlier writing I have suggested that some useful ideas for understanding learning in settings of collaboration could be found in the works of the American Pragmatist philosopher, John Dewey. I have argued that Dewey's notion of transactional inquiry offered a third metaphor for thinking about learning, one that overcomes the limitations of viewing it as a purely cognitive or purely social matter (Koschmann, 2001). Further, I have argued that meaning-making practices are at the very core of our research interests in CSCL and that Dewey offered some clues as to how we might go about studying such practices (Koschmann, 2002).

In his later writings, Dewey devoted much attention to the topic of inquiry. He (1991/1941) wrote, "[I]nquiry begins in an *indeterminate* situation and not only begins in but is controlled by its specific qualitative nature" (LW14:181). Dewey defined inquiry as "the set of operations by which the situation is resolved (settled, or rendered determinate)" (LW14:181). But, the problem or aspect of the situation that renders it indeterminate is not given; it must be discovered through the processes of inquiry. Dewey wrote, "The conditions discovered, accordingly, in and by operational observation, constitute the *conditions of the problem* with which further inquiry is engaged; for data, on this view, are always data of some specific problem and hence are not given ready-made to an inquiry but are determined in and by it." (LW14:181). Inquiry, in Dewey's hands, was a foundation upon which he hoped to develop a new form of logic (Burke, 1994). Dewey went on:

> As the problem progressively assumes definite shape by means of repeated acts of observation, possible solutions suggest themselves. These possible solutions are, truistically (in terms of theory), *possible* meanings of the data determined in observation. The process of reasoning is an elaboration of them. When they are checked by reference to

> observed materials, they constitute the subject-mater of inferential propositions. The latter
> are also operational in nature since they institute new experimental observations whose
> subject-matter provides both tests for old hypotheses and starting-points for new ones or at
> least for modifying solutions previously entertained. And so on until a determinate
> situation is instituted. (LW14:181-182).

Deweyan inquiry is neither a purely cognitive, nor a purely behavioural process. It
may have phases that might be described as psychical/mental/cognitive, but it must
also effect "*existensial* transformation and reconstruction of the material with which it
deals" (Dewey, 1991/1938, LW12:161). Inquiry is for Dewey an "outdoor fact"
(Hickman, 1998).

When multiple participants engage in inquiry together, new meanings are created
as a by-product of the activity. Dewey (1991/1938) wrote:

> [T]he meaning which a conventional symbol has is not itself conventional. For the
> meaning is established by agreements of different persons in existential activities having
> reference to existential consequences. ... For agreement and disagreement are determined
> by the consequences of conjoint activity. (LW12:53)

If the goal of argumentation is to produce a well-reasoned judgment (*warranted
assertion* in Dewey's terms), then argumentation could be construed as a form of
Deweyan inquiry conducted conjointly. Inquiry for Dewey, was not the only means by
which learning could take place, but he did consider it the most productive. If
argumentation can be considered a form of inquiry, then, by implication,
argumentation is also a form of learning.[6] This represents a new way of
conceptualising the relationship between argumentation and learning. Instead of
treating argumentation as a means to achieve learning (arguing to learn) or treating
learning as a process of achieving competent participation (learning to argue), the
view proposed here is one of taking argumentation as a form of learning in its own
right, conducted collaboratively and available to direct study. What implications
would such a move hold for future research on argumentation?

## STUDYING ARGUMENTATION PRAXIS

First off, let me say that studying argumentation is, in my opinion, a step in the right
direction. Traditionally, CSCL researchers have concerned themselves more generally
with how people learn in settings of collaboration. But collaborative learning is such a
broad and vague topic, it is difficult to sustain a common focus. Limiting the scope of
inquiry to argumentation serves to more sharply focus our attentions and this should
prove beneficial in the long run.

Argumentation provides a site for doing inquiry into the very processes of inquiry
itself. Early work on argumentation focused on studying the logical structure of
argument construction (Eemeren, et al., 1996). More recently there has been a shift
toward studying discursive or pragmatic aspects of argumentation (Eemeren &
Grootendorst, 1999). Adequate attention has yet to be paid, however, to the methods
participants employ in *doing* argumentation. That is, there is a need for research
carefully documenting how argumentation is accomplished as an interactional
achievement, as a form of enacted practice. We know little, for example, about how

argumentative discussions are occasioned, how participants engaged in argument offer a "source or basis" (Pomerantz, 1984a) for their claims, or how assessments for such claims are offered and received (c.f., Pomerantz, 1984b). Though some researchers are beginning to examine such issues (e.g., Goodwin, Goodwin, & Yaeger-Dror, in press), this is a wide-open area for exploration.

Research of this type has great practical significance for those of us interested in instructional issues. Absent such inquiry, we have no way of beginning to answer the question of why, as we saw in many of the chapters here, it is so difficult to foster productive argumentation in instructional settings. Furthermore, research on argumentation praxis is a necessary prerequisite to dissemination of any sort of instructional reform initiative based on argumentation. If we are not able as researchers to articulate what forms of interactional practice we value, how can we reasonably expect to persuade others to adopt these practices in their teaching? Finally, but most importantly for us as members of the CSCL research community, how can we hope to understand the role of designed artefacts in supporting argumentation without first developing an appreciation for the fundamental meaning-making practices by which argumentation is accomplished?

## AFFILIATION

*Timothy Koschmann, Department of Medical Education*
*Southern Illinois University, P.O. Box 19622*
*Springfield, Illinois, 62794-9622, U.S.A.*

## REFERENCES

Anderson, R., Chinn, C., Chang, J., Waggoner, M., & Yi, H. (1997). On the logical integrity of children's arguments. *Cognition & Instruction, 15*, 135-167.

Baker, M. (1999). Argumentation and constructive interaction. In J. Andriessen & P. Coirer (Eds.), *Foundations of argumentative text processing.* (pp. 179-202). Amsterdam: University of Amsterdam Press.

Bell, P. (2002). Using argument map representations to make thinking visible for individuals and groups. In T. Koschmann, R. Hall, & N. Miyake (Eds.), *CSCL 2: Carrying forward the conversation* (pp. 449-485). Mahwah, NJ: Lawrence Erlbaum Associates.

Bruffee, K. (1993). *Collaborative learning.* Baltimore, MD: Johns Hopkins University.

Burke, T. (1994). *Dewey's new logic.* Chicago: University of Chicago Press.

Chinn, C., & Anderson, R. (1998). The structure of discussions that promote reasoning. *Teacher College Record, 100*, 315-368.

Dewey, J. (1985). Logical objects. In J. A. Boydston (Ed.), *John Dewey: The middle works, 1916–1917, Vol. 10* (pp. 89-97). Carbondale, IL: SIU Press.

Dewey, J. (1991/1938). Logic: The theory of inquiry. In J. A. Boydston (Ed.), *John Dewey: The Later Works, 1925–1953, Vol. 12.* Carbondale, IL: SIU Press. [Originally published as Dewey, J. (1938). *Logic: The Theory of Inquiry.* New York: Henry Holt & Co.].

Dewey, J. (1991/1941). Propositions, warranted assertability, and truth. In J. A. Boydston (Ed.), *John Dewey: The later works, 1939—1941, Vol. 14* (pp. 168—188). Carbondale, IL: SIU Press. [Originally published in 1941]

Dewey, J. & Bentley, A. (1991/1949). Knowing and the known. In J. A. Boydston (Ed.), *John Dewey: The later works, 1949–1952, Vol. 16*. Carbondale, IL: SIU Press. [Originally published as Dewey, J. & Bentley, A. (1949). *Knowing and the known*. Boston: Beacon Press].

Doise, W. & Mugny, G. (1984). *The social development of the intellect*. Oxford: Pergamon Press.

Eemeren, F. van, & Grootenhorst, R. (1999). Developments in argumentation theory. In J. Andriessen & P. Coirer (Eds.), *Foundations of argumentative text processing*. (pp. 43-58). Amsterdam: University of Amsterdam Press.

Eemeren, F. van, et al. (1996). *Fundamentals of argumentation theory: A handbook of historical backgrounds and contemporary developments*. Mahwah, NJ: Lawrence Erlbaum Associates.

Felton, M., & Kuhn, D. (2001). The development of argumentative discourse skill. *Discourse Processes, 32*, 135-153.

Gee, J. P. (1992). *The social mind: Language, ideology, and social practice*. NY: Bergin & Garvey.

Goodwin, M., Goodwin, C., & Yaeger-Dror, M. (in press). Multi-modality in girl's game disputes. *Journal of Pragmatics*.

Hickman, L. (1998). Dewey's theory of inquiry. In L. Hickman (Ed.), *Reading Dewey: Interpretations for a post-modern generation* (pp. 166-186). Bloomington, IN: Indiana University Press.

Hutchins, E. (1995). *Cognition in the wild*. Cambridge, MA: MIT Press.

Koschmann, T. (2001). A third metaphor for learning: Toward a Deweyan form of transactional inquiry. In S. Carver & D. Klahr (Eds.), *Cognition and instruction: 25 years of progress* (pp. 439-454). Mahwah, NJ: Lawrence Erlbaum Associates.

Koschmann, T. (2002). Dewey's contribution to the foundations of CSCL research. In G. Stahl (Ed.), *Computer support for collaborative learning: Foundations for a CSCL community* (pp. 17-22). Mahwah, NJ: Lawrence Erlbaum Associates.

Kuhn, D., Shaw, V., & Felton, M. (1997). Effects of dyadic interaction on argumentative reasoning. *Cognition & Instruction, 15*, 287-315.

Kuhn, T. (1962). *The structure of scientific revolutions*. Chicago: University of Chicago.

Lave, J., & Wenger, E. (1991). *Situated learning: Legitimate peripheral participation*. NY: Cambridge University Press.

National Research Council (2001). *Scientific inquiry in education*. Washington, D.C.: National Academy Press.

Perret-Clermont, A.-N., & Schubauer-Leoni, M.L. (1981). Conflict and cooperation as opportunities for learning. In P. Robinson (Ed.), *Communication in development* (pp. 203-234). NY: Academic Press.

Pomerantz, A. (1984a). Giving a source or basis: The practice in conversation of telling 'how I know.' *Journal of Pragmatics, 8*, 607-625.

Pomerantz, A. (1984b). Agreeing and disagreeing with assessments: Some features of preferred/dispreferred turn shapes. In H. Atkinson & J. Heritage (Eds.), *Structures of social action: Studies in conversational analysis* (pp. 57-101). NY: Cambridge University Press.

Saxe, G. (2002). Children's developing mathematics in collective practices: A framework for analysis. *Journal of the Learning Sciences, 11*, 275-300.

Sfard, A. (1998). On two metaphors for learning and the dangers of choosing just one. *Educational Researcher, 27*(2), 4-13.

Stein, N., & Bernas, R. (1999). The early emergence of argumentative knowledge and skill. In J. Andriessen & P. Coirier (Eds), *Foundations of argumentative text processing* (pp. 97-116). Amsterdam: Amsterdam University Press.

Stein, N.L., & Miller, C.A. (1993). The development of meaning and reasoning skill in argumentative contexts: Evaluating, explaining, and generating evidence. In R. Glaser (Ed.), *Advances in instructional psychology* (Vol. 4, pp. 285-335). Hillsdale, NJ: Lawrence Erlbaum Associates.

Veerman, A. (2000). Computer-supported collaborative learning through argumentation. Enschede, Netherlands: Print Partners Ipskamp. Retrieved December 11, 2002 from the World Wide Web: http://www.library.uu.nl/digiarchief/dip/diss/1908992/inhoud.htm

Veerman, A., Andriessen, J., & Kanselaar, G. (2002). Collaborative argumentation in academic education. *Instructional Science, 30*, 155-186.

## NOTES

---

[1] All references to John Dewey's work in this chapter can be found in The Collected Works of John Dewey edited by Jo Ann Boydston (1969-1991). This critical edition consists of thirty-seven volumes divided into The Early Works (EW), The Middle Works (MW) and The Later Works (LW). Each reference will provide a volume designation followed by a page number or range of pages.

[2] For other examples, see Bell (2002), Veerman (2000), or Veerman, Andriessen, and Kanselaar (2002).

[3] See Baker (1999) for alternative formulations.

[4] See, for example, Michael Baker's figure (p. XXX).

[5] For further discussion along these lines, see the raging debate concerning what should count as 'science' in educational research (cf., NRC, 2001).

[6] Dewey himself would seem to have anticipated this conclusion. Writing about scientific discourse, he observed:

> In advancing fields of research, inquirers proceed by doing all they can to make clear to themselves and to others the points of view and the hypotheses by means of which their work is carried on. When those who disagree with one another in their conclusions join in a common demand for such clarification, their difficulties turn out to increase command of the subject. (Dewey & Bentley, 1991/1949, LW16:3)